**Counterfeit U.S. passport photo of the author
as "Gerald Ezekiel Sawyer," 1978**

The author dropped out of five prestigious colleges and spent his twenties in a wilderness therapy community. In 1980 he stumbled back into the world and learned who Fleetwood Mac was, and in 1985 he graduated from UCLA law school. The driving force of his adult life has been his passion to tell the world what happened at the psychedelic Shangri-la without getting himself killed or hurting other people. This book is his best effort.

Steve has written extensively for the legal community on the child custody rights of gay and lesbian parents and other human rights issues. He has been a frequent contributor to *Christopher Street*, *The James White Review* and *Manzanita*, and is a well-known participant at the Squaw Valley Community of Writers.

He practices law in San Francisco, specializing in the needs of people with life-threatening conditions.

Moving Finger Press

PEOPLE FARM

A LARGELY TRUE STORY
OF EXPLOITATION, REDEMPTION AND
ORGANIC SEX IN A THERAPY CULT OF THE
EARLY AQUARIAN AGE

BY STEVE SUSOYEV

PUBLISHED BY

Moving Finger Press

MANUFACTURED BY

Produced by Falcon Books,
San Ramon, California

"Moving Finger Press," by the way, is the author's imprint, which means he started the company to publish his book. He plucked the name from the most-quoted quatrain of *The Rubáiyát*, whose try-and-stop-me tone is appropriate because certain people have suggested he take his story with him to the grave, preferably sooner than later:

The Moving Finger writes; and, having writ,
Moves on: nor all your Piety nor Wit
Shall lure it back to cancel half a Line,
Nor all your Tears wash out a Word of it.

The author derives comfort from the illusion that a trendy publisher snatched up his manuscript, perhaps during a bidding frenzy. The truth is that seventy-six self-addressed, stamped envelopes boomeranged back from top-drawer literary agents who declined the privilege of representing this work ("You must name names, because the market wants blood . . . despite the high literary quality, nonconsensual sex is wrong for the current market"), and from a few porn-fringe publishing outfits that accept unsolicited manuscripts (". . . awfully literary, and where's all the nonconsensual sex promised in your cover letter?").

To purchase copies of *People Farm* for everyone you know, please visit your neighborhood independent bookseller and express shocked incredulity if they don't yet carry it. Or you may search **amazon.com** for **People Farm** or **Susoyev**. Even if you have enough copies, visit **peoplefarm.com** and let the author know what you think of the book.

Library of Congress Control Number: 2002096395
ISBN 0-9727225-0-5   SAN 254-9972

"Moving Finger Press" and the hand logo are the author's registered trademark.
The hand logo was designed by Burton Clarke.

I believe I have cited all sources appropriately (see the Bibliography on page 408) and obtained permission where necessary. If you disagree, please don't sue. Write me and let's work it out. No, on second thought, sue me! I could use the publicity.

Manufactured in the Land of the Free

People Farm is dedicated
to the Vistans,
who know who they are.

The crocodile isn't evil, he's hungry.
He doesn't care who plops into his
pond. Ghandi? A platypus?
Either is a tasty snack.

Cyrus Aaron

PART ONE

Much will be gained if we succeed in
transforming your hysterical misery into
common unhappiness.

> Sigmund Freud
> *Letter to a patient*

>> People blather on about
>> "Unconditional Love" as if it were
>> stocked beside the frozen corn-dogs at
>> the supermarket. Most people will
>> never experience unconditional love.
>>
>>   Cyrus Aaron

**I'LL SPARE YOU THE CLICHÉS ABOUT PROTECT-
ING THE INNOCENT.** Nobody who lived at the Ranch is
innocent, and some of us are dangerous. I've invented locations,
and changed names and automobile makes and models, to
protect myself. The old man once instructed me matter-of-factly
to fling acid in a girl's face and kill her mother—not very original
for a man whose creativity had been celebrated so widely, but as I
reminded myself at the time, he was under a lot of stress. On that
occasion I didn't do what he wanted, but still I've abandoned any
illusions about presenting myself as what literary types call a sympathetic, or likable, character.

"Revenge," a great spiritual teacher once told me, "is the
greatest motivation for writing. If people hadn't wanted you to
write about them, they should have treated you better." I was

nineteen when I met the old man. He gave me my first taste of evil. When we finally turned each other loose, I was thirty—exhausted and broken and facing the likelihood of eighty years in prison. But even after the story began to pour out of me, I denied any thoughts of revenge. I told myself, and the therapists whose bills eventually totaled sixty-eight thousand dollars, that I was writing *People Farm* in order to "reach" the man who had hijacked my youth in exchange for saving my life—as if, having read my lucid explanation of his psychopathic behavior, my erstwhile mentor would experience a spontaneous recovery. Having thus been reached by me, he could live out his golden years free from the burden of denying how he'd injured scores of people who had entrusted their souls to him.

This is important because he does fear he is a psychopath—one of those charismatic and often brilliant characters who seem to have no conscience and who inevitably turn everything they touch to shit, beginning with the lives of anyone foolish enough to love them. My knowledge of his fear is the source of my only power in our relationship. When I was his student he believed that psychopaths could be cured. I'm not sure what he believes any longer. I talk to him once a year, on his birthday. He's often stoned when I call, and I practice the listening skills he taught me.

While I'm fishing for excuses for having devoted my entire adult life to figuring out how to tell this story, I mustn't forget the public-service angle: I am educating the world about charismatic charlatans and their cultish ways, to spare others from the traps that ensnared me at such a tender age.

To anyone who isn't living inside the tortured terrain of my head, it must be obvious I want the son of a bitch on his knees. While he begs for my mercy I will sneer, "Forgive *you?* I prefer to publish everything that didn't make it into the court transcripts."

But I have decided to take a less direct route to exposing the most dangerous person I have ever known. Unless you inhabited the tiny world in which his star burned so bright during the 1970s, you won't recognize him here, but the scary old fuck knows who he is.

SO, OKAY. I DO WANT REVENGE, and I want to reach the old man, perchance to save his soul. I want to punish him, to protect the world from people like him, and even to thank him. But primarily I am writing our story because I am hungry for understanding and acceptance—the two things I sought most desperately when I followed the pied piper into the wilderness.

He came into my life on the Tuesday I had scheduled for the fulfillment of my destiny. I intended this day to be exempt from regret, but watched with a sore heart through my ratty curtain while the dawn degenerated into a day the color of lentil soup. Then I snorted. Had I expected to wake up to a blue sky, with anything like my old energy and purpose?

The day grew as bright as days would be until the windy spring rains rinsed the air, long after I stopped caring. The freeways that intersected nearby were in full roar. Songbirds clung to the sooty branches of the walnut tree outside my window and chirped feebly into the din. They had flocked to Orange County for the mild winter, like retirees.

"If you have any sense," I muttered, "you'll head further south before you fucking asphyxiate."

I was going to miss my parents' twenty-fifth anniversary and the end of Richard Nixon's regime in the White House. "No regrets!" I reminded myself, and rose to begin for the last time the ritual I had observed every morning for months. From my sock drawer I removed a Vitamin C jar, and spilled its contents onto a chipped white plate. I sorted powder-blue Valiums, dung-brown Thorazines and translucent ruby Chloralhydrates—forty-odd pills, enough to put a Clydesdale into a coma.

The candy coating on the Thorazines was mottled from bathing in psychotics' saliva. I worked in an insane asylum, one of California's oldest regional state hospitals, where the patients often pretended to gulp down their pills while they shuffled away from the dispensing window. I hadn't induced the deception, but upon discovering this "cheeking" of pills I'd worked out a cordial confiscation routine to further my plan.

From the hip pocket of my bell-bottoms I fished out a creased envelope that contained the fruits of my most recent expropriation, five bubblegum-pink Mellarils. I dumped these onto the plate with eight gleaming "Black Beauties"—seamless gelatin bullets of Methedrine I had bought for twelve bucks from a fellow attendant. The speed was superfluous, of course, but why not skip out with a smile?

I scooted my pills around to form a psychedelic sunflower with a hollow center. Today I would acquire the flower's lethal scarlet seeds—a fistful of Seconals. Thorazine and Valium were as common on my assigned ward as chewing gum in a sixth-grade classroom. But Seconal, a Schedule II barbiturate, was kept in a double-locked cabinet that could be opened only by two registered nurses using separate keys. Seconal tablets—"reds"—were available exclusively for cash. Since summer I had eaten in the patients' canteen, smoked seeds and stems, frequented the public library instead of bookstores, and sacrificed in other ways to save toward this day, when the guy who'd sold me the Black Beauties had promised he would deliver four dozen reds, in exchange for two hundred and forty dollars I had paid him on Friday.

For practice I scooped a handful of pills into my mouth and closed my eyes. The chalky Valiums immediately began to melt into a bitter paste. Overdosing was so easy, I marveled that millions of people didn't do it every day. You could probably check out with Pepto Bismol or Ex-Lax, if you swallowed enough.

I gagged up a pill that slipped into my throat and spat out the whole gooey mess. "Deliver us from evil," I rasped, the closest I was willing to come to prayer, and indeed my deliverance was at hand. I pulled my bush of red hair into a ponytail and tied it with a strip cut from an old tee-shirt. I scratched my stubbly cheek. A pimple festered on the side of my nose, too unripe to pop but so large it loomed in my field of vision. My parents would surely insist on a haircut and a shave. Would the mortuary drain my zits and plaster makeup over my ravaged skin? Would they notice I hadn't showered? I'd taken the precaution of going without food since the previous afternoon, knowing first-hand from rotations on the geriatric wards that the bowels tended to empty at the moment of death. The thought of being found with a load in my trousers appalled me.

Annoyed with myself for thinking any of this mattered, I poured my arsenal back into the vitamin jar and jammed it into the bottom of my knapsack, under *The Spy Who Came in From the Cold* and other library books I wouldn't live to finish reading. The plate I returned to the sock drawer, which held my only precious possession, a scrapbook. Between yellowed newspaper clippings, which confirmed I had once been known as a boy with a bright future, lay the goodbye note I had agonized over. I read it one last time and folded it into my back pocket.

I slipped into a wrinkled but clean white shirt while my roommate, Lydia the Sunshine Girl, splashed around in the bathroom. We worked together—it was thanks to her I had a job and a place to live—and I usually drove her to the hospital. We were scheduled to assist in the morning's series of routine shock treatments. I had agreed to accompany her at eleven to the funeral of a former patient, a teenager I had known slightly.

She was up to something, of course. The dead boy had killed himself, and Lydia was weary of my ongoing ode to suicide. I figured she meant to shock me into reality by bringing me face-to-face with self-induced death.

Or maybe she just wanted me to get it over with. Even Lydia's patience had limits.

Her huaraches slapped the plank floor and she called from the hallway, "Steve, whatcha doin'?" Her fingers drummed on my door. "It's almost six for—"

"I'm planning my future!" I snapped the knapsack shut and opened the door, then sat on the bed to yank on my cowboy boots.

She gasped in mock horror. "We've lived together two years and I didn't know you owned a tie!"

"I stole it from my dad." Her white cat Cleo wandered toward the doorway and eyed me while I clumsily knotted the red paisley silk. "I hope people will dress up for *my* funeral."

Lydia abruptly left my room, braiding her wet dark hair, and sang out, "We've got a busy day ahead of us!"

"We sure do," I muttered, stung by her evasion. I reached down to stroke Cleo, and she bolted down the hallway.

PERDIDO VALLEY STATE HOSPITAL had commandeered my childhood nightmares, a gothic horror castle that crouched behind mossy granite walls. As a boy I had held my breath in the back seat when my parents drove near the place. Don't let me end up in there, I had prayed, and peered through the iron gates for a look at the asylum's most notorious inmate, Hermione Pitt—a woman who had killed and eaten her twin babies.

Now nineteen, I was one of the hospital's countless long-haired, disgruntled attendants, and Hermione was the star of my art therapy group. My nickname for the asylum, *Los Perdidos*— Spanish for "The Lost Ones"—had caught on among the demoralized staff, an acknowledgment that we were as lost as the patients. Even Lydia, so infuriatingly upbeat, sometimes slipped and called the place "Los Perdidos" when she spoke with patients' beleaguered families.

Lydia and I approached now in my rusty Karmann Ghia. A guard in a bulletproof kiosk yawned and pulled a lever that opened the front gate. I parked in the dirt lot and walked with Lydia to Oregon Trail Hall, a decrepit Edwardian wedding cake of a building, surrounded by eighty acres of scrubby lawns and similarly funky old structures. We reported to separate sections of Oregon Trail's basement.

Under a recently-adopted policy, we didn't have to change clothes—the then-current progressive approach to mental health treatment allowed patients and staff to wear street clothes. The stated objective was a non-institutional atmosphere from which patients could graduate more smoothly into the real world when ready for discharge. In fact, I rarely saw a patient discharged. The principal results of the policy were savings in the hospital's uniform and laundry budgets, and my frequent inability to distinguish patients from staff.

At seven forty-five I rolled a gurney into Oregon Trail's cavernous recovery room. Strapped aboard, in hospital-issue pajamas that he had tie-dyed purple and pink, a patient named Rupert Seville lay on his back. He kept his hands folded tightly over his chest. On several fingers he wore silver rings wrought with arcane and incompatible religious symbols, and he clutched a rose quartz rosary. His size-fifteen feet bounced past the end of the gurney's thin black pad. He was six and a half feet tall, with auburn hair uncut since his first admission to Los Perdidos over five years before. This huge man had become my friend during our two years together at Los Perdidos.

I couldn't have admitted it at the time, but other than Lydia, Rupert Seville was my only friend. He gently thumped my shoulder with his huge hand. "Why do you call this the 'recovery room,' li'l buddy? Do people really recover in here?"

"Not my name for it." I'd spent hundreds of numb hours in this horror palace, but for the first time in months I took it all in. How must it be affecting Rupe, who was seeing it for the first time? Like every enclosed space at Los Perdidos, the room stank of pine-oil cleaner, roll-your-own cigarette smoke and feces, all rather comfortingly familiar. But ancient iron hooks had trailed russet stains into the grout of the white tile walls. From the hooks, side-by-side with bedpans and stomach-pumps, hung canvas straitjackets and leather straps, cuffs and harnesses: equipment engineered during psychiatric prehistory to restrain violent lunatics, and still employed when Thorazine and other psychotropic drugs failed to subdue. Or when the treatment of choice required terror, torture and degradation.

I sighed and recited the standard crap. "Dr. Turner says shock treatments give depressed patients new hope."

"Everybody tells *me* this is my last stop on the road to the turnip bin."

I chewed a clump of my hair, a habit that disgusted me, and looked around for a distraction. Other attendants came and went. Inert men and women lay cinched to gurneys, staring into space as they did when waiting to be fed or hosed down or put to bed. Some had already been wheeled back from the shock treatment room and were sleeping off their short-term sedative.

"It's true," I admitted. "Shock treatments turn people into chronic patients. A lobotomy's probably the only thing that can fuck you up worse." I avoided the eyes of my friend, who would wind up in the vegetable bin even if I didn't swallow fistfuls of pills today. Feebly I murmured, "Buddy, I want to get you out of here," suspecting that a braver person really could accomplish such a thing.

Rupert dug into his pajama pocket and pulled out a handful of colorful plastic discs, the currency of the hospital's token economy system. They looked like poker chips, and many patients did gamble with them. The tokens spilled off the gurney and rattled onto the floor. He flashed a bright smile. "I've got buckets of these under my bed. Could I buy my way outta this?"

The psychiatrist who was administering this morning's shock treatments had driven onto the grounds just ahead of Lydia and me. "Dr. Turner's got a brand-new canary-yellow Coupe de Ville," I told Rupe. "Probably doesn't need tokens." I removed a bottle of Pepto Bismol from my knapsack and drank a double dose, then offered it to my friend. Rupert curled his lip. Neither of us bothered picking up the tokens, the wages Rupert had earned by mopping floors and performing other chores. Most patients hoarded tokens to buy coveted brand-name "tailor-made" cigarettes and candy. But unlike most, Rupert always seemed to have money, and gave away his ration of the free tobacco that was the hospital-issue staple.

Across the room, toothless old Bertha Flippe had wriggled free of her cinch strap. "Say, sonny," she demanded of a young attendant, and groped his crotch. "How many inches you got?"

The teenager teased, "Bertha, not when I'm on duty, okay?"

Rupert hugged himself and shot me a sulky stare. "I coulda

walked, man. I ain't no turnip yet. You didn't have to roll me down here on this loony cart."

I hoisted myself onto an empty gurney. "You're really in trouble this time. After your shock treatment I'll definitely have to roll you out."

"Is this really happening because I told Doc Burner my correct diagnosis?"

"Turner, for Christ's sake! And yeah, that might have something to do with it." A week earlier Nathan Turner, a senior psychiatrist, had led a fresh crop of interns on rounds and introduced them to Rupert. He'd declared, "Mr. Seville here exhibits symptoms of a psychopath, a chronic schizophrenic and a drug addict," then challenged the greenhorns to interview and diagnose the big nut.

Before any of them could formulate a question, Rupert brightly informed the group that under current diagnostic guidelines he wasn't a chronic schizophrenic but a paranoid schizophrenic. He explained the subtle differences and pointed out, "The term 'psychopath' is antiquated. In appropriate nomenclature, the fire I started on the U.S.C. football field was symptomatic of a character disorder." He added that he suffered from a psychotic depressive reaction, "Two-nine-eight-point-zero in the Diagnostic and Statistical Manual."

"It'd be worse," I observed now, "if you'd told him who gave you the manual. We could both be getting shock treatments today."

THE LIGHTS DIMMED and the power system moaned for two intense seconds that felt like ten minutes, while a patient in the treatment room across the hall received an electric shock to the forebrain. Rupert and I watched each other's faces through the subsequent rumblings of the muffled but violent struggle, an upholstered seizure.

He slowly shook his head. "How many of these brain-fries you been in on?"

"Every Monday morning for the last two years. Helluva way to crash from a hangover."

"Today ain't Monday, li'l buddy." He counted on his fingers and pantomimed a retarded patient reciting the days of the week. "It's, uh, *Tooz*-day." He cuffed my arm. "So you came in special 'cause it was me gettin' fried?"

I shrugged. "Lydia's here for you, too."

"Hold my hand when they zap me?"

A gurney crashed through the stainless steel swinging doors across the room. Lydia wheeled in an unconscious, sweat-drenched and still-twitching patient. I saw the shadow of revulsion in Lydia's clenched jaw as she wiped electrode cream from the woman's translucent temples with a cloth. Then she caught sight of Rupert. Suddenly buoyant, she swished her full white cotton skirt and skipped to his side, snapping her fingers like castanets. He cooed in the light of her attention.

Bertha Flippe, next in line for a treatment, roared out in a raucous melody, "Otto Wundercummer, how I've missed you!" She spotted me and howled, lips flapping over toothless gums, "Stephenson! Whadja do with that goddamned three millions dollars I gave you? Invest it in the Radio Corporation of America, or give it to that goddamned *whore* I saw you with last night?"

The head nurse Esther Cathcart appeared at the double doors, wielding a syringe and flanked by two attendants. I grinned like a lunatic at the beefy attendant on her left—Norton, supplier of Black Beauties, promisor of Seconals—but he looked right through me.

Lydia and I helped hold Bertha down. Like a champion dart-thrower, Cathcart stabbed her needle into a withered bicep. Almost immediately Bertha's maniac eyes fluttered shut. Again I tried to catch Norton's attention, desperate for a nod or raised brow, any acknowledgment I could interpret as *I've got your pills*. But he turned and followed Cathcart back toward the treatment room. "Don't *ever* approach me, man," the big thug had once warned me with a gap-toothed scowl. "No telling who's watching. If I got your shit, you'll know."

Rupert unbuckled the strap that held him on his gurney, and sat upright. From the hallway Cathcart called, "Flippe, Bertha Flippe!"

Lydia gestured to me to walk with her. She navigated Bertha through a logjam of loaded gurneys and said softly, "Make sure they give Rupert Amytal."

I stared at her. "What? They always knock 'em out with it. Jesus, don't they?"

"When Turner has it in for somebody, Cathcart just shoots 'em up with water so it looks like she's following the rules."

I cringed from the thought of a zillion volts shooting through the brain of a fully conscious victim.

Bertha groaned and her head lolled to one side. A glistening filament of her drool pooled on the gurney's black vinyl cover. Lydia drew a face cloth from her skirt pocket, folded it to a clean edge, and wiped Bertha's chin.

Dr. Turner bellowed from beyond the doors, "Flippe!"

Lydia grimaced and ran toward his voice, with Bertha bouncing on the gurney. Rupert and I listened to the rattling wheels and the muted, bored voices echoing from the treatment room. We hunched together silently, waiting for the lights to dim, then shivered through the pulsing power drain, the dull silence, then the savage, padded struggle.

The convulsions moved past the thrashing phase and an eerie peace issued from the treatment room. "Let's not piss 'em off," I said. "Get back under the belt, buddy." Rupert lay back and fastened his cinch. I hopped to the floor and steered my friend forward by the shoulders.

The steel doors swung open and Lydia pushed the wet and vibrating Bertha into the recovery room. She stopped and squeezed my hand. Flat on his back, with a look of bemused detachment, Rupe was fashioning a cat's cradle of his rosary.

IN THE NARROW TREATMENT ROOM, six of us techs positioned Rupert's gurney beside the massive leather-upholstered treatment table. I unbuckled his strap and waited for Dr. Turner to snarl orders.

The chief psychiatrist took his time reviewing Rupert's chart. He was a lank, stringy man, middle-aged, with features pinched by contempt for humanity. Sometimes I watched him during these sessions, surprised to realize he wasn't really ugly. Turner had full, shapely lips, long dark lashes like a girl's, and wavy salt-and-pepper hair. What would he look like with the meanness drained out?

Rupert scooted onto the table. In spite of myself I felt a rush of adrenaline. Like all the attendants, I hated electro-convulsive therapy—but couldn't repress the awe that overwhelmed me in its presence.

While Turner scribbled in Rupert's chart, Cathcart prepared an intravenous injection. Arrayed before her were little glass bottles of what looked like the appropriate medications.

"Jesus," Norton muttered, "can we hold this mother down when he starts rockin' and rollin'?"

"I won't convulse, man," Rupert said. "I'll use yoga. Yogi Rajananda took ten hits of acid and beat some English duke at chess. I saw it in a documentary."

I sighed. My friend had blown it already. Keen and articulate, Rupert clearly hadn't taken meds for several days. If Turner even suspected him of cheeking his Thorazine, he could order the nurses to give him daily shots instead of pills.

The attendants jostled for position. "Hey," Norton said to me, "don't you always take the leg from the knee down?"

"Lately I've gotten into torsos." I took Rupert's hand tenderly in mine, bent the enormous arm and snugged it against his ribs. I had planned to behave mechanically and avoid conspicuous intimacy, rather than give Norton and the others cause to whisper the dreaded word *Queer* behind my back or growl it in my face. But Rupe had asked me to hold his hand, and there'd be plenty to whisper and growl about when the guards found my limp body among the concrete tombstones in the patients' cemetery.

The others had trouble maneuvering into position because of Rupert's size. "Seriously, Doc, this guy's huge," Norton said. "How we gonna hold onto him when he convulses?"

Turner continued writing, and I glared at him. Everyone knew the state law: patients must be held by "human restraints" that allowed their limbs to flail during the violent, full-body convulsions triggered by the electric shock. If Turner allowed the attendants to strap Rupert down, the big guy could snap a bone. Before I swallowed my pills I would write a detailed report on the morning's proceedings—not for the hospital, but the Los Angeles *Times*.

"Doc?" Norton persisted.

Turner peered over his glasses. "Sit on him."

Rupe smiled up at me. "Don't end up on Ward Six. You sit on me too."

Turner glanced toward the ceiling and spat out the words, "There is no 'Ward Six' here, young man." He began writing again. "This hospital's treatment units are named for highlights in the history of the western United—"

"*Ward Number Six* is a Chekhov story," I said. "About a psychiatrist who befriends a patient and ends up getting committed himself."

Turner fiddled with the dials on the primitive black transformer. "Sounds instructive," he said, and began reciting his standard newcomer's speech. He spoke more loudly than necessary, as a cruel child might address a captive lizard in a jar. "Mr. Seville, we are treating your depression with *electro-convulsive therapy*—E.C.T. We will pass a mild electrical current through your forebrain. As a result your body will undergo a convulsion, which will begin to diminish your depression. You may experience a temporary lapse of short-term memory not unlike that occasioned by marijuana."

Rupert's smile broke into a grin. I glanced back at Norton and muttered, "Oh, brother," but he ignored me.

"You will not feel this convulsion or remember it," Turner said, "because Nurse is about to give you an injection that will send you drifting into a brief but peaceful sleep."

Rupert forced out each breath, sucking his stomach tight, then slowly drew in air. Turner concluded, "Science doesn't yet understand why the convulsion caused by our electrical therapy alleviates depression, but it does. You will receive twenty-one of these treatments in three series of seven. Subsequently we will determine whether you will benefit from another series."

Rupert cried, "Wow! It's all in sevens, just like in the Book of Revelation!"

Nurse Cathcart squeezed his jaw, forcing his mouth open, and positioned a hard, green plastic tube between his teeth. Because no one else was going to explain, I did: "Rupert, Nurse is putting this airway in your mouth to keep you from swallowing your tongue during your treatment." I wished he would look at me, but his gaze was locked on the ceiling.

Turner never spent so much time on the transformer. I strained my neck to see what he was up to, but wanted to watch Cathcart too. She splinted Rupert's forearm and prepped the area around the plumpest vein. Then she jabbed him, drew a stain of blood into one vial of a double-barreled syringe, and met my stare eye-to-eye.

If she did her job, the Amytal from one chamber of the syringe would knock Rupert unconscious, and the Valium from the other would relax his muscles for the convulsions. But if she followed the orders I felt sure she'd received, Rupert would be fully conscious for the electric jolt and the resulting savage seizure, with only a few cc's of sterile water in his blood.

She pushed in the plunger. Even if she was giving him the proper medications, I worried that she hadn't increased the dosages to compensate for Rupert's size. Quickly she withdrew the needle and removed the splint, then stood behind his head.

She lifted two metal paddles—like flattened spoons connected by threadbare cords to the transformer—and pressed them against his temples. Turner rotated the dial into the red zone, to 180, by far the highest voltage I had ever seen administered. I swallowed back the taste of bile. Rupert lay helpless and still—his brain absorbing the full impact, his body waiting to catch up. The doctor's finger tapped on the upholstered table, a slow count of three. The finger hesitated and tapped a fourth time, and only then Turner cranked down the dial. Cathcart set aside the paddles and met my horrified glare with tired eyes.

I had never seen a patient receive four seconds, even at a lower voltage. Turner could probably use Rupert's size to justify the intensity and the duration. But to whom? Other than Lydia and me, nobody gave a shit.

Rupert seemed to float peacefully, in what the attendants called "the calm before the storm." Purple shadows soon splotched his face. His eyes flew open, and I saw in them the terror of a fully conscious man. His entire body vibrated. His eyes rolled up in his head. Spasms rippled through him, then the thrashing began. The attendants holding his legs flew off their feet as they desperately, ridiculously, tried to hold him flat. Norton clambered onto the table and straddled Rupert's thrashing hips like a bronc buster. Helplessly I whispered near Rupert's ear, "We're holding you down so you don't get hurt." I saw no response but felt Cathcart's eyes on me from the corner of the room. "This is a rough ride," I continued, "but hold on and I'll buy you an ice cream later."

I gripped an arm with both hands but it wrenched away, slick with sweat. I flung myself across Rupert's chest. My own face dripped with sweat and tears as the convulsions persisted with sickening jerks that ripped through my friend's body. I reached for the flailing arm again, weak with the knowledge that a true friend, a true human being, couldn't let this happen.

2

AS IF SHE KNEW I WAS TRYING TO SCORE a bucket of Seconals, Lydia showed up in the recovery room ten minutes before I expected her. "For gas," she said, and slipped a dollar into my shirt pocket. "Since you're doing all the driving."

We sat with Rupert and each held one of his hands while he moaned. Every creak of the double doors jolted me, but Norton never showed up. Finally another orderly came to wheel Rupert away. I dragged myself out to the parking lot with Lydia and wondered if Norton was deliberately holding out just to fuck with my head. After my affectionate display toward Rupe in the shock treatment room, I felt lucky not to get slammed in the face with a bedpan.

Lydia winked when I held open the Ghia's passenger door. "I hate funerals," she said. "Thanks for coming with me. But please, nothing weird. Don't kiss the body."

I stalked around the car, got in and slammed my own door. Lydia was known for her sensitivity, but she could be so cold. "Garth was a sweet boy," I muttered. "I like to think people will kiss *me*."

"I should talk to Garth's mother today," she said pointedly. "What can you tell somebody whose son has committed suicide?"

"Good Christ." I stomped on the gas and the Ghia sailed out of the hospital driveway. A cement truck's horn bellowed, then faded into the din of the surrounding traffic. Lydia peeled both hands from her face and I shouted, "If coming back to the state hospital was Garth's alternative you say, 'Excellent choice your boy made.' You say, 'Congratulations! He avoided years of agony. He took care of things *once* and for *all.*'"

For her sake I stopped smoothly at the next red light. But when it turned green I jammed into first gear and popped the clutch to race ahead of the other cars.

She made a "hmm" sound. "I know you think about doing yourself in if you don't have a Nobel Prize or at least a couple of Ph.D.s by the time you're twenty."

"There's more to it than that." For years I'd had a recurring nightmare: a boy I loved held my hand and leaned close to kiss me. With my eyes closed, I felt his hot sweet breath on my lips, and surrendered to the kiss but was knocked to my knees. I recoiled from a combat boot flying into my face, but it caught me and broke my jaw. My lover had vanished, and a gang of Marines stomped me bloody until I woke up screaming.

I ached to tell Lydia, but describing the nightmare would breathe life into it. Instead I proclaimed, "A teenage suicide is a thing of lyric tragedy, the failure of a tender root to take hold in poisoned soil." I downshifted to zip past a jacked-up black pickup.

She grabbed my thigh and her voice shot up. "That redneck's not gonna let you in. Don't push it!" Her hand remained tense on my leg while I swung past the truck and zoomed down a side-street. "Jesus," she shouted over the rattling engine, "not everybody's susceptible to your dimples. And that way you crinkle your nose."

I revved the motor pointlessly and recited my personal mantra: "If you wait 'til you're twenty to kill yourself, you look like a loser who couldn't hack life."

"Fine. Just don't let me come home and find you've hacked your *wrists*. If you cash in your karma, please make it neat. Leave a bloody mess in the bathtub and I'll never fucking speak to you again. I certainly won't kiss you in your coffin." When I didn't respond she added softly, "I care about you. I wish you'd tell me why you don't think you deserve to live. And now I'm scared. Your twentieth birthday's what, a week from Friday?"

I gripped the wheel—offended, though I couldn't have explained why, that she had memorized my birthdate.

"My one comfort," she went on in her earlier tone, "is that Garth beat you to it. You're too original to play follow-the-leader."

Unable to thank her for caring whether I lived or died, I silently cursed the dead boy for upstaging me. I'd originally asked Norton for Seconals two months earlier; if he had come through a little sooner, I would have beaten Garth to it.

Lydia fiddled with her braids and remarked, "Hermione is up for release in a few weeks. Have they asked you to testify at her hearing?"

"Nobody's interested in my opinion."

"She's the only talented patient in your art group. We've come a long way, huh?"

"Speak for yourself." I remembered the *National Probe* headline from my childhood—*Mother Boils, Eats Twin Babies*—and my terror that Hermione Pitt would escape from the state hospital and eat *me*. Dear Lydia, I thought, struggling to draw me out of myself. I smiled feebly. "As a kid I was afraid I'd end up elbow-to-elbow with her in Los Perdidos, slurping lunatic gruel from a trough."

"Because you thought you were crazy?"

"Because if my parents found out I was—you know, how I felt about other boys—they'd have me committed."

"What an outrageous bid for sympathy. Your parents are progressives!"

I sniffed. "From the waist up, maybe." The lefties of my parents' era who had marched for the Rosenbergs, and the flower children of my own generation who wept in the streets for Cambodians, had carried on the tradition of hating homosexuals—perpetuating a world in which my love was a curse.

I FOLLOWED HER into a contemporary warehouse of faith whose one refinement was a skylight that bathed the glass-fronted baptismal pool, behind the pulpit, in sunlight. An oil painting of the Jordan River suggested itself as the source of the pool's sacred waters, flowing from between two hills. But the pool was dry and a green garden hose drooped behind its glass face.

I felt cheated when I saw that the rosewood casket's lid was shut. As compensation for coming I had hoped to look into the face of death. The sparse floral displays were spaced for best effect, little islands of red and yellow, white and pink, with lots of green filler. I shuffled behind Lydia across the industrial-gray carpet. From speakers high on the cement walls oozed an organ solo of *Abide With Me*, but the organ wore a dust cover.

"In the front pew with the two kids," she whispered. "Garth's mother, Vivian Elfinger."

"Where's his dad?"

"Killed in 'Nam."

We settled in an empty pew behind a clutch of Los Perdidos administrators. The grieving mother looked about forty. Bright freckles stood out against her pale skin. When she bent to smooth the boy's cowlick and, moments later, to adjust her daughter's barrettes, she turned and glanced behind her. Was she aware that people had tried not to sit too close? Did she notice how they fiddled with their mimeographed programs? In case her dry, red eyes met mine, I tried to smile. I wanted to tell her that her dead son was better off now, finally free of his misery.

A gangly, black-suited young man with a crewcut approached Vivian, deposited a limp-looking hand in hers, then progressed to the dais and perched on a folding chair. He studied notes that were tucked like a bookmark in his Bible.

"When my time comes," I said, "get me a minister with a little more hair." Lydia examined her program and hummed along with the organ recording. I considered returning to the hospital to hunt down the elusive bastard Norton.

A couple entered through a side door and sat in the front pew, far to the side and apart from everyone else. Among the scattered, ordinary mourners these two, with their glamour and maturity, were stunningly out of place. I jutted my chin toward them. "Who are *they*?"

"That distinguished pair? Huh. They do look familiar."

The man's white hair crested a rugged profile. Leprechaun eyebrows gave his otherwise classically handsome face an approachable look. He sat in a meditative posture with his broad shoulders back, hands in his lap, strong jaw relaxed, eyes closed. His white hair and the crinkles around his eyes made him appear about fifty, but with the animation and bearing of a much younger man. His sleek suit outclassed the rumpled tweediness of the hospital administrators and the cheap sheen of the minister.

The woman beside him had exquisite features softened by a small veil, and skin the color of richly creamed coffee. She appeared young enough to be his daughter. Her alert obsidian eyes discretely surveyed the room. She wore a soft gray suit with a black velvet collar and a tiny hat cocked at the side of her silky black hair, which was pulled up in a modernized Gibson Girl. Her hand rested on the man's shoulder.

"That's the biggest diamond I've ever seen," Lydia said. "She's not his first wife."

No one remotely like this sophisticated pair would be at my funeral. My parents would wear tweeds, Lydia her white eyelet dress with the flounces. Who else would even show up? Maybe Rupe, if he could get a day pass.

I was envying Garth an awful lot. His mother continued to stroke her two surviving children, then tilted her head slightly when the minister reached inside the pulpit. The recorded music stopped with a crackle. The guy consulted his notes and hunched over the microphone. "Dear, dear beloved friends, we gather today in the house of God to mourn the tragic passing of a young man . . ."

The mother, Vivian, pressed her lips to her children's hands while the drone went on, "I would fail my duty as a minister of the Gospel if I did not remind you that Jesus came into the world to deliver us from our sins . . ."

Lydia yawned noisily. "Burying her son isn't enough. Poor woman has to listen to this shit."

I shrugged. I wanted to tell her I had decided to ditch the suicide note in my pocket and compose my own eulogy. Instead I said, "*I've* been washed in the blood of the lamb."

"Please. I know your parents. Susi's an Episcopalian and Alex is a secular humanist."

"Which is why they were ashamed to tell you I became a Southern Baptist when I was ten. We'll be whacked with the terrible swift sword any minute." I stared at the closed casket. Appalled by my urge to look inside, I clasped my hands so Lydia couldn't see how they trembled. "You know how he did it?"

"Let us pray," the minister intoned.

"Shot himself," Lydia said.

"Heavenly Father, we come to you today in humility. We ask you to walk with us on our path of grief . . ." Once again Vivian kissed her squirming children's hands. ". . . for it is in Jesus' name we pray. Amen." The minister coughed. "Garth Elfinger had so many good friends that his tragedy is difficult to comprehend. With us today is a man who worked with Garth and understood his struggles."

My hands contorted into fists. The Los Perdidos doctors hadn't helped Garth. They may as well have loaded his gun. For one of them to speak here was an outrage!

"Doctor Cyrus Aaron, a psychiatrist known for his work with young people, has agreed to say a few words to help us." I shrugged at Lydia. Who the hell was Cyrus Aaron?

The white-haired man in the elegant suit rose, clasping a book. "What's this guy gonna do," I said, loudly enough for those around us to hear. "Read to us from the diagnostic manual?"

With a light and youthful step Dr. Aaron strode toward the trio in the front pew. He knelt before them in a gesture of humility like nothing I had ever witnessed in a psychiatrist. With a hand on the boy's knee he spoke to Garth's mother. He smiled sadly into her face, then winked at the little girl. He straightened, walked to the casket and stood among the flowers.

"Garth Elfinger was a gifted young man," Aaron began in a soft but resonant voice. His cobalt eyes seemed to look deep into Vivian, but she avoided his gaze and busied herself with her little boy's cowlick. "But we do not honor gifted young people in this brutal society. We stone them to death."

The minister grimaced behind Dr. Aaron, and several mourners gasped. I wanted to yell *Shut up!* at the muttering crowd.

Aaron ran a hand through his magnificent hair. "We are not here to mourn a suicide. We have gathered to grieve the slaughter of a talented young man." Ignoring the murmurs that rumbled through the church, he smiled gently at Vivian. This time she didn't look away. "When Garth Elfinger was fourteen he wrote a prophetic poem. He *knew* he was marked for destruction by a school system, a religious hierarchy, a vicious pecking order that demanded he either conform to rigid standards of mediocrity, or die. We are blessed that he did not take his life the day he discovered the hypocrisy into which he had been born, but withstood the suffering for several more years, because he lived to give us his special view of the world."

An enchanted calm descended on me. I whispered to Lydia, "Would you read one of my poems at my funeral?"

"Make it easy on everybody. Hop in the coffin with Garth when nobody's looking. Here, gimme your car keys so I don't have to hitchhike back to work."

I sat back, deflated.

Dr. Aaron studied the crowd. "I won't read this entire poem. It's intensely personal, and particularly in his death let us honor the young man's privacy. Can we learn from our fatal mistake before we destroy yet another gifted child? But these few words may teach us how we, the human tribe, betrayed Garth:

> *"I ask you why and you say with a sigh,*
> *Not now, silly boy, not now.*
> *You won't care when you're grown*
> *so don't ask and don't moan,*
> *and we won't even hear if you cry."*

Again Aaron seemed to speak only to Vivian, although his words resounded. "It's not a mature poem. Indeed, Garth earned a 'C-minus' for the effort from his English teacher, who commented here in red ink, 'The rhyme is strained.'"

Fiercely I inspected the crowd, wondering in which rumpled suit or tasteless dress the wretched teacher slouched.

"But can we look past that for a moment?" Aaron continued. "This young man longed to participate in decisions about who he was to be. Garth sought only what we all seek: to be *understood*, to be *accepted*."

My heart raced and I worked my fists, sensing for the first time in my life that I was in the presence of greatness. I forced myself not to run up the aisle.

Aaron raised his silver eyebrows. "Garth came to me as an outpatient. In our sessions he sometimes read me passages from his favorite book, *Beneath the Wheel* by Hermann Hesse. Hear Garth's voice in the words of this writer who touched his soul: 'In young beings there is something wild, ungovernable, uncultured which first has to be tamed . . . Thus it is the school's task to subdue and control young people *with force* and make them useful members of society.' Of course Hesse is being ironic. The book's hero is a gifted boy who dies trying to satisfy the bureaucrats who believe their duty is to tame him."

Aaron looked up and appeared to gaze directly into my eyes. With his sad, wise smile the man seemed ready to comfort anyone who heard his words. I squeezed my hands between my thighs. "Garth's struggle was the same. A gifted boy whose 'strained' rhymes offended his teacher, whose loneliness frightened people and secured his isolation." Aaron's voice broke. "Garth, we all betrayed you. The ultimate tragedy is that we will blame *you* for refusing to fit in. We will learn nothing from your death. The next time a gifted youth struggles to accept his own uniqueness, desperate for understanding, we will stone him, too."

I clutched the hymnal caddy in front of me so hard the wood cracked. Lydia placed a hand on mine.

"Listen finally," Aaron said, "to Hesse's description of a young man being hauled beneath the wheel of conformity: 'No one detected in the slight boy's helpless smile the suffering of a drowning soul casting about desperately.' I am guilty. I knew Garth had serious problems, and I didn't insist that he get the help he needed. He ended up in a notorious state hospital. The result lies before us in this wooden box."

I had known Garth was lonely and desperate. Terrified of absorbing the troubled boy's pain—or being accused of queer-mongering—I'd avoided chances to talk with him, to know him. "We helped them kill Garth," I murmured, and Lydia squeezed my arm.

And why should the fuckers have the satisfaction of seeing

still another sensitive young man take his own life? If I followed through, it would be two-to-nothing.

After a pathetic closing prayer—how dared the crewcut sermonizer try upstaging Dr. Aaron?—I followed Lydia to the front pew. I stood back, reluctant to meet Garth's mother and be recognized as a representative of the nation's most notorious mental hospital. People fidgeted while Vivian spoke with Dr. Aaron. "Call us any time," he said, and handed her a card. "The Beverly Hills office always knows where I am."

I stood back while Lydia inched ahead with the other mourners. Aaron buttoned his suit jacket like a diplomat tactfully taking his leave. His wife lifted the veil from her face, giving her hat an informal, almost sporty, look. Arm-in-arm they walked through a side door into the gloom.

I stood in a torment of indecision. If I followed them what would I say? Would they see I was about to become a casualty? I worked my fists. Aaron spoke beautifully, but could he believe that even sexual degenerates deserved understanding and acceptance?

Lydia chatted softly with another hospital worker, and I pushed my way through the mourners and out the door. Outside I looked in every direction but saw only a red dump truck pulling out of the church parking lot. The Aarons had vanished.

When I returned, Vivian Elfinger was confessing to Lydia, "I didn't know my boy was reaching out for understanding with his poetry. I couldn't see why he loved Dr. Aaron and wanted to live at his ranch. I told Aaron, 'My son belongs with me.'"

While Lydia hugged Vivian, I avoided the hollow faces of her two children, terrified of what I would see in their eyes.

3

IN THE CAR I confessed I had looked outside the church for Dr. Aaron.

"I knew that guy looked familiar," Lydia said. "A few months ago, some magazine—the *Radical Therapist*, maybe—ran a story about his setup in the boonies. He's supposed to cure alcoholics and schizophrenics with LSD. Right on! And I think he wrote a book, *Quest for Unconditional Love* or something." She tilted her head in the charming way she always used before asking a loaded question. "Going to your therapy session today?"

I shrugged. My routine Tuesday appointment had not been part of today's plan. A year before, I'd needed a letter for the draft board and found Dr. Sutton in the phone book. He confirmed in writing that I was psychologically unfit for military service, then offered, "I can cure your homosexual yearnings."

Today I owed the quack fourteen hundred dollars and my yearnings were intact.

Dr. Aaron's eulogy flooded through my mind: *Understanding*, he had said. *Acceptance*. Simple words for what I craved. In the past I'd been desperate enough to tell Sutton many details of my entirely unrealized sexual life. "I wonder," Sutton often intoned, and would no doubt repeat if I did show up today, "if what you want is permission to go ahead and be homosexual. Or if, as you claim, you're serious about wanting a full, normal life."

"I don't want to be a misfit," I always replied. But I had never tried telling Sutton the truth, and it gnawed at me. What if I said, Yes, I want permission to be who I really am! Maybe after Sutton overcame his surprise, he would teach me to be myself without shame or fear or the desire to die.

Lydia impatiently re-braided her hair as if reminding me that she was awaiting an answer.

No, I knew Sutton too well to expect acceptance or understanding from him. After discoursing on perversions, inversions, maladaptation and psychoneurosis, he would hit the hard sell, puffing at his pipe and claiming that thousands of men had been relieved of their homosexual urges. I cringed and imagined the tinny edge of fear in my voice as I asked, With shock treatments? Sutton, the peevish dragon, would exhale smoke, and repeat the weekly shit: "We've been over this. You view homoerotic photo-graphs. A sensitive instrument detects any arousal and conducts a negligible electrical impulse to your genitalia, just sufficient to circumvent an erection. You're then shown appropriate images, of heterosexual relations, without the electrical impulse. And you learn to re-channel your urges."

I always squirmed and changed the subject. The prospect of repeated electrocution of my private parts was reason enough to take an overdose. Sutton was the only person I had told about my pill stash, and he always renewed our "weekly contract"—meaning I dutifully promised not to do anything self-destructive before the next session. As if this stupid vow could make a difference to a desperate man.

Lydia now eyed me with concern—she was probably worried that skipping my session with Sutton meant my suicide obsession was peaking. "No," I said finally, trying to sound casual. "No therapy today."

She shrugged and left me to my driving.

THE HOSPITAL LIBRARY DIDN'T CARRY the *Radical Therapist*, but the magazine was popular among many social workers. In their lounge I found a stack of back issues, and shuffled through articles on "The myth of Mental Illness" and nude bioenergetics, and interviews with Timothy Leary and R.D. Laing, hoping to find some mention of Dr. Aaron and his therapy ranch.

An editorial advocating suicide as a viable option for certain depressed patients reminded me that Norton could be in the staff lunchroom by now with my reds in his pocket. I gathered the magazines to dump them back where I'd found them, and an image leaped out at me that made my heart thump. On the cover of the next issue in the pile, a white tipi glowed before a stormy sky. I read golden words emblazoned against purple thunder-heads: *Inside Cyrus Aaron's Wilderness Revolution.*

I found the feature story and caught my breath. In a full-page photo, Dr. Aaron, shirtless and in shorts, walked among a herd of baby goats. His powerful chest bristled with white hair. The caption said Aaron's therapy center was a three-hundred-acre Colorado retreat called *Rancho Vista*, a highly successful psychiatric innovation. In other photos, bulbous red sandstone cliffs cradled vast meadows and channeled two serpentine rivers. The young "Vistans" laughed as they harvested pumpkins and played guitars. In cutoffs and gauzy shirts they rode horses and tended beehives, hiked with oversized backpacks, held hands in a large circle near a waterfall, and crowded together in the back of a red dump truck.

I ran my trembling fingers over photographs of an other-worldly life, as if I could absorb the joy and hope those photos portrayed. The people in the pictures were under the care of a man whose healing tools were understanding and acceptance. Could that circle possibly include a degenerate like me? I caressed a photo of two teenage boys who stood close together in a high, open home washed with light. The tipi's canvas skin was stretched over rough-hewn wooden poles, and from these hung plants and tapestries.

Social workers trailed into the lounge from lunch. I stashed the magazine in my knapsack and hurried to the one place where I could have privacy, my "art therapy studio"—a lean-to at the back of the laundry building with a view of the hospital cemetery. I read hungrily.

Skeptical of the miracles I had heard about that supposedly took place in Aaron's organic Shangri-la, the article began, *I traveled to the unpaved reaches of Colorado and descended into lush canyons of softly-contoured sandstone. I arrived at Rancho Vista in time for a dinner of home-grown quail and yams. My doubts melted in the warm light of the Vistans' care. Their enthusiasm delighted me—shortly before my visit, they had hosted Arthur Janov and were practicing Primal Screams during their bowel movements and orgasms . . . . My only regret is that I had to leave.*

The Colorado sky shone crystalline blue. Beside a photo of a beautiful young woman astride an Appaloosa, I read, *Cyrus Aaron calls Rancho Vista a spiritual community. His few detractors call it a "bisexual harem." To his students, Aaron is the leader of America's most inspiring intentional community, a cradle of unconditional love.*

More like a promotional brochure than the hard-boiled skepti-cism I expected from this magazine, but I read hungrily on about the Vistans' home-made rock 'n roll and blues, the showers they took under a sparkling waterfall, their marathon group therapy sessions and grueling wilderness survival training. *These young people have the freedom to be who they really are! Many, articulate and clear-eyed, showed me their rap sheets and psychiatric referral papers. They talked of the close calls they had experienced before Cyrus Aaron rescued them. There's an epidemic of rampant self-acceptance among these kids. Could Dr. Aaron be the world's greatest therapist?*

The clock on the wall read one-twenty. I had planned to be dead by now. I would see Norton at a staff meeting scheduled to start in ten minutes. I hiked across the grounds muttering, *"The freedom to be who they really are."*

I TOOK NORTON'S FAILURE to show up as a good sign: he must be making his connection for my Seconals. Cathcart droned on about the problem of patients cheeking pills, and I continued reading in the back of the room—astounded by Aaron's bold discussion of the LSD studies he'd conducted in Canada in the 1950s, and blown away by the reporter's passion for him and his work: *Cyrus Aaron is a Pied Piper for the Aquarian Age, a psychiatrist who speaks the language of youth. Troubled kids in his care, who have been given up on by everyone else, become whole. Their families and insurance carriers pay as much as $4,800 a month for residential psychotherapy, a bargain compared to the cost of maintaining one delinquent or depressive in a public institution.*

I felt as if I'd been kicked in the gut. I could afford about twenty minutes at the place.

I re-read the closing paragraph several times: *Cyrus Aaron employs Christ's parable of the seed to explain that these juvenile delinquents and would-be suicides merely needed fertile soil in which to thrive and bloom.*

Why did fertile soil have to cost forty-eight hundred dollars a month? I returned to the photograph of the two young men in the tapestry-hung tipi. One, darkly beautiful with an impish smile, held a saxophone. His handsome companion, tall and white-blond, strummed a guitar. Two who had been losers, outcasts maybe a little like me, now thrived in Dr. Aaron's fertile soil.

Norton finally appeared for two o'clock group therapy, but looked right through me as he had during Rupert's electrocution—no wink, no upturned thumb—and slipped out before the session was over. I hung around the nurses' station, hoping the big thug would return. I hadn't expected to live long enough to complete my paperwork, but nervously I pulled charts, since I had no other legitimate excuse to hang around. *Mrs. Pitt expresses guarded optimism about her upcoming probation hearing,* I wrote. On Rupert's sheet I added, *Mr. Seville reports he was fully conscious for his first E.C.T. treatment, and is able to quote conversations that took place . . .* Nice try, but the entry wouldn't protect my friend from further violations by Dr. Turner.

Looking beyond my own notes in Rupert's chart would normally have felt like rifling through Lydia's underwear drawer, a little creepy and unlikely to yield any relevant information. But I flipped to the physicians' notes section, eager to read Turner's lies about today's treatment, and found what I expected: *ECT 130 volts—1.5 seconds. 1.2 cc's sodium amytal, 30 mg Valium I.V...* Rupert's history of depression was contrived in densely-typed entries, each terminated by Turner's tight blue signature. The first fabrication was dated six months earlier: *10/11/71. A pattern of lethargy, sleeplessness, lack of interest· in life outside his own obsessions . . . suicidal ideation evident in ritualistic self-destruction . . .*

I'm the one with suicidal ideation, I thought bitterly, and Rupe never spent a sleepless night in his life. But the manufactured symptoms conveniently qualified him for electroshock. Turner had backdated his notes to justify legal torture, but I had no way to prove it. And to whom? No one else cared except Lydia, and she was as powerless as I was.

In the correspondence section of the bulky chart the only letter written in the past year was dated two weeks earlier, from Turner to a lawyer in Philadelphia, with a request for consent from Rupert's guardian for electro-convulsive therapy. No response—probably because Turner hadn't mailed the original. A week-old entry in physicians' notes stated the treatment would be administered under emergency authority.

With a thrill I realized that before I cashed in my tokens I could help Rupe. Cursing the monstrous Turner under my breath, I photocopied dozens of pages and circled each inconsistency in red. I wouldn't survive the day, but the Orange County editor at the *L.A. Times* would receive a folder from a dead man that would shine light into the secret corners of this torture chamber, and send the vermin scurrying.

In the legal documents section I read a six-year-old court order designating a guardian for Rupert, Irma Seville—also named as manager of his trust fund. I copied that as well, returned the chart to its drawer, and only then realized what I held in my hands.

I folded the photocopies, tucked them into my knapsack and ran to the art therapy room. Frantically I phoned directory assistance for Beverly Hills. *Cyrus Aaron, M.D.* and *Rancho Vista Corporation* were listed with the same number. In a low voice I rehearsed, "Dr. Aaron, please," then dialed, sucking on a tuft of my hair.

An answering service operator offered to take a message. In a tone that amazed me, I demanded that Dr. Aaron phone me immediately. "I can only call him in an emergency," the operator replied.

"This *is* an emergency," I insisted. "It concerns a suicidal patient."

"One moment." The phone clicked and went silent. I held my breath for what felt like an hour. Finally the phone clicked again and rang. The great man said, "Aaron here."

I exhaled and spoke in my rehearsed baritone. "Doctor, my name is Steve Susoyev. I am calling from the Social Services Department at Perdido Valley State Hospital, because we have a transfer to Rancho Vista underway—"

With only a trace of the morning's warmth, Aaron replied, "Transfer? I agreed to accept this call because of a suicide."

"Doctor Aaron, I am the deputy director of social services—"

"You're calling because I publicly told the truth about your hosp—"

"At Garth Elfinger's funeral."

Aaron snorted. "I couldn't restrain myself from pointing out that the poor boy had been in the most inhumane asylum in the country. But the press has already extracted quotes from me about that, and at this moment my wife is waving her arms, admonishing me to keep my big mouth—"

"Dr. Aaron, I was at the funeral. What you said was true. I'm calling about a suicidal patient."

"I'm sorry," he said, in a suddenly soft voice. "How can I help?"

Stirred by the gentle resonance that had first touched me, I wanted to shout, *You can rescue me like you couldn't rescue Garth!* I steadied my breath and continued my subterfuge. "I'm working with a young patient. I read that you've developed a cure for schizophrenia. Our psychiatric staff is trying to turn this fellow into a chronic." My voice was rising, and I lowered it. "They gave him a shock treatment this morning—"

"Hold on," Aaron said, his patience sounding strained. "I'm sorry, but Rancho Vista is a wilderness community. We work with high-potential dropouts. Wounded, sensitive kids. We can't handle back-ward cases."

"This fellow dropped out of U.S.C." I dredged up everything I knew about Rupert. "He's a talented guitarist and speaks French, he practices yoga, he's read Dante—"

"Unusual for someone in your position to be worried about a

chronic patient receiving shock treatments." Aaron made a "hmm" sound. "Are you concerned about countertransference?"

Without bothering to control my voice I blurted, "I'm concerned about suicide!"

"The patient's or your own?"

Could the man read my mind? My hands shook but my voice remained low and calm. "Dr. Aaron, a psychiatrist here fried Rupert's brain this morning with an illegal dose of electroshock. I'm desperate. He has a trust fund that can pay your fees."

"Okay, we're finally getting somewhere. You're bucking the system, probably risking your job, to rescue someone you care about." Aaron let out a slow, relaxed laugh. "Good for you. You say the patient's name is Rupert?"

I invited him to interview Rupe immediately. But I had reached him at a hotel in San Francisco, and he and his wife were leaving soon for Canada. He promised that Willow Buckingham of the Rancho Vista staff would travel from Colorado and interview Rupert by the end of the week.

My hands trembled so badly I barely managed to hang up the phone. Then I yanked at my hair and crazily replayed the conversation in my mind. My voice had risen half an octave until I'd sounded more like a deranged patient than the social services administrator I was pretending to be. It was ludicrous to think I could get Rupert to Rancho Vista. And Jesus!—why had I used my real name? What if Aaron called the hospital and learned that Steve Susoyev was a lowly attendant who wheeled drooling patients around on loony carts?

But what if it worked? Rupe's family had money. Maybe a suicidal liar *could* get him into the care of the man the known as the world's greatest therapist.

I danced through the art studio. Yes! I would get Rupert transferred to Rancho Vista, and more—I'd find a way to accompany Rupe into the verdant canyons. Fuck the surly Norton and his red death pills! Fuck my stash of blues and browns and pinks and blacks. Together Rupert and I were going to thrive in fertile soil. Fuck Los Perdidos!

I rifled through the copies I'd made and found the number for Rupert's guardian in Philadelphia. Irma Seville would have to be informed of the transfer and arrange for routing payments to Colorado. I dialed, connected with the Seville Foundation, and left a message including my home number.

In the administration building my heart raced. I calmed my

voice and distracted a secretary with a complex request from the file room. While she was away from her desk I grabbed a stack of hospital letterhead and envelopes, and tucked them into my knapsack.

I was scheduled to supervise a volleyball game between the patients of two adolescent units. Usually I joined in, but today I sat on the sidelines with a blind patient named Michael. Though on perpetual suicide watch, and diagnosed with an exotic species of paranoia, Blind Michael was known among patients and lower-level staff as the one truly gifted psychotherapist in the hospital. In his fifties and with the flowing hair and beard of an Old Testament patriarch, he listened better than anyone I had ever known. With his profound understanding of pain, he often wept for others when they couldn't weep for themselves. I told him about Garth's funeral and Dr. Aaron's critical analysis of the Los Perdidos psychiatrists.

Michael's opaque eyes seemed to focus on the endless sky above. He reached for my hand and said softly, "This Dr. Aaron gave you hope."

I started to reply but sobs burst out of me like death rales. I allowed Michael to hold me. As much as I wanted to talk about my plan to liberate Rupert, I was afraid of jinxing it.

After the volleyball game I emptied my pill jar down a storm drain, and laughed as my stockpile clattered into the bowels of Los Perdidos. I dug the suicide note from my pocket. The words I'd written were barely recognizable. *Don't blame yourselves*, I had admonished Lydia and my parents. *I wasn't meant for this world*. I ripped up the note and sent the pieces fluttering down after the pills. No, I wouldn't let the world off that easy.

GIDDILY I PEERED into the shadowy corners of the Mission Hall dining room where the cigarettes of restless patients burned. I couldn't wait to tell Rupert about the pills and dumping them, and about Aaron and his psychedelic ranch. But I also had to prepare him for his interview with the Vistans, and find out how much money was in that trust fund. The scheme rested on assumptions I had drawn from a six-year-old court order.

Rupert was sitting up in bed when I found him, smoking a cigarette in violation of the hospital's most brutally enforced rule. If caught, he could spend a month in seclusion with no hope of meeting any outsiders. "Rupe," I wheedled, "please don't make things worse—"

He flicked the half-smoked cigarette into a pile of dirty clothes. I retrieved it and stamped it out. He pointed a huge finger at me and roared, *"And the devil that deceived them was cast into the lake of fire and brimstone where the beast and the false prophet are, and shall be tormented day and night for ever and ever!"*

The shock treatment had triggered a psychotic episode. I forced myself not to recoil from the face of madness. Rupe scratched at the welts on his temples, the brands left by Turner's electrodes. Rivulets of dried blood had caked down the sides of his face. Uselessly I stared at him, wondering if a shot of Thorazine would help.

Rupert spat out his next words: "That devil is in our midst!"

"Hey," I said as gently as I could, "you want something to eat?"

"Oh, buddy," he parodied in a maudlin voice, *"I want to get you out of here. Let me buy you an ice cream."* He flexed his hands. "One thing you said was true," he went on, suddenly sounding absolutely sane, and meeting my gaze eye-to-eye. "The brain barbecue did eliminate my depression. Thoughts of homicide are quite effective at knocking out suicidal ideation."

"Rupe—"

"I do belong here." He spoke quietly, as if to himself, but his steady eyes bored into me. "I was crazy enough to believe you would help me." He clawed the welts, so fresh blood oozed down his face. "Go," he commanded, and pointed toward the door. "Serve your masters!"

I ran to the nurses' station. It would be hard to get Rupert transferred even if the big guy coöperated. In his current state he would sabotage salvation. The one person who seemed capable of wooing him, Lydia, had left me a note and gotten a ride home. I rushed to the art therapy room and called her, but the line was busy. In panic I ran to my car, wishing I'd prepared her for the calls I was expecting.

The phone was ringing as I tore across the porch and through the front door. I grabbed the receiver out of Lydia's hand and answered in my deputy director's voice, "Good afternoon, Steve Susoyev." Lydia sat down, looking more entertained than annoyed.

An elderly-sounding woman said, "Mr. Susoyev, this is Irma Seville. I understand there is an emergency involving my grandson Rupert."

"Thank you for calling so quickly, Mrs. Seville." I smiled grimly at Lydia and she winked. "The social services department wishes to transfer Rupert to a wilderness center. But this would require his guardian's consent." I explained that Rupert had insulted an influential psychiatrist and received the first of several scheduled shock treatments, at an illegal dosage.

For several long seconds I heard nothing. Then Mrs. Seville said dully, "It is my responsibility to prevent something like this."

"Would you like to talk to Dr. Aaron at the wilderness center?"

"For the moment, my attorneys will obtain an injunction to prevent further shock treatments. We can discuss alternative facilities after—"

"But he is in real danger," I insisted. Lydia raised her fist in support. "Illegal levels of electroshock are only one of many painful punishments he may have to endure."

Mrs. Seville asked for Dr. Aaron's number, and offered her address and home phone. I promised to send her copies of all correspondence.

Lydia was reclining on Old Glory, the overstuffed couch she had upholstered with an enormous American flag. "Wow," she said when I hung up the phone. "What'd you do to your voice, gargle with oven cleaner or something?"

I felt as if I'd just guzzled ten cups of coffee. "When Rupe hears about the LSD therapy, he'll hitchhike to Colorado." I cut out the *Radical Therapist* article, excising the sexier photographs and references to bowel movements and orgasms. With relief I noticed a short list of rates: some high-functioning patients paid as little as twelve hundred dollars a month—still daunting, but on a more human scale than forty-eight hundred. I rolled a State Hospital envelope into my typewriter, addressed it to Mrs. Seville, then folded the clippings and slipped them inside with a simple one-paragraph letter reiterating my concerns.

After flourishing my signature on the letter, I opened the door and chortled, "Rupert doesn't know it, but I'm rescuing his ass."

"Not to mention your own," Lydia called out.

I turned to face her. "Huh?"

"You haven't referred to suicide once since you got home. Ten minutes is some kind of record."

I grabbed an apple, my first food all day, blew her a kiss and bolted out for the post office. After mailing the letter I would go to the library and read up on the quest for unconditional love.

WE SQUINTED INTO THE FLUORESCENT GLARE of the Western Winds dining room. "A dance in this dump'll trigger a depressive episode in anybody who shows up," I said.

Lydia tweaked my earlobe. "Especially the chaperons."

"But we've gotta do something."

"If you say so. You know the power you're confronting."

The bilious green of the concrete walls and ceiling seeped into everything: the stainless steel tables and the patients' doughy skin reflected the sickly hue. But at least the place was clean, because patients continually mopped and scrubbed to earn tokens they could exchange for tobacco and candy. And, so soon after the evening meal, the smell of pine-oil cleaner overpowered the stench of cigarette smoke and excrement.

I had to contrive a party atmosphere in the next half hour, and it would take more than the dance music I had brought from home. Lydia had done her part by wearing her turquoise margarita dress, and now she headed for the ward office to catch up on paperwork. The patients, bleary on their after-dinner Thorazine, shuffled around the brown linoleum, smoking roll-your-owns. Most wouldn't care whether they shuffled in time to music from the old record player or their private, inner orchestras.

I unrolled a pink crepe-paper streamer and looked for someone coherent enough to help string it up. I saw only droolers who squatted with their hands in their pants, mumbling to themselves while they masturbated or scratched themselves raw. I stood on a chair and tied one end of the streamer to a fire-sprinkler pipe.

Western Winds was a more modern and spacious facility than Mission Hall, the windowless dungeon where Rupert lived. I had arranged this location to impress a pair of special guests: Willow Buckingham had phoned me mid-week from Rancho Vista to confirm that she and another member of Dr. Aaron's staff would arrive on Friday. I invited them to a dance so they could meet Rupe informally.

He had stopped raving about the eternal lake of fire. When I asked, he shruggingly agreed to act as tonight's disc jockey, a role in which his sweet spirit and high level of functioning could shine. I hadn't mentioned Rancho Vista because I wanted him to discover the Vistans on his own. And I didn't want him to know about the transfer because I feared he would brag about it. If word of the scheme reached Dr. Turner before Rupe's grandmother arranged the transfer, Rupe would never make it to the enchanted canyon of Dr. Aaron. He would rot in seclusion.

I twisted the streamer and tied its other end to a light fixture in the opposite corner. Of course Lydia was right about the power we were up against: Perdido Valley State Hospital didn't turn anyone loose without a fight. Most patients who'd been hospitalized as long as Rupert eventually graduated to the geriatric wards—and from there it was a short journey across the cyclone fence to the weed-choked cemetery. While Rupe and other chronic patients waited to be buried there, low-level employees like me settled in, shellshocked and bitter, with nothing to look forward to except eventual absorption into the state retirement system.

"Dance tonight, everybody," I announced, and wondered how the Rancho Vista visitors would react to the weirdness that I found so disturbingly familiar. In the men's dayroom, a few coherent old-timers in pajamas played checkers and smoked roll-your-owns, ignoring a quiz show that blared from the television, while droolers languished on the floor.

I returned to the dining room and found that Blind Michael had commandeered the turntable and the mood: Mozart's *Requiem* shook the walls. A choir of satanic angels heaved accusations at humanity in an ancient tongue, their voices animated by fiendish intensity. Michael interpreted for little Paloma Carillo, "The angels of heaven are fighting over the soul of the departed with the hungry angels of hell." Poor Paloma. Her grip on reality was tenuous enough without Michael's interference.

Still, the terror of the music made Michael's interpretation sound reasonable. The *Dies Irae* exploded from the record player, the most violent section of the mass—concerning the Day of Wrath which, as Michael liked to translate, "shall change the world to glowing ash." I cringed and used my fishfork-shaped key to turn off most of the ceiling lights. Determined to make this gathering into a dance before the Vistans arrived, I steeled myself to confront Michael. A week earlier the blind patriarch had played a recording of *The Volga Boatmen* forty-two times while the patients bet hard-earned tailor-made cigarettes on how long the staff would let it continue.

Approaching Michael, I caught sight of Lydia—busy with a patient who had thrown up all over himself. She pointed frantically across the room, to where Bertha Flippe was pulling off her panties and belting out a gravelly *Wild Irish Rose* over the howl of the *Requiem*. I ran to Bertha's side. "You promised you wouldn't take off your panties for anybody but me," I cajoled.

"I'm sorry, Stephenson," the old manic said with her goofiest smile. Her hooked nose nearly touched her chin. "Nobody but you can get my panties offa me tonight." She pulled them back up under her shapeless cotton dress. "Unless Otto *Wunder*cummer shows up!"

I surveyed the place nervously and hoped no serious trouble erupted. In a red sweater ensemble and high heels—pushing the limits of the "street clothing" policy—Hermione Pitt mixed orange punch. Two young guys stacked tables and chairs along one wall.

The dance could start as soon as the music was under control. I headed for the nurses' station to call Mission Hall and find out where Rupert was. I had left visitors passes for the Rancho Vista guests at the guard gate. The passes would expire at eight p.m. It was now almost seven. The Vistans needed to roll in and meet Rupe, fascinate him with wilderness ranch tales, and disappear.

Before I could leave the ward, Paloma scuffed toward me, pinching the last ember of a roll-your-own between blackened fingers. "Toothache Giraffe eat leaf from top of tree," she declared, in what I hoped was a reference to Rupe. She was the only resident of his ward who had already appeared for the dance.

"Have you seen Rupert?" I asked her.

Paloma gripped my arm and dug her nails into my flesh. As I wrenched away she hissed, "Toothache Cobra hide in grass, bite giraffe at water hole," then screamed and flailed at her face with tiny, furious fists.

A security guard appeared from the nurses' station, hand on pistol. A nurse followed him with a loaded syringe. Paloma bolted out through a patio door. Another guard, two nurses and Lydia ran out after her. The head nurse shouted at me, "Keep the patients calm!" then scuttled out across the patio.

Michael sniffed the air, his milky eyes wild.

"In the two years I've worked here," I told him, "Paloma's never turned into the Toothache Cobra so fast."

"Rupert's shock treatment unleashed a savage power here. Haven't you observed the signs?"

"I've observed that you're even more cryptic than usual. And speaking of Rupert—"

Hermione approached, announcing herself to Michael by humming "Stardust." She stroked his beard and accepted a squeeze of the hand, then winked at me on her way to the women's dayroom.

I reached for the turntable, ready to lift the needle off the record. Firmly I asked, "Michael, do you know where Rupert is?"

He lowered the turntable to the floor and secured it between his boots. The needle barely skipped. "Haven't seen him."

More patients came in, ready for the closest thing to a party they ever got to enjoy. A few attendants trailed behind them. Alert to the presence of guests including staff from other wards, many Western Winds residents went to work bumming cigarettes. The young coherent ones, most on jail diversion from drug-related convictions, distributed punch in tiny paper cups. My twisted streamer drooped above them.

I eyed Michael. "This is supposed to be a dance." Golden-throated angels of heaven were singing a simple, stirring melody, the "Recordare"—*Remember, loving Jesus . . . lest fire unending be my fate . . .* But the music would soon turn violent again. "Let's put on *Rubber Soul* before the angels of Satan storm back in. Or *Sticky Fingers.*"

"The *Requiem* is appropriate," Michael replied. "As long as you confiscated Mellaril and Thorazine I knew you were merely playing at suicide. When I heard you'd ordered Seconals I thought, Oh, this sounds serious. But the black beauties! Methedrine could scuttle your—"

"How the hell—"

"I survive here by paying attention."

"So I guess you canceled my order with Norton. I gave him two hundred and forty bucks and he doesn't even look at me when I try to talk to him."

Michael extended his thickly-muscled arms, palms up. The skin from wrists to biceps was ridged with heavy keloid scars, the chronicle of suicide attempts made with shards of broken glass, and the trail of intravenous injections administered during hundreds of shock treatments. "Since childhood I've tantalized myself with the prospect of death. Have you ever put pills in your mouth and tripped on the thought of swallowing them? Like a rehearsal?"

"I don't remember giving you permission to read my mind."

"Welcome to the Society of the Constant Possibility of Suicide. Perhaps you're not truly suicidal, but you desperately want something and—"

"This is very interesting but I'm going to change the music now. And since you know so much, where is Rupert?"

"Whatever you want, you can arm-wrestle me for it."

Michael was a blind suicidal intellectual, but his powerful arms and chest strained the seams of his extra-large tee-shirt. He routinely did five hundred pushups before breakfast. I understood this challenge to mean, You will entertain us for a moment, then I'll answer your questions and you can play your damned rock 'n roll.

I watched the doorways, hoping the Vistans didn't show up until Rupert was placidly spinning dance records. Michael cranked up the volume on Lucifer's dark-voiced minions, who now wailed about the sentence of piercing flames to be passed upon the damned. He scooted his chair to a low steel table, and I sat opposite him and gripped his big hand. Patients immediately crowded around to make bets.

I focused my concentration on Michael's arm. "Ultimately," he said between measured breaths, "it is death's power to transform that fascinates and humbles us."

Two tailor-made cigarettes landed near his elbow. Blue, red and green plastic tokens clacked beside the cigarettes, then a pack of tobacco and a Tootsie Roll. A stick of gum, then two quarters. No one put anything on my side of the table. An old-timer dumped a pocketful of change at Michael's side and chortled, "He'll slam the kid in ten seconds!"

Sweat trickled down my face and neck. Only a dewy perspiration gleamed on Michael's forehead. A full pack of Camels landed at his side. Hermione drifted over, placed a tailor-made cigarette at my elbow, then left the dining room. I wanted to jump up and hug her.

The security force returned with Paloma and carried her now-flaccid form through to the women's dayroom. Michael remained maddeningly calm. My arm vibrated and I struggled to stay in my chair. "Jesus!" I sputtered, spewing saliva and sweat into his face.

Three figures approached, and I recognized Lydia's turquoise dress among them. The *Requiem*'s "Confutatis" reached its infernal crescendo. The pressure building in my arm turned to urgent distress—the wrenching of sinew in my wrist, then my elbow and finally my shoulder. I was risking injury, but had come too far to stop. I clung to the presence of the lone cigarette Hermione had wagered on me. If I succumbed to the ridiculous impulse to check and see what brand it was, Michael would flatten my hand on the steel tabletop.

Hermione strolled in from the women's side, a red blur, and called out, "Hey, Steve! How 'bout some dance music?"

Michael groaned and his wrist quivered. I tightened my diaphragm and pumped my breath, forcing his arm down until the huge hand vibrated within an inch of the tabletop. I exhaled abruptly and slammed his hand against the cold metal. The powerful arm went limp.

After a moment of stunned silence the patients cheered. Michael rose and shook my hand with dignity. "I hope your disc jockey arrives soon," he said. "Who could dance to this noise?" He walked out through the patio doors with his white cane hanging from his arm. Hermione scooped her winnings into a colander and began distributing money, tokens, candy and cigarettes to droolers who hadn't participated in the betting.

I worked my arm and knelt to retrieve the turntable from under the chair. When I glanced up a pair of wolfen gray eyes accosted me. I looked into the handsome face of a tall, blond man who stood beside Lydia in a fringed buckskin jacket—the guitarist from the *Radical Therapist* photographs. The woman with him had appeared in the same article, astride the Appaloosa. She was now swathed in silk batik and wore her ginger-colored hair in a top-knot. She smiled warmly and graciously, as if she found these surroundings charming.

"Meet our guests," Lydia said, and introduced Willow and Eric from Rancho Vista.

Willow's green eyes sparkled. She offered her hand and I took it gently. "Hi," I said, amazed to be in the presence of people who knew Cyrus Aaron.

Soft wisps of hair spilled from her topknot and framed her large eyes, delicate nose and generous mouth. "You're younger than we expected," she said, with an amused smile that showed off her dimples. "You impressed Dr. Aaron so much he sent us a thousand miles to meet you."

"Dr. Aaron sure impressed *me*, at Garth's funeral."

The handsome Vistan called Eric cocked his head slightly. "Do you always deflect compliments like that?" I looked into his sunny face, wondering what the comment could mean, and shook his outstretched hand. Eric was over six feet tall, with shoulder-length blond hair and gray eyes that gleamed. He smiled, flashing large, even white teeth. His slightly crooked nose did not detract from his beauty but merely brought it down to earth. Like Willow, he looked directly, unflinchingly, into my eyes.

"I just need a *second*," I said, "to change the music."

I bent over the box of records, aware of the gray eyes that followed me. Lucifer's angels abruptly stopped screaming, and moments later the Rolling Stones' "Brown Sugar" filled the room. Lydia invited the Vistans to help themselves to punch, but Willow ignored her and asked, "Where's Rupert Seville?"

I fought the urge to chew on my hair, and looked all around the room as if expecting to see Rupe. "I didn't tell him you were coming, in case you couldn't make it. He's had so many disappointments. I'll go find him."

From the nurses' station I phoned Rupert's ward. The attendant there assured me Rupert had left for the dance. When I returned to the dining room, Eric was dancing with Bertha Flippe. I approached to remove the panties from her head.

"Otto my darling," Bertha cooed to Eric, "how many inches do you have?"

"Twelve big ones, just for you!" he crowed.

A wave of heat passed through me. I was shocked by the unprofessionalism of this wilderness bumpkin, but there was more. Could I be jealous? It had taken me months to establish a comfortable, teasing rapport with the patients, rapport that came so easily to the blond Vistan.

And I was jealous of the attention this beautiful man was giving to someone who wasn't me. I let Bertha keep her panty cap, and grilled a few stragglers from Rupert's ward. None knew where he was. In a fit of frustration I pushed past them into the warm evening, hiked the fifty yards to Mission Hall and stormed into the men's dorm. There I found Rupe's bed made, with the heavy old army blanket stretched in a sharp fold across the top. Two pairs of shoes were lined up under the bed's edge. I checked the bathrooms and dayrooms and the dining room, all more dismal than usual, populated only by droolers too lethargic to attend the dance, and an attendant holed up behind glass, paging through a magazine.

I returned to the dormitory and stared at Rupert's bed. He never made his bed more neatly than was needed to earn him breakfast each morning. And he certainly never lined up his shoes. Something else was wrong: Rupe wore size fifteens, and these were closer to my size, eight-and-a-half. His stuffed white rabbit with the gold earring was missing. His bejeweled slippers, hand-made by Hermione Pitt in art therapy, were gone from their place under the pillow.

My legs buckled and I sat on the bed to face the truth. Rupe had gone "U.A."—on an Unauthorized Absence, the state hospital version of AWOL—a violation punishable by three months in seclusion once the police returned him. He would spend much of that time spread-eagle, strapped to a tiny bed and staring at the concrete ceiling or the apocalyptic visions in his head. After that he would have to earn back all privileges. A year might pass before he could have visitors, much less be considered for a transfer anywhere. And I would lose the thing for which I had traded the jar full of pills—my hope. I would never speak face-to-face with the great healer Dr. Aaron, never feel the tremendous rush of understanding and acceptance.

From the privacy of the art therapy room I phoned Lydia at the Western Winds nurses' station. "Don't tell the Vista people," I said, "but Rupert's gone over the wall."

"This is your scheme. I'd just fuck it up if I tried to explain."

I described what I had found, and she chuckled. "Now all the weird stuff tonight makes sense. The Toothache Cobra showing up with no warning, Michael letting you win."

"Michael—*what?*"

"I wonder if it was a conspiracy! Paloma kept the guards busy and Michael tied you up arm-wrestling while Rupert got away. Even Bertha, shucking out of her panties all night. When Hermione asked you about the dance music she might have been signaling Michael that Rupe had made it out of here."

"Oh. God. Oh God, okay."

We brainstormed about people I could call, places where I might track Rupert down. "There's some good news," Lydia said finally. "Willow's teaching everybody the hula. She and Eric have business in Beverly Hills on Monday. I invited them to spend the weekend with us."

I made several dead-end phone calls, then went to my car. On the front seat I found a shopping bag packed with pungent, red-haired Cambodian pot. From Norton, obviously, in lieu of the paid-for Seconals—another conspiracy masterminded by Michael, this one intended to save my life.

I drove in circles for hours, asking in blues clubs and late-night cafés if anyone had seen a six-and-a-half foot tall chain-smoking nut with hair down to his ass, wearing a rose quartz rosary. For once I wished I could call the police—but if I did, the hospital would receive a copy of the resulting missing-persons report.

Back at the Mission Hall nurses' station, I documented that the patient was on a weekend pass with his grandmother, and forged Dr. Turner's tight blue initials on the approval form. The deception was safe for the time being. I left for home, touched in spite of myself that a task force of blubbering psychotics had beaten me at the rescue game.

5

GENERATIONS OF LYDIA'S FAMILY had sold off chunks of their citrus orchards and left the log house to sink into what remained—an acre of soil wedged between a tire factory and a motorcycle parts distributorship. The surrounding squalor deepened the magic of what we called the "grove." Arching walnut trees formed a curved tunnel that led into a hidden paradise of overgrown wisteria and jasmine, limes and oranges. The house harbored relics of a lost age: a lion-footed bathtub and wood-burning stove, cabbage-rose wallpaper of a style popular before my parents were born.

Usually I entered the little haven of greenery with relief after a day in the smelly surrounding sprawl. Tonight I returned home frustrated, with only a feeble lie for the Vistans. The house welcomed me with the skunky-sweet aroma of freshly-smoked pot.

I found Eric in the kitchen, rinsing Lydia's latest crop of radish sprouts. "The girls went out," he said cheerily. Cleo the cat, ordinarily aloof, was rubbing sensuously against the Vistan's long legs. "I took my chances you'd come home." His clear eyes zeroed in. "Find the patient?"

I sighed and reached to stroke Cleo. She arched her back and ran down the hall. "He's in seclusion for smoking in bed. They can keep him in there for a month and deny him visitors. I might be able to get you in to see him Monday."

Eric nodded. "So it's you and me tonight." His face brightened. "How about a hike in the hills? The moon's almost full."

I tried to relax. I made room for myself on Old Glory, squeezing in among the Vistans' duffel bags, guitar cases, pillows and clothes, and rolled a few fat joints for the hike. Lydia had left a pan of enchiladas in the oven, and we devoured a few before we set out into the warm night.

I left the Ghia's top down and took side streets, avoiding the clogged freeways on the climb into the foothills east of the city. A few days earlier I had pursued Cyrus Aaron into a parking lot, ready to throw myself under the wheels of the great therapist's car. Now I had one of Aaron's protégés in my passenger seat, the most beautiful man I'd ever seen, and didn't know what to say. If

Rupert didn't show up by Monday these wondrous people would retreat to their Shangri-la and forget the pimply-faced kid who had lured them into the cesspool of Los Perdidos.

I didn't have to contrive conversation. Eric talked easily, and complimented me—"You're natural with the patients, they really trust you . . . you and Lydia have created a beautiful home in the middle of this city . . ." He discoursed on the theories of Cyrus Aaron and life at Rancho Vista. I learned that when Bertha Flippe sang odes to Otto Wundercummer and groped young men's genitals, she was exhibiting symptoms of *Great Golden Weenie-Itis.* "GGW is the most common psychological disease among women," Eric explained. "Right up there with *Lifeboat-Itis*, which men get, too." He described parties where everyone danced naked around a bonfire then jumped into a sweatlodge. The Vistans shared responsibility "for tending the alfalfa, the vegetable gardens, the baby goats, and each other's souls."

I shook my head. "I feel like I should be taking notes."

"Yeah," Eric replied, apparently missing my intended joke, "even when heavy shit comes down in Group, we're all writing in our notebooks."

"Our experiences with group therapy are pretty different. I have to fight to stay awake."

Eric laughed. "Nobody ever has that problem when Cy's running the show."

I parked behind a golf course and led Eric to a ridge above the glittering sprawl of overlapping suburbs. Vehicles chugged through a uniform grid of streets and sailed along meandering freeways. The county's few remaining orchards hunched in dark squares in the smoky distance to the south. Directly ahead hung the russet moon, and beneath it spread the ashen Pacific.

I shrugged. Why had I brought him here? "I'm embarrassed to show you this filthy place. My dad says this county is called 'Orange' because the smog makes the sun looks like one." I pulled a joint from my pocket and struck a kitchen match on a rock to light it.

Eric accepted the joint with a glowing smile. "You've got more people within five miles of you here than we have in all of Colorado. Population of Abraham County's nine hundred. More cattle and horses than people." He passed me the joint and told me about his conviction for selling speed to an undercover cop two years before, at eighteen. "It's a wonder I hadn't gotten myself killed by then—I'd fucked over every friend I ever had. Cy

Aaron peered in my jail cell and saw me for the steaming turd I was. But he also saw something in me he could nurture, my golden kernel, and he gambled I'd be willing to rip open my soul for growth. Wow. Good dope."

"I hope so," I said, handing back the joint. "If I don't get really loaded every night I have these—dreams."

"Cy says dreams are gifts from our subconscious."

"Mine are the booby prize."

"You'll want to talk to Cy about that."

I grinned, excited by Eric's casual assumption that I would be talking to Cyrus Aaron, about my dreams or anything else. "Does everybody have a golden kernel?"

Eric stood and stretched. "In some people it's buried pretty deep. Let's hike." He leaped to his feet and took off, and I scrambled to catch up. "But in *The Quest for Unconditional Love*," he was saying, "Cy claims even psychopaths can be touched by other humans. Some people are 'life generators' but others are 'sucks' and 'feeders,' and there are subtle degrees of energy ripoff in between. A lot of people act like grunts because they're so encapsulated, but when they come out of their shit they have a lot to offer."

Lost in the jargon, I trotted along to keep up and thought with amazement, *I'm actually glad to be alive.* I mentioned trying to find Aaron's book on unconditional love: "Must be popular. The library's copies have all been stolen and the bookstore had to back-order it."

Eric walked with a lanky gait and spoke breezily, but there was nothing casual about the way he changed subjects and recalled the first words I had spoken to him. "You said you heard Cy speak at the funeral. Garth's mom just moved to the Ranch with her other two kids."

"Since Tuesday?"

"She was feeling suicidal herself."

"Little kids can go to Rancho Vista?"

He nodded. "Mostly little geniuses, IQs off the scale. Imagine growing up in an environment with congruent input. Speaking of which, are you from here?"

"Grew up on a farm in Arizona, but we spent a lot of time here when I was little." My personal history struck me as intensely boring. I pointed toward a bauble in the distance. "That's Disneyland. It opened when I was three, back when the citrus trees still outnumbered the cars. I escaped and went to college back east. But I dropped out and dragged my ass home."

I hated the guttural bitterness in my voice, but when Eric made an encouraging "hmm" sound I couldn't stop myself. I sat on a patch of grass at the summit and gestured at all of Southern California. "Our principal commodities are sulfur dioxide and carbon monoxide. On bad days the solvents in the air dissolve nylon stockings, and gummy soot settles on cars. So women have been liberated from stockings, and there's a car wash on every corner."

Eric said in a sweet tone, "On our way into town Willow and I watched a beautiful sunset."

I re-lit the joint and tipped my chin toward the dark sea. "The chlorinated hydrocarbons in the air give our sunsets the ravishing iodine blush that incites lovers strolling on the beach. People keep hauling babies into this filth. Would fish spawn in a stagnant pond?" I passed the roach to Eric. "God, I sound cynical."

"Cy would say you're in high reality. Never comfortable." Eric stretched and yawned, and lay back in the grass, hands clasped behind his head. "Steve, why didn't we get to meet Rupert Seville? Please tell me the truth."

I heard myself make a tiny noise—a whimper of shock and shame. "He ran away. Lydia told you, huh?"

"*You* told me, with your eyes. You couldn't look at me when you made up that story about him smoking in bed."

"I didn't tell him about Rancho Vista. I wanted him to discover you at the dance without me intervening. He doesn't trust me since I let 'em give him a shock treatment."

The Vistan's strong hand stroked my shoulder. "Sounds like you really care about the guy. Cy says you're rescuing him."

I rocked back and forth, afraid I would cry if I tried to speak. *I need to go to your ranch*, I wanted to say, *but I'm broke and I don't have anything to offer.*

Eric's hand remained on my shoulder. "If you dropped out of college, how'd you get out of the draft?"

"Told 'em I was gay."

Eric sat up and his face swooped in close. "*Are* you?"

"I was—in love with a guy once, when I was really young." To be worthy of the Vistans, I sensed that I would have to tell everything I knew about myself, but all I managed was a tired platitude: "We're all bisexual, I think."

"That's what Cy says."

And? But?

"I haven't done much exploration in that area. Yet." He looked toward Disneyland. "Where back east? The college you dropped out of."

"Columbia. NYU after that."

"Exclusive, huh? And expensive."

Look him in the eyes this time, I told myself. "Oh, I guess," I said casually, desperate to blaze a trail into Rancho Vista, in case Rupert never showed up. "My family set up a trust for my education, and anyway I had a scholarship." The second half of this was true. I'd been a scholarship student at five colleges, until proving myself unworthy of another dime.

Eric sat up abruptly and leaped to his feet. "Let's run." When he bounded down a slope, his long hair glistened in the reddish moonlight and bounced behind him like the tail of a proud horse. I managed with great effort to keep up, sweating and panting. I was lean and wiry, had been a tennis star in high school but hadn't exercised in years, and was no match for this wilderness strider. We climbed a steep trail and reached a gap that opened to the dusky valleys east of the city. Eric watched me catch my breath, then asked, "So, Mr. Bisexual, is Lydia your lover?"

Of course the Vistans were more interested in my cheerful housemate than in a depressive pervert like me. If anyone possessed a golden kernel it was Lydia. "Do you mean, will I shoot you if you sleep with her? The answer's no."

"That's not what I had in mind. If I sleep with *you*, will *she* shoot me?"

I sat down hard on a rock. "Look, I know there's a sexual revolution going on, but I'm—I haven't—"

Eric sat very close. "Being a virgin is nothing to be ashamed of. Kind of surprising, though, a handsome guy like you."

My cock twitched. "I haven't made love with anybody in a pretty long time."

"Wow. You've got a story to tell. Well, I'm a good listener."

I stared out over the city. I could see my parents' neighborhood, now choked with shopping centers and housing tracts where once there had been orchards and horse pastures, and a boy who loved me. Beside me sat a beautiful man who offered to open the door on a new world. The money it cost to live at Rancho Vista was incidental to the true cost: Cyrus Aaron worked only with people who were blessed with golden kernels.

My throat felt so tight I wheezed as I said, "I've never talked about this stuff to anybody. I'm sorry."

Eric's gaze was gentle but direct. "Cy says it's important to explore every part of ourselves."

"Everything always comes back to Cyrus Aaron, huh?"

"People say he's the world's greatest therapist."

I looked away, confused and suddenly afraid. To me Eric's words meant, *He'll get you to rip open your soul.*

THE GROVE WAS DARK WHEN WE RETURNED. "Looks like girls' night out," Eric said, and lit a candle. He sat on Old Glory and picked up his guitar. The notes of a blues progression slithered through the house, setting a melancholy but sexy mood. In the kitchen I mashed tangerine slices into a saucepan of red wine and prepared a batch of sangria. I filled two mugs and sat on the rug, feet tucked under me, and imagined an evening of home-made music, sipping hot wine by candlelight—in a tipi. Eric began to sing the Beatles' "Yesterday" in a solid, natural baritone. I harmonized, winning a broad smile. When we sang "Michelle" I took the melody and Eric harmonized. On "Cripple Creek," a song I had never heard, Eric repeated each verse so I could learn the words:

> *I gotta gal at the head of the creek,*
> *I'm goin' up to see her 'bout the middle of the week*
> *Kiss her on the mouth, just as sweet as any wine*
> *and she'll wrap herself around me*
> *like a sweet potato vine . . .*

Suddenly he drained his second mug of sangria. "I bet that clawfoot tub's big enough for two." He picked up the candle.

I swallowed hard and followed him to the bathroom, turned on the water and dumped in a generous amount of organic bubblebath. When I turned around Eric was folding his clothes, appearing utterly at ease in his impressive nakedness. The Vistan's long body was well-muscled but naturally graceful. He splashed into the tub, sat back in the bubbles and announced, "Definitely room for two."

Was this an invitation, a therapy lesson? I lit a stick of sandalwood incense, then pulled off my shirt but kept my pants on. Slowly I scrubbed Eric's wide shoulders with a natural bristle brush. He moaned, and I slowed and intensified my scrubbing.

"Let me do this for you too," he said. He rose from the bubbles and his meaty, half-erect cock flopped against his thigh. He chuckled as if embarrassed. "That felt good. Looks like I got too relaxed or something." He gestured to me to join him, and sat back down.

Acutely aware of how irrational I was to feel ashamed of the nearly erect state of my own cock, I peeled off my bell-bottoms and splashed quickly into the bubbles. I sat with my back to Eric. He squeezed my shoulders, kneaded the tight muscles in my neck. I closed my eyes and drifted in the warmth, savoring the strong hands that coursed over my back, shoulders, neck and chest. For long moments the only sounds were the gurgling of the bath water and my moans. Finally, without speaking, Eric removed the plug from the tub, wrapped me in a towel and led me out of the sandalwood-scented steam.

The bedroom's tired lace curtain caught the moonlight. Against it I studied the silhouette of Eric's cock, now smaller than it had appeared in the bathroom. My own erection sprang out ahead of me. I dried myself, gulped the last of my sangria then lunged to the far side of the bed, pulling the comforter over my hot, naked body.

When Eric sat on the bed it sagged like a second-hand trampoline. He drew a pillow out of a duffel bag and bounced as he settled under the comforter, facing me. I turned my back and we fluffed our pillows.

"Goodnight," he whispered, and I echoed it, stirring a little. Eric's foot moved against my calf, and stayed. He yawned lazily. His hand stroked my hair and relaxed against my shoulder.

My cock was so hard it ached. Of course I knew I could respond to his affection, meet him half way, but the idea terrified me. Sex shredded the fragile web of trust that grew so rarely between people. I had loved someone once—but because of our "play" my friend had been ripped away from me forever.

Eric's hand stroked my shoulder blade and the big hot body spooned in close. An arm encircled my chest, fingers tickled the hair around my nipples. His lips grazed my ear. Moist breath warmed my face. I squirmed and arched my back, and Eric pulled me closer. His great bowed muscle nestled into the damp crevice of my butt.

And rested there. Over the roar of the freeways, the rhythm of Eric's breath was hypnotic. His cock softened, and gently tugged at me as it shrank. I allowed my breath to ride along with his. My body relaxed, my cock drooped, my mind drifted. Sex destroyed, but affection like this nurtured me. With half-closed eyes I watched the moon drift behind the wisteria, and melted in the heat of the body that held me, drifting into luxurious sleep.

I awoke on my back, full of overpowering sensations. Eric was kneeling over me, cascading his silky hair across my belly, stroking my chest. He reached for my hands and clasped them. Suddenly his mouth was everywhere, licking my nipples, my navel, blowing on my cock, kissing the head, licking the shaft, tickling my balls. Eric encircled the head with soft lips, tried to swallow it, gagged slightly but didn't withdraw. With determination he squeezed my hands tighter, closed his lips around the shaft and worked his tongue slowly down to the base. He set no regular rhythm, made no fast movements, just continued to lap with his tongue, finally swallowing the entire length of my cock in one slow, slobbering gulp, withdrawing just enough to exhale, inhale, and again swallow, lap, withdraw, breathe, swallow. His lips and tongue worked slowly, teasing and milking.

I was out of my mind. My sensual pleasures were limited to the rush that came with the first hit of good pot, and an occasional soak in the tub. I had developed a hasty, dry masturbation routine, true self-abuse that forced me to fight back memories of childhood joy-turned-nightmare. I knew climax mainly as the relief of pain. Eric gave me sensations I'd never imagined, with a tongue that invented dances across the contours of my cock. One crystalline, rational thought burst through my confusion and excitement: My God, I almost killed myself and missed this!

Now Eric established a rhythm and swirled his tongue to welcome my cock into his throat, then tightened his lips on each maddening withdrawal. Though I tried to lie still, I thrust my hips with growing insistence.

I watched by the dim scarlet glow of the sky as the mass of blond hair cascaded over my stomach and hid Eric's face. Every night at Rancho Vista, warmed by spiced wine, we would give each other this, and more. Every night—

"Stop!" I cried, and tried to free my fingers from Eric's. "I want to do this for you, too."

He grasped my hands tighter and moaned deeply, two syllables that might have been "Uh-uh." The moaning vibrated deep in his throat and pulled me into a swirling vortex of light and color and overpowering sensation. With each swallow, Eric gobbled more of me, milking with his lips, tongue and throat. I flailed and kicked the comforter off the bed. My heel clipped his shoulder, and my cock jerked powerfully, but he rode the spasms and never let me leave his mouth.

I shivered and my juices gurgled up. When the thunder finally ripped through me, Eric gagged but quickly recovered and drank my semen in deep gulps and continued to clasp my hands while he licked me clean. I trembled, overcome by his vulnerability. Finally he released my hands, moaned groggily and collapsed onto his back at the far edge of the bed.

I rolled over to him, stroked his hair and kissed his cheek. With gentle fingers I traced a path down his body. He remained quiet and still until I reached the bush below his navel. Then he grasped my hand, moved it to his collarbone and held it there.

"Can I kiss you?" I asked, wishing my face weren't stubbled with whiskers.

"That was about all I can handle," Eric answered in a flat voice. "I told you I haven't explored much with guys." To the ceiling he said, "I sort of drifted into a fantasy."

I squinted at his silhouette against the curtain. "Me, too. About your tipi."

"You know that girl in last month's *Playboy*, riding the zebra?"

I grunted, "Yeah?" as noncommittally as I could.

"I fantasized I was riding the zebra with her, and she was facing me, sitting on my cock."

The confession felt like a kick in the stomach. I breathed slowly, calming myself. The stab of anxiety I felt over the zebra girl was as foreign as the sensations of sex had been a few moments before. I was jealous of a picture in a magazine, and I had been jealous when Eric flirted with nine-hundred-year-old Bertha Flippe.

Eric now silently moved his lips, with eyes closed, as if in prayer. I savored the memory of his gift, the lingering scent of our lovemaking. He began to snore. Finally I released my breath and allowed myself to sleep.

I SMELLED FRESH-BAKED BREAD and opened my eyes on a pink morning. From the kitchen I heard Eric's voice, and Lydia's, and a trilling laugh that had to be Willow's. The freeways weren't roaring yet—on Saturdays they started late—and the birds sang joyously.

In the bathroom mirror I saw that I looked as different as I felt: a keener expression, a funny set to my chin, a glint of delight in my eyes. Last night Eric had made love to me, and I would never be the same. Vistans were free to be who they really were. Eric was discovering himself, and had chosen to explore new territory with me. Together at Rancho Vista we would learn all of life's secrets.

The kitchen was strewn with bags of bulk tea, brown rice, potatoes, dried fruit, beans and rolled oats, which the Vistans shuttled from the trunk of a red Mercedes sedan they'd driven from Colorado. Already, while I snored, Eric had baked two loaves of bread and made oatmeal.

Our guests sat on Old Glory, with papers and photo albums spread on the hookah table, and wrote an agenda for a phone call to Cyrus Aaron. From the kitchen I heard enough to understand that the entire Vista community—Dr. Aaron, his wife Zoë, and the patients and staff—were coming to Southern California in six weeks to attend a historic conference.

The voices in the living room softened. When I entered from the kitchen Willow said, "Here comes Steve now. No time like present time."

"Yeah, guys," I said quickly. "What's up?"

Lydia sat near the window and met my eyes. She bit her lip but said nothing. I could hear the tightness in my voice as I added, "We talk about everything. Forget the preliminaries. What's happening?"

"You need to get oriented," Willow said. "Eric has to express some things to you."

I felt like an alien being in my own living room—observed, monitored, gently but firmly corrected by a superior species. "It's cool," I snapped, then added as softly as I could, "Just tell me whatever's going on!"

Eric gave me a hang-dog look. "I have to express something about last night."

My heart thumped. "Sure. Should I be sitting down?"

Willow nearly laughed. "We always have Group sitting down, unless the process requires somebody to stand." Eric scooted onto the floor and sat cross-legged facing an empty space.

Lydia handed me a pillow and I sat opposite Eric, struggling to steady my breath.

"First," Willow said, "is there really such a person as Rupert Seville?"

I caught Lydia's slight shrug. From Willow's expression I saw that Eric had filled her in about my lie. "I don't know where he is. I'm sorry."

Willow chuckled. "Cy would say the ends justify the means in this case. You lied to keep the Rancho Vista door open for your friend. You don't know Cy, but he's a man of his word. Rupert will have a place at Rancho Vista when he's ready."

"When I met Cy," Eric said, "I was in jail. I told him the cops had framed me. I was afraid he wouldn't accept me at the Ranch if he knew I was a real criminal."

"And I told him I was in a rock band," Willow confessed with a smile. "He immediately figured out the truth, which was that I was *fucking* the band. I was their whore. Except I think whores get paid." She and Eric shared a chuckle while my skin burned with panic. "Anyway, Eric, what do you feel like saying to Steve?"

"Last night I broke a pretty serious rule," Eric began. "I told Steve—"

"Talk to him," Willow gently admonished.

The gray eyes zeroed in. "Steve, I told you about my zebra girl fantasy."

"You had a fantasy," Willow asked, "about balling a zebra while you two were getting it on?"

"A naked woman in *Playboy* was riding a zebra, and I fantasized I was facing her, fucking her. So Steve, I need to ask, how did that make you feel?"

"I thought it was pretty weird."

From beside the window Lydia commented, "I think it's weird that the liberated Vistans read *Playboy*."

"Eric's asking you a different question, though," Willow said, ignoring Lydia. "What you *thought* isn't relevant, Steve. He asked how you *felt*. In a relationship, that's what matters."

Thrilled at the sound of "relationship," I answered, "It scared me a little."

Willow prompted, "You felt scared of—?"

"I felt like we'd been so close." Remembering that she had prompted Eric to talk to me, I turned to him now. "And it turned out you weren't really with *me*. You were with the zebra girl."

"Which," Willow explained, "thwarted the intimacy."

"Intimacy between you and me," Eric clarified, with a sad look that touched me.

"Eric," Willow pressed, "you asked for this group. Do you have more withholds?"

"More whats?" I asked, hating the metallic annoyance in my voice.

"Things he's withheld," she replied. "Secrets. They block the flow of communication."

I wanted Lydia to look at me. She was stroking Cleo absently.

Willow's voice was deep and soft. She seemed to look right into me as she asked, "Is it hard to discuss this personal, sexual stuff in front of us?" I nodded and she continued, "*That's* what we mean about intimacy. Cy says the sex isn't the intimate part of a relationship. True intimacy is *communication*. If we don't talk about difficult things, we keep ourselves encapsulated. Isolated."

I wanted to scream. These people spoke in tongues. Did they accept me and understand me, as Cyrus Aaron said was so important? Did Eric care for me, or had he merely challenged himself in some strange way by making love to me? *Could* Eric love someone who wasn't a Vistan? They knew so much about me, and in spite of what I had read and heard, I knew damn little about them.

What I did know was that my heart was thudding, and that they had opened a narrow door while countless others remained closed.

Practicing Vistan eye contact, I told Eric, "Thanks for telling me your Withholds."

"We feel like you're a growth case," Willow said. "Otherwise we wouldn't bother trying to communicate with you like this."

A growth case must be someone who showed some hope. Hope of going to Rancho Vista.

"There's one more problem," Willow said. "Eric, you know better than to run your own case like this, especially with some-body who doesn't know any better, like Steve. You really acted like a grunt."

"It was fine about the zebra," I said.

"It wasn't fine," Willow insisted.

Eric shook his head with a pained expression. "It wasn't fine, Steve. You went into your shit afterward."

"He did what?" Lydia demanded. "I don't see that *Steve* did anything shitty."

Eric reached open hands toward Lydia and explained, "No, being in his shit just means—" He turned to face me. "You've been sort of withdrawn and sullen this morning. When you came in the room a minute ago, your voice was cold and hard."

I protested, "It was?" but of course he was right.

Willow sighed. "When you've been trained to communicate you'll hear these things in your own voice as well as other people's. You sounded angry when you told us not to waste time on preliminaries." She looked at the ceiling, then back at me. "Which is all beside the point. What Eric told you about the zebra girl would put anybody in their shit. Lydia, I know that sounds severe but it's just our way of saying Steve got depressed and preoccupied, and withdrew."

"Wow," Lydia said. "I thought Eric's zebra timing was strange, but it did seem like he was being honest."

Eric pulled his knees under his chin. "I'm sorry, Steve."

How could I keep from smiling? The two women looked on Eric and me as a couple!

"How does all this make you feel, Steve?" Willow asked.

I reeled in my smile and watched Eric's eyes squeeze shut. "Manipulated, I guess. You know, what you said did upset me, and I didn't get to talk about that with anybody."

Eric held his hands out toward me. "I'm sorry I manipulated you like that."

Willow asked if I felt like saying anything else. I forced my hands to stay in my lap although I longed to reach for Eric's.

"Yes. Eric, your attraction to the zebra girl is part of you. I wouldn't want to take that away."

"You're more advanced than most people," Willow said.

Eric nodded so his hair bounced. "I admire you a lot for sharing this stuff with us." He gazed into my eyes. My heart opened, and my cock stirred.

In a wry tone Willow prompted, "Do you appreciate anything else about Steve?"

Eric blushed. "You have beautiful eyes. And a beautiful body. And—you know, I've never gone that far with a guy before, and you made it really easy. You're hot."

"This is cool," I said brightly, "talking about stuff." I sought Lydia's eyes, but she was gazing out into the wisteria.

Eric scooted across the floor and took my hand, and we fell into a rocking hug. I felt like a Vistan, sobbing in my lover's arms.

ERIC AND WILLOW SEQUESTERED THEMSELVES IN MY BEDROOM to telephone Cyrus Aaron, and I made a quick study of their suede-bound photo albums. Aaron's young wife, Zoë, appeared in more photos than anyone—carrying a backpack, comforting a small boy, sitting at the wheel of another red Mercedes, a classic roadster with the top down. I recognized many faces from the *Radical Therapist* article, and felt haunted by an overweight girl with what looked like a teardrop tattooed on one cheek. The photographs of tipis showed exotic spaces with soft diffused light, rich carpets and inviting beds. Willow wrote at a gilt-edged desk surrounded by ferns; Eric sprawled shirtless across a bear skin. A group of Vistans appeared to be praying in a circle before a cliff covered with ancient picture-writing.

Lydia looked over my shoulder. "How many red Mercedeses have they got in their fleet, anyway?"

"Look at this rusty blue house-trailer in the background. It's one of their offices. Pretty humble, I'd say."

I saw none of the forced smiles common to family photo albums. The Vistans never seemed to be posing. They appeared comfortable with themselves and one another in a way I had never felt, with myself or anyone else.

But I dimly understood something I imagined Lydia was grasping already, and that my political father would recognize: for all the talk of community, two kinds of people lived at the Ranch. The "grunts" were unreliable patients whose families or insurance companies paid thousands a month for their therapy. The "growth cases" drove a big Mercedes on recruiting trips. Willow had called me "advanced," and hinted I might belong among the elect—but no one was inviting me to join the Vista community. Without Rupert's coattails to grab, even if I could sell my rusty car and second-hand books for enough to buy a month of therapy, I would be riding in the back of a dump truck with the manure and the other grunts.

Soon Eric and Willow packed to leave. They talked about a conference the Vistans would be attending in six weeks, in Beverly Hills, but didn't ask me to meet them there. After distracted hugs they rolled their Mercedes down the curved drive. I wanted to cry and run after them. They hadn't had time to reach the freeway before I sat down to write Eric a letter. I typed and retyped it three times. I left out "You've changed my life" from the final version, though it was true.

MASTURBATION HAD ALWAYS LEFT ME IN STARK ISOLATION, and I'd hoped sex would disappoint me. I had looked forward to telling Lydia, *It's so overrated*, had been prepared to feel sympathy for the poor souls who expected sex to make them whole. My night with Eric had abolished these notions, and aroused the hope that he and I could share a life of love and joy. He had awakened my hunger for unbridled pleasure. I slathered lotion on my cock with both hands to remind myself of his wet mouth. In my new fantasies, Eric and I kissed and cuddled and made love for hours, naked on his bear rug. The idea of death now seemed a million years away. I embraced my new life in a way I'd never thought possible, even though I still wasn't sure what life I was living—that of a liberated homosexual? Hell, I didn't care. For now, to live was enough.

But on Monday I woke up in dread. Turner might already know Rupert was gone. He'd certainly learn of it on Tuesday when Rupert didn't show up for his shock treatment. After torturing a full morning's complement of patients the bastard might also check closely enough to learn that his initials had been forged on a pass-approval form. I could be fired by noon.

But the psychiatrist wasn't in E.C.T on Monday, and I relaxed. Nurse Cathcart presided with a greenhorn resident. One of the other techs said Turner had taken an unscheduled vacation.

Later, in the staff lunchroom, I carried my tray around looking for a place to sit. The only available table was a small one already occupied by Cathcart. She smoked a cigarette and read a paperback book. Before the Vistans came into my life, I would have taken my tray outside rather than sit with her. But now I beelined for the empty chair and put my tray down across from hers. She ignored me.

"Turner hurt the wrong person this time," I announced cheerily. "Rupert Seville's grandmother has an army of lawyers who are about to take this place apart brick by brick."

Cathcart drew on her cigarette and didn't look up, but she exhaled her smoke straight at me. "I'm retiring in three months. I don't give a good God damn what happens to this snake pit or anybody in it."

"I have copies of his notes and I'm gonna testify against him. Will you join me, after you retire?"

"I used to be like you." She stubbed out her cigarette and slitted her eyes at me. "If you're lucky they'll fire you while you're young enough to find something useful to do."

WHEN HE DIDN'T RETURN FROM THE PHONY PASS, Rupert officially became a missing person. On Tuesday, at home, I received a Mardi Gras postcard from New Orleans.

Seeing the world, man. Leaving for Paris today, then to Marrakesh. You did your best. Now I'm doing mine. Keep on truckin'. R.

Lydia read the card with a smile. "Aren't you relieved he isn't damning you to the lake of fire? And look, he's having some fun, instead of resigning himself to life in a back ward."

I grunted. "He could have gone to Rancho Vista!"

When I phoned his grandmother, she remarked, "I'll never forget the panic in your voice when you first phoned me. I didn't know how strongly Rupie felt about leaving that hospital."

"Obviously none of us did."

"If you hear from him, please get him to Dr. Aaron, and worry about calling me later."

Get *myself* to Aaron, I thought.

6.

"IMAGINE MY SURPRISE," Turner whined, "to find that while on vacation I had approved a pass for a depressive pyromaniac paranoid schizophrenic, three days after his first E.C.T. treatment." He looked up from Rupert's chart. "Can you imagine my surprise?"

I studied the carved edge of his oak desk. About two minutes after returning from vacation, Turner had detected Rupert's name in the Unauthorized Absence register. He now jabbed a finger at the forged initials on the approval form. "A patient who has overstayed his visit with Grandmama by six days."

I yawned and didn't bother to cover my mouth.

The doctor chewed and licked his lips, then slammed a fist onto the chart. "I've talked to the Attorney General!" Shrilly he catalogued provisions of the California Penal Code and various federal laws I had violated. "Before the legal system's through with you, you'll wish all you'd lost was your job. We know you helped this patient escape. He is a danger to himself and others. The blood of his victims will be on your hands, Mr. Smartass."

Relishing my position beside Rupert in the *dangerous* category, I rose to leave.

Turner's lips stretched into a cruel line. "You'll have ample time to ponder the results of your behavior. In prison."

As if operated by remote control, the door opened abruptly and a security officer entered, hand on holster—a guy near my age, who sometimes joined the patients and me at the volleyball net.

I yelped, "I have the right to a lawyer!"

"Come along," the officer ordered. With one hand he clutched his pistol, and with the other grasped my elbow. I flattened myself against the wall and faced Turner. "You can send me to the firing squad but you've tortured your last patient." The guard tugged at me. I clung to the doorway and screamed, "You're finished, you fucking monster! The papers know all about you." Turner's smirk didn't fade as I allowed myself to be dragged into the dim hallway, wailing, "People are giving depositions!"

Once we reached the sunlight the guard loosened his grip. I wished I'd kept my mouth shut about exposing Turner to the press. The guard could confiscate the copies I'd made from Rupe's chart. "I'm not opening my knapsack without a search warrant," I declared.

"No firing squad, no searches," the guard said. "Turner *would* have me shoot you if he could, but he's bluffing as bad as you are. I'm just supposed to escort you to your car. Then you high-tail it on out of here." He released my arm. "Do you have any idea what a deposition is?"

I climbed into the Ghia. "Something very fucking legal."

Before meeting the Vistans I would have burned rubber. Instead I nodded to the officer and drove away quietly. Once outside the hospital gate I pulled over on a side street and cried. My final words to Turner had felt so good to say, I'd almost believed them.

Lydia often asked why I stayed in a job I so clearly hated, and I could never admit that I didn't think I was capable of much else. Herding droolers at Los Perdidos had felt like my destiny, the proper livelihood for a five-time dropout, the one thing I had believed I couldn't fail at.

AT THE GROVE I TORE OPEN A LARGE ENVELOPE from Eric, containing a hard-cover copy of *The Quest for Unconditional Love*. This was exciting enough, but my heart leaped when I opened the book and found a letter, red ink on both sides of a sheet ripped from a yellow legal pad: *My feelings for you aren't strong, but they are good feelings . . . Since we made love, I've experienced a quantum leap with my guitar playing, new chords and picking patterns . . . Cy says we need to define our relationship.*

I sat in the porch swing and read the letter several times. What did it mean to "define" a relationship? How could Eric acknowledge that he'd grown as a musician after our lovemaking, but claim his feelings weren't strong? The Vistans were highly developed, but they lived in twentieth-century America where men who loved other men were shunned. Eric would need time to get used to his true feelings.

Hours later I was still in the swing, working on my fifth draft of a letter to Eric and surrounded by the crumpled earlier attempts. Lydia came home and snuggled beside me. She confirmed that Turner had been bluffing about prosecution, since there was no real evidence I had helped Rupe escape. Los Perdidos was buzzing over my outburst, which several people had heard from the halls.

I nodded absently, then read Eric's letter aloud and dithered about its meaning.

"You're more concerned about a letter from him than losing your job?" When I shrugged she presented me with a folder. Inside, in lush script on creamy paper, I read, *Proclamation Concerning Steve Susoyev, Genius Compassionate*, above the signatures of a few dozen patients and three or four staff members.

"Blind Michael?" I asked.

"He dictated it to Hermione. She did the calligraphy."

I ran a finger down the eccentric signatures. "I bet nobody's asked Bertha Flippe to sign anything in forty years."

"Only when you registered her to vote," Lydia reminded me. "I can put the Proclamation in your personnel file so it follows you when you go job-hunting."

"No way. I'm framing this. Besides, can you imagine what kind of place would hire Los Perdidos castoffs?"

She flashed a sly smile. "You're going to Rancho Vista with or without Rupert, huh?"

Before I could respond she stood and grabbed the garden hose, then swaggered across the porch with a generous length swinging between her legs. In a dumb-bunny voice she said, "I'm curious but yellow. Hey, let's bunk together! I've never fooled around with guys, but I'll give you the best blow job in history and maybe you'll fall in love with me."

"Ha, ha."

She dropped the hose. "I'm not worried about Rupert. He's a schizophrenic survivor. Do whatever *you* need to survive."

We sat quietly while the sky darkened. Cleo sprang into my lap and hunkered down—since my night with Eric, even she could tolerate me.

Lydia finally broke the silence. "When you talked about suicide all the time I shielded you from some things. I owe sixty grand in back taxes on this place. About twice what it's worth."

"My God," I tried to joke, "you sound like a grownup."

She humored me with a weak smile. "Remember when we moved into this dump? We were gonna save the world."

"Eradicate racism, war and poverty."

"Greed. Envy. Jealousy!"

We recited the many things we *had* accomplished during the two years since assuming stewardship of the tiny abandoned island of burned-out citrus and walnut trees. We'd established a sanctuary for anyone bold enough to believe, even after Kent State, that human society could do something noble. We registered everyone we knew to vote. I counseled young men of all sexual persuasions on how to persuade the draft board that they were flaming fairies. Lydia housed Chilean refugees in the barn and married a Polish activist to get him a green card—Ryczard, a "documents specialist" who once explained to me in detail how to create a U.S. passport using a dead baby's birth certificate, "Easy like to make bomb from household cleaning products."

She took my hand. "Bulldozers will show up soon. I'm going south. Far south. Ryczard is doing relief work. I'm helping."

"You mean he's running counterfeit passports to Chilean refugees, and you'll risk prison to prove you're not a tool of the oppressors. Didn't he slap you once?"

"Shall I attempt an equally incisive analysis of your decision to move to the psychedelic Shangri-la?"

I pulled her tight against me. "No, thanks."

I WOULD ALWAYS KNOW THE WAY to my parents' house, but had stopped calling the place *home* while I still lived there. Except for certain street names, almost nothing in the neighborhood was familiar. The field where I'd flown kites, the horse barn that sheltered my aborted explorations of love, the dirt lane where my father trotted alongside while I learned to pedal a bicycle—all had been swallowed by a shopping mall. The creek I'd learned to swim in ran silent now, somewhere under the shopping center's vast parking lot.

I cruised past the turnoff to my parents' street and tried to rehearse my appeal. At this hour my mother should still be able to walk and talk. I wanted her to be tipsy but not drunk, and hoped she'd be drinking the sherry my father encouraged rather than the gin she preferred. Which argument would convince my parents to fund my move to Rancho Vista: Lydia's concern over my suicide obsession, or Dr. Aaron's belief that it was a crime not to live up to one's potential?

The house had been built twenty years before, in honor of my anticipated birth. Long and low and flat-roofed, constructed of pink bleeding brick and rough beams, it looked like a Mexican jail dolled up with climbing roses. Its strangeness had embarrassed me when I was a child, but Lydia had taught me to appreciate that it didn't resemble the stucco cookie-cutter tract units that sprang up near it.

When I pulled into the driveway, my father opened the kitchen door and waved. Tall and dark-haired, with a lean, well-defined body, Alex Susoyev grew handsomer as he aged. Lydia called him a fox. Only people close to our family knew that the distinguished-looking man was pussywhipped by the tiny she-devil known as Susi.

My father shook my hand, then put my dollar-fifty rosé on ice. From the living room came my mother's lovely voice, singing a lied of Schubert. I went to the piano and bent to kiss her. She acknowledged me with a nod but continued the song, one of my favorites. Her dramatic phrasing and slow cadence infused pathos into a ballad about lovers planning a tryst at a garden gate. Tonight she had the icy-sharp breath of gin. On a small table I spotted the crystal tumbler containing the remains of her martini.

From the mantle I retrieved a lipstick-stained coffee cup half-full of what smelled like cream sherry and moved it to the little table, then gulped the inch of gin that remained in the tumbler.

In the kitchen Alex sipped at the glass of scotch I knew he would nurse all evening. He had prepared a huge pot of his famous spaghetti, with corn on the cob. We discussed horse racing and the likely fate of the soldiers court-martialed for the murder of civilians at My Lai. "By the way, I ditched the martini," I said. "I need to talk to you both about something serious."

Alex shrugged. "It's a little late for that in the concert hall, but you can talk to me."

"Maybe she'll eat something."

He chuckled. I set the dining table, lit the candles and stood behind my mother at the piano to announce, "Dinner's served!"

"You could respect an artist at work," Susi answered, and continued singing. Even on martinis she had a lovely voice. I enjoyed the last refrain then watched her reach for the sherry mug. She took a sip and rose to join Alex and me in the dining room, with no comment on the disappearance of her gin.

Alex served the meal and filled three glasses with my rosé. Susi pushed food around on her plate. Feeling the gin in my belly and head, I began to speak with no idea where my words would lead. "I met a psychiatrist who works with people my age," I ventured. Susi and Alex smiled pleasantly, having heard many entertaining mental hospital stories. My mother looked tiny in her captain's chair. Slowly she gnawed at an ear of sweet corn—her standard bluff to create the illusion of eating—then thrust aside the mangled cob, leaving long rows of toothmarks.

"He calls me a high-potential, overwhelmed dropout," I continued. "He has a ranch in Colorado, three hundred acres in the mountains." Alex smiled. Money didn't impress him but acreage did. I marched into my story. "At first I thought I would get training from him, and I may do that later. But right now I need his help *personally.*"

My father's smile faded. "Another therapist? What's wrong with you now?"

Susi threw back her head. "He goes to those charlatans to punish us for giving him too much freedom. Too much respect. Too much *love!*" She sipped delicately from her sherry mug.

"What's wrong with me now?" I took a deep breath and my head reeled as if I were stepping out of a high-flying airplane without a parachute. "I've recently realized I'm a homosexual."

The silence felt like the false calm of a shock treatment, after the electric impulse and before the convulsions. Susi gulped the last of her wine. Alex's fork stopped twirling spaghetti. He opened his mouth to speak, but Susi slammed down her empty mug and beat him to it. "You didn't think you had us fooled."

"He sure as hell had *me* fooled!" Alex yelled. "But this is all going according to your plan, starting with the Oscar Wilde *fairy* tales you read him when he was six."

"He was reading on his own by that age," she snapped. "Thanks to *me.* And yes, he read whatever interested him. Wilde is an important writer. If you knew anything, you'd know his tragic life was an advertisement for heterosexual conformity."

Perfect. They were sniping at each other and I was ready to slip out the back door. I could return in a day or two, after this battle fizzled, and present my Rancho Vista proposal.

"Those 'Blame the parents' theories are passé," Susi asserted. "It was the DeWitt boy, wasn't it, who made you this way."

I looked at her, shocked into sudden grief, and bit my lip to keep from saying, *If anything, I made Dean that way.*

Her eyes blazed. "He wasn't normal. They killed him for it in reform school!"

I hadn't heard Dean's name in years, had rarely thought of my boyhood friend since Susi mailed the modest obituary during my second, and final, semester at Columbia. I crossed my arms over my chest and wondered why I'd been stupid enough to seek comfort here.

Alex took over. "That fruit took pricks up his ass and then

put them in his mouth. What tricks did he teach you?"

"Where do you come up with this shit?" I snarled, then shut up. This wasn't an argument. I wanted twelve hundred dollars.

"Maybe we should have sent you away," my father continued, "like Dean's parents did with him."

"To be murdered?" I swallowed dryly and looked to my mother, a questionable source of support, but now my only hope.

"We thought we'd heard it all," she said with false amusement. "You've gotten a kick out of shocking us—that fright wig you call your hair, the hitchhiking trips to New York when you were fourteen. And what was the point of being the youngest student ever admitted if you were going to drop out before the end of your freshman year? I guess *that's* where you met the perverts who got you involved in this, if it really wasn't Dean DeWitt."

Alex pointed a finger at me. "After a few years you'll lose control of your bowels. You'll spend the rest of your life with a rubber bag strapped to your leg and a hose up your ass."

My laugh was a sharp, amazed bark.

He pounded the table. "What's so goddamned funny? Are you a homosexual or are you just trying to provoke us?"

"The Draft Board rejected me because of it."

I knew this would distract my father, whose distrust of the government had endeared him to Lydia the moment I introduced them. "Enormously sophisticated computer systems keep track of everything about you!" he ranted. "You can't keep your exemption confidential."

Susi flattened her hands on the table, suddenly the voice of pragmatism. "All right. What does this psychiatrist propose to do for you that you can't do for yourself?"

"He can *cure* me," I improvised.

While they absorbed the lie, I recalled Willow's words: *Cy would say in this case, the ends justify the means.* "I want a normal life. My therapist wants to use electric shock on my genitals." I looked from Susi to Alex and spoke slowly. "I'm telling you my most shameful secret because I need your help. I can start therapy at Rancho Vista for twelve hundred dollars."

"Or you can stop this malarkey right now, for free," my father replied. "Your mother insists we didn't make you a homosexual. I agree. So we don't have to pay to fix you."

I sat up straight. "I tried to kill myself last week."

"You must not have tried very hard." Alex walked to the mantle and picked up a framed newspaper photo of a ten-year-old me, standing among much older kids, holding up a spelling trophy. He stood the gilt-framed picture in front of me. "I've always known my son would never fail at anything he tried."

I glanced at the bright-eyed boy in the photo, a child with too much promise and no future, accepting an award for spelling "crossopterygian". How pathetic that my father thought my ability to spell six-syllable words was a guarantee of success in life. I didn't bother reminding him that I'd washed out of the statewide competition, by misspelling "erudite."

I looked up to see my mother's earrings dancing in the candlelight. "You do seem unhappy. You were such a happy little boy."

I slumped over the photograph. "I'm mentally ill! I didn't manage to kill myself because I have still have a shred of hope. But I'm desperate. Please help me."

LYDIA CREPT INTO MY ROOM early in the morning and kissed my cheek. I pretended to be asleep, afraid I couldn't handle saying goodbye to the one person who had never let me down. If she remembered today was my birthday she didn't let on. I waited until I heard her old minibus roar out of the grove, then got into the tub and shaved, exposing my face for the first time in months. I wanted the Vistans to see who I really was.

I dressed and folded my father's twelve-hundred-dollar check, payable to Cyrus Aaron, M.D., into my shirt pocket. Alex had handed over his Hasselblad camera as a birthday present, and I carefully packed it in my knapsack. My parents' love was conditional, dependent on my promise to become normal. But at least they loved me for something.

I packed my Army surplus camping gear and books into a foot locker, clothes into a duffel bag. What didn't fit I jammed into pillowcases and boxes. I left my stash of red-haired Cambodian for Lydia, along with the hookah. At Rancho Vista, in the care of the world's greatest therapist, I would welcome the dreams I'd so vigorously suppressed with my nightly dose of marijuana.

On the seat of the Ghia I found Lydia's worn copy of the *Rubáiyát*, her favorite passage marked by a satin ribbon. *Happy Birthday, vaya con dios* was inscribed on the flyleaf. I squeezed it into the footlocker with my Oxford English Dictionary and Cavafy poems, and *The Quest for Unconditional Love*.

First I drove east, through Riverside, and soon the smog thinned to reveal a pale blue sky. The day turned cold and I put up the car's rag top, then discovered the heater didn't work. I turned north on Highway 395 and drove past Death Valley and through broad canyons of patchy desert, where I stopped to put on a turtleneck and the only two sweaters I owned.

I had hitchhiked through this country and peered at it from airplanes, but never considered a place with fewer than ten thousand people per square mile a *destination*. Each little wind-scrubbed town reminded me that I'd been living in a cesspool. No wonder death had looked so good.

The Ghia began thumping at midnight, beyond Reno, and the thump turned into a clang just past the Utah line. Soon after that I coasted onto the gravel shoulder. A highway patrolman called a tow truck and the driver diagnosed a thrown rod—"Rebuild the engine or sell 'er for scrap." I accepted fifty dollars for my car, then used ten to buy the driver's knitted cap and insulated gloves, and said goodbye to more of my possessions in the boxes and pillowcases. I hit the side of the road on the outskirts of Blair with my foot locker, duffel bag and knapsack.

Even at this hour cars poured into Nevada, and the few that went the other way whizzed past me. I stood before a road sign, with my hair tucked under the cap. My Army surplus parka, too heavy for the climate I'd come from, now felt like tissue. A sharp wind bit through the feeble seams. Finally an oil tanker stopped and took me into the night. I slept through Salt Lake City and the Colorado border, and the trucker woke me up at the junction to the two-lane state highway that led southeast to Keystone.

Stunned by the cold, I kicked crusty snow from a patch of ground, then shimmied into my sleeping bag and sat against a sign that read, "Welcome to Abraham County."

I tightened the sleeping bag's drawstring around my face and waited in my feather cocoon. Waves of exhaustion swept over me. I shut my eyes against the stinging wind and considered the legendary pleasure of freezing to death—a warm sleep enveloped you and you never woke up.

My nose ran and the snot froze on my lip. I closed my eyes and time froze, too. I drifted, ready for any destiny. Later I stirred when I felt fleas biting my face, and opened my eyes on a swirl of tiny snowflakes.

When headlights approached, I leaped to my feet like a giant caterpillar, fighting with the drawstring. A pickup rattled by, then the fluttering snow in its wake burned deep red in the glow of its single brake light. Once out of the bag I ran to the truck and encountered a cowboy of about my age in a ten-gallon hat and faded clothes. "I'm goin' up home," the young man said, "clear to the end a the road. Ninety miles past where the pavement ends."

I accepted his help with my gear. "I'm going to Keystone."

"Oh my heck, that's past the end of the *dirt* road."

"I'll pay you to take me."

The pickup flew past dreamy rockscapes. What might the cowboy know about Rancho Vista? I began to formulate a circumspect question but was spared the effort when the kid said, "You must be goin' to Dr. Aaron's oasis."

"Well, sort of," I answered carefully.

The cowboy offered his hand. "Dove. Dove MacKenzie."

I shook the strong hand. "Steve Susoyev." I didn't want to care what the kid thought of me, but wanted to hear the local opinion of Cyrus Aaron's ranch. I added, "I'm a reporter."

"A hitchhiking reporter?"

"Free-lance. My car blew up outside Reno. Gotta deadline for a magazine article on Vista. So here I am." I fished my father's impressive camera out of my knapsack as evidence. "So what's the scoop on Dr. Aaron?"

"He's got a hareem out there at the rancho. Me and my dad helped 'em put in their water system. In the summer you can hike up to the edge of their canyon and see 'em skinny-dipping' in the river. Good show with binoculars. You might finish your magazine story and decide to stay."

"I'm not much of a back-to-nature type." I watched fresh snow flying past as if the pickup were in a wind tunnel.

"It's cushy out there. No phones or lectricity, but they got a steambath and a D8 bulldozer. And in town Dr. Aaron's got a jacuzzi at his trailer."

"He lives in a trailer?"

"A triple-wide. Three trailers, as big as would make it over these roads, all bolted together. Mom says it's like a fancy restaurant inside, with orchids and Oriental rugs and whatnot. They got another old ratty trailer they call the 'Blue Worm.'"

"I saw a picture of it."

The highway narrowed. I dozed, too tired to think straight. Some time later I jolted awake when Dove stopped at a signal light in the center of a town—the only signal light, as far as I could tell. The cracked pavement abruptly ended and the truck regained speed on a washboard road. Snow accumulated steadily and formed a thick pad that softened the bumps. I couldn't read the mileage signs through the blasting snow. "I might have died out there if you hadn't picked me up."

"Sometimes two days go by without no cars on this road."

"Jesus!"

Dove flashed a toothy smile. "You can cuss in front a me, but don't be takin' the Lord's name in vain around my mama."

I made a pillow of my jacket and pretended to sleep, wondering what I was getting into. Lydia seemed to think I was traveling beyond the end of the road merely to be with Eric. I believed Eric was my soulmate—reason enough to come to the wilderness, but something even more vital drew me. Yes, I loved Eric, was fascinated by Willow, and wanted for myself the easy grace I'd seen in the Vistans' photographs. But the destination of my journey was Cyrus Aaron, the man whose miracle-working energy was merely channeled by the cheerful Vistans.

An hour or so later the truck barreled over a narrow plank bridge. The blizzard was weakening. The muddy road twisted into a serpentine ridge Dove called the "Razorback," flanked by canyons two thousand feet deep.

The cloud-cover broke apart. Moonlight revealed a silver strip of river glimmering at the bottom of the left gorge, and giant white boulders lining the right. Soon the road widened and we passed between snowy fields dotted with dark houses, and the tidy farm where Dove lived with his parents and seven brothers. A few miles beyond, a lane cut past an abandoned motel. "That's the road to your rancho," he said. "Another ten miles east. I'll drop you at their office here in town."

Beside a frozen pond he showed me the Keystone Post Office, like an outhouse with an enormous flagpole planted in front of it. A hundred yards farther, in a large clearing, stood the Vistans' trailers, each wearing a tall hat of snow. The closer one—Dr. Aaron's home—was as big as a warehouse, with a wrap-around deck and brass light fixtures.

Dove stopped in front of the small, rusty Blue Worm. A dim light burned inside. "Lotta stuff for a few days," he remarked. We hoisted my foot locker and hauled it to the covered porch. He waved away a five-dollar bill, climbed into his truck and drove off the way he'd come.

Between the mountains and the clouds, a strip of sky grew violet with a trace of dawn. I knocked at the door of the Blue Worm. When no one answered I tried the handle and found it was locked. Or, from the look of it, rusted shut.

7

CLOUDS OF FAIRY-GLITTER SNOWFLAKES whirled around me. Beyond the white field that surrounded the Vistans' town trailers, a monolith of red sandstone emerged from the frozen mist, a vermilion cliff at least a thousand feet high and a mile wide, shining gold in the day's first light.

I ventured across the powdery snow and sank to the tops of my Army boots. The little icy snowflakes stung my face. I considered walking the ten miles to where the Vistans actually lived. I would see Eric and rock in the cradle of unconditional love before nightfall.

Or be turned away like the intruder I was. Suddenly I couldn't believe I'd come all this way without a single practical thought. The Vistans thrived on honesty and directness. What could be more dishonest than showing up unannounced? But if I confessed I'd been fired, and that this was my last detour off the road to a Seconal overdose, the world's greatest therapist would demand far more than twelve hundred dollars for a month's treatment. And even if Aaron took me in, how could I possibly earn my keep after my parents' twelve hundred bucks ran out?

The snowflakes warmed into splashes of rain. I ran to the protected porch of the Blue Worm and watched black clouds roil in from the southwest. The sun struck me from beneath the storm's eastern lip. Across the hostile sky streaked a bolt of lightning, then a sharp crack of thunder rattled the windows of the old blue trailer. Rain poured down. The surrounding snow retreated into patches that seemed to float inches above the ground, held aloft by the dense winter-dead grass. The wind shifted. I moved to the far end of the little porch but the rain still soaked my pants and duffel bag.

The black clouds collided with the redrock monolith and emptied themselves. Crystal water splashed down the crevices in the rock and glittered in the slanting sunlight. The cliff face spouted countless waterfalls. Lightning struck a hazy point to the east, in the realm where the heart of Rancho Vista lay. Thunder rumbled from every direction.

A shocking explosion on the cliff face jolted me. Even more terrifying was a huge dead pine tree that catapulted over the edge in a torrent of red-brown water, with boulders that looked as big as cars. The tree spiraled in freefall and splintered with a deafening crash at the base of the stone mountain.

The thunderheads churned toward the phantom land to the east, past the great ridge of rock that lay like a sea-wall between town and the canyons I had seen in photographs. The rain slowed and came in spasms. The monolith, now in darkness, spewed half as much water as a minute earlier. The flood followed the storm east toward Rancho Vista.

I gazed toward the canyons. A pygmy forest of sage and juniper stretched for miles over brilliant pink sand. Patches of snow survived around several bushes. Somewhere out in those canyons Eric lay in his bed, possibly thinking of the magic night he had spent in Perdido Valley. He was an early riser. By now he was probably heating water on the wood stove for a morning cup of tea. If I were with him we would be planning our day, holding each other under the bear rug. Defining our relationship.

The wind whipped tall skeletal poplars that ringed the clearing around the trailers. The rain stopped but the sky seemed darker than before. I sloshed with my knapsack through the wet, dead grass toward the road and approached the huge triple-wide trailer that Dove had said was Aaron's home. It was set high off the ground, with pale gray wooden siding and blue trim. Soft lights glowed through swagged draperies in two corner windows. As I came closer, I heard a woman's voice, too low for me to understand, seven pointed syllables, then a man's voice, very distinct: "You fucking cunt." After a pause the woman spoke again, the same seven syllables, and the man repeated mechanically, "You fucking cunt." Again a pause, again the woman's indistinguishable words, again, "You fucking cunt."

Horrified and fascinated, I moved closer and caught the woman's words, in a French accent, "You are a pervert, Aaron." Again the man said, "You fucking cunt."

Sneaking still closer, I brushed past an ancient cottonwood tree and kicked over a snowbound bucket full of rusty car parts. The voices stopped and a window opened. I ducked behind the tree.

"Who's there?" Aaron called.

I listened to the thumping of my heart.

"Who the hell is that?"

I froze in terror of having done everything wrong. "Dr. Aaron?" I asked. "Cy?" I peered around the tree and saw the big man's shirtless silhouette in an open window.

"Who's there? Why are you hiding?"

"It's Steve Susoyev. From Perdido Valley."

There was a sickening silence, then "You found the Seville kid!"

I stepped toward the window. "I—no."

Aaron turned away and the woman said something unintelligible. "It's Eric's boyfriend from California," he told her. "Susoyev. He's brought Rupert Seville."

"No," I repeated loudly. "I brought myself."

"What?" The silhouette faced me again.

"I've come to ask if I can stay." I took a long, slow breath and approached the window. "I want to spend a month at Rancho Vista."

"Good lord!" He chuckled. "Meet me at the front door."

The hardwood door was ajar when I reached it. Desperately aware of my imposition, I entered a large bright room whose parquet floor gleamed under a rock-crystal chandelier. Glass doors protected a sky-lit atrium where a tiny waterfall tinkled into a pool dense with moss and purple water flowers. I recognized the scent of jasmine, and gawked at yellow-white flowers that bloomed on bamboo lattices. Even in L.A. the place would have felt extravagant. In this muddy wilderness it was an enchanted oasis.

"Welcome," Cy called out. I walked toward the voice across a silky Persian rug in shades of rose and turquoise. "Honey, do you want to join us?" Cy asked in a distant room.

"*Mais oui*," the woman answered. "But I am awaiting Sally's *call* from Geneva. If I sit over here I can talk to her without disturbing your *beece*-ness discussion!"

"We'll be a moment," Cy called to me.

A door closed far down the hallway. I shut my eyes and inhaled the intoxicating scent of tropical flowers. My socks squished inside my boots and I saw with panic that I had tracked mud across the rug. Frantically I jerked off my boots, rushed to set them on a grass mat at the front door, and hurried to the kitchen where I dampened a dish cloth.

Aaron approached in a pair of white briefs and navy dress socks, and found me on all fours mopping up my bootprints. The sight of the famous psychiatrist in his underwear shocked me into silence. Then I blurted, "I made a mess. I'm really sorry."

The skin around Aaron's cobalt-blue eyes crinkled. "At least you're cleaning it up. A grunt wouldn't even notice." He waited for me to finish, then led me into the hallway. He was built like a football player. His powerful body was elaborately patterned with silver-brown hair. Even his calves bulged. He looked like someone who ran ten miles before breakfast.

I peeled off my jacket and followed Cy into an enormous, cluttered bedroom, the entire width of the three trailers, carpeted in soft blue. Marble steps at one end led up to a square tub. Two king-side beds dominated the other end of the room. Bookcases took up most of the wall space, and the floor was stacked with books and magazines. Shallow cardboard trays on the beds and floor overflowed with cassette tapes and tiny spiral notebooks.

"Etienne!" Zoë Aaron exclaimed, with the animation of a six-year-old. She stood to offer her hand and I was startled to see that she wore only white panty hose. Her full breasts were beautifully shaped with enormous, dark nipples. At Garth's funeral she had appeared serious and mature. Now, with her black hair secured by red lacquer chopsticks in an eccentric topknot, she looked like a grown-up little girl. "You are a hero to us! You gave Eric the new *lease* on life."

My mother claimed that even modern women were enchanted by a kiss on the hand. Following her advice had earned me a seat in the front row in kindergarten. I gently took Zoë's hand and drew it to my lips.

"Cy!" she squealed. "Etienne is a genius, a growth case *and* a gentleman."

Her husband fiddled with a professional-looking tape recorder mounted in a bookcase. He lifted off both reels without rewinding the tape and set them on a shelf. The repetitive argument I had heard from outside now made sense—the voices had been a recorded snatch of conversation played over and over. Aaron reached for a fresh tape and reel, set them in place, and turned abruptly to look straight into my eyes.

The contact was like an electrical current—frightening but absolutely compelling. I couldn't disengage from the gaze once it gripped me.

Aaron gestured for me to sit on the empty bed. I hesitated, afraid of soiling the rose satin spread. I folded my jacket inside out before dropping it onto the carpet.

"So your poor friend Seville is still at large?"

"I haven't found him," I admitted. "I took time off from my job. I'd like to study here with you. For a month." I tried not to look again into the piercing eyes that searched my face. "I brought twelve hundred dollars."

"Etienne," Zoë said, "it is not un*us*ual for a young person to seek us out, but we must under*stand* the motives. Can you truly be a growth case? Eric thinks yes, and he knows you—hmm—*een*-timately."

"Yes, I want to grow." I blushed but enjoyed the sweetness of Zoë's tone. She didn't mock my love for Eric, and even seemed to think it was reciprocated. "I've reached a plateau." I hoped I sounded like a growth case, mature and self-determined.

Aaron flipped a lever on the tape machine. A red light glowed and the reels turned slowly. "Steve Susoyev, you've manipulated me before," he teased. "Very impressively."

I watched the needles of the recorder's little gauges jump as Aaron spoke. I caught myself chewing on a stray wisp of my hair. The tape reels turned and the needles danced as the machine recorded a distant peal of thunder. "As Zoë says," Aaron went on, "we have to understand your motives. Where do you see yourself functioning right now on Maslow's hierarchy of needs?"

Oh, Jesus. I stifled a groan. Abraham Maslow and a ladder of needs, something I'd once seen on the blackboard in one of the many psychology classes I had dropped.

The phone rang and gave me a moment to think.

Zoë sang into the receiver, "Bonjour!" then turned away and continued softly in French.

I remembered only the bottom and top rungs of Maslow's multi-tiered ladder, and ad-libbed, "No longer struggling at the edge of survival but stymied on the way to self-actualization."

Aaron laughed. "An A-plus on the glib scale. But I know you're capable of something real."

I looked up at the ceiling, white acoustic tile trimmed with strips of golden bamboo—and crossed with the cables of four hanging microphones that led to the tape recorder. "I feel like a failure because I didn't prevent Rupert's shock treatment. He had to run away because I couldn't protect him. He really *is* struggling to survive."

Aaron smiled thoughtfully. "How could a bright, sensitive kid like you help administer shock treatments to someone you care about?"

"I couldn't handle it." I was tempted to confess I'd been fired. "That job is a dead end for me. Your work is dynamic."

Aaron pulled a chair close and faced me. "You've mentioned a sense of failure."

I mumbled in agreement.

"As if you've reached the end of your rope?"

I nodded.

Aaron spoke gently but firmly. "We learned you weren't on the state hospital payroll a few days ago. We tried to reach you there after we heard from Mr. Seville's grandmother."

My face blazed. Why was he torturing me? Those electric-blue eyes were trying to grab me. I wanted to bolt from the room, out into the mud.

"You lost your job," Aaron said flatly, "but came in here telling us you're on sabbatical." Zoë, still on the phone, dismissed her husband with a wave of her hand and winked at me.

I stared at the clutter of books and notepads on the floor. The Vistans would sit in one of their sessions and listen to this tape and laugh at the lying buffoon, laugh until the news of my suicide reached them. But I wouldn't return to Southern California for Seconals. I'd leap from a two-thousand-foot cliff at the ridge the locals called the Razorback.

"Imagine a mind like yours," Cy said, sounding bitter, "and they had you holding down convulsing psychotics." He smiled, his face suddenly warm and open. "What's the *worst* thing you've endured, Steve? I mean ever, not just at the snake pit."

"I'd better go. I'm sorry I lied to you. I was afraid you wouldn't accept me if you knew I'd lost my job." I rose and bunched my jacket under my arm.

"I can see you're desperate," Aaron said. "Give me credit for knowing my job. I remember your pinched face at Garth's funeral, the fear and pain in your eyes. Please sit back down. Your month at Rancho Vista started when I turned on the tape recorder. Don't waste the time you're paying for. You owe it to yourself to answer my question."

I took a deep breath and sat on the bed, still clutching my jacket. "The worst thing I've endured?" Where had it begun? When I realized the world was a dangerous, hostile place for people like me. My nightmares had cemented the knowledge that if I lived as myself I would be destroyed, a fag literally beaten to death, and the murder not even investigated. The decision to kill myself had emerged as the only rational alternative.

But had there been a moment even before the nightmares? Yes. The rare times I let myself remember it, I vomited. I had resolved never to tell anyone.

"Some guys," I said, dizzy-sick. "When I was thirteen. Hurt me."

"They hurt you." Cy Aaron's voice was as soft as his eyes.

In a year of sessions with the genital-electrocuting Dr. Sutton, I had never considered humiliating myself by speaking of this. Urged by Cy's concerned expression, I heard the words pour out of me: "Four guys shoved a bar of soap into me, up my ass, in the gym shower. After a tennis match. There was blood, more than you'd think."

A twist in my stomach, nothing more. Cy held his gaze and asked matter-of-factly, "Did any of them have hardons?"

I stared at him, astonished by his intuition. "One did. How'd you know?"

"I've been studying people a long time. Those goons *raped* you. It's a miracle you've held onto your humanity. But look at the cost."

Zoë was now speaking German into the phone, then said a few words in a language I had never heard. With a final giggle she hung up.

"Honey," Cy said, "Steve was raped at thirteen."

She turned her gentle attention on me and asked, "Did you tell your parents, Etienne?" I shook my head, dumbfounded at the thought. She moved from the shadow with feline grace and sat beside me. "Was there *any*one you could tell?"

I continued to shake my head. "The coach knew. He——."

She watched me for a moment. "He heard you scream for help, but did not respond?"

"That's right." I felt sobs rising up but feared I would collapse if I let them out.

Cy said, "Life hadn't beaten the expectation out of you that people would respond to your cries for help. Your coach had the power to save you or destroy you. The bastard probably thought he was promoting morality by allowing a young homosexual to be violated." There was so much more, the evil jokes at school—*Maybe you need a Clorox enema next time*—the terrifying thought that I deserved torture.

Zoë slid the chopsticks from her hair and let it cascade past her bare waist, then leaned close to me. "You cried *out* for protection but you were betrayed."

Cy cradled my face in his hands. "My son, everyone suffers from impacted resentments and guilt. Your failures are your soul's cries for help. You seem to be punishing yourself for something." He paused until I nodded in agreement, then continued. "The source of your resentments is clear enough. Kids who tortured you, adults who didn't protect you. We can assume that like all victims you blamed yourself. But when the boys who raped you answer for their sins, what will *you* be answering for?"

I reminded myself to breathe. Susi had told me, *Dean DeWitt wasn't normal. They killed him for it.* I shook my head.

"What was that, right there?" Cy asked.

I looked into his probing eyes. Even before Eric made love to me, I'd decided I would rip open my soul if this man prescribed it. "My best friend got killed in reform school," I said softly.

"Tell me about your relationship with him." Cy pulled his chair closer.

Zoë smiled her little girl smile. I let out my breath, barely containing the sobs that tried to shake me. "Dean was my first love, I guess." Another thing I had never told anyone. Until now I had never even thought it.

"Your first love," Cy said with reverence. "How old were the two of you?"

"Both thirteen."

"How did he die?"

I stared at my hands. "He—got in trouble. A kid in the state school killed him."

Cy's eyes held me. "Gotta do a Relationship Workbook on Dean as if he were alive. Explore your part in this to get clear with him and yourself, and the human race."

Tears spilled from my eyes. Cy had let me off the hook only temporarily without even knowing the details. He seemed to be saying that my role in Dean's death was the point of my pathological need to punish myself. Until this moment I had never wanted to speak Dean's name or even think of him. Now I wanted to talk on and on about what had happened. Could I so easily cast off the burden that had caused me to sabotage every good thing life had given me? A Relationship Workbook, whatever that was, would lead me on the first step.

Zoë drew me close and I buried my face in her hair. One of her nipples nudged my sleeve while she rocked me.

"You're coming home now, Etienne," she said, "where you will *not* suffer betrayal!"

Zoë's words rang in the air. *Coming home.* Cy nodded silently, slowly, and finally said, "A month at Vista will set you on a new path, my young friend." I lost myself in the crinkles around his eyes and he went on, "We're a family here. An *intentional* family, not like the families most people are born into randomly, with such disastrous results. You and Eric aren't Primary Significant Others, not yet, but you're certainly more than Relevant Others. You'll get a chance to define your relationship."

Even these obscure concepts comforted me, promising a world beyond anything I had imagined. I withdrew my father's check from my pocket. "Hope you don't think I need the forty-eight hundred-dollar program."

Cy accepted the check, and he and Zoë discussed my living situation. Should I stay with Eric—who would be astonished to see me—or "tipi-hop," staying with lots of people? Zoë felt I should have the privacy of my own home, but a tipi cost over five hundred dollars. She seemed to assume I would be staying longer than a month.

"I brought a camera," I offered. "It's the only thing I have that's worth any money."

Cy raised his wondrous eyebrows. "What make?"

This detail nailed the negotiation. I would have my own tipi in exchange for my father's Hasselblad. "After the end of your first month," Cy said, "we'll invite your parents to a marathon group in Beverly Hills and offer them an opportunity to invest in your mental health."

A week ago this would have sounded like a shady investment. Today I was willing to bank everything I had, or would ever have, on my own happiness. I even believed my parents would want a piece of the action.

THE PHOTOGRAPHS I'D SEEN OF THE RANCH— taken by professionals under dramatic lighting conditions—had made the place look like a paradise of rainbows, pink sand beaches, and sky-high salmon cliffs that bore the picture-writing of ancient, vanished tribes. Even the black-and-white shots portrayed majestic shapes and unearthly proportions: waterfalls that made the horses grazing in nearby meadows look like toys, gardens as big as football fields. I had prepared myself for disappointment. Nothing could be as beautiful as those photographs.

Cy drove a white Land Rover through red soupy mud, along the lane Dove MacKenzie had pointed out. As if they knew my back-seat ride to the Ranch was a religious experience, Cy and

Zoë were silent. The tires crunched over icy spots that were sheltered from the warming rain by overhanging ridges of brittle-looking limestone. Pink hills rose, grew into bulbous cliffs, and arched over the road until the sky above us was a curvaceous strip. The cliffs on either side seemed to press ever closer together, as if reminding me that to get through the narrow passage to self-understanding I must allow defensiveness and fear to be squeezed out of me.

At the road's tightest spot, a half hour from town, Cy stopped the Rover and snapped me out of my daze when he asked gently, "Would you get that?" A few feet ahead a great iron gate blocked the road. Hand-carved in medieval script, a curved wooden sign read, *Rancho Vista*. Beneath it hung a plaque that counseled, *Abandon All Dope, Ye Who Enter Here*.

I hopped out and unhooked the chain that held the gate. After the Rover rolled through I carefully secured the chain. No horses would escape due to my negligence.

I trotted ahead to jump back into the vehicle, and stopped a moment. Somewhere in the distance I heard a roaring sound like the San Diego freeway at eight a.m. I hopped into the back seat and asked, "What's that noise?"

"We call her the Mother River," Zoë replied with a wink, "because she gives us life."

The canyon widened and the Rover passed over a sturdy wooden bridge. A reddish torrent raged below. Cy drove through a crystalline wonderland of cattails, then a grove of ghostly leafless trees. Dove had called Keystone *past the end of the road*. That tiny town now seemed like a hub of civilization. Rancho Vista was truly in the wilderness. It had no telephones, no electricity, no radio or TV reception. Nothing but love, reality and congruent input, whatever that was.

Past another bridge the river separated into two streams. Horses stood in a grove of dormant willows and drank from the river's left fork as it meandered across a field. The channel to the right disappeared at the edge of a pasture where the canyon walls grew higher and further apart. We drove into a round sandstone canyon like a mile-wide bowl. High in the cliffs, stands of bluish trees perched on narrow shelves of rock. The truck crossed a final bridge and a canyon opened to what I thought must be the north, a vista that stretched into the mists. Upstream, below a waterfall, the two rivers met again.

"Rancho Vista is an island," I said. "Like Manhattan."

"Maybe more like Avalon," suggested Cy.

I had come to this land hoping to fall in love with it. Peering up narrow side-canyons thick with evergreens, I felt that the land itself had the capacity to love me in return.

The Rover dipped into a tight, steep turn, crossed a trickling stream and groaned up a rise just as the sun broke out. At the far end of the round valley, dozens of white tipis gleamed against a receding bank of graphite clouds. A dozen field workers leaned on their shovels to wave. The Rover passed a coal bin and a covered wood shed, a pen of brown goats and another of white turkeys.

Half a mile down the road, the cookshack, at the center of everything, was alive with activity. People ferried bushel baskets between the L-shaped building's front porch and a half-buried root cellar. Others hiked to the surrounding plateaus where the tipis stood.

I steeled myself. Would Eric rush up and hoist me off my feet? Or hang back, chagrined that the guy he'd explored shameful sex with was violating his sanctuary? And how would the others regard the confessed queer?

By the time Cy parked in front of the cookshack all work had ceased. Children ran toward the Rover. Faces I knew from photographs rushed in from all around. I thought I recognized Vivian—who'd buried her son less than two weeks ago—now in jeans, swinging a little boy by the hands.

Willow waved from the cookshack porch and pushed through the throng. I stepped out of the Rover and my new family gathered around, cheering. She leaped at me with tears in her eyes and exclaimed, "My God, you *are* a growth case!"

Over the clamor I heard the river, a water song already calming me. People I had never met pressed close and touched my hands, stroked my hair and kissed my face. "I'm—here," was all I could say.

PART TWO

Touching evil brings with it the grave peril
of succumbing to it . . . The wrong we
have done, thought or intended will wreak
vengeance on our souls.

      Carl Gustav Jung
      Memories, Dreams, Reflections

> To eliminate their overwhelming
> power over us, we do not attempt
> to slay our secret demons. Instead
> we welcome them at the table of
> the human family.
>
> Cyrus Aaron

"WE CALL HER THE MOTHER RIVER," Zoë had told
me, "because she gives us life." For days I assumed this was her
poetic description of the irrigation system that watered the
gardens and pastures. But soon I came to understand: the river
was the emotional constant in the Vistans' lives, the source of
infinite melodies as waves caressed sandy shores, the rhythm of
water patiently eroding stone, the music of personal growth.
Echoing this song, the community's love caressed wounded souls
and, oh-so-gently, eroded defenses.

    The Mother River greeted the Vistans each morning and set
the pace for their work in the fields and livestock pens, keeping
them company as they hung cloth bags of goat cheese to ripen in
the root cellar. Her song accompanied their mealtime conversations in the cookshack and comforted them there during Group

when they plumbed the depths of their pain and shared the miracle of acceptance and understanding. The melodies ebbed only for their parties, when the walls of the womb-like canyon echoed with guitar and tambourine, harmonica, saxophone and soaring voices, when the writhing, leaping young bodies peeled off thermal underwear and glistened with sweat by lamplight.

When growth, work and celebration finally left the Vistans exhausted, the song of the river eased them back to sleep in their tipis.

I HAD RECEIVED NO MORE FROM ERIC than shocked silence, followed by a hesitant hug of greeting and an unconvincing, "I'm glad you're here." We would not "define" our relationship for some time, it turned out, because Cy and Zoë left for a conference in San Francisco before I knew north from east.

"Don't waste time," Cy advised me cheerfully before he and Zoë drove away. "Plunge into your shit as soon as possible!" After a few more days of evasion I wondered if Eric was ignoring me deliberately to further this goal.

Other people helped me with the things I wanted Eric to do. I went along and concealed my disappointment. The saxophone-playing, dark-eyed Ken, whom I had nicknamed "The Great God Pan" when I studied his mysterious smile in the *Radical Therapist* photos, hiked with me to choose a tipi site. Ken was compact and wiry, with sun-streaked brown hair and full, red lips, and wore shorts with a down vest. His perpetual smile sometimes looked like a smirk, sometimes like a shy invitation to friendship. But he'd perfected the Vistan art of eye contact. He made sure I met his gleaming brown eyes fully, then nearly ran up the steep rise into the salmon-red foothills while I scrambled to keep up.

For my site we chose a rock terrace in the western cliffs with a sweeping view of the canyon. The gardens, orchards and fields far below, gray and haggard, awaited the kiss of spring. A dozen tireless Vistans spaded compost and manure into the sandy soil.

"Eric's guitar playing got a lot better after he spent that week-end with you," Ken remarked. "Helluva weekend, huh?" Without waiting for an answer, he went on to point out the path to a grotto where fresh water dripped from a rock, "A private spring."

So, I thought, if everyone knew about our lovemaking and accepted it good-naturedly, why did Eric duck out of every chance to be alone with me as if he were ashamed?

Before I could pursue such questions, Ken bounded down the hill, hollering to the others. A burly hippie named Travis, who ran the cookshack like a mess sergeant, promptly organized a tipi-raising party. Workers loaded a truck with lumber and tools, buckets of nails and bales of straw, and hauled them up the hill as far as the truck would go. We carried the materials the rest of the way by hand across a makeshift path. Everyone helped. One crew built a sleek platform, twenty-by-twenty feet, and packed straw bales underneath for insulation. Another team felled sixteen slender cedar trees and used a two-handed tool called a draw-knife to shave off the branches and bark. Kids came and went with chilled lemonade and platters of sandwiches that Vivian sent from the cookshack. Once the decking was ready, a tripod of the raw poles was set on it, then more poles were stacked to form a conical skeleton. The canvas was tied to the tip of the final pole, raised high and stretched over the framework. Finally a quilted liner and flap door were attached. Almost as an afterthought, Travis hammered together a simple plank bed and closet.

The entire effort took six hours. The sight of my own home on Vistan rock, erected by strangers who welcomed me like a long-lost brother, made me cry with delight.

A freckled, furry-headed fellow who called himself "Puck, the ex-schizophrenic" set up my pot-belly stove, cut a slit in the tipi canvas for the stovepipe, and installed asbestos plates to protect the cloth from the pipe's heat. He demonstrated how to build up the fire and bank in the coal, then dampen the air-flow to keep the fire smoldering all night.

Travis delivered an empty half-gallon wine bottle and explained, "Pee in this thundermug at night so you don't have to go out in the cold. Just don't tighten the lid, 'cause if you go to bed drunk and forget to bank your coal, your pee's gonna freeze and crack the bottle and leak all over." He watched my face a moment, then added, "If you shit on newspaper and throw it in the fire, the smell goes up the pipe with the smoke."

"So much for the simple life," I said, overwhelmed with the details but relieved I wouldn't have to hike to an outhouse in the middle of the night.

Willow gave me scarlet silk pillows and a worn but pretty Turkish rug. When I was settled she helped get me started on my Relationship Workbook, then listened without comment to my fears and frustrations about my love for Eric. Gently but firmly she repeated Cy's admonition, "Your first project is to go into your shit."

As much as I wanted to demand that Eric notice me, I couldn't complain about being starved for attention. Many Vistans stopped by to offer tipi-warming gifts—cooking utensils, a lightweight foam mattress, a kerosene lantern.

One dreary afternoon a plump girl named Teddy delivered a box of Oreo cookies and a dozen Hershey bars. Photographs of her face with its teardrop tattoo had haunted me. When I met her the tattoo had seemed grotesque. Today, at the end of my first week at Rancho Vista, it was as familiar as Lydia's braids had once been.

"Ask me anything," Teddy offered now, and peeled off her ski coat. Under it she wore a white leather miniskirt and a halter top. "Unlike some people around here I won't bullshit you." She flipped straw blonde hair with glossy brown roots out of her face.

I made hot chocolate, using the exact proportions of goat milk and Hershey bars Teddy recommended. She helped herself to a handful of the Oreos, and explained cookshack politics. Travis padlocked the little half-door that opened into the kitchen area— "But that can't stop us grunts from climbing over the serving counter to wash our hair in the sink." The "official line of crap" was that Travis and his work crew were going to build showers at the Ranch "real soon." Meanwhile, when the weather was warm enough, the Vistans bathed in the river with biodegradable soaps. "The other eleven and a half months of the year we wait for trips to town where we get one-minute showers at the Blue Worm. Or we heat up buckets of water on our wood stoves. I prefer to hop over the fucking serving counter and wash my crusty ass in the sink."

Before I could digest the idea of such rebellion, Teddy paused and abruptly asked, "So, how was it?"

"The ride up here? Well—"

"I don't bullshit you, you don't bullshit me." She sprawled face-down on the bed. "How was it screwing Eric? I can't wait 'til I'm seventeen so I can have him. I've screwed hundreds of guys, but everybody wants Eric. And no offense, but it hurts that some *fag* from L.A. gets him and I have to wait."

"I didn't 'screw' Eric," I nearly shouted. How in hell was I not supposed to take offense to such a comment? I steadied my hand to pour hot chocolate into a mug and gave it to her. "We made love. It was wonderful, but I think he's forgotten all about it. Or wishes he could."

"Poor baby, you got a lot to learn." Teddy dipped an Oreo into her mug then sucked the liquid out of it. "Eric's a sex surrogate. It's his *job* to give people experiences they need, but to not get involved. So you can't take any of it personally, the screwing or the detachment."

My face burned, but if she saw I was blushing she didn't mention it. She said Puck was her own sexual surrogate, "like a concubine." While she rattled on, I stirred the molten chocolate in my little saucepan. Her revelations raised more questions than they answered, but already I'd heard more than I wanted to know.

I'D NEVER IMAGINED LIFE WITHOUT ELECTRICITY, but the cookshack operated as a modern kitchen with refrigerators, wall-mounted lights and a two-hundred-gallon water heater, all powered by propane. Several times I volunteered for compost duty, a surprisingly popular task. The Vistans did everything by committee, but the compost job allowed the solitude of a stroll to a small garden with a bucketful of kitchen garbage that had to be dumped into a stinking pit. A muscular teenager named Lucky taught me to milk the goats and to mix the mash of soybeans, rice and corn that the turkeys ate.

As I watched and learned each new task, I dithered about what a "sex surrogate" could be, but promised myself I wouldn't ask anyone. I decided Teddy was a fat, stupid, jealous juvenile delinquent who wouldn't know love if it bit her, who threw around words like "detachment" as if she understood them. *I* understood that Eric naturally needed time to accept his deep feelings for me.

Each morning I heated water in my tiny saucepan and bathed privately in my tipi, though Teddy, Puck and others invited me to join them when they bathed in the cookshack sink. I was determined to have clean hair and fingernails at all times, to give the staff no reason to see me as a grunt because of filthy habits or mutinous behavior.

One reminder of my past caused me serious anxiety. I froze whenever Vivian Elfinger looked at me. I couldn't stop picturing her son as a patient at Los Perdidos—Garth, who had marshaled the courage to deliver himself from misery. During breakfast one morning I wandered around with my tray and avoided the seat across from her. "Won't you join me, please?" she asked, and pleasantly recalled seeing me with Lydia at the funeral. Later she invited me to her tipi.

At the funeral Vivian had worn her pale hair in a tired, teased pile that sharpened her narrow face. The dark rings under her eyes and her slumpy posture belonged to a broken and cast-off doll. I had guessed she was about forty. In the weeks since then she'd gained a few pounds and now filled out her jeans nicely. She kept her hair pulled back in a simple, blunt ponytail, wore a little lipstick, and looked closer to her actual age of thirty-three. Her tipi was a museum diorama of Orange County, transplanted into the Colorado wilderness. It featured avocado shag carpeting and bean-bag chairs covered in rust-red corduroy. Like me, she had stacked cinder blocks and boards to fashion a bookcase. But unlike me, even in her grief, she'd taken the time to stain the boards and paint the bricks.

Her children, seven-year-old Mikey and twelve-year-old Elizabeth, already had their own tipis. One morning they and the other six Vistan children hiked upriver with Ken, the Great God Pan, for a ten-day backpacking adventure called "Trail." I watched them go with a wistful desire to be included. Soon after, Vivian invited me to join her for a walk upstream. "Watch out," she warned. "I'll try to mother you, and I haven't got a great track record in parent-child relationships."

"Me neither," I muttered, then told her of my near-suicide. She listened in silence. When I finished she began to turn away but I touched her arm and we shared a spontaneous embrace. I confessed, "I never thought how my mother would feel."

The Relationship Workbook prompted these thoughts—page after pastel page of double-spaced blank lines with such headings as, *AT THESE TIMES I MAY HAVE MADE YOU FEEL DESPERATE*. Vivian and I wrote together and discovered a common experience: she blamed herself for Garth's death, and I blamed myself for my childhood friend Dean's. My first assignment from Willow had been to fill out the journal thinking of Dean. But I obtained a second fresh notebook from her, and began to answer the questions with my parents in mind. Beneath *AT THESE TIMES YOU HAVE MADE ME FEEL HOPEFUL*, I wrote, "When you gave me the money to come to Rancho Vista."

In Cy's absence, Eric and Willow ran daily Groups and did individual sessions in their tipis. Eric had duties even at the nightly party, where he gave guitar lessons. From the propane refrigerators Travis removed jugs of chilled homemade beer, cheap wine and "Dandelion Joy Juice," which looked like lemonade and tasted like honey-sweetened rubbing alcohol.

At night I sat up reading Cy's best-selling book, *The Quest for Unconditional Love*, a slim volume whose simple message was hope for the human race. In places it read like a doctoral dissertation, with footnotes and citations to Freud, in others like a spiritual guidebook—as when Cy offered Christ on the cross as the ultimate symbol of unconditional love, or quoted the Kabala and ancient Vedantic texts. And periodically his personal view of humanity shone through: *People blather on about "Unconditional Love" as if it were stocked beside the frozen corn-dogs at the supermarket. Most people will never experience unconditional love.*

Cy seemed to believe that no individual is capable of loving others unconditionally. He explained that we grow up in straightjackets of our parents' making because their love is conditional; thus we are programmed so that our *self-love* is conditional as well. We feel unworthy when not living up to these conditions—however irrational or inconsistent they may be.

Cy's theory gave me hope. "We need to work together," the book repeated often. Thus Cy chose to work in a community rather than an office. Thus he had created Rancho Vista.

Despite many little pleasures and a lingering sense of hope, my depression came slithering back. Every day the sky dumped snow, rain or some slushy mixture. With each sodden dawn my stomach and heart ached more. I missed Lydia, the privacy of her grove, such simple comforts as soaking in the lion-footed tub. At least once a day I agonized about what might be happening to Rupert. On my tenth night at the Ranch my most fearsome nightmare returned, with a twist. As always, a boy I loved held me and murmured, "Can I kiss you?" When the gang of jack-booted Marines inevitably appeared, the lovely boy didn't vaporize as he usually did, but joined them in kicking and stomping me until I was blinded by my own blood.

I woke up terrified, wondering how in hell I'd landed in a place that forbade marijuana, the one reprieve I'd ever enjoyed from my evil dreams. Was I here to become a self-accepting homosexual? If such a thing were even possible, would it stop my nightmares? Did my happiness depend on Eric's accepting himself too? And what was the point of being the only self-accepting homosexual in a world that hated me?

All my questions seemed to point to a straightforward conclusion: centuries of medical research had arrived at a simple treatment for people like me—an electric current to the genitals, to re-channel maladaptive urges.

But what treatment could re-channel the urges of my heart?

ERIC NARROWED HIS EYES at the children. "Dammit! We've been sitting here for two hours. Who stole the fucking peanut butter?"

I crossed my eyes to stay awake. I'd enjoyed the scene that opened Group, when the kids sat in a circle on the cookshack floor to process the events of their backpacking trek. But soon they reached an impasse that involved the disappearance, on day three of their ten-day Trail, of a major source of protein and the closest thing they had to candy. Willow dubbed it The Case of the Purloined Peanut Butter, but the session lost its entertainment value as the afternoon waned and the thief failed to come forward.

· My stomach lurched with the growing tension and I wished I'd smuggled a few quarts of Pepto Bismol into the organic Shangri-la. Cy and Zoë had been gone for over two weeks. Would Eric and I ever "define" our relationship, as I'd been led to expect? We hadn't spent a minute alone since my arrival. Half my money had been eaten up while the drama of Rancho Vista's daily life unfolded in Group on the cookshack floor. Couples argued and broke up or reconciled. People screamingly reconstructed scenes of childhood trauma. They confessed to having sabotaged the cohesion of the Vista community, usually by doing something they called "subgrouping." And at today's new low point, Eric was trying to cajole a confession from the peanut-butter thief.

At six, Otis was the youngest child. Vivian's twelve-year-old daughter Elizabeth was the oldest. A few, like her and her brother, were the children of adult Vistans. And some had arrived through the court system—abused and neglected waifs who'd been plucked out of foster care because their remarkable IQ scores distinguished them as Vista candidates.

In their circle on the cookshack floor, with matted hair and grubby hands, they all looked like the spawn of Devil's Island. I lifted my numb butt and re-folded the jacket I was using as a seat cushion at the edge of a cookshack picnic table. Eric and Willow sat in low camp chairs. The remaining Vistans perched on tables or sat on the floor, cushioned like me by parkas and sweaters. No one seemed to find it strange that a group of children had been taken backpacking for ten days in the snow. Several people passed index cards to Eric or Willow, containing comments that the two Group leaders read aloud—"Otis looks Withholdy. . . . If I confess *I* stole the damn peanut butter, can we move to something else?"

"Hell, I'm ready to confess," Eric joked, then instructed the kids to take turns telling the anonymous thief how they felt about the loss. I admired his strategy—the guilty kid would overplay the outrage or underplay it, and stand out either way.

"I felt ripped off," Otis grumbled.

Seven-year-old Humphrey whined, "The fucking peanut butter was our only dessert."

Elizabeth's turn came. "Whoever did this, you *violated* us!" Her flame-red pigtails flew about while she screamed, "I feel used and pissed off and *hurt!*"

"I didn't do it on purpose!" her little brother Mikey cried. Vivian gasped at her son's confession. He stared at his feet and continued, "I was so hungry. I was just gonna take one bite, but when I tasted it I lost contr—"

"Specious bullshit!" Elizabeth declared. Could I be the only person present who didn't know what "specious" meant? On the faces of the other Vistans I saw relief that someone had finally admitted to the crime. People's hair hung in dull strings they flipped out of their faces with coal-stained hands. Some wore clothes that hadn't been washed since before my arrival. But there was a clarity in their eyes, an earnest directness, that I trusted. Even the kids spent their time in Group with spiral notebooks open and pens poised, scrawling personal insights. One obvious feature of a growth case was this eagerness, bordering on zealotry, to explore the depths of one's own soul.

The only adult on the children's Trail had said little during the past two hours. Now Ken held out his sinewy hands, palms up, and said tenderly to Mikey, "I can understand being hungry, sneaking and getting out of control. But you didn't need to lie about it. After more time at Rancho Vista you'll understand that you don't have to lie about anything." He looked to Willow.

"That's right," she agreed, then mimicked a fundamentalist preacher. "It's in the Bahble—'Fer *awl* have sinned and come short of the glory of Gawd.' But you can't accept the C.S.O.'s forgiveness until we know you need it."

I wrote the initials on the last page of my notebook, a mush-rooming glossary. The C.S.O. was some kind of significant other. Comprehensive? Consolidated? *Composite*, that was it. I reviewed other definitions: *P.S.O.* = *Primary Significant Other. In My Shit* = *depressed & preoccupied. Withhold* = *secret. Subgrouping* = *??* People talked about subgrouping all the time but I understood only that it was bad.

I'd expected Mikey's confession to end Group or at least trig-ger a break, but the seven-year-old's outburst of honesty launched a new process. Eric instructed the boy to demonstrate how he had gained access to the peanut butter. Someone provided a backpack, and Travis retrieved a large jar of peanut butter from the locked pantry.

"You need to *show* us what you did," Eric explained, "so we can give you our acceptance. Otherwise it's just words."

I smiled toward Vivian, but she was too involved in her son's process to notice. Mikey's bangs hung over his eyes as he reënacted the midnight raid on the food pack and scooped a dollop of peanut butter into his mouth with a coal-stained finger.

Bored now, I paged through my notebook to a letter from Lydia that I'd read at least ten times since its arrival a few days before. It was barely a page long, hastily written to enclose my last meager paycheck from Los Perdidos. She had jammed the bad news into one paragraph: *The grove's been bought by a developer who's already applied for a permit to build a car wash . . . Blind Mike's on a hunger strike to protest your termination, and I'm afraid it's his latest suicide strategy . . . Hermione's probation was denied because they figured out she helped Rupe escape. That post card from New Orleans was the last word from him. . . . Dr. Sutton turned you over to a collection agency for the money you owe him . . . The library is charging you for some books you never returned.* Casually she added that she and Ryczard were leaving for "down south" in a few weeks. Next she shared the juiciest gossip ever to emerge from Los Perdidos: *Remember the unscheduled "vacation" Turner took right before he fired you? Well, his son Tobey had just been arrested for possession of pot. The poor kid's sixteen and Turner won't go his bail.*

I read and re-read the final paragraph. *I'll always love you, Steve, wherever either of us may wander. Vaya con dios, mi hermano.*

Tears welled in my eyes and I looked up. Through a filthy window, for what seemed like the first time in weeks, I saw the blue sky. The slushy snow had stopped falling. I'd assumed no birds would appear until summer, but a pair of hawks surprised me, diving and soaring in the small gray garden beside the cookshack. My gaze wandered to the pomegranate glow of the sharp distant cliffs and the rounded knolls nearby, still wet and now gleaming in the raw sunlight. If the weather stayed clear, I thought with a thrill, and Group ended before midnight, I would ask Eric to hike with me in the moonlight as we had done in Perdido Valley, that magic night we made love.

With Mikey's reënactment complete, the boy was told to sit in the center of the floor—the "hotseat"—where he looked alone and afraid. Elizabeth made a connection that apparently had escaped everyone else. "Nobody can eat—Travis, what's that jar hold? Two pounds?"

Behind the counter Travis nodded with a faint smile.

"In one sitting!" she raged at Mikey. "Did you shovel it into a ziplock bag and hoard it in your pack? Every time you disappeared into the woods to shit, you must have carried it under your parka and gobbled more. No wonder you took such long shits."

Eric told Mikey to return to the demonstration. The little boy showed how, as his sister guessed, he had rolled a large plastic bag into his long underwear to hoard the peanut butter, and ditched the empty jar in a ravine. The delayed confession made things worse for him. Each child expressed some version of "Betrayed," "I hate you," "Like you don't give a shit about us, and I don't give a shit about you." The last to have a turn, Humphrey, wept about the week of deprivation he had suffered—"With no peanut butter for my groat cakes!"

I didn't enter this new term into my glossary. Whatever "groat cakes" were, I didn't want to know.

Mikey wailed as if he were being horsewhipped, and Vivian ran to him. "Let him have this pain," Willow softly admonished her. "He needs to remember this the next time he's tempted to steal." Vivian grimaced and returned to her seat.

Willow sat beside Mikey in the center of the floor. She stroked his shoulder and encouraged him to look around the room. "Mikey," she said, "have you heard everyone's anger?"

He sniffled. "Yes."

"What do you feel like saying to us?"

His face relaxed for the first time, and a light seemed to come on in his dark little world. "That I'd be mad, too."

Willow next moved him through a process of asking his companions for positive feedback to balance the negative. Elizabeth laughed when her turn came. "I guess you felt so guilty about the peanut butter, you dried my wet socks by the fire. I *love* you for that." Others expressed respect for his honesty, and praised his hiking skills.

As dreary as the hours-long inquisition had been, I saw that Mikey had needed to be primed for the confession. The Vistans deserved their no-stone-unturned reputation. One by one, each person in the room told the boy what they admired about him. He began to look newly born, radiating hope in the center of the cookshack floor.

When my turn came I said, "You licked the peanut butter off your fingers with a big smile. *That* was honest."

Eric finally called for a break. Travis set out dried fruit and nuts, thick slabs of homemade wheat bread with honey, preserves made from wild "Vistaberries," and the demo jar of peanut butter. Elizabeth helped her brother with his parka, then took his hand and walked with him onto the porch.

While people wandered outside, Eric poured a mug of tea.

"That was beautiful with Mikey," I said.

Eric grunted. "Willow did the beautiful part. I wanted to kick the little fucker when he finally fessed up."

"So," I continued as casually as I could, "the sky's finally clear. How about a hike after dinner?"

Eric's hesitation sent a stab of humiliation through me. Finally he mumbled, "I usually take patients with me."

"I'm a patient." I wanted to add, *I've got six hundred dollars' worth of therapy still coming.*

"Let's see how late Group ends."

The session continued for several hours. Rainbow and Lucky worked on ending their relationship, and how to handle the pain and jealousy of watching each other date new people. In overalls and matching flannel shirts, with bowl haircuts and pink cheeks, they looked like twins. Both were younger than me. Did they know what they were throwing away? I opened my Relationship Workbook and looked for the right place to enter the first negative feeling I had allowed myself toward Dean. On a page headed, *I AM SAD ABOUT THESE THINGS YOU HAVE SAID OR DONE*, I wrote, *You got yourself killed in reform school. If you were alive we would be lovers.*

While Lucky and Rainbow hugged goodbye, Willow asked, "Who else has some shit?"

Teddy said she felt people hated her because she was overweight. Eric asked if she wanted to try doing a Body Image without Cy present. "I trust you, Eric," she answered, in a flirtatious tone that made my stomach flip-flop. While she removed her leather miniskirt and gauzy blouse, revealing a womanly pair of full breasts unencumbered by a bra, Travis carried a full-length mirror from the pantry and propped it against a wall. She stepped out of her panties and flipped them across the room with her toe. Puck dove and caught them, then blushed so hard his freckles disappeared.

I chewed a clump of my hair. Cy wanted my parents to come to a Group. It would be a freak show for them! Dressed in tweeds, they would walk in on the underwear-clad doctor and his bare-breasted wife, the tattooed delinquents and filthy-mouthed children—then run out to call their lawyer with instructions to leave everything to a hospital for crippled rabbits. Without their support I would lose my feeble grasp on Rancho Vista.

I had considered Lydia and myself utterly free of hangups because we sometimes chatted while one of us took a bubble bath. I hadn't experienced the skinny-dipping of summer, or the much-giggled-about sweatlodge, and was amazed by Teddy's— and everyone else's—comfort with her naked body. She pulled her two-tone hair into a ponytail. The movement made her breasts swing. I found her pale, thick body strangely beautiful. Her cheesy blouse had strained at the seams, and the leather skirt rode up her heavy thighs. Unclothed she looked like a powerful peasant woman who could pull a plow.

"Oh!" Eric exclaimed. "Before we start, Teddy, have you got any Withholds?"

"What the hell's that got to do with anything?"

"Cy says Withholds get in the way of receiving love. You want to let in our love during your Body Image."

"Oh, okay." She gouged at a pimple on her chin. "Vivian, I subgrouped with Elizabeth that if you were my mom I'd be embarrassed by your hairdo. Which is ridiculous because *my* mom's in prison with a terrible hairdo, and you've stopped ratting your hair and it's real pretty."

"Thank you," replied Vivian. "I guess."

"Steve, I subgrouped about you in my head before I even met you. When Cy said you were a genius I thought you were an egghead. When Eric told us about blowing you I decided you were an egghead fag. But I'm just threatened."

"Thank you," I said, more confused than ever about "subgrouping," but thrilled to know Cy thought I was a genius and to hear my night with Eric so freely acknowledged.

She looked around the cookshack. "And I've subgrouped in my head that you're all idiots. We're not supposed to take baths in the kitchen sink, but I do when staff's not around, which is when they're in *town* on important *business* and taking *showers*, and I won't stop 'til Travis builds a fucking shower out here."

"Thank you," Eric and Willow said in unison. It occurred to me that Willow's ginger-colored hair always bounced as if she'd just washed it and brushed it dry. Which, since she went to town every day to talk with Cy on the phone, was entirely likely.

Relieved of Withholds, Teddy stood nude before the mirror and named everything she disliked about her body, beginning with the size and color of her nipples and the bushiness of her pubic hair, and continuing through an exhaustive catalogue of what Eric called "self-negatives": her "boring hair, jagged fingernails, monkey ears, this chipped tooth"—which, she claimed with a leer, she had broken while opening a beer bottle.

I sensed that behind the bluster she hated herself. Her brassy voice cracked when she pointed to a scar on her shoulder. "A dude who was fucking me put out his cigarette here."

Vivian cried out. Travis slapped the serving counter and muttered, "Bastard!" I thought of Blind Michael at Los Perdidos, who wept for people who couldn't weep for themselves. Teddy had a room full of Vistans to weep for her.

She finally finished her self-negatives. At Eric's gentle prompting she asked, "What do you all dislike about my body?"

I couldn't imagine asking such a question, much less standing naked in front of thirty people. I understood that Teddy's willingness to do this made her a growth case. My opinion of her was changing dramatically. At fifteen she had lived more of life than I would ever experience. She hated herself but had something I wanted: courage.

Eric spoke first. "Your complexion's still blotchy from all the drugs. The teardrop tattoo's a suck, but I guess you got it to show the world your pain. And your hair'll be pretty after that bleached blonde grows out, but right now it looks like shit."

"Thank you for your feedback, Eric," she said.

I was used to the Vistans' habit of thanking one another for every utterance, but how could Teddy mean this? I sat quietly, embarrassed to imagine what these people would criticize about *my* body. *Scarecrow hair, pizza skin.* Beginning with bashful Puck—

Teddy's "concubine," I recalled—several Vistans agreed her teardrop tattoo was a "suck." I wrote, *Suck = attention-getter?* As if to compound Teddy's humiliation, Willow asked people to repeat certain comments so her notes would be accurate.

When my turn came I commented on Teddy's roughly-chewed fingernails—which she could do something about—and admitted I needed to stop chewing my own cuticles.

Other Vistans were painfully direct. Willow said, "You're about thirty pounds overweight," and left her camp chair to point out which of Teddy's still-perky bulges would droop and sprawl if she didn't get her weight under control before age twenty.

"Thank you, Willow," came Teddy's reply.

Next she was directed to name the things she did like about her body. The only feature she was really happy about was the teardrop tattoo, but with Willow's encouragement she continued to scrutinize herself in the mirror. "My hands aren't pretty," she said after a pause, "but they're strong as hell. I guess my eyes are a nice color." I wanted to cheer even at these modest acknowledgments. She was the most honest person I'd ever met. She deserved to like herself.

With the self-positives complete, she asked, "Everyone, please tell me if you like anything about my body."

Eric instructed her to re-state the question—"Please tell me *what* you like . . ." He was the first to respond. I paid close attention to his positives, which included the word "voluptuous." Eric was hot for Teddy, bulges and all.

Puck enthused, "I love your pussy. It gets so *juicy*, like a big ripe peach!" Willow matter-of-factly transcribed this with the other comments.

I recalled the thing Teddy most disliked. "I like your nipples," I said. "They're nice and big, and they look suntanned."

She scowled. Damn, she knew I was just trying to make her feel good. But she replied, "Thank you, Steve."

Rainbow had been among those who agreed the teardrop tattoo was a suck, but now said she admired the artistry in the delicate shading. *Two sides to everything*, I wrote in my notebook.

"Body image" was a hot topic in the psychology magazines. Talk of it had even reached Los Perdidos' training rooms. But what went on outside Rancho Vista was just that—talk. Nowhere else in the world were people standing naked in crowded rooms doing inventories of their self-concepts, then adjusting how they felt about themselves with the guidance of a loving Composite

Significant Other. And Cyrus Aaron was a thousand miles away! Eric, a twenty-year-old kid on probation, was conducting sophisticated therapy based on Cy's teachings.

Though Group was in its eighth hour, Eric and Willow slowed the pace so Teddy could absorb everyone's positive comments. The little boys agreed that she was "stacked," and she smiled. When Elizabeth said, "I want to be as strong as you when I'm older," Teddy began to cry. The positives continued to flow. Travis came out of the kitchen to say, "Your eyes are a beautiful shade of brown, with little flecks of gold. They go soft when I least expect it."

"Your hands *are* pretty, honey," said Vivian, "you just need to learn to care for them."

For me, the Body Image had begun as the embarrassing spectacle of a naked overweight teenager picking her face with jagged fingernails. Now Teddy was in tears—for the first time, she claimed, since age ten—and accepted a hug from each of the Vistans. She made a date with Vivian to do her nails, accepted Willow's offer of yoga lessons to improve her posture, and said flatly to Travis, "No more of your coffee cake, pal. I gotta lose a couple hundred pounds."

She stuffed herself back into her miniskirt. After the tearful crescendo of the Body Image, I was sure we were about to start dinner. The aroma of roast turkey had filled the room for hours. Travis lighted the webbed mantles of the propane wall fixtures, washing the big square dining room in bright light. Then, inconceivably, Group continued. I watched in exhaustion as the proceedings devolved into a dispute over whether Lucky or Puck was responsible for changing the tractor's oil. Why did thirty people go hungry over something Travis could swiftly and arbitrarily decide?

But even this apparent absurdity proved to have a purpose. Everyone was involved. Each Vistan had a different memory of how the tractor duties had been assigned. Some gave feedback on how Lucky and Puck handled other responsibilities. The children's comments received the same respect as the adults'. Like Teddy during her Body Image, the two young men thanked each person who pointed out their shortcomings. "I don't want to be a grunt my whole life," Puck said, prompting me to add, *Grunt = irresponsible person?* to my glossary.

After nine o'clock we finally pulled the picnic tables from the walls. Travis howled, "Soo-eee!" as he did before each meal, and everybody lined up for turkey with zucchini, mashed potatoes and fried beets—all home-grown. I was so hungry I almost flung myself at the food. Eric announced that Cy would be returning the next day, then sat with Willow and Ken. The three of them picked at their dinner while anxiously writing an agenda for a morning staff meeting in town with Cy.

When the time came for the kids to wash the steel food trays, Travis opened the gate into the kitchen. I stood up and called to Eric, "I'm going up to work in my journal. Still want to go for that hike?"

Without looking up Eric mumbled, "We're almost done."

FROM THE PORCH I FOLLOWED THE GENTLE RISE past the outhouses, known as "shitters," up into the leafless orchards that spread out on either side of the path. I'd dropped my gloves somewhere, and without the familiar cloud cover the air stung my face and bare hands. The moist sand had frozen into humps and ridges that didn't give way under my boots.

A noise above my head startled me. Skeletal tree branches were dueling in a gust of wind, and I gazed into the phenomenon far above. The canyon's black lips framed the star-dusted indigo sky. The Milky Way seemed to have oriented itself precisely above the canyon so its tapering tails pointed toward the river's mysterious source and its destination.

Past the orchards I reached a crunchy frozen marsh and reached for my flashlight. It didn't work—apparently I'd left it burning in my jacket pocket the night before, and the batteries were dead. I felt my way along the riparian's northern edge. My feet found a narrow natural stairway in the rock and I headed for the dimly-silhouetted pair of ponderosas that stood on each side of my tipi.

Once there I untied my quilted canvas door, ducked through the oval opening and felt for my box of wooden matches. I knocked my pocketknife off the makeshift bookcase. Finally I found the matches and lit the kerosene lamp. I adjusted the wick, and tiny sparks sputtered up the sooty glass chimney. Next, as Lucky had taught me, I stirred the hot stove embers and made an A-frame of dry sticks. I opened the damper to get the air flowing, then blew on the kindling until it flared. I stacked on larger pieces of wood and, finally, fist-sized hunks of coal.

I could find my way among the trees in the dark but still had no idea how to navigate the constantly changing territory of my mind. I coveted the clear-eyed purpose of the other Vistans. Even Teddy, though she hated herself so much she'd let men use her as an ashtray, was on a path toward self-acceptance. Cyrus Aaron seemed to think there was a place for me on that path, but two more weeks at Rancho Vista would not get me to the end of my journey.

I stepped outside to pee into the ravine. The quarter moon was cresting the canyon rim. Ragged clouds crossed the horizon like scraps of tissue. I looked out across the Ranch as awestruck as on my first night. The canvas skins of the scattered conical dwellings diffused and warmed the lamplight inside, so the tipis glowed like little spaceships from a very friendly planet. I most loved Eric's home, furnished with a desk, chairs and bed carved from logs. A trap door in the floor covered a coal bin. The comforter on his bed was the skin of a bear killed by his grandfather. Willow's was the largest and most extravagant of the tipis—a sheik's tent festooned with silk and carpeted with Persian rugs, and furnished with an enormous armoire and Louis XVI desk. Travis's place was probably the most comfortable: he had built a sleeping loft to take advantage of the warmer air at the top. Set far apart on a plateau, Cy and Zoë's tipi sat on a huge terraced deck that commanded a view of the entire canyon.

The horses stomped about in the near pasture and a goat cried out. I pictured coyotes circling the paddocks. I'd been transplanted not only in place but in time, to the age of coal heat, oil lamps and bed warmers.

Footsteps sounded a short way below and Eric called out, "Winter's hanging on."

I heard a zipper open and pee splash onto the rocks in the ravine. I asked, "Did you bring a flashlight?"

The zipper zinged shut, and Eric appeared out of the juniper shadows. "We won't need a flashlight," he said with a hint of contempt. "The moon's coming up."

"Oh, sure. Sorry."

"I need to be back soon. Let's just hike up Ophelia's Nipple."

"Whose what?" I laughed, careful not to ask why Eric had to rush back. I tied the quilted door in place to hold the heat inside my tipi.

"The Mormon codgers who settled this county had a sense of humor, and considerable repressed sexual energy. You can see on the government survey maps how they named every little hill after some woman's body parts. Ophelia's Nipple, Sarah's Mound."

We climbed without speaking until I was out of breath, then paused on a ridge. Eric's long yellow hair caught the moonlight as it had done in Orange County the night we hiked above the glittering sprawl. But now the stars glittered above us, and nothing else seemed the same as that night.

The tiny, glowing tipis dotted the landscape far below. From up here the twin rivers that meandered through the Ranch gleamed like silver ribbons. Desperate to resurrect the intimacy we'd shared in Perdido Valley, I commented, "Everything you said when I met you seemed surreal. Now I see what you were talking about."

Eric shrugged. "I don't know what that's supposed to mean, but it doesn't matter."

"It does!" I insisted, then added softly, "I care what you think."

"You need to be here for your*self*."

I heard myself complain, "We haven't had a conversation since I got here. I don't think it's much to ask."

"We're having one right now."

The question that had run through my mind every frigid night, sometimes until Travis beat the garbage can lid he used as a breakfast gong, now leaped from my mouth: "Why did you make love to me if you didn't want to have a relationship?"

"Cy thought it would be a good process."

"That was Cy's idea?" I recalled Lydia swinging the garden hose between her thighs. "I thought you were curious about those feelings in yourself."

Eric pitched a rock into the night. "I was."

I managed not to ask the obvious, *But not now?* Silently I studied the sky, found the brightest star, and began to formulate a wish. *Let our relationship become as it was, free and easy, exploring and sharing, funny and sexy . . .*

He hawked up a wad of phlegm and spat. "We'd better head back." As we descended, he commented on Teddy's courage in requesting a Body Image. "Pretty impressive for a juvenile delinquent."

"I can't imagine getting up like that in front of everybody," I agreed. "Especially with that big ass."

Eric snorted. "She's what I'd call voluptuous."

"Right. But like Willow said, in a few years it'll sag."

The wolfen eyes gleamed at me in the moonlight. "Willow's too thin," Eric said dryly. "And you sound like a subgrouping little jealous bitch."

That night I hardly slept. When I did, I dreamed that vultures were feasting on my entrails, ripping my flesh with jagged beaks. Even more than Pepto Bismol I missed pot, suppressor of evil dreams.

TRAVIS PULLED ME OUT OF THE BREAKFAST LINE and handed me a folded piece of yellow paper. "Eric went to town to meet Cy and Zoë," he said. "He left this for you."

I read the note where I stood:

> *I'm sorry I was so rough on you last night. With Cy away I've had too much responsibility and I took out my frustrations on you. I need your friendship. You were brave to come to the Ranch. I'm envious because you did it on your own, and I came to get out of a prison sentence. With love and reality, Eric*

Swooning, I sat with Mikey and Humphrey. They giggled and plucked chunks of potato from each other's plates. Clearly, one of the wonders of life at Rancho Vista was that nobody held grudges. People spewed their shit during Group and let go of it.

Travis announced that Cy and Zoë would be at the Ranch in time for dinner, and asked for a volunteer to help refurbish the sweatlodge. I raised my hand and Travis nodded. "We could use a few more like you around here."

The sweatlodge looked like a primitive dwelling, a domed lattice of willow branches with an enormous brown tarp stretched over it. The round space inside was about twelve feet across, lined with homemade benches in concentric circles. A deep central hole about three feet wide held a tub full of cracked limestone rocks. I helped Travis haul out the rocks, toss them down the hill, rinse the tub in the holding pond, hose off the benches and put it all back together. While we worked, Travis explained that he'd come to live at the Ranch after jail time, a stint in the Army with a dishonorable discharge, and impregnating a few women. "I'm safe here," he said. "Cy knows I'll work hard, and he doesn't try to scramble the insides of my head."

"You're not a patient?"

"I'm the outfit's only employee. Even his secretary Elsie is a patient, so she gets time off to go in her shit. I get room and board and ten bucks a month."

I hadn't imagined anyone was exempt from therapy, or would want to be. "I don't know what to do," I confided. "Everyone else is so busy, I feel guilty."

"It's your 'process' to go into your shit," Travis said. "Which includes being unproductive, so you'll feel worthless."

Our final project looked like the hardest—lugging fresh rocks up from the river. Travis sauntered to a green Volkswagen bug parked beside the root cellar and blasted the horn in a staccato pattern of beeps. Promptly several children appeared.

"Who doesn't want to wash dishes tonight?" he called out.

"I don't!" the kids all yelled.

"Then pile up a hundred rocks. You know the size to get. Gather enough wood for a bonfire, big enough to welcome Cy and Zoë home. An hour's work keeps you off kitchen patrol tonight. If anybody slacks off, I trust the rest of you to bring it up in Group."

Travis then led me to the root cellar and opened a quart bottle of homemade honey beer. We each took a long sip of the cool, sweet brew. In a far corner, beneath bags of goat cheese, he showed me a series of five-gallon glass bottles and a kettle capped with coils of copper tubing. "Dandelion juice goes in this contraption."

"You've got a still in here!"

He winked. "Rural self-sufficiency."

We shared the beer on a walking tour of the irrigation and culinary water systems. "Cy designed all of this, from the cistern at the spring to the waterwheel," Travis said. "We paid a water engineer to check the plans. He couldn't find a thing to improve on."

"You're saying Cy's a pretty smart guy."

"Smartest I've ever met."

"Why are you showing me all this? When I asked Lucky how the water systems worked he didn't know, after a year on the work crew."

"I think the place could use a higher employee-to-patient ratio. And something tells me you're gonna be here a while."

Anticipating Cy and Zoë's return from their travels, the Vistans swept tipis and beat rugs, swabbed the cookshack floors and squeegeed its windows, and grew more excited as the hours passed. Travis held up dinner until six, then the whining kids persuaded him to go ahead without Cy and Zoë. He put plates aside for them.

People stopped eating when the Land Rover finally roared through the last tight turn past the steep, muddy swale. A greeting committee ran outside. Cy and Zoë entered the cook-shack a minute later with Eric, Willow and Ken immediately behind them.

"Welcome home!" we cheered.

A mousy young woman came in last, laden with travel bags— Elsie, I soon learned, Cy's secretary. Her hairdo, a bun held together with a hairnet, would have been appropriate for a librarian in her fifties. She apologized to people for bumping into them. I was amazed that no one offered to help her with the suitcases and bags.

Cy's tanned face blazed with energy and his handsome features crinkled into a smile. Alertly he surveyed the room and announced, "Zoë and I have been out in the 'real world.' We need a party!" Several people whistled in agreement. "Is the sweatlodge together?"

Travis beamed. "Steve helped. I'll fire up the rocks."

"Wonderful," Cy said. His eyes bored into me for a moment. "Oh, good. Steve's managed to plunge into his shit right on schedule. Is anybody in desperate need of a session with me? Is Vivian here?" He looked past her and did a double-take. "My God, honey, you look fantastic! I was worried about leaving you, but you've thrived. You took my advice—*When you can't function, move the body.*"

She rose for hugs from Cy and Zoë, then gave my hand a squeeze before putting on her coat.

"Etienne," Zoë said, "you and Vivian are friends!"

I accepted her hug. "Welcome home."

"Eric will treat you right," she whispered, leaving me to wonder what the staff had said about me in town.

The men unloaded treats Cy and Zoë had brought from the city—bags of fresh citrus and tropical fruits, cases of champagne, boxes of books, and a bronze gong from San Francisco's Chinatown, to replace the garbage can lid Travis hammered on to announce meals. Willow took a flat of strawberries and two bottles of champagne, and invited the women to her tipi for a "pre-party."

Travis entrusted me with the squeezing of oranges for Cy and

Zoë, and gave me a funnel and sieve to strain the juice into a thermos bottle. "Cy doesn't drink," he said, "not even my home-made organic brew. But he sure likes fresh O.J."

I laughed in surprise. "Hard to imagine he puts up with all the Joy Juice flowing if he doesn't drink himself."

"He gets a kick out of watching us make fools of ourselves. And of course the foolishness brings up material for Group."

During the afternoon Travis had overseen construction of a tower of logs around the pile of freshly-gathered rocks, between the sweatlodge and the banks of the holding pond. He now ignited the kindling at the tower's base, and the bonfire soon raged a hundred feet into the sky. The women came down the road with their hair spilling in sensuous curls and crowned with feathers, eyes sparkling with color, cheeks deeply rouged. They wore lacy slips and négligées under parkas, and carried glasses of champagne with strawberries floating in them. The laughter of a secret sisterhood danced across the sands.

The Vistans frolicked like nymphs and satyrs around the fire. Clothes disappeared as the moon rose higher. A few people stripped down to shorts, but I felt like an old-timer and followed Eric's example, flinging off everything. Vivian and Elizabeth wore flowered bathing suits with little skirts that screamed *Orange County!*

Cy and Zoë, both nude, shared a thermos of orange juice. Everyone else passed around a gallon jug of Joy Juice. Lucky played a harmonica and little Mikey accompanied him on percussion, striking a coal bucket with a pine bough. Ken appeared with a tenor sax, quickly shed his clothes, and tore into a raucous blues number that Willow joined, singing, "There's a red house over yonder, Lord that's where my baby stays . . ." Everyone danced in the hot, flickering light.

Travis suddenly leaped naked through the flames. The children whooped and chased one another around the fire. I danced with Willow and tried to ignore Eric's shimmying with Teddy. As the liquor warmed my insides, I savored the freezing air at my back and the stark heat in front of me. I enjoyed myself thoroughly until I noticed Eric's flopping cock was nearly erect. I gulped more Joy Juice to quell the jealous fire in my chest.

Once he judged the rocks ready, Travis lifted one in a shovel, tossed it in the air to dislodge the clinging ashes, and dropped it into the tub in the center of the sweatlodge. He followed it with several more. We kicked off our boots and charged in to claim seats on the benches. I found a spot between Vivian and Elizabeth where I wouldn't have to watch whatever Eric was doing with Teddy. Outside, Travis broke the sheet of ice on the holding pond and plunged a bucket in, then came inside the sweatlodge and waited until Lucky pulled a tarp across the entryway. The glowing rocks provided the only light.

Travis poured on a few ounces of water, and the rocks popped and sizzled and billowed steam. "Want more?" he called out.

"YES!" we shouted.

He splashed on more water. The rocks cracked and shot out choking clouds of steam. I gasped for breath and howled along with the others.

For the next hour we ran from the lodge to leap into the freezing water of the holding pond, then back inside to the steam until we were again ready for the water. Travis kept a steady supply of fresh hot rocks coming from the fire.

Finally the revelers dried off in the heat of the coals, exhausted and drunk. Willow invited everyone to her place and went running up the road, taking Elizabeth with her.

I dressed and fell in beside Eric, who carried his guitar in a battered case. We walked silently until I got up the nerve to say, "Thanks for your note this morning, but I knew you were under a lot of pressure. I *was* acting jealous. It was my shit." I congratulated myself for sounding so mature.

"I'm glad you're here," Eric said. I wanted to put an arm around his shoulder, and resisted by jamming my hands into my pockets. Near Willow's tipi we heard her high, clear voice, singing an English ballad. Inside, the Vistans sat shoulder-to-shoulder or on each other's laps, lounging in dazed comfort. Cy and Zoë giggled together like teenagers. Ken had brought his saxophone, and he and Eric began a soft bluesy melody. I drank Joy Juice, beer, a jar of red wine, and still more Joy Juice. I spent part of the evening lying on the floor cradling Eric's foot while he played his guitar. Later Cy talked to me about something I couldn't understand, and gave me a cute nickname. Later still, I clung to the icy edge of Willow's tipi platform and vomited into the snow.

9.

I AWOKE TO THE ECHO OF WHOOPING SCREAMS.
A bowel movement or an orgasm, I reminded myself, and
opened my eyes to see I was in my own tipi.

Obviously the screaming was manufactured to impress Cy,
since there'd been no primal carryings-on during the leader's two-
week absence. I heard a truck toiling through sand, then more
screams.

My mouth tasted like mildewed wool, and my head pounded. I
had no memory of leaving Willow's tipi. My own place was
unaccountably warm—my breath wasn't visible and there were
no ice crystals in the water bottle, so I knew someone had banked
my stove. When I sat up, my head reeled and I vomited onto the
rug. I pulled on my boots and stumbled outside to pee against a
tree. The grinding of truck gears reverberated off the cliff walls. I
squinted into the bright, early sun. People were already working
in the fields and gardens, though the breakfast gong hadn't
sounded and the canyon below me was still deep in shadow. Such
bustling, like the screaming, must also be due to Cy's return.
Even Travis rarely worked outdoors before breakfast. The dump
truck crawled through a distant field, loaded with children in
parkas. They shoveled clumps of compost off the back.

The brisk air cleared my head enough that I worried about
being considered lazy, but I felt too rotten to do anything about
it. I could feel the sun drawing the poison out of me. On the
salmon-red plateau where my tipi sat, an etching of frost covered
the surrounding terrace of flat, smooth stone. Over the centuries,
sand had collected in shallow basins in the rock. Young scrub
oaks and cottonwoods, cedars and pines had taken root in these
patches. Some had died at the tender height of two or three
inches, while others crowded them out and flourished.

While I mopped up the vomit with an old tee-shirt, wondering
what force determined which sprigs would thrive and which
would wither, the new breakfast gong rang out in tempo with the
thumping in my head. I splashed cold water on my face and
brushed my hair, bracing for the humiliation of facing the other
Vistans. My only hope was that they had guzzled as much alcohol
as I had, and wouldn't remember how I'd thrown myself, literally,

at Eric's feet.

In the cookshack Travis whistled while he served fresh fruit, pancakes and scrambled eggs. Elizabeth and her brother gabbed at me while Cy and Zoë spoke in low tones with Vivian. Eric seemed deliberately preoccupied. During cleanup the children gleefully carried out the compost buckets. Lucky and Rainbow laughed together as if they hadn't drearily ended their relationship a few days earlier.

The high spirits continued while we shoved the tables against the dining room walls for Group. Cy sat in a low camp chair surrounded by nylon pouches of food, a daypack full of books, and a huge canvas shoulder bag whose cargo of cassette tapes, batteries, recorders and camera equipment spilled over. Zoë straddled a bench behind him, wearing riding pants and a sun-hat adorned with silk fuchsias. She stroked his hair and whispered in his ear.

Elsie turned on a portable tape recorder, and the Vistans promptly stopped their chattering. "On our trip," Cy said, "Zoë and I met a man who claimed his parents raised him with unconditional love." People snorted as if he'd said, *We met a man who said his dog reads Greek.* "It turned out he'd grown up doing exactly what his parents wanted. He went to the schools they chose, became a lawyer like his dad, married the girl they approved of instead of the one he loved. At forty he divorced his wife, bought a hardware store and married his high school sweetheart. His parents said he needn't bother visiting for Christmas. The poor guy told us, 'Their love became conditional.' We explained it had been conditional all along, but continued to flow as long as he met all the conditions."

I transcribed the essence of this last statement in a spontaneous shorthand I hoped I could decipher later. Cy continued to report on his travels with Zoë, and each observation seemed full of meaning, worthy of a seminar or even a book: "The Needy Gland is connected to the genitals. That connection keeps us alive as a species, and provides steady work for therapists ... Politicians think they're running the show but they still have to pay taxes. The guys with the real power are hiding behind the pulpit, invoking the tax-exempt mercy of the Coconut God ..."

With a cramped hand I wrote *Coconut God?* then capped my pen and simply listened. Cy asserted that psychiatry, in its enforcement of an arbitrary standard of "normality," was like the Procrustean Bed of Greek legend. "When anyone didn't fit into the bed at his little inn," Cy explained, "Procrustes stretched their bodies or chopped off their feet to make 'em fit." The kids giggled nervously. "True therapy lets you participate in designing your own bed."

Some people were destined for personal growth, he said, like those whom John Calvin called the "Elect," foreordained for spiritual salvation. Cy had hand-picked each Vistan for this quality. "I won't invite anyone who isn't a growth case to join our community. Each of you contains a golden kernel, a divine gift. However low on the scale of humanity you fell while living among the carnivore, you're willing to face down the demons inside you and pursue psychological health."

None of the Vistans wrote now. Many closed their eyes and seemed to pray with thanksgiving. Cy continued, "Let me tell you about the theory Zoë and I are developing on subpersonas and polyselves."

Eric and Willow nodded along with Ken, apparently having heard something about this theory while in town. I began to relax. Cy described the little girl within Zoë who had longed for a puppy since her girlhood in Tahiti, and the five-year-old within himself who still waited for his mother to return from her trip to town—although his adult self understood she'd been struck and killed by a car in 1927. These two children were imprisoned in the pain and longing of their early years. Everyone had inner "sub-personas," unacceptable selves who awaited a key to unlock their prison doors. "Ninety percent of our emotional power is locked up in those excluded personalities we keep hidden," he explained. "People go to their graves never having let that power express itself. Today—." He paused with a pleasant tone of drama. "We shall begin observing what happens when that child is gratified."

After a commotion in the pantry, Travis emerged and presented Zoë with a fluffy white Husky puppy. She jumped up with speechless delight. Amid the squeals and laughter that filled the cookshack, I tried to smile naïvely, but wondered how much Eric remembered of the previous night's party. I must have passed out on the floor. Had he shoved me away with his foot, or was that part of a nightmare? Other memories were so clear: He had sung "Kentucky Woman" and "Michelle," songs about beautiful, powerful women, while I coiled around his foot, breathing into his red wool sock. Gallons of Joy Juice had flowed. Maybe nobody remembered much.

Zoë named the puppy "Wolfie" and kissed Cy in thanks. He

flipped through index cards people had been passing to him, then casually asked, "Who was at Willow's tipi party last night? Steve—actually he named himself *Sniveling Stevie* during the festivities—demonstrated his unrequited love for big Eric."

A spasm wrenched my gut. A growth case wouldn't stare at the floor. I forced myself to look into the other Vistans' eyes, and kneaded my hands together to avoid clasping them over my hot face. People nodded and murmured. Vivian and a few others gave me smiles of concern. "He·lay on the floor and curled about the foot of his beloved. Eric ignored him and played his guitar. I wonder if Sniveling Stevie—or should we call him *Sneevie*—could show us more now."

While Cy whispered with Zoë, I listened for the song of the river, trying to remember. Had I wrapped myself around Eric's foot before or after Cy began calling me "Sniveling Stevie"? Could I possibly have dreamed up that nickname myself?

"Of course that wasn't Group last night," Cy explained, "only a therapy party, like all Vista parties. But Steve took advantage of the opportunity to show us a needy *polyself* who dwells within that handsome professional man we see when we look at him. The first time we talked, when he tried to rescue his friend from the snake pit, Steve convinced me he was the head of social services for a psychiatric hospital. So we already knew he was resourceful and compassionate. Last night we saw his courage. Don't you all agree Steve was brave to let Sneevie out last night?"

Vistans agreed, "For sure, Cy" and, "Yes, indeed!"

I squirmed like a bug impaled on a pin.

"And from what Sneevie told me," Cy said, "the neediness he showed at the party was the tip of the iceberg." He gestured toward the center of the room.

I scooted to the hotseat, afraid I would throw up if I tried to speak. What had I told Cy while full of Joy Juice? The Vistans hunched on the picnic tables and benches, and along the serving counter, some of them silhouetted against the windows. Outside, two turkey buzzards flew in lazy circles, like the nightmare vultures that recently had eaten my innards.

Across the room I found Zoë's comforting gaze, then Vivian's. Elizabeth wiggled her fingers at me. "Let's make this easier for you," Cy suggested. "Why don't you stand up?"

My stomach surged dangerously, but I imagined the Vistans would see vomiting as an important part of my process. I knelt to steady myself, then stood with my hands in the pockets of my bell-bottoms. Cy placed a hand on my shoulder. "Eric, come help your buddy."

Eric slid from his perch on the counter and stood about a yard in front of me, his face frozen in hollow detachment.

"Sorry, kids," Cy said. "We're handling adults-only material. Everybody under seventeen's got to leave. Except Teddy, who's seen everything. And—Vivian, do you mind if Elizabeth stays? I think she's certainly mature enough to handle this."

Vivian replied that whatever happened, she trusted Elizabeth to know her own limits.

"Amazing," Cy said. "A parent who treats her child like someone who will grow up to make her own decisions." He waited until the kids were bundled in coats and out the door, then asked Elsie, "How's the tape?"

"A few minutes left on this side. I'll flip it now."

"Here we go," he said. "Sneevie, what do you feel like saying to Eric?"

Don't make me talk, I thought. Growth cases didn't hesitate, but I was beyond pretending I was anything but a twitching glob of neediness. And I *did* want to say something before I left these people whose kindness I didn't deserve, this place where I didn't belong. "I want to tell him—tell you, Eric—I'm sorry. All I wanted was to be your friend."

Cy explained in a seminar voice, "The issue is familiar for us all: needy and graspy behavior," then softened the message by affecting an Irish brogue. "Me boy, that graspin' is pushin' away the one you *seem* to love, though you protest you feel only friendship for the lad."

I acknowledged this with a nod. Cy sat down and added, "But that wasn't Steve who pushed Eric away. Who was that?"

Why was he doing this to me? I had responded to the humiliating name only a moment ago, like a dog named *Shithead* who obediently came when called. "Sneevie," I muttered.

"But maybe somebody else, even more *powerful*, is rambling around in the dank basement of your personality." Cy sat forward, elbows on knees. "Eric, ask him how much he cares."

I saw in Eric's pinched face and flexing fists that this was wrenchingly difficult for him, too. "Steve, how much—"

"For now," Cy broke in patiently, "he's Sneevie."

I snapped, "I hate that name."

Cy rose to stand beside me. Softly he said, "Your nickname embarrasses you because it reflects your shame about being needy. But we all have a deep pit of need inside us. We're with you, man. I admire you *tremendously* for exposing your need." He pitched his voice over my head. "Does anyone else admire Steve?"

Tears stung my eyes at the sound of my real name. With a hand on my shoulder Cy slowly turned with me while hands reached for the ceiling. "See that?" he asked gently.

"Sneevie," Eric recited with a look of pity, "how much do you care for me?"

"I love you," I said, looking past him out the west window. High clouds like mounds of whipped cream were gathering beyond the canyon walls.

"Ohh," Zoë cooed, and I felt the balm of her attention. "I love you," I went on recklessly, "and it's really fucking hard 'cause you don't love me."

"And now," Cy said, "it's time for you to *show us*."

Eric's jaw tightened. "Sneevie, please show me your love."

Now Cy spoke as if only he and I were in the room. "Maybe you could start where you left off at the party."

I was withering. I sank to my knees and crawled toward Eric. Recalling how bravely little Mikey had reënacted his theft of the peanut butter, I reached for Eric's ankle and settled into the fetal position, realizing I would *embrace* this process and welcome any chance to touch Eric, even in the mendicant rags of Sneevie.

"That's right," Cy said. "Curl up around your beloved's feet."

I stroked Eric's red wool socks and lay my head on one of his feet. Two smashed kernels of corn loomed before me in a knothole in the pine-plank floor. I closed my eyes and huddled in my cocoon, attached to him. Suddenly I was beyond anxiety or shame and felt strangely safe, as I'd once imagined I would feel when I succumbed to a Seconal overdose. I could comfortably lose consciousness, and if I never woke up I wouldn't know the difference.

Whispers rustled through the room, then footsteps clopped to the pantry and returned. I was startled by the sound of a guitar immediately above me. Eric began picking the melody of "Michelle"—and I realized there was nothing spontaneous about any of this. Cy must have planted the guitar for ready retrieval, as he'd done with Zoë's puppy. Slowly I melted into the floorboards, briefly opening my eyes, and saw with huge relief that others seemed to be tuned into something besides my shameful drama: Vivian held her head in her hands. Beside her, Teddy sat with glazed eyes and nodded out of time with the music.

Cy suggested Eric sing *Cripple Creek* so the others could join:

> *When a Cripple Creek girl's about half grown*
> *she'll jump on a boy like a dog on a bone.*
> *Gonna roll my britches up to my knees*
> *and wade up Cripple Creek whenever I please . . .*

I hummed along and rocked myself with eyes tightly shut. When the singing stopped Eric continued picking the notes softly. "How's it feel in there?" Cy asked.

His voice seemed to reach me from the end of a long tunnel. "Mmm," I replied.

"Remember what we said about polyselves?"

I nodded with no idea where this was leading.

"You, Sneevie, are a polyself of Steve Susoyev. Because Steve wants to grow and doesn't want to stay sick for the rest of his life, he is allowing you to display yourself to us, unashamed. You represent the needy beast each of us keeps chained in darkness. As Steve Susoyev allows this neediness to possess him, he takes a leap of growth and we grow, too."

Cy's voice was now so close I thought he must be on his hands and knees beside me. Still I kept my eyes closed.

"Eric," Cy said, "keep playing. How's this feel for you?"

"It's a little—*cramped*, I guess."

I heard scattered titters, and listened for the river's soft roar to calm me.

"Let's be gentle, people," Cy admonished. "If you're tempted to laugh, just picture yourself on this hotseat." The room fell silent. "Eric, may Sneevie curl up around your feet any time he wants to show you some lovin'?"

For a grueling moment Eric was silent. He finally answered, "I don't think so. It sounds confining. It does feel real, though."

"Confining, like the boy from town is trying to build a white-picket fence around you?"

"Feels more like a white-picket force field."

I felt as if I'd been kicked in the stomach. I heard a woman, probably Vivian, groan in sympathy. Eric continued, "Usually he's not this up-front."

"Sneevie," Cy asked, "can you *show* Eric some of the power of your love?" I snuggled tighter against Eric's foot. I heard whispering and kept my eyes shut tight.

"Let's try this," Cy finally said. "Do any of you women find

Eric attractive?"

My eyes popped open. Every woman in the place, including Elizabeth, held a hand high. The room turned crazily.

"Girls, show Eric how cute he is! Come stand over here." He herded over a dozen women into the space before the wood stove, then knelt beside me. "Can you get up now, Sneevie, and watch this?"

In agony I peeled myself from Eric's leg and stood with Cy.

"Who's got the hots for Eric?" Cy asked. "Don't be shy, and don't be afraid of hurting your pal Sneevie. He needs to size up the competition." While Cy stroked my shoulder, a sudden thought gave me hope. The women might lust for Eric, but none could show she *loved* him as I did.

Willow spoke barely above a whisper. "Eric, you're a beautiful man."

Cy asked gently, "How's that make you feel, Sneevie?"

Cramps twisted my stomach and I shook my head.

"That's all right," Cy said, and gripped my shoulder. "The feelings and words will come. Who else has something? Vivian?"

"If I were younger," she said, with a concerned look in my direction, "or Eric, if you were a little older and I thought you were interested, I'd think about—."

"How about *that*, Eric?" Cy asked. "Is Vivian too old for you to find her attractive?"

Eric laughed. "You're one of the sexiest women I know."

A hollow space opened inside my bowels, and a sharp pain ripped through me. I heard myself grunt. Cy asked in that tender but persistent voice, "How's it feel to hear that, Sneevie?"

"It's—okay. I mean, I *know* Eric's horny for all the women."

"Please let us know when it stops being okay. Girls, move in closer and see if you can get rid of that shirt. Don't anybody be shy today."

The women surrounded Eric and almost ripped away his flannel shirt. I heard a harsh electrical buzz in my head. "Let's *show* big Eric how attractive he is," Cy called out. "Somebody rub those muscles. How about stroking that lovely face?"

Vivian reached for his shoulders. Willow stepped behind him to braid his hair. His face broke into a broad smile. With a giggle, Elsie stroked his high, round ass through his jeans.

I was melting into the floor. "Isn't anybody interested," Cy asked, "in that wand of love Eric's known for?"

Willow reached from behind to stroke Eric's chest and stomach, then his crotch. "Ooh, it's ready for action!" she announced. I contorted my blazing face into a mask of laughter, pretending to be entertained.

"How does that make you feel?" Cy asked in a soothing tone.

"I—it's horrible."

"To watch the man you love, pawed at by bitches who only want his body but don't appreciate his soul as you do? What can you do about it?" With a hand on my shoulder, Cy pulled me in a circle around the profane spectacle. "Keep it up, girls," he added, and everyone chuckled because of Eric's conspicuous erection. "Sneevie will figure out what to do."

I continued circling with Cy. He asked softly at my ear, "What can you do?" I shook my head and stared into the womanflesh that slithered between me and Eric. When my body began to move on its own, Cy backed slightly away and followed me. I circled closer to Eric and the women. Like a neglected machine, they finally seemed to be losing energy. A few women returned to their seats. Eric's erection subsided.

"They're getting tired," I observed.

"Insulting your beloved!"

"I need to be patient."

The remaining women licked their lips and winked sluttishly. The faces swam past me.

Willow did a low-down hoochie-coo. I continued to circle. Spasms rolled through my gut, forcing me to hunch over and hug my waist. The Vistans smiled at me with loving eyes that illuminated my disgusting insincerity toward them all. I didn't like anything about pudgy Teddy's nipples, but had praised them during her Body Image in a pathetic attempt to make Eric jealous. And Eric had gotten only snide sarcasm from me.

Eric now appeared neither detached nor lusty. In his eyes I saw the shimmer of terror.

"Show us patience," Cy said quietly. "Don't explain."

I felt a beast chewing through my gut, gnashing membrane and tissue, organ and gristle. I hunched lower with each step and soon was walking sideways, dragging one foot, wringing my hands, possessed by a predator that studied Eric and the women with glazed, unblinking eyes.

"What are you waiting for, Sneevie?" Cy asked.

"For them to weaken." I spoke in the reedy, lizard voice of the creature that had eaten its way into my throat. "I'll be ready when they wear down."

Eric was radiant, his strength and beauty magnified by his fear. Some of the women yawned and walked off to sit down. I smirked. Cy suggested, "You gals are getting tired, huh?" The remaining women returned to their seats, leaving Eric alone to face my twisted body and wringing, clawlike hands. Cy spoke again in a quiet voice, "Show us, Sneevie. Show us who's screaming to get out."

I circled closer, hunched, lusting and leering, triumphant. I grabbed my crotch and slowly licked my lower lip, exulting in the power that surged through my contorted flesh. People were crying. I closed in on Eric. A wave of pain convulsed my insides, and the room spun into darkness.

I OPENED MY EYES ON VIVIAN'S UPSIDE-DOWN FACE. My head was in her lap and the Vistans sat in a tight circle around me. "He's coming to," she said. "Are you okay, honey?" I nodded in my far-off place. Ken and Willow held my hands. Zoë rubbed my feet. Travis brought a mug of cold water. Vivian held it while I drank a sip. It tasted of fresh lemons.

Gently Cy asked, "Who was that you let us see?"

I opened my mouth to speak, not knowing how to answer. The lizard creature crouched below my throat. I heard a child's voice say from inside me, "A monster."

"What kind of monster?"

I lay paralyzed in a pit of darkness, unable to hear the song of the river or coöperate with my rescuers. I closed my eyes. "A big, slimy lizard. But not mean. He's sad."

"Like Gollum?" Cy asked. "More needy than dangerous? In *The Hobbit*, Gollum's the reptilian creature who paddles around the underground lake protecting his 'precious,' the ring. But so overwhelmingly needy he's become dangerous." He paused and knelt beside me. "To eliminate their devastating power over us, we do not try to slay our secret demons. Instead we welcome them at the table of the human family."

Please let me go now, I wanted to beg, but Cy continued in his gentle tone, "We will integrate Gollum into your personality. He will live in the light. You will tap into his power some day."

I shook my head, swallowing my nausea. "Okay, people," Cy said. "Raise your hand if you have something inside you that feels as shameful as what Steve has shown us."

Every person raised a hand. Some smiled joyfully, and some,

including Vivian and Elizabeth, Willow and even Eric, with tears. Suddenly the space around my heart opened. No one spoke. Several minutes seemed to pass before Cy broke the sacred silence, speaking for me as Christ spoke for the adulteress. "Look around at your friends, Steve. Everybody here is harboring something at least as horrendous as Gollum."

"Or worse," Ken added.

"Of course," Cy said. "Who feels they have something inside that's *more* monstrous than what Steve has shown us?"

I laughed uneasily. Every hand stayed up, and some shot higher. The light of the Vistans' understanding poured into me. I felt my tears trickling down my jaw. Vivian stroked my hair. "The love of this community is truly unconditional," Cy said. "It is greater than the sum of its parts. Vivian, you have no trouble accepting Steve?"

"No," she whispered.

Gollum was deep in hiding. I crouched inside my own skin, in a tiny spot the monster had not fouled.

The Vistans pressed in tight and slipped their arms under me. Suddenly I was airborne, rocking in a human cradle as my new family drew me away from lingering horror. "Your pallbearers carried you to the land of the dead," Cy told me. "Now your midwives are delivering you into the land of the living."

Willow began to sing a simple melody, *"Sometimes I feel like a motherless child, sometimes I feel like a motherless child . . . a long way from home . . ."* As the others joined in, I felt myself sliding, as through a birth canal. "This is your new family," Cy said, "able to protect and nurture you as your original family was so sadly unable to do." With hands joined beneath me, everyone rocked the sobbing babe. They sang Willow's simple line again and again. Many more were weeping. "Behold Steve's pain," Cy told them, "and share your pain with him. Take away inspiration for your own growth from his Breakthrough." He gripped my hand. "These people love you unconditionally. Here you will become whole."

I looked up into the Vistans' gleaming eyes. I had come home.

10

I WAS STARTING TO UNDERSTAND: PAIN WAS HUMANITY'S LIFELONG COMPANION. Cy didn't bother contriving pain for anyone, he merely illuminated it and taught people to develop a productive relationship with it. Before Cy came into my life I had named my pain "loneliness" and blamed it on jealous schoolmates and brutal teachers, on my mother's alcoholism and my father's contempt for fruits like me. Rocked in the loving cradle of Rancho Vista, I would find my pain an exquisitely complex companion, something I couldn't reduce to intellectual concepts like loneliness.

I emblazoned across a fresh page in my notebook, *Self-acceptance is the goal of Aaron therapy.* The catalyst for this miracle of healing was the unconditional love of the Composite Significant Other. People needed this surrogate family because their original families were, for some pre-ordained reason, incapable of unconditional love.

Occasionally this all made sense, and I felt something like tranquillity. When I fully accepted who I was, Gollum and all, I would be happy. But most of the time the surrogates and composites and catalysts scrambled in my head. I cried for no reason while milking Rosebud, my favorite goat, or found myself laughing hysterically in one of the shitters over a snip of graffiti I'd read twenty times. I agonized. Why was I befriending the reptile inside me instead of chopping off its head? How could thirty muddy misfits give me anything that my earnest and well-read parents had not imparted?

At each Group I waited for Cy to make sense of it *permanently.*

I KICKED OFF MY BOOTS NEAR THE STOVE where other soggy footwear lay—cowboy boots, Frankenstein-style hiking boots, nylon snowmobile boots with soles like automobile tires, once-white leather sneakers stained the red of Rancho Vista's clay. The cookshack air was thick with steamy foot odor and the essences of toasted sock wool, broiled leather, coal-smoked hair. Cy was expounding on another of his proliferating theories. He talked like a diligent but challenged child, reciting a difficult rote lesson. "The Darling is the one for whom we save our really stinky poo-poo."

Rainbow and Lucky slumped in the middle of the floor, looking forlorn.

The community was so sick of this couple's constant bickering, Cy had to come up with increasingly entertaining approaches to dealing with them. By now I wasn't surprised by Groups that lasted all day and into the night, or started at nine p.m. with no warning except the ringing gong. Emergency Groups over kids caught skipping chores. Adults-only Groups held when a couple went in their shit over sex with a third person, whether consummated or merely desired. And even boring Groups, which today's threatened to be until Cy announced, "Okay, enough of you two. We've got some important business."

In each Vistan's face I saw the same question that flashed through my own mind: *Oh, shit, will this business involve me?*

"The Six-County Department of Health has received anonymous complaints about hygiene out here, and about sex among the minors. A rancher with binoculars, no doubt, spied some skinny-dipping last summer and spend the frozen winter embellishing his tale. We had a call from the county Health Inspector. He's coming for a look-see, but promises not to show up unannounced. I explained we're doing therapy with some very sick people whose privacy is my top priority."

Ken responded with a Quasimodo walk across the dining-room floor. Cy joined the laughter but cut it short. "Kids, we must make our oasis presentable. This man, Dr. Folsom, represents one of the institutions responsible for maintaining the planet's hypocrisies." He looked from face to face. "You, Teddy, could live in a condemned warehouse, content to get gang-raped every night as long as the rapists gave you drugs." He paused to let her remember—and, I realized, to let everyone else reflect on our own versions of her experience. I closed my eyes for a moment and saw the high school coach who'd hidden in his office while a boy was attacked by thugs in the shower.

"Those Gestapo assholes!" Willow declared. "We're serving a sacred mission here, and they revel in their power to crush us."

I stared at her, alarmed by her vehemence.

Cy chuckled and said, "Honey, listen. The people in power in this little county appreciate us. Our patronage brought over a hundred thousand dollars into the local economy last year." I relaxed into Cy's even tone. "Your leader has purchased eggs and irrigation pipes and petroleum products from local sources. Against the advice of penny-wise, pound-foolish members of his staff." Elsie sat up straighter. "The MacKenzies bought their new tractor with money we paid them to install our water system. Many locals want us to succeed. We have to win over the others. Everybody, think how to do that while we finish with our problem pair."

Group rambled into a seminar on the functions of the Needy Gland, which led back to Lucky and Rainbow. They fought when together and pined for each other when apart, and drained the community's energy either way.

"You're jealous when I talk to anybody," she complained.

"You're projecting," he snarled. "*You're* jealous!"

"What a joke. You're always projecting on *me*."

Folded index cards made their way toward Cy. He read and sorted them while he spoke over the heads of Rainbow and Lucky. "Zoë and I are developing a theory called *Polysex*. We feel if two people truly share love, and not just neediness, they can *enjoy* each other's attraction to people outside the relationship. In Polysex, you don't 'cheat' on your Primary Significant Other, you pursue your attraction to a guest with your P.S.O.'s affirmation."

The Vistans were uncharacteristically silent. I tried to imagine feeling happy about Eric making love with someone else. Cy broke the silence by reading one of the cards he'd received. "Elizabeth asks, *What's projecting?*" He smiled. "Isn't it refreshing when people can admit there's something they don't know? Steve, you're here on loan from your career as a mental health professional. Can you answer Elizabeth's question?"

I explained as simply as possible, "Projection is one of the eight defense mechanisms identified by Sigmund Freud. It involves assigning to others those negative qualities that we subconsciously fear are features of our own personali—"

"Thank you," Cy interrupted. "A very serviceable clinical definition. Ken, you have some life experience with defense mechanisms. Can you elaborate?"

Ken grinned. "Elizabeth, projection is when I have dog shit on my shoe and don't know it. I walk into your tipi and say, "Pee-*you!* It smells like dog shit in here!"

I joined the laughter but a flush of heat spread up my face. "Great example," I conceded.

Rainbow and Lucky meandered into an argument about whether they were ready to try Polysex. I opened my notebook to a letter I'd begun writing to my parents. On the next page I wrote, *How to be a Growth Case*, then jotted down some ideas.

"What's likely to happen," Cy asked, "if I claim I love Zoë yet continually try to limit her opportunities for pleasure and happiness?"

Ten hands shot up and Cy recognized Elizabeth's. She said, "She will figure out what you call 'love' is more like 'ownership.'" Others nodded in approval, and Vivian beamed.

"Steve is isolating with his notebook?" Cy said, reading from another card.

I looked up, startled.

Cy spoke softly. "May I read what you've written there?" I shuddered but handed over the notebook. Cy flipped to the previous page. "*'Dear Susi and Alex.'* On a first-name basis with your progressive parents! *'Rancho Vista is amazing,* dot dot dot, *cost of room, board, therapy all included in the monthly fee. Two more months will ensure I meet my goals,* dot dot.' Damn good letter home. Right to the point, no bitching about the food."

"Excellent letter home," Travis agreed from behind the serving counter.

Cy turned the page. *"How to be a Growth Case. Work hard. Shut up when other people are talking. Listen and strive to understand them, especially when they're giving me feedback."* He looked around the room then read slowly, with uncontrived reverence, *"When in doubt, do the process."*

"The 'shut up' part is harsh," Willow remarked.

"Steve," Cy said, ignoring her, "will you print this on cards for newcomers?"

I nodded, feeling thrilled. Instead of being scolded for isolating I'd been praised. I pictured a design for newcomers' cards, the headings I could create if I had templates to trace elegant letters onto a mimeograph stencil. Maybe Elsie would let me use the machine that produced the Relationship Workbooks.

Cy smiled benevolently. "Not bad for a kid who had a funeral here a few days ago."

I basked in the smiling respect of the others. In Cy's crinkley eyes I saw possibilities I'd been afraid to hope for until now.

THE NEXT MORNING WAS COLD AND WET. After breakfast, I returned to bed and sat up elaborating on the letter to my parents. My tipi was comfortable for the moment, but only lumpy black dust remained in my coal bucket.

I recognized all the Ranch vehicles by the sound of their engines, and heard the Land Rover and the Volkswagen climb out of the swale, bound for a staff meeting in town. When the roar faded into the lower pasture the round valley was again full of birdsong and the echo of the twin rivers. Why couldn't Cy make any decisions? Did he need Eric, Ken and Willow for everything? Today even Travis was going to town.

I put on my boots and waterproof poncho—green Army surplus held together with silvery duct tape—and carried my empty bucket down the hill to Eric's tipi. Our last time together we had filled his coal bin. I felt justified in borrowing back a few chunks of what I'd hauled.

The interior was still cozy from the morning fire. I removed my boots and filled my bucket, barely denting Eric's supply, then carefully replaced the Navajo rug over the trapdoor. The tipi was rich with animal hides, primitive but ingenious hand-made furniture, and tapestries. The bed smelled of Eric's musk. I climbed under the bearskin and enjoyed a moment of intimacy with the sheets.

My intention hadn't been to snoop, but suddenly I could almost smell Gollum's fetid breath as I began to ravage Eric's sanctuary. I peered under the bed and found a crate that overflowed with Relationship Workbooks, notebooks and scribbled-on scraps of paper. Systematically I thumbed through everything in the top of the pile, both relieved and hurt to find nothing about myself. Helping myself to cheese and bread, I stoked the fire and made a pot of tea. Inhabiting Eric's private world thrilled me.

I knew I was creating a Withhold that some day I would reveal. But I was powerless to stop. I dug in the crate for more writings and touched a bag of filmy plastic, tightly packed with a crunchily familiar substance. I pulled out the bag and saw a pack of Zig Zag rolling papers tucked against unmistakable sage-green leaves.

The discovery infuriated me. I'd left my stash with Lydia, believing Vista was drug-free. In the city I'd shared my best dope with Eric. I rolled and smoked my first joint in over a month and pawed through the whole collection of writings. How I'd missed getting stoned! I settled into warm well-being, free from the loneliness and fear that still dogged me in this soggy desert outpost. Unearthing the letter I'd written in Lydia's porch swing gave me mild comfort—at least Eric hadn't burned it.

For hours I pursued my investigations in a haze of contentment. I savored a second joint. Journal entries concerning someone named *Mr. M.* raised hairs on the back of my neck: *If you're such a stud,* Eric had written, *how come you need young guys like me to ball your wife?* I read the sentence half a dozen times, wondering what it could mean. When daylight faded I lit two kerosene lamps and rolled my third joint. I ignored the dinner gong and feasted on slabs of cheese and homemade bread, and lit another joint when a raucous version of "Gloria," on guitar and harmonica, drowned out the Mother River's song.

Long after dinner, twelve-year-old Elizabeth called to me. Soon I heard her right outside, kicking the mud from her boots. I opened Eric's antique Bible in my lap.

"So this is where you've been hiding," she said, and poked in her head around the quilted door flap. "Didn't you hear the music?"

"Just studying a little."

"Come with me. My mom's having a party." Her wry smile told me she understood what I'd been up to, but I didn't bother trying to explain. I returned the writings and baggie of pot to their crate, straightened the bed and blew out the lamps, and followed her to Vivian's tipi, carrying my coal bucket.

When Eric was around, Lucky played a restrained guitar. But tonight he launched into some raunchy riffs that made the Vistans grin and shimmy in appreciation. Puck did a hot suck-and-blow on a harmonica, and little Mikey beat syncopated rhythms on a bucket with a wooden spoon. I sank into my most pleasant mood. At my first Ranch party everyone had danced and fire-hopped nude. Without the staff around, the grunts and patients relaxed, perhaps less compelled to put on a show. Their gentle laughter filled the night.

Puck let Teddy take a turn on his harmonica and sat beside me. "When you let Gollum out," he said, "it was the bravest thing I've ever seen."

Lucky twanged out a musical agreement. "Yeah," Rainbow echoed, "fucking *brave.*"

Teddy made the mouth-harp wail like a train whistle. "You made me glad I've never loved anybody."

"Not even Puck?" I asked.

"He's not my boyfriend," she said, and winked at him. "Cy

just wants to keep me happy because of my trust fund. Puck's underage, like me, so there's no legal problem. Big dick, sweet disposition. We like each other, but he can do what he wants in his time off."

"So you've really never loved anyone?"

"I like it that way."

A vehicle roared into camp, and soon Travis showed up pushing a wheelbarrow loaded with bottles of homemade beer and Joy Juice. "Staff's staying in town for a party," he explained. "I'd rather be with you grunts."

I hadn't imagined separate parties. Clearly there was a world of experience denied me, from staff parties to Eric's ministrations for "Mr. and Mrs. M." And as much as I wanted to be at Cy's side, a trusted growth case, I enjoyed the easy comfort of the grunt party.

AT GROUP IN THE MORNING, CY SORTED THE CARDS PEOPLE PASSED IN. In a newsy tone he said, "Looks like somebody violated Eric's privacy. Goldilocks made a pot of tea and left the kettle to burn on the stove."

I heard myself make an animal noise and looked at Elizabeth, realizing if I feigned ignorance I would drag her into my Withhold. It was too late anyway. People were staring at me. "I went into Eric's tipi yesterday," I confessed. "I spent the day there. I read his journals and smoked a few joi—"

Eric let out an unintelligible howl. He leaped from his perch on the counter and backhanded me across the face.

I fell over and rolled into a ball, with a hand clasped over my stinging cheek. Travis, Ken and Puck restrained Eric while he pawed the air.

Cy raised his eyebrows high, but his expression held the hint of a smile. "You brought *drugs* here from Perdido Valley?"

I sensed I was being tested and that I would fail if I fingered Eric. "Just three joints," I ad-libbed. "I finished them off."

"You endangered everything we've worked so hard to accomplish. Worse than the lowest grunt!"

"He's a zit on the face of this community," Eric snarled. "A carbuncle. A *pustule*."

I wanted to scream that this was unfair. I forced myself to look into the eyes of people around the room and found no comfort. "I'm really sorry, Cy. Everybody."

I sat on the hotseat and listened as the Vistans told me how disappointed they were in my irresponsible behavior. The distrust in Travis's eyes and the sadness in Vivian's pained me.

During the break, Willow took me for a walk around the pond. "Some of the staff keep marijuana," she said. "Cy's inner circle. We use it for therapy. But the grunts can't know about it. I don't think Eric was as mad as he acted. He just wanted to stop you before you confessed to stealing some of *his* stash. Cy's pleased you caught on so fast."

"When did he tell you that?"

"After you've known Cy a while, you'll sense it."

"A lot of what goes on here flies right over my head. I guess burglarizing a staff member's tipi doesn't exactly catapult me toward being let in on more."

She looked away, but I didn't miss her tiny, private smile.

EACH DAY WAS WARMER THAN THE LAST and brought more hawks, eagles and owls into the canyon. A pair of black swans appeared one day and took over the holding pond, chasing out the emerald-necked ducks that had arrived a week ahead of them. The ducks relocated to the marsh below, where young cattails were rising above dense new grasses.

I stayed out of Eric's way and tried to avoid everyone else. After being exposed as a thief and a sneak, I enjoyed a strange relief in realizing I was a grunt after all. If I never rode in the front of the truck with the staff, no one would expect me to live up to labels like "growth case" and "genius."

I recorded my nightmares in my journal and wrote to my dead friend Dean. Mindful of Cy's admonition to "keep the body moving," I rubbed my bookshelves with stain and refinished a warped armoire someone had abandoned outside the root cellar. Puck helped me haul it to my tipi as an elegant replacement for the makeshift closet. Over my bed I mounted the Proclamation the Los Perdidos patients had signed to protest my firing. Occasionally, after becoming lost in work, I was surprised to find myself content in my own company.

I made myself useful, especially to Travis—who teased me about my espionage skills and seemed to have let go of his disappointment without a struggle. I knew others appreciated my willing attitude. But where was all this leading? I didn't feel more or less homosexual, or self-accepting, than before. My time at the

Ranch was running out. I had flashes of panic at the idea of returning to L.A.

THE RED TRUCK RUMBLED UP THE RUTTED ROAD with Elsie at the wheel. I straddled the gearshift and Cy hung an arm out the window. The purpose of this trip up the mountain wasn't clear to me, but as usual Cy was saying profound things. I worried I should have brought a notebook. My paid-up time at the Ranch had expired three days before, and I worried that any day I'd be dispatched to the nearest Greyhound stop.

"Personal growth is an onion," Cy was explaining. "Most people peel away one layer at a time—if they have the courage even to go near the stinky thing."

Elsie nodded. I listened attentively, relieved to be the focus of the leader's private attention at last. But how was I going to pay for it?

"In your case," Cy continued, "because you're willing and desperate, we peeled away several layers all at once during your Gollum session, and a few more when Eric whacked you upside the head. Meaning you're still raw and exposed. Am I right?"

Actually, numb was how I felt. "Raw" had worn off a few days before. "My therapist in the city taught me 'coping skills,'" I said, "when he wasn't trying to electrocute my genitals."

"Sorry to interrupt," Elsie said. "This sounds like a good story. But should I drop you guys at the turnoff to the lake?"

Cy said the turnoff would be perfect, and asked if she'd paid certain important bills. She replied that she would hand-deliver a check to the man who supplied the Ranch's diesel fuel.

I knew that some Vistans hadn't spent a moment alone with Cy for months. Why was I about to be honored with a personal session of walking therapy? Maybe he would use the hike back to town to confront me with the debt that was now mounting by the minute. My last therapist, Dr. Sutton, had let me run up a debt of over a thousand dollars before he started sending nasty letters. Elsie was probably keeping a tab. Twelve hundred a month was forty dollars a day, meaning I already owed over eight hundred bucks I didn't have.

"Ah, yes," Cy said, turning back to me, "the popular coping skills treatment for the wounded soul. It's as if the surgeon says, 'I'm not competent to remove that malignant tumor on your face, so we'll cover it with this nice Band-Aid. Thus you can cope with it until it spreads through your lymph system and kills you.' Garth Elfinger was learning those skills from the therapist his mother sent him to when she refused to let him come to Rancho Vista." In his tone I heard tremendous sadness, and a trace of bitterness. "Anyway, the length of our walking therapy session won't be determined by fifty minutes ticking away on a clock. It'll time itself organically. If you get into something deep, we'll naturally walk more slowly to savor the reality. If you bullshit me, we'll walk faster to get it over with."

"The record is thirty-five minutes," Elsie said, "from the turnoff to the trailers in town. I should know. I was the shallow, unreal patient who had to run to keep up with Dr. Love and Reality here."

"Trying to convince me she wasn't interested in losing her virginity to Eric," Cy said, "while everybody else at the Ranch wished they still had some virginity to offer him." I laughed with them, but the joke poked me in a tender spot. I'd been jealous even at Los Perdidos when Eric danced with toothless, ancient Bertha Flippe. Dowdy Elsie seemed like a bigger threat.

Cy and I hopped out where a hand-lettered sign pointed toward Moose Lake. He gestured at the truck as Elsie slowly drove away. "There's personal awareness in action. Notice anything unusual about her driving?"

The truck disappeared around a bend and I guessed what Eric or Willow would say. "She didn't blast dust in our faces. Most people would rattle off without noticing."

"You have amazing sensitivity." Cy surveyed the morning, then led off and set a brisk pace back toward town. "You're in post-operative recovery since your Gollum session. You need a chance to heal without forming thick scar tissue. To switch metaphors—are you ready to peel the next layer of the onion?"

Money, I thought. This was my first and last private session with the world's greatest therapist. "Cy, I have no idea what's next."

"Of course not." He patted my shoulder and seemed to slow his pace. "Few people go to the emergency room knowing they need an appendectomy. They only know they're in pain. It's the doctor's job to diagnose and treat the cause."

I drank in the cool air and let out a deep sigh. Crows shrieked at two young deer who watched us from a meadow. A rabbit sprang from a low oak scrub and bounded like a wind-up toy

across the road and out of sight. Spring had fully arrived for the
pregnant green buds on the aspen trees and poplars, the watercress that cascaded from the wet rock walls of the grottos.

"I always enjoy these walks," Cy said, "but there's a special
reason I had Elsie bring us up here today."

My chest tightened and I nodded seriously.

"This is the wilderness, one of the few congruent environ-
ments left on the planet. Even Keystone down there, with its
hundred-some humans and ten thousand head of cattle, is full of
chatter and distracting input. Televisions blaring in the farm-
houses, radios blaring from pickup trucks that rattle down the
washboard roads."

"It's lovely up here," I agreed, moved by the beauty of the
misty labyrinths that cradled Rancho Vista's tiny island below us,
to the east.

"Beautiful and *healing*. It's time for you to go on Trail. Ken's
taking a group tomorrow. Out there you'll have the chance to
become *emotionally self-sufficient*. The time away from Eric will let
you contemplate the real reasons you came here."

We walked silently. I couldn't relax into the idea that Cy was
planning further treatment as if money were not an issue. The
words "emotionally self-sufficient" echoed in a lonely corner of
my mind, and I fought the urge to protest that I had *not* come
here to be with Eric.

"The entire community will leave for Beverly Hills the day
after you return from Trail," Cy continued. "Among other things,
we'll be doing a Marathon Group down there. In the wilderness,
work through a Relationship Notebook on your parents to
prepare for the session. We'll invite them to our Marathon. That's
usually the core of the onion, our relationships with our
O.P.S.O.s."

"Our—Obligatory Primary Significant Others?"

Cy whooped. "Oh, that's a good one! Is it a joke? No,
O.P.S.O.s are *Original* Primary Significant Others, but I'll remember 'Obligatory.'" From his shirt pocket he withdrew a tiny
notebook, wrote a line, and chuckled. "Let's identify other
important relationships. The boys you grew up with, were they *all*
cruel thugs?"

"Yeah," I replied automatically. We paused in the road for a
moment. I saw acceptance in this man's eyes and told myself
there was no point in harboring unturned stones. "Not all," I
continued. "There was one, a boy I loved."

"Dean."

"You remember his name."

"He may provide the key to your self-destruction, your string of failures, much of your grief. You told Zoë and me he died in reform school. But he wasn't a tough guy?"

"No! It was my fault he went there."

Cy spoke with the softness I was beginning to count on. "Tell me how it happened."

Thus the surgeon's scalpel pierced the spot where I had buried my pain when I had no words for any of my feelings. I described growing up with Dean in semi-rural Orange County, the hours we'd spent riding horses, building forts in the hay, sharing chores to make the drudgery tolerable. As puberty approached, our roughhousing turned to wrestling, which turned slow and sensual. I went on in detail about kissing and cuddling that led to delicious hours of rubbing our young bodies together.

"What the French call 'frottage,'" Cy remarked.

"One day we were in the hay loft at his place."

"Frottaging?"

"We'd gone beyond that. I was inside him, with my pants pulled down. He was naked."

"A true roll in the hay."

"We used a blanket." I smiled weakly when I realized I'd missed the joke.

Cy buried his hands in his pants pockets and stopped walking. His eyes penetrated my fear. "And what happened?"

"Suddenly we heard his dad down in the barn, really mad, yelling, 'Dean, what the hell're you doing up there? Who's with you?' He started up the ladder."

"Jesus." Cy began to walk again, but very slowly, towing me with his eyes. "Were you afraid he'd attack you with a pitchfork?"

"He kept a rifle in his pickup and I was afraid he'd shoot us. I pulled up my pants and shimmied down a rope hanging off the back of the barn. Dean never made it out. His dad caught him, and told my parents he was sure I'd been in the loft doing something nasty with his son. I cooked up an alibi."

"Nasty!" Cy punched the air with a fist. "Sex play is a normal developmental process. Unfortunately for kids, it's the *first thing* most adults forget from their own childhoods."

His voice softened. "You said Dean died in reform school. Did his father send him there because of what he'd caught you boys doing?"

Cy's tone allowed all possibilities, though he made this one sound as monstrous as it truly was. "Yeah," I answered. "He told the judge Dean was 'ungovernable.'"

"So Dean was put away, and you went to Columbia."

I looked toward the canyons so Cy couldn't see my eyes. "Nobody ever told me what really happened. My mother says he was killed for being a homosexual. My guess is she doesn't know any more than I do. Maybe that's wishful thinking."

"Am I making excuses for you if I guess you dropped out of college, and began your cycle of failure, when Dean died?"

"Everybody raved about what a fantastic kid I was, but I ran away and let him go to that hell-hole to be murdered."

"Did you write or visit him in reform school?"

I stared into the canyons, allowing my silence to answer the dreadful question.

Cy explained that my journal entries and mock letters to Dean were a good start. Now I would work in Group on my relationship with my lost love. "You'll ask your dead friend for forgiveness so you can begin to forgive yourself." I nodded as if this made sense, as if I believed my parents would pay for more therapy at the Ranch.

"A powerful, brilliant man lives inside you," Cy said, "committed to growth and eager for a full life. I've seen what he's capable of—that inspired deception on behalf of Rupert Seville, the courage to hitchhike to Rancho Vista in search of healing. The way you bared your soul in Group to Eric, then caught yourself and took the heat for bringing dope into the Ranch."

I trembled with gratitude. Cy understood and accepted my role in the tragedy of my childhood, and believed I could grow past it. We walked past Keystone's ramshackle rodeo grounds and weedy cemetery. As we approached the Blue Worm, he said, "In your first love we may have found the key to your freedom."

The question, *How am I going to pay for this?* dogged me, even though Cy hadn't yet mentioned money. Susi and Alex expected me to be cured of homosexuality by now. When they learned this goal hadn't been accomplished, they would refuse to pay another nickel. And with Gollum rearing his slimy head, I couldn't expect to earn my own way at Rancho Vista.

The session ended with silent ambiguity. Cy trotted ahead to take a phone call in the triple-wide. I watched him go and decided not to mention my debt, and just run a tab until he threw me out.

11

THE RIVER SOAKED MY CANVAS HIGH-TOPS AND NUMBED MY FEET. The canyon ahead zigzagged up between jagged stone cliffs that were swallowed in mist. Seven hikers marched abreast into the boundless, menacing wilderness—for me, until this morning, a place to be explored on educational television or peered at from an airplane window.

We were in the care of Ken, the terminally cheerful yet strangely distant Great God Pan. A mysterious smile, sometimes cocky, sometimes sweetly vulnerable, often played on his shapely lips. Only a few months older than me, also a dropout and with no credentials, Ken had somehow established himself as a "wilderness survival" expert and the leader of Rancho Vista's flagship Trail program. Barely five-feet-six and a hundred forty pounds, he bounced along under a ninety-pound backpack, far heavier than anyone else's. Trudging behind, I was embarrassed even to joke about my own seventy-pound burden much less actually complain.

Ken couldn't boast the tall, blond rock-star looks of Eric, but in his compact, sinewy, sun-kissed way he had intoxicating beauty. Eric had erupted into my life, asking a hundred questions and making love to me the night we met. Ken's slightly lopsided smile hinted at trust and even playful affection, but I sensed I must earn both through impossible feats of manhood.

The sun melted a bank of steamy clouds. The only remaining shade clung to crevices in the forbidding side-canyon walls. Ken said we would spend much of the next ten days walking through water, but mustn't drink from the river or creeks. He paused at the base of a narrow zigzag trail that ascended past a crystalline waterfall. Once he had everyone's attention he announced, "Puck and I are trained to keep you alive." He pulled his full red lips into a serious line.

I smirked with a private wink at Teddy. "We haven't lost anybody," Ken went on more loudly, "and don't intend to. We know this country, which water is safe and which'll give you diarrhea you'll take to your grave—"

I asked in a cut-the-crap tone, "Terminal diarrhea?" which won a snort from Teddy.

"Cramps'll make you pray for death," Ken said with forced patience. "Animals drop dead in the creeks and their rotting shit is loaded with parasites. The parasites seep out of the animals' guts and into the water. Some amoebas stay with you for life." He stepped up onto the narrow trail that led upstream. "We'll pass springs with safe water."

He hiked ahead, a huge backpack with taut brown legs, and Puck stayed with the group, quoting Cy on the nature of Trail. He had pulled his corkscrew curls into a tight ponytail, giving his usually goofy face a more serious look. "It's a chance to learn self-sufficiency, the most important goal of therapy, in the congruent environment of the wilderness."

Text memorized from a brochure. Yesterday I'd hiked alone with the world's greatest therapist. How had I gotten stuck on this desert jaunt with Nature Boy and his sidekick? Was it a cheap way of getting rid of me until they dumped me in L.A., since my money had run out? Whatever psychobabble Ken and Puck employed to consecrate this ordeal, Trail was a chance for people to walk in a big circle for a week and a half, then drag themselves back to the cookshack famished and sunburned with bleeding, blistered feet.

But Ken's self-assurance was also a challenge. When he dipped his bandanna into the stream and re-tied it around his neck, I did the same. Cold rivulets coursed down my chest and hardened my nipples. A nylon cinch held my pack on my hips, relieving my shoulders of the burden. I twisted my hair in a topknot to keep the backpack from pulling it, and wrinkled my nose at Teddy when she said this made my head look like a bushel of wheat.

At times I deliberately fell behind and watched my companions. Ken, in a sleeveless shirt and cutoffs that showed off his hard little body, kept himself in the lead, but stopped often to lecture on the arcana of wilderness survival. Teddy and Vivian hiked together, the tattooed street girl and the petite Orange County housewife, with matching pink paisley bandannas tied over their hair. Puck bounded along, pausing frequently to help others. Rainbow and Lucky ignored everyone else, arguing while they hiked and necking during breaks.

Ken countered the hazards of the wilderness with practical survival tips. "Don't sleep under a cottonwood tree 'cause rattlesnakes have standing reservations. But they won't fuck with you unless you fuck with them first . . . You won't starve in the desert. There's watercress growing in bunches at every spring. Pull out your pocketknife and the menu grows considerably. Look at the juicy meat inside this little cactus . . . Let's high-tail it through that narrow slot canyon in case there's a flash flood." For scorpion bites he prescribed a poultice of willow leaves and creek clay. "One theory says stay calm, don't let the venom race through you. I've tried that and stayed sick for days. Or you can run around, drink gallons of water, get dizzy, but chase the shit out of your system. That's my preferred method."

I quipped to Teddy, "My preferred method is to bite the fucker before he has a chance to bite me."

Ken's dark eyes flashed but he assumed a clinical tone. "I have Benadryl to help you recover from a scorpion or wasp attack. But if a rattlesnake fangs you, stay calm. I carry a snakebite kit. Puck and I learned the hard way how to use it."

Puck knelt and deliberately jabbed the heel of his hand into a prickly-pear cactus, then demonstrated how to remove the spines using the tweezers on his deluxe Swiss Army knife. On the insides of his wrists I saw thick parallel cords of tell-tale suicide-attempt scar tissue, like Blind Michael's. I wanted to embrace this exuberant, goofy boy, who didn't need comforting.

Ken carried the Hasselblad that had once belonged to my father, and captured the hikers when we helped one another over slippery river rocks and down steep sections of a narrow path, or sliced apples and blocks of sweaty orange cheese during breaks. Puck picked handfuls of lemony "squawberries," like hard red currants, and I accepted some for my canteen.

The hikers followed faithfully when Ken forded the river or pointed out fossilized shells in a canyon wall, proving this desert had once been a sea. He passed around binoculars so everyone could see the tiny caves in a cliff where ancient people had hidden grain. "The Anasazi disappeared mysteriously," he said. "No one knows why they left these canyons."

"Steve," Teddy asked, "isn't there a place like this in Orange County? Oh, I remember—Frontierland. But when people disappear it's no mystery. They're in the bathroom barfing up their cotton candy."

Several people chuckled and I joined in. But I saw how Ken's horseshoe-shaped tricep quivered, and thought better of encouraging Teddy and alienating the leader completely. In silence everyone followed Ken to a ferny grotto where cool, sweet water dripped from a fissure in the sandstone. We drank our fill and topped off our canteens, then climbed out of the main canyon and faced a moonscape of smooth, bleached-looking rock strewn with volcanic boulders. I had never paid much attention to the texture of the ubiquitous sandstone, but now noticed that crusted lichens of chartreuse and rust-orange clung to every surface. A baby thunderstorm rolled through, pelting me with hail for several minutes before the fierce sun reappeared. Acres of damp rock steamed with tiny white hailstones. I walked alone. I would exert myself only enough to keep the others in sight.

A mile or so farther along Ken came to a water hole and flung his hands out to both sides. The hikers behind him stopped, then inched ahead. "Oh, brother," I whispered, infuriated by Ken's melodramatic advance on every mouse turd.

"Puck," Ken called. "How old you think these tracks are?"

I sauntered toward the group with a yawn, ready to study rabbit prints in the sand.

"She came through since the hailstorm," Puck replied. "Last half hour or so."

"She?" asked Vivian.

Ken answered with reverence, "It's the female cougars who hunt. You won't find a male out in the open like this. The dudes stay down on the river."

I figured "cougar" was another name for bobcat, an adorable animal with tufted ears, so ferocious a popular sports car had been named after it. I imagined the little beast stalking toads in the cattails around the water hole. But when I came close enough to see the tracks, I shivered. The prints were six inches across. "Wow," I said. "What do they eat?"

"Deer, cattle, elk, people—anything that runs." Ken glanced around, making sure everyone got the point. "Don't run from a mountain lion. Don't act like prey. Stand and stare her down. She'll mosey right past you."

Teddy asked the question I would not. "So a cougar's a mountain lion?"

"Only thing here deadlier than a rattlesnake," Puck replied.

I stayed closer to the others after we resumed hiking. Soon Ken fell behind and stopped to roll out his worn topographical map on a flat rock. He placed a compass on it, motioned to me to join him for a look, then pointed to twin pinnacles of rock a mile away. "Those spires are these seven thousand-foot points here on the map."

"Molly's Nipple," I read, "and—Molly's Other Nipple?"

Ken traced a crooked path on the map. "We'll pass between them. The switchback trail gets us to this ledge, where we'll lower ourselves to Walters Creek."

The ledge's elevation was marked sixty-two hundred feet, the creek's six thousand. "How do we 'lower ourselves' that far?"

"We'll rappel down."

"I'm gonna dangle two hundred feet from a rope?"

"You're gonna walk down a vertical cliff, perpendicular to the rock face. You'll control the rate of your descent. It's fun."

"Who's carrying ropes that long? All I've seen in our packs is lentils and rice."

"The equipment's buried in barrels. See here?" Ken pointed to a cluster of tiny circles on the map, labeled *Ropes*.

"There must be a trail."

"You won't have to look down. You'll be walking backwards. Looking up."

The idea filled me with a mixture of terror and contempt. "It's like summer camp. You're manipulating us into 'facing our fear.' I faced mine when I let Cy drag Gollum out of me."

Ken sighed. "There'll be some frightened people on that ledge. I counted on you to be a role model. I didn't need that sarcastic shit about your preferred method with scorpions." He gazed into my eyes. "I think of you as a courageous guy. When you showed us Gollum, when you admitted you'd gone through Eric's stuff and gotten stoned, hell, when you showed up at the Ranch, I thought, That guy's got balls. Which is why I figured I could count on you now." Impatiently he continued, "Besides, rappelling is the only way to get to Walters Creek. If we run out of water up on the ledge, you'll see how much summer camp there is in death by dehydration."

I recognized the "role model" maneuver as something I had used on Rupert and other patients at Los Perdidos, when I wanted them to do something my way. But I was eager to earn a good report, and imagined Cy reading aloud from a card in Group, *Steve was a disruptive, uncoöperative pain in the ass . . .*

"I won't let you down," I promised, and felt a knot tighten in my stomach.

Soon the hikers passed between the twin, sky-high peaks. The steep switchback trail led up to a wide rock shelf where Ken and Puck moved aside large flagstones to expose the buried storage barrels. They pulled out a great coiled purple rope and webbing of turquoise nylon. I shuffled as close to the cliff's edge as I could, trying to see the creek, which was barely audible far below and hidden by an overhanging lip of rock—the overhang Ken claimed all of us were going to walk over. Backwards.

Ken looped the longest rope around the base of a sturdy cedar tree and tied it in a fancy knot. "We'll go down one at a time," he explained. "Puck first, to show how it's done. He'll wait at the bottom for each of you, then we'll lower the packs. Okay, let's start."

Puck stood with his feet wide apart while Ken fashioned a harness of turquoise straps over his shorts. I watched closely when Ken threw the rope's free end over the edge of the cliff. The coiled bundle unwound itself until only the section knotted around the tree was left in sight. Puck snapped three metal clips around the purple line, passed the rope around his waist and over one shoulder. "These aluminum karabiners provide the friction to stop me," he said. Ken checked his rigging, then Puck shuffled toward the cliff. He leaned back at an impossible angle, to demonstrate how he could stop his descent by pulling the rope close to his belly. With no further preparation he back-stepped to the edge, leaned into the breeze, let out rope, and with a calm glance over one shoulder hopped off the cliff and disappeared.

My stomach did a flip. Vivian squatted, looking as if she might throw up. Teddy wandered away with both arms clutched around her middle.

"This cliff's too steep for us to watch him," Ken said. "But we'll stay in contact."

Puck's voice echoed up to us, "About twenty feet down!"

"No fucking way," Teddy said. "You can call a helicopter and fly me back to Juvie, but I'm not doing this."

The rest of us stared ahead, silent and wide-eyed. Lucky poked at a coiled rope as if the risk we were expected to take had become sickeningly clear. Panic seemed imminent. "Is it possible," I asked Ken, "for two people to go down together? Teddy, would it be easier if I went with you? We'll run out of water if we stay up here."

"Fifty feet," Puck called up.

"No," Ken said with a tight smile. "It's only safe for one person at a time."

"Horseshit!" Teddy kicked at a heap of rope. "I'm hiking back to the river. I'm thirsty for parasites."

"I'll go over next," Vivian offered. "I haven't much to lose."

Ken replied, "Great," in an upbeat tone that shocked me.

"Let's get you into a harness." At the Ranch, Cy would stop everything to explore Vivian's hopelessness—but obviously Trail was not used to investigate feelings.

"Half way down," came Puck's echo.

"I wonder why nobody's listening to me," Teddy said. "Even you, Vivian, always acting like my big sister. I'm walking back to the Ranch right now." She drank from her canteen and strode away, leaving her backpack in the sand.

"What are you going to do?" Vivian asked Ken.

He spat. "She's pretty used to getting her way."

I hoisted on my pack. "Well, she can't go alone." I called out, "Wait! I'm not doing this either," and ran to catch up with her.

She regarded my pack with surprise. "We gotta reach the Ranch before dark. That load'll slow you down."

I shrugged. "Guess I could dump out some rice. I've got four huge bags. But let's keep going for now."

We walked on silently and stepped with caution down the steep switchback of loose rock chips. I said, "When Puck went over the edge I thought I'd throw up."

"That's the scariest thing I've ever seen. You're a brave fucker to say you'd go down with me."

Again we walked in silence. I was willing to hike all the way back to the Ranch, but knew I would earn Ken's respect if I got Teddy, and myself, over the cliff.

"Hope we don't run into that mountain lion," I said. "I don't care what Ken and Puck say, I couldn't stare her down. I'd run for the nearest tree."

Teddy slowed her pace. "Lions are cats. Cats climb trees." She looked around. "And I see exactly one tree, that scraggly runt over there."

I eyed the brittle juniper she pointed to. "You're right. Could you stare down a lion?" She slowed even more. My voice cracked. "I'm terrified. It could get dark before we find the Ranch." I turned to face her.

She leaned in close to me. "Would you really have gone over that cliff with me if Ken had said it was okay?"

"Not just for you. I wanted to go with somebody because heights freak me out."

We looked at the lone tree, and at each other.

"I fucking hate to admit when I'm whipped," she said.

I spat, Ken-like. "Especially to Nature Boy back there."

From somewhere above, a handful of pebbles tumbled down

a sandstone slope, making a ghastly rattle. Both of us flinched. "That happens a lot," I said, trying to sound casual. "The wind, or a bird, or something."

"It's the 'or something' that scares the shit out of me."

Without another word we turned slowly and retraced our steps, increasing the pace as we went higher, and finally hiking with flat-out urgency up the switchback. When we reached the ridge only Ken remained, re-coiling the rope. "Welcome back," he said, and mouthed to me, *How'd you do that?*

I helped Teddy into a harness. She practiced maneuvering the "brake rope" and found it simple, requiring no brute strength. With a fierce look of determination she rehearsed Puck's leaning routine, then walked backwards over the edge and whooped all the way down.

I took deep, shuddering breaths while Ken rigged a harness around my waist and thighs. Like a good soldier I followed instructions, leaned back and walked, letting out rope slowly. I managed my terror until I was half way down the cliff, then made the mistake of looking over my shoulder. The creek spun far below me. I slapped the brake rope against my belly, stopping myself cold, and screamed. Sweat stung my eyes while I stood like a fly on the vertical rock cliff. After a moment I realized I had a free hand to wipe it away. Teddy and the others shouted incoherent encouragement from below. Hours seemed to pass before I let out an inch of rope, then another, and resumed my descent, taking longer steps, finally enjoying this sense of being airborne. Eventually my feet touched down on a broad pink beach. I was shaking, but without fear, so full of adrenaline I felt ready to climb back to the top, hand-over-hand, chewing cactus and scorpions.

My pack descended and I untied it. The purple rope rose out of sight. Puck explained that Ken would re-bury the ropes and hike down by a different route. *So there is a trail*, I thought, feeling deceived, yet too exhilarated to complain.

We camped on a plateau near the water but—at least according to Puck—high enough to be protected from flash floods. Everyone hauled river rocks for the fire ring, then pulled wrinkled brown bags full of vegetables from the lined-up backpacks. Leeks, onions, potatoes, carrots and celery, all trimmed and rinsed before the trip, were cut and dumped into the stewpot. Teddy returned from the spring with handfuls of watercress for a salad. Plastic bottles of safflower oil and eggs, and bags packed with spices, powdered milk and parmesan cheese, were arranged along a log for the cooks' convenience. I recognized the peanut butter jar from Mikey's Group, an event that now seemed lost in the mists of time though it had taken place just a few weeks before. I felt a stab of anger that rice wasn't being used; my pack held twenty pounds of the stuff. Tonight's dinner relied heavily on potatoes, carrots and the lentils that were a part of everyone's load. The vegetables boiled and the sweet Bermuda onions fried. Puck lay back in the shade of a willow to blow a blues riff on his harmonica.

I stood in a driftwood pile collecting fuel for the fire until a swarm of hornets drove me out. Vivian ran to me, then laughed hysterically when she realized I was all right. She appeared free of grief for the first time since I'd known her, and did a full-body shimmy as she dumped handfuls of chopped leeks into sizzling oil. Teddy stirred the soup and smiled without her usual twist of sarcasm. Puck's harmonica sobbed on.

Trail made the Ranch look like a luxury resort, but the food was plentiful. We ate like the inmates of a French prison and savored our dessert of "groat cakes," a thick flour-and-oat batter dollopped onto hot coals and eaten with a drizzle of honey. After a spectacular but fleeting sunset, a chill fell over the canyon and we bundled into sweatshirts. Ken hiked into camp, his down vest ripped and his face and legs covered with scratches from "some serious brambles." He gulped everything in his bowl. Once again, I had to admit to myself he was right. He'd taken a treacherous trail while the rappel had been easy. After rinsing his bowl, he disappeared to set up a private campsite, and I silently marveled at his lack of fear.

The rest of us dragged out our sleeping bags and within minutes everyone else was snoring. I lay squeezing my sore muscles, torn between pride in my rappel and humiliation over my fear of it, between resentment and reverence for Ken. The creek finally sang me to sleep.

Ken marched into camp at dawn. "Trail 101," he announced. "Leave the campsite as we found it."

Puck jumped out of his sleeping bag, naked and with a startling erection. He built a frame of fresh twigs atop the remains of the fire, blew on the coals until the twigs ignited, threw on chunks of wood, then scampered to the creek and leaped in.

People wandered into the bushes with personal rolls of toilet paper—and, following another of Ken's Trail guidelines, returned to throw the soiled tissues into the fire.

After a breakfast of oatmeal and oranges, everyone drowned the fire's hot coals, scattered the rocks and buried the ashes, wiping out all evidence of having been there. I decided to rise beyond Ken's challenge. After heaving on my pack, I waited until the others left the campsite, then swept it clean with a willow branch, obliterating even our footprints.

I spent the morning hiking with Vivian. "Until yesterday I didn't think I resented my parents," I told her. "Don't dads teach their sons to hike and fish and track cougars? All Alex taught me was how to read a racing form."

Vivian nodded distractedly. "It's unfair. Garth wanted to come to the Ranch but I wouldn't let him. Now I'm here."

I slung an arm around her. "Based on what I knew of Garth at the hospital, I think he'd be happy that you and Elizabeth and Mikey are taking care of yourselves."

EACH DAY KEN DID HIS OWN FORM OF WALKING THERAPY with one person after another. The group stopped for cheese and carrot breaks, and jumped naked into the streams while the sun was high. We camped where and when Ken decided, and tackled chores in a way that would have thrilled Travis. There was an abundance of firewood at every twist in the waterways—branches of aspen and cottonwood, sometimes entire trees, carried by the spring runoff and left behind when the waters receded. After recovering from the exhaustion of the first days, the hikers often joined Ken for moonlight walks.

Having broken my habit of hiking alone, I heard about Puck's suicide attempts and Lucky's polygamous Mormon grandfather. Ken described the countless whippings he'd received as a child, and during a swim showed the shadowy, crescent scars left on his butt by his father's belt buckle. Teddy matter-of-factly described how her mother had poisoned her father and received a life sentence. "Crime runs in the family," she added. "Dad was convicted of insider trading. I stole a Camaro when I was thirteen. Cy rescued me from juvenile hall."

The season of slush was a faint memory. Every afternoon a thunderstorm rolled through the canyons and settled the dust. Some hikers tied ponchos over their packs and themselves. I let myself get drenched, as I saw Ken was content to do. The clouds dissipated within a half hour, giving way to a sunset that blazed far above the canyon.

By the fourth day my body no longer ached. My hair was matted and my fingernails were ragged but clean from scrubbing pots with river sand. I had never felt so alive.

After each night's groat cakes, people scrawled in their journals while the sky faded. The fifth evening out, I wrote in my journal, *Dean, It's time to tell you how pissed I am you got yourself killed in reform school. I'm sick of blaming myself for your death. It's also time to stop using you as my excuse for not living my own life.*

OVER BREAKFAST KEN ANNOUNCED, "SOLOS TO-NIGHT." Each hiker would camp alone, he explained, cooking and sleeping in a private site. At first this seemed like a nice idea but by midmorning I had changed my mind. The two hundred-foot rappel felt like a Cub Scout field trip compared to solitude. Of course this was another test, a chance to be scared to death. Never mind that I'd slept on the ground for the past five nights surrounded by the other Vistans. Sleeping solo while rattlesnakes and scorpions crawled over me was terrifying.

That afternoon the group hiked along the meandering creek behind Ken, and dropped off participants at intervals of a quarter-mile or so. When my turn came, I nervously chose a site at the base of a cliff. Ken and the remaining hikers disappeared upstream.

Muttering to myself, I dragged branches and logs together for my fire. Flames soon leaped twenty feet in the air. "Snakes, cougars, bears," I growled, "I fucking dare you!" I'd planned an evening of singing and writing, but the sun set and the moon rose while I carried wood and tended my fire. Then I fretted that I should have built the blaze in a circle—a great flaming doughnut, with my sleeping bag in the center. Then, even if the fire died out, the mountain lions would have to cross hot coals to eat me.

Long after dark Ken stopped by. "It'll take a few seasons of high water to replenish all that wood," he commented dryly. He added that it was likely to rain, and I had been wise to camp well above the water. After a quick hug he moved on downstream.

I threw on more logs and stuck out my tongue at Ken's back. I looked around for more fuel. An enormous, weathered cottonwood branch, the better part of a dead tree, cast a house-sized dancing shadow against the cliff wall. I rolled and tumbled it nearer the blaze and saw my own shadow, like an ant toting a

stick twenty times its size. I hoped the branch would burn all
night so I could sleep without feeding the fire.

The sky flashed far upstream, and thunder rumbled through
the canyons. I thought with wild resentment that Ken seemed to
be right about everything, even rain tonight. Again I dragged at
the branch. Something tickled the back of my hand and I swiped
at it, then felt a stab of pain like an icepick. I dropped the branch
with a yelp. A musclebound scorpion writhed, its tail stinger
buried between my index and middle fingers. I backhanded it
against the cottonwood, ran down to the creek and thrust my arm
into the cold water. When my hand went numb, I pulled it out.
The scorpion, a jerking, smashed mess, still clung to my flesh by
its tail. I scraped it off in the wet sand and crushed its body with
my shoe. My hand swelled as I watched it, red streaks running
past the wrist.

My heart raced. Dizzily I remembered Ken prescribing willow
leaves and creek mud. Again I plunged my blazing hand into the
cold water, grateful for the moment of numbness before the
throbbing resumed, and tried to slow my breath. I stripped leaves
from a willow and wrapped them around my aching hand, packed
mud over them and hunched beside the creek. The next flash of
lightning lit my camp like a floodlight. The creek water had
turned the color of peanut butter, opaque with mud from the
storm that raged miles upstream.

Rain splashed on me, then poured down. Waterfalls danced
off the cliff. My fire sizzled and billowed smoke. From the edge
of the creek I steadily waddled back from the advancing water.
While I replenished the mud poultice, an ominous, uniform
rumble echoed down the canyon.

My hand pounded with the racing of my heart. The ground
itself shook. I told myself I was hallucinating from the scorpion
venom that surged through me, bearing insanity and death. I
began to cry. The rising brown water swallowed my shoes.
Another flash of lightning illuminated my misshapen hand.

The creek rose even higher and threw me into terrified confusion. A ghostly tree crashed past, smashing a branch against a
granite island that a few minutes earlier had been a landlocked
boulder. Soon the willows that had been at the creek's edge were
halfway under the raging water. I'd camped close to the cliff wall,
so that a waterfall now pelted rocks and mud on my sleeping bag.
My fire was dead.

Above the water's roar, I thought I heard someone scream my

name. More hallucinations. But a second scream came distinctly from downstream. I grabbed my flashlight and ran. Floodwaters had swallowed the creekside path. Desperately I climbed between two scrub oaks. My flashlight beam illuminated bullet-like raindrops and blinded me to everything beyond the rocks at my feet. I took one short step at a time and crested the hill. About fifty yards ahead, another flashlight waved crazily. The screams reached me clearly now, and I signaled with my own beam.

"Steve!" Teddy shrieked, "hurry!"

I reached her and she pointed her flashlight at something that billowed in the roiling, muddy water, caught on a big rock about four feet from shore. Her sleeping bag, I thought, then realized the billowing form was Ken, clinging to the rock. "Hold me." I shouted to her. I lay face down on the sand and she sat on my feet. I crawled hand-over-hand through the torrent to a rock a yard downstream, then braced myself against it to reach for Ken.

Teddy's light struck his face and his eyes flashed like a wild animal's. Then the muddy undertow swallowed him. I gulped a breath and ducked underwater, swinging my arms in a huge blind embrace. I grasped his submerged body and struggled to rise for air. Teddy hauled me out of the water by my ankles. Together we dragged Ken to a flat spot and rolled him onto his back.

His body was cold and limp. In the halo of Teddy's flashlight I saw a gash on his forehead. I felt his neck for a pulse and thought I detected a faint response. First aid at Los Perdidos, I remembered. CPR. If there's no heartbeat, crack the sternum. Do the steps first, I told myself, struggling to stay calm.

I pinched Ken's nose, tipped his head back and blew a sharp gust of air into the lifeless body, counted to three, blew another, then another. I heard a ghastly gurgling sound and turned him onto his side. Teddy wailed when water poured out of his nose.

"It's okay," I gasped. "His heart's beating!" I shifted him onto his back and resumed breathing for him, lung-swelling exhalations that left me light-headed. "Ken!" I yelled between breaths. "Teddy, talk to him. Bring him around."

"Ken!" she shrieked. "Don't die, you little motherfucker!"

I gasped and whooshed air into him, dizzy with the venom that raced through me. Finally Ken began to cough. Teddy cradled his head, weeping with relief. I fell back and surrendered to darkness.

ON OUR TENTH AND LAST NIGHT in the wilderness we
dined on fresh rainbow trout hand-caught by Puck. He claimed
the fish voluntarily surrendered to him because he'd once caught
the grandpa of them all on a hook. The old one had bargained his
own life in exchange for the knowledge of how to tickle the
youngsters into submission. Teddy studied the mouths of the
trout he delivered to be cleaned. Finding no evidence of hooks,
she announced, "He's not shitting us."

"Trail's over," Ken said after dinner. The cut on his forehead
was healing and he carried his left arm in a tee-shirt sling. "Write
down your issues for Group. We'll handle everything back at the
Ranch. In the morning we'll hike to town for some hard-earned
showers. I am so proud of you all."

His self-satisfied smile faded and he admitted he'd been foolish to check on campsites by hiking along the flooding creek
instead of through the hills. The surging water had overtaken him
immediately. "I would have raked any of you for doing the same
thing." He leaned forward to place a hand on my knee, then
added in a faltering voice, "My life was saved by a brave man."

Here was the respect I'd craved from Ken. Heat rose in my
face and I turned to Teddy and said, "You told me once you'd
never loved anybody. That looked like love when you screamed
at Ken not to die."

Before the sun abandoned the canyons I wandered over a
sandy rise and spotted a narrow ravine a short way upstream. I
decided to sleep solo since I'd missed the first opportunity. I built
a modest fire close enough to water to make a poultice if another
scorpion attacked. I sprawled naked across my unzipped sleeping
bag. As soon as darkness fell I was swimming in the stars, glad
for a warm night. The fire burned bright in my sandy alcove, but
I hadn't stockpiled driftwood. Two meteors streaked and died
within moments of each other. Out of the Milky Way wandered a
slow and steady star. I watched the independent voyager in
wonder until it disappeared into the black horizon. The enchantment broke and I said aloud, "Sputnik or something. Telstar."
The narrow rock walls danced with the shadows of the trees in
the firelight. I stared into the flames until they burned out to soft,
gray ash that glowed hell-red from within.

Frogs and crickets called out for mates among cattails rooted
on a tiny island of rock in the middle of the stream. Closer to me,
grasshoppers leaped in tussocks of buffalo grass. Under the
sounds of their courtship, I listened to the song of the water

spirits and floated on my raft of flannel. I slept and dreamed of hiking, of wading through cold water, of lying in the hot sun, of someone sucking my cock. Someone tentative, someone I couldn't see who grasped and suckled at me as a baby takes the breast, moaning lightly. Then a real person transcended the dream, drawing me out of sleep and firmly into my own body. This was no dream—and the head of curly hair that bobbed at my crotch was unmistakably Ken's.

I lay still, caught between shock and pleasure. Ken stopped to wet a hand with spit, then resumed his suckling while he stroked his own cock. I became fully aroused, loving the sensations I hadn't known since my night with Eric. I longed to hold Ken and kiss him, but remembered Eric's determination to perform this same service as if I had been asleep—the Vistan way, apparently. Ken took no more than half the length of my hard cock in his mouth, stroking it only with elusive swallowing motions of his lips and tongue. He scraped me with his teeth, making me fight not to cry out, then settled into a pleasurable rhythm using his tongue. As I replied with subtle thrusts, he clung to his position and intensified his tiny tongue movements and self-stroking, and still his teeth got in the way. The whole effect became frustrating and I nearly laughed out loud when the cliché "It's the thought that counts" passed through my mind. My elusive orgasm finally approached through concentrated effort. Ken seemed focused on deriving his own pleasure simply from holding a cock in his mouth. My tense, squirting release triggered Ken's own, and I felt the hot splash of his semen on my thigh.

I lay as still as I could, observing my night visitor through slitted eyes. Ken was naked except for socks and sneakers, and the sling on his left arm. He took a sock from his nearby backpack, wiped his semen from my leg, stashed the sock, hoisted his pack and disappeared into the willows.

I watched the sky a moment, wondering if I would feel so lonely right now if I hadn't pretended to be asleep. What was it with the Vistans and their night rituals, anyway? They talked about absolutely everything. But I had been made love to twice now, by men who seemed capable of loving me only while I pretended to snore.

12

AFTER A COLD-CEREAL BREAKFAST THE SEVEN OF US HOISTED OUR PACKS and followed Ken off the mountain toward town, chattering about showers and cheeseburgers and other much-missed treats. As we passed the rodeo grounds, the others began walking faster and were nearly running by the time they reached the cemetery. I strolled on. I would happily stay on Trail for the rest of my life rather than join tomorrow's journey to Southern California. Ten days ago I had treated Nature Boy with contempt. Now I could admit, was in fact proud, that rappelling, sleeping alone outside, functioning in spite of the scorpion attack, had delivered the promised "self-sufficiency." With my new confidence I felt prepared to face my parents, tell them what I needed, and demand that they pay for it.

And with their familiar mulishness, they could remind me they'd paid to get a heterosexual son.

Outside the Blue Worm, Ken lectured on shower protocol. "Get wet, turn off the water, soap up, rinse, make way for the next guy. Three minutes, tops." Then he disappeared to the triple-wide. The hikers stuffed their filthy clothes into the battle-scarred Maytag and entered the shower two at a time. Hunched over a Selectric typewriter in the front room, Elsie ignored the pandemonium. I hopped into the shower behind Vivian, amazed at how comfortable I had become with nakedness, intoxicated by the campfire musk that steamed from our wet hair.

When we were clean we approached Elsie and offered to help. She brightened and led us to an alcove. On a worktable made from a door, she had arranged twenty stacks of paper—the pages of an article Cy would present at a conference in California. She took a sheet from each pile to assemble a set. "All the copies might not be straight," she confessed, then returned to her other work. "Please check the page numbers before you staple 'em."

The Problem of Socially-Constructed Pathology, I read. In a sociology class I'd vaguely grasped the idea that a culture's truths were "constructed" out of its mythologies and prejudices. As I scanned the first page, a paragraph leaped out at me. "Listen," I said to Vivian, "right in the introduction: 'Homosexuality may not deserve a place in our catalogue of mental disorders. We have

known since the 1940s that far less than half the adult U.S.
population is exclusively heterosexual. Many homosexuals live
productive, happy lives, and share lasting, loving relationships. Is
there a rational basis for ranking a common experience as a *sexual
deviation*, equivalent to intercourse with corpses and animals?'"

Vivian whistled. "Pretty radical, huh?"

"My ex-therapist'll be selling pencils on the street when his
genital-shock business collapses." I continued reading giddily. On
page two dysphoria was misspelled disphoria, and I spotted other
problems. "We've got some typos," I called to Elsie.

She appeared at the doorway, lugging an armload of file fold-
ers. "Cy'll shit," she said, and read over my shoulder. "His peer
review committee wanted the article last week. I'm up to my neck
in insurance reports to prepare before we leave tomorrow. Can
one of you type a stencil?"

The rest of the Trail participants piled into the truck bound
for the Ranch, but I stayed at the worktable in the Blue Worm.
Ken gave me a one-armed hug and whispered, "Thanks again,
brother," then kissed me quickly on the cheek. Arousal stirred in
my shorts. When the Blue Worm's front door slammed, I wished
I'd returned the kiss.

I proofread the article and marked it with several suggested
editorial changes, unsure whether Cy would be impressed or
insulted. I agonized over one comment, then wrote in the margins: *Why waffle by saying homosexuality MAY not be a mental disorder?
Just say it isn't one. You've already offended the old guard. The rest of the
world will applaud your courage.*

I delivered the marked-up manuscript to the triple-wide. Back
in the Blue Worm Elsie was rifling through a worn copy of the
Diagnostic and Statistical Manual, the book Rupert had used to
diagnose himself and humiliate Dr. Turner. "I'm pretty familiar
with that material," I said. "Can I help?"

She peered through a curtain of hair. "Puck isn't schizophrenic since Cy cured him. But he still needs a diagnosis, or his
parents' insurance won't pay our bills."

I thought for a moment. "At the very least he's having an
adjustment reaction to adult life," I suggested. "Or maybe—can I
see the index?"

In the next hours I diagnosed Puck, Vivian and her kids, and
six other Vistans, learned that Puck's real name was Gene,
Rainbow's was Sarah, and Lucky's was Harvey, and tabulated the
hours each insured patient had spent in group and individual

therapy during the past month.

Long after dark, Cy burst into the Blue Worm waving his article. "Brilliant changes!"

I looked up, startled. I'd forgotten about it in my absorption with the insurance reports.

"Should have asked you to read this weeks ago," Cy went on. "You're so young I forget you were Chief of Social Services. You're right about deleting the qualifiers. And you got the point exactly—the only mental disorder inherently related to homo-sexuality involves the hatred you absorb from your families and society, and then turn inward."

In the manual I held my finger on the term I'd been looking for, and beamed. "It's an ego-dystonic reaction."

"Perfect! Work that into the text."

Elsie glanced up from her typewriter. "Steve has a perfect diagnosis for Puck: Adjustment Reaction to Adult Life. We've got half these reports done."

Cy thumbed slowly through several clipped bundles of paper, nodding, making little humming sounds. Then he whistled. "Steve, you may be right. Rainbow's passive-dependent behavior probably does mask an affective disorder." He flipped through the remaining reports. "Jesus. This is wonderful."

"And I think I told you I was the *Deputy* Chief," I said with a shy smile.

ZOË SERVED DINNER at the triple-wide and Elsie poured wine. I sat stiffly at the fruitwood table, afraid of breaking the stemware with my Trail-roughened hands. Cy read the reports between bites of steak. He explained that health insurance reports accounted for forty thousand dollars a month of Ranch income, but drained his creative energy and prevented Elsie from getting other work done. "Listen to this, honey," he said to Zoë. "'Gene's clinicians encourage him to recognize the indicia of improvement in his condition.' Steve, you're a pro! 'Nightmares remind him of the severe psychotic episodes he survived until recently. He is still considered a suicide risk.' You've got the perfect mix of clinical language—*indicia*, for Christ's sake—and real information. You really know Puck."

I drank in the respect of the others at the table. Before Elsie and I returned to the Blue Worm and our typewriters, Cy added, "One more thing! Ken exaggerates about the rough-and-ready life on Trail." He looked into my eyes. "But he's usually the hero of his adventure tales. So when he says a kid from Disneyland saved his life out there, I listen."

I acknowledged my role, and Teddy's, in rescuing Ken, but felt an unexpected sting of disappointment. Ken hadn't mentioned the lovemaking.

Cy stood over me and squeezed my shoulders. "I phoned your well-spoken mother this afternoon. She agreed to come to the Beverly Hills Marathon. With your father." I let out an involuntary squeak and he assured me, "Don't worry. We'll all be there to support you."

WHILE ELSIE TYPED THE REMAINING INSURANCE REPORTS on a manual machine, I used her Selectric to redo the stencils for Cy's article. I finished stapling the newly-printed pages at three a.m. Too exhilarated to sleep, I typed one more stencil, *Growth Case Guide*, printed four cards per page on pastel sheets, and sliced them on Elsie's paper cutter into eighty neat rectangles.

I slept a few hours and woke up with stomach cramps, obsessed with Cy's article. It was sure to generate publicity. When Susi and Alex learned the great Dr. Aaron didn't believe homosexuality could be cured—or even needed to be—they would realize I had lied about my reasons for going to Rancho Vista. And without their financial support I would have to leave. I could never pay my way writing a few insurance reports. I'd seen in the files that Vistans who worked very hard, like Puck and even Ken, had families or insurance coverage that paid thousands of dollars each month. And even if money were not an issue, I would have to confront my parents in Group. Only Cy knew the goal of the confrontation.

The trip was a major event for the community. Only a few people would stay behind at the Ranch, to take care of Zoë's puppy Wolfie and the livestock. At least twice a year, Elsie said, Cy took everyone to Southern California. "He likes to show us off to the world, and his dentist takes care of us for free." I didn't bother questioning the economics. Ninety miles away in Gentile was a dentist whose services certainly cost less than rooms for thirty people at the Beverly Hills Hotel. But Cy had his eye on a much bigger picture.

The Ranch vehicles arrived in Keystone as I finished my

shower. While others jockeyed for their turns to bathe, I went to the phone and dialed my old number, then held my breath, eager to exclaim, *Lydia! I'm coming to L.A.!*

After four rings a disembodied voice crackled, "The number you have dialed is not—"

I listened in shock, then slammed down the receiver as if it had bitten me. While I wandered in the wilderness, Lydia had moved on to her own version of the "real world." By now she could be in Chile or Argentina or some other battlefield of U.S. imperialism, traveling with a fake passport, scared to death, risking prison and worse. Had I abandoned her to extreme danger? Considering her comments about Rancho Vista, she probably felt she'd done the same to me.

Before dawn Elsie led the caravan at the wheel of the red dump truck. Ken and I sat up front with her while twenty Vistans with duffel bags and parkas huddled in the back. Two Land Rovers, a Volkswagen, a Mercedes roadster and Cy's Mercedes sedan followed.

Ken straddled the gearshift. I waved an arm out the passenger window, trying to act casual while I read his every glance, recalling the night visit that had left me so lonely. We settled into traveling postures and I measured the pressure of the sinewy thigh against mine before answering with shy pressure of my own.

The one-lane razorback road doubled back on itself like intestines, and terrified me in the daylight even more than the night I'd ridden into Keystone with Dove. The drop on each side was two thousand feet. Ken remarked that while hiking through the canyons below he'd explored the rusted hulks of smashed pickups, victims of the ridge's soft shoulders. I tried to keep my eyes on the road ahead.

The pavement began ninety miles later, just short of Gentile. Cy stopped the caravan and called for Puck to ride with him and Zoë. Lucky and Rainbow climbed out of the Mercedes and into the bed of the truck. Elsie asked me to keep track of their therapy time. "So far it's two and a quarter hours each for next month's insurance records," she said.

"I could start writing the reports right now," I joked.

She didn't laugh. "Can't hurt to get a head start."

On a fresh page in my notebook I wrote, *Individual psychotherapy, 2.25 hours* for Rainbow and Lucky—and wondered whether, with diligence, I *could* earn my way.

THE WORLD LOOKED DIFFERENT NOW. The communities along America's highways, where I imagined rednecks used homosexuals for target practice, were drained of their fearsome power over me. I saw them as sad home towns for the lonely kids trapped in them. The smoggy cities we passed through oppressed me more dismally than ever.

After the caravan gassed up outside Las Vegas, I logged the latest change of passengers in the big Mercedes and offered to drive the truck. Elsie thanked me but explained, "Our vehicle insurance is tricky. Besides, no one drives until Cy rides with 'em on a test drive."

"Some of us'll never take the wheel," Ken said. "Like me, 'cause of my rap sheet."

"Your what?" I couldn't see the upright Ken—who wouldn't leave a scrap of toilet paper in the desert—committing a crime.

"On my sixteenth birthday my dad beat me, one of his famous whippings with the buckle end of his belt. That night my brother shot me up with morphine for the first time. Once I'd tasted that, street drugs couldn't touch my pain. I craved pharmaceuticals. My brother and I broke into drug stores. I stole syringes and learned to cook up pills in a spoon."

"So you're on diversion from prison like Eric?"

"Diversion from death. I got probation for a burglary, but then I took an overdose. My parents sent Cy to see me in the hospital. When I came out of my coma I thought a white-haired angel was in the chair next to my bed. He said, 'I'm Doctor Aaron and I'm here to make your miserable little life worth living.' And he did."

After an awkward silence I turned to Elsie, hoping to lighten things. "So you get to drive for eighteen straight hours because you don't have a police record?"

"I came close," she said without her familiar giggle. "I was waiting for a chance to shove my mother down the basement stairs. Then I saw Cy on TV, talking about self-acceptance. He had such conviction, and I knew there was hope. I wrote and offered to work without pay if he got me away from my family." She talked about her childhood in the Church of the Burning Bush, and her mother's branding her a "whore of Satan" because she was reported to have worn lipstick at a Bible college dance. "If I look uptight now, you should have seen me then."

On Trail, I had crammed two Relationship Workbooks with bitter resentments against my parents. Did I have work to do in the empty pages dealing with appreciation, respect and joy? Susi and Alex had never struck me, forced religion on me, or even called me dirty names. "So," I ventured, "have you both resolved the problems with your parents?"

"I didn't kill my mother," replied Elsie. "Definite resolution."

Ken chuckled. "I got a Breakthrough with my father. We did the beating process."

A wave of nausea swept through me. "My God, you used the buckle end on *him*?"

"Cy's work is subtle. My parents came to a Marathon and *I* got the beating with a belt, from Willow. I begged her to use the buckle but she wouldn't. My process was to take lashes until I'd shown my father how much emotional pain he'd given me."

"How many?"

"Seventy-two. I wanted to go 'til I passed out. My back was streaming blood. Finally Dad jumped up and screamed, 'Stop!' He held me and dressed my wounds and cried. He'd never hugged me before, and I'd sure never seen him cry. A Breakthrough—I got to see he loved me, in spite of his sickness."

"Wasn't your mother there?"

"Mom is what Cy calls a *painted iron tit*—she watched the beating and didn't say a word, since the problem was between me and my dad. Just like when I was a kid. She always said if I was stupid enough to piss him off, I deserved what I got."

My heart was racing. What would be my version of the beating process? Was Susi a painted iron tit? How would Cy provoke my parents into proving their love for me?

After doing individual sessions with a series of passengers, Cy and Zoë sped ahead into the darkness. I leaned back sleepily and pretended not to notice Ken's hand on my thigh.

A sign near Bakersfield announced Los Angeles was ninety-eight miles away. "I don't know what I'll do at the Marathon," I said. "What does Cy expect of me?"

Ken squeezed my leg. "To be a basket case. He'll tell some of your story, name the prestigious schools you dropped out of. You'll sit on the floor looking smart and handsome."

His eyes sparkled in the dim light of the truck cab. Our moment under the stars was the only unturned stone I had encountered in the Rancho Vista soil, and I wouldn't be the one to dislodge it. I would go on pretending I had slept through Ken's toothy blow job, and enjoy whatever attention he gave me.

ELSIE HAD RESERVED ONE SUITE AT THE BEVER-
LY HILLS HOTEL FOR ZOË AND CY and another in her
own name for the rest of us. At two a.m. we all hauled our gear
up a back stairway of the elegant old resort.

The double room Travis called the "Grunt Suite" immediately
looked like a flop-house, with the contents of thirty duffel bags
strewn over the damask love seats and heaped in every corner.
Vistans crashed five to a bed, snuggled on the sofas and sprawled
on the floors. I rolled out my sleeping bag on the vine-shrouded
terrace and climbed in. Eric brought out his own bag, knelt to
hug me and said, "We'll get you through tomorrow."

I wanted to cry when he left to bed down across the terrace. I
gazed into the opaque sky, like the dome of a bell jar harboring a
biological experiment gone savagely awry. The city roared even at
this late hour and in this chic part of town. Cars cruised Sunset,
sirens screamed in Westwood, helicopters did night surveillance
in East L.A., and the racket penetrated every boundary. I pined
for the Mother River's crickets and frogs, the song of the water
spirits. How had I survived, breathing this noxious air all my life,
smothered by this noise?

I drifted into a pained sleep and awoke with my stomach doing a nervous tango. Inside, Vistans were ironing and mending
clothes, taking showers, wielding blow dryers. I bathed and
dressed quickly and helped Elsie organize props for the Marathon, including a nurse's cap—to be worn by anyone who tried to
shield others from necessary psychological pain—and a hat made
of rubber turds called the "Brown Crown," for people in their
shit. A foot-long rubber penis, fitted at the base with the bulb of
an ear syringe, flopped out of a plastic bag. "The Saturday Night
Special," Elsie said matter-of-factly. "For reënacting scenes of
sexual trauma." She squeezed the bulb and a load of lotion shot
onto my arm from the dildo's tip. I gasped, then giggled with her.

She sent me to the gift shop for a fresh supply of lotion. While
there, I bought a bottle of Pepto Bismol, guzzled a double dose
then hid the bottle under a fern near the pool. If the Brown
Crown didn't send Alex and Susi running, the Saturday Night
Special would give them heart attacks.

13

I MANAGED MY ANXIETY by rearranging chairs against the walls of the ballroom—a vast, chandelier-lit space that was papered, carpeted and upholstered in champagne tones. When a group of UCLA graduate students dragged in bean-bags and giant pillows, I introduced myself as a Vistan and declined any help with arranging their seating closer to the center of the room. The neon paisleys and earth-tone corduroys stood out in homey contrast to the fleur-de-lis wallpaper.

I was struck by the youth of my adopted tribe. Most Vistans were under twenty, and many of the strangers who streamed into the room looked at least forty. Though known for his work with troubled youth, Cy drew a largely middle-aged crowd. Maybe my parents *could* feel comfortable here.

Having moved every free chair at least twice, I leaned against a wall and sipped a club soda. Zoë, Willow and Eric circulated among the early arrivals. Ken worked with Elsie on setting up the recording system. I imagined Cy would appear after the crowd settled down.

I listened in on conversations around the room and learned that most people hoped to get to the hotseat and work on personal issues. A soft-spoken man with a bushy goatee introduced himself as George Larkin, the psychologist who organized a Marathon Group whenever Cy came to town. When I told him I was a new member of Cy's community, his face relaxed and he told me he had enrolled eighty-three participants, at two hundred dollars each, to attend today. Then he zoomed over to someone else and again offered his hand.

A woman in cashmere and pearls, checking in with patients she had invited here, referred repeatedly to "Cyrus Aaron, the miracle worker." A few others in the crowd were therapists who also referred difficult patients to Cy, then observed the results. Anyone who didn't respond to fifty-minute sessions or weekly group therapy needed the miracle worker.

I both envied and pitied these people who showed up with money to tap into Cy's brilliance and compassion. They didn't live in tipis or tend goats, would never know the self-sufficiency of Trail, the thrill of the sweatlodge, the taste of Joy Juice. Few would even get to "work in Group" on the hotseat today. Most could only observe and hope to gain fringe benefits.

The graduate students sat together, looking very shy. In their midst I recognized a professor whose class I'd taken during my one semester at UCLA—Dr. Homer, author of a popular textbook on abnormal psychology.

More strangers poured in, and soon the ballroom swarmed with people who embraced and exclaimed to one another, "You look wonderful!" They filled the chairs along the walls and spilled onto the beanbags and pillows. I awaited my parents' arrival with the same dread that had attacked me when I'd stepped off the cliff in the rappel harness: It was too late to pull myself back up.

Across the room, Willow listened intently to a wiry old cowboy in a plaid flannel shirt and Wranglers who could have been a refugee from Abraham County. His glittering oval belt buckle, like a turkey-platter, was evidently a trophy from some well-endowed rodeo event. The young man beside him wore an outrageous suit made of tapestry panels. His mane of auburn hair shimmered with gold highlights.

I caught myself chewing on a clump of my ragged hair. I dug a rubber band from my pocket and secured the unruly mess into a pony tail. Across the room Vivian looked as lonely as I felt. I bee-lined toward her and knelt with my head in her lap. "I'm scared to death," I said, and she stroked my shoulder with a trembling hand.

I froze at the sound of my father's voice a short distance behind me, asking in his distinctive, charming tone, "Could you direct us to the restrooms, please?"

Frantically I imagined the worst reasons his father might have for requesting restrooms for "us." Scenes of life with Susi flashed through my mind: In my third-grade Christmas pageant I'd played a Wise Man, and she had mounted the stage to claim the jewel securing my turban. At numerous poetry recitals and spelling bees she'd interrupted other children's performances to embrace her mortified son. She'd passed out in the aisle at my junior-high graduation ceremony.

"We're looking for our son, Steve Susoyev," she said, in her shy, sober voice.

Vivian winked at me. "It's time," she whispered.

"There he is," Alex said.

"His hearing's even worse now than when he was an adolescent," my mother remarked. I stiffened and she asked at my back,

"Young man, are you still our son?"

I rose to face them. Both looked as if they would rather be wrestling sharks than attending a group therapy session. I kissed my mother and sniffed, but detected no alcohol, only her delicate perfume. Alex shook my hand and searched my face like a Vistan, as if looking for signs of the sexual transformation for which he'd coughed up over a thousand dollars.

I led my parents to the restrooms, wishing I had the nerve to reach into Susi's purse and confiscate whatever was sloshing inside. When they returned I sat on the floor in a spot where I could watch their faces.

Soon the psychologist George Larkin announced, "Thank you all for coming," and gestured toward the open double doors. "I'm honored to introduce Dr. Cyrus Aaron, author of *The Quest for Unconditional Love* and founder of Rancho Vista."

The Marathoners stomped, clapped, whistled and howled like the audience at a quiz show. Cy strode into the room, smiling and waving. Someone had trimmed his thick, white hair, leaving it stylishly over-the-ears but dignified. He wore a creamy turtleneck under a midnight-blue blazer. I had begun to take him for granted. Any grunt in the cookshack could demand his attention. Here among wealthy and sophisticated people, the authors of famous textbooks, he was a celebrity. George Larkin and Dr. Homer, and the cashmere-and-pearls woman, settled into chairs to observe the miracle worker.

Cy bowed slightly and said, "Thank you." The room immediately fell silent. He took his seat beside Zoë, paused dramatically, then called out, "Do you want to grow, or stay sick for the rest of your lives?"

"We want to grow!" came the wild response.

"Then let's get to work."

"No sub*group*ing," Zoë called out. "Don't say behind the back what you would not say to the face." I was grateful for the definition of a term whose meaning until now had eluded me. "When you are on the hot*seat* you always feel the whispering is about you. Keep the energy focused in the *cen*ter of the room."

Cy gestured toward Elsie and she began passing out stacks of index cards. "Write your questions and comments and pass them to Cy," she said. "Remember that everything you hear in this room is confidential. You can count on others to honor your privacy, and they're counting on you for the same respect." She also passed out my "Growth Case" cards, and Cy introduced me as their author.

My parents maintained a look of controlled dignity. Alex wore a tweed suit with wing tips, Isabel a tastefully fitted knit dress and spectator pumps. Though I'd had dinner with them a few months earlier, I hadn't really looked at them in years. My father appeared thinner, which showed off his magnificent bone structure. My mother had gained a few wrinkles and a little gray. To anyone who didn't hear the sloshing in Susi's purse, or Alex's rabid denunciations of fruits, they would pass as a typical middle-class couple.

"Let's start with reports from last time," Cy said, and asked a balding man to describe a confrontation with his boss.

The man enthused, "Everything you taught me worked! I just reminded myself to *listen*, like you said. My boss is human, with fears and problems just like mine. For the first time, he treats me with respect. Trust, even."

"Which means," Cy prompted, "the most powerful organ in the human body is—"

Dozens of people chorused, "*The ear!*"

"The ear," Cy repeated with reverence. I hadn't known the answer, and marveled. "*Listening* is the most intimate of all human interactions. People often sexualize my question about the most powerful organ—but what's sex without communication? Just pork chops rubbing together! Many people come to Rancho Vista expecting to get laid. They don't realize that the Vistans first expect them to learn to communicate. For some, that price is too high. The sex at Rancho Vista is organic, like the zucchini."

Susi yawned meaningfully. Sitting on the floor nearby, I gave her a weak smile and added the possibility of my parents' boredom to my worries. When would the Saturday Night Special start squirting? When would the beatings begin?

A middle-aged man and a far younger woman walked in, kissed, and took separate seats. I was sure the woman winked at Eric. Could this couple be Mr. and Mrs. M., for whom Eric did stud service? I scratched at the spot where the scorpion had stung me, and missed the manageable anxiety of Trail.

Cy asked a bedraggled woman if she had anything to share. She reported that since the last Marathon she'd registered for adult school classes—a big "win," since she'd supported her husband through his Ph.D. then suffered humiliation when he divorced her. She grinned while everyone including Susi and Alex applauded her. I smiled at my parents, relieved that they approved of something.

Cy turned to his stack of index cards, but a tiny woman with a perky haircut waved and called out, "Dr. Aaron, aren't you going to ask how *I'm* doing?"

He regarded her with a look of confused interest.

She stood and grinned. "You don't recognize me, do you?" She didn't sound hurt, but thrilled.

"I'm so sorry. Please refresh my memory."

"Three months ago you told me I didn't have to live with God's practical joke. I got a nose job a week later. Then I got that haystack of hair cut off, since I didn't have to hide under it any more." She flourished her left hand so an enormous diamond ring flashed in the chandelier-light. "Now I'm engaged."

"Tracy!" Cy exclaimed, and stepped forward to hug her. He led her to the center of the room and studied her face. "Gorgeous. Does everybody remember Tracy? God gave her a nose like a camel, but look how pretty she is now."

"Dr. Aaron," she said, holding both his hands, "you're the only person who ever told me the truth about my damned nose. *Thank you.*"

"I want the name of your surgeon," a woman called out. Tracy took a proud little bow to much applause.

"Amazing," Cy said. "Why are we still surprised when love and reality do their job?" He sighed as if to himself, then consulted an index card. "Josh, are you ready?"

A muscular, ruggedly handsome man in a polo shirt and jeans walked to the center of the room. I smiled at my parents, sure Alex would identify with Josh and see there was nothing unmanly about exposing oneself in therapy. "I'm a card-carrying failure," Josh said, before Cy had a chance to prompt him. "Here to turn my life around." He gestured toward a poised woman with a blonde chignon. "Charley and I were college sweethearts. On graduation day she made me the happiest man in the world by agreeing to be my wife." Obviously not the first time he'd told this story. "Right out of school she landed an executive position with a major insurance company. Now she's a VP. I've done nothing but embarrass her."

"That's not true." The blonde woman shook her head. "Josh has his teaching certificate. He's smart and good-looking." A chorus of humming women, including my mother, confirmed this opinion. "All he lacks is self-confidence. He's skipped job interviews because he's afraid of being turned down."

"What's this mean?" Cy asked. "Are you working, Josh?"

"I'm currently what you could call a sanitary engineer, specializing in the short curlies."

Cy considered this for a moment. "You clean restrooms." His tone would not have been different if he had said, *You're in the diplomatic corps.*

"In one of your nicer resorts, thank you."

Except for the deep imprint of pain on Josh's face, I could have believed he felt as blithe about his career as his words suggested. Cy urged him, "Tell us more."

Until recently Josh had worked as a garbage collector, in a job that paid well but humiliated him. "The moment I dreaded arrived last month. I was clinging like a maggot to the tail-end of a garbage truck. At a red light I looked down and there was Charley, riding in her boss's Jaguar to an important meeting."

My parents were nodding, clearly as engaged as anyone in the room, as Josh continued: "She was too ashamed to wave or even smile."

"No!" cried his wife Charley. "I *wasn't* ashamed. I could never—" Her voice trailed off.

Of course she'd been ashamed. Why deny it in this loving atmosphere?

Cy involved Josh in a role-play to reënact his moment of shame. I found myself more interested in Charley than in Josh. I watched her closely, expecting signs of compassion or humiliation. Instead, her softly-shadowed eyes followed Cy everywhere. Beneath the tasteful makeup and richly-dyed golden hair, the creamy tailored suit, subtle nail polish and steely jewelry, she was plain. Her thin lips and small eyes were skillfully outlined to look larger, and she'd blushed her sallow cheeks in a shade that complemented her plum lipstick and violet blouse. She made me think of a Ford Fairlane dolled up with leather tuck 'n roll and a diamond-finish paint job.

The big man stood on a chair with his arms wrapped tightly around himself, and Cy guided him to the center of his pain. "When you're ready, Josh, let go. Let the words flow."

All at once Josh's arms flew toward the ceiling. "No more garbage!" he bellowed. "Honey," he cried out to Charley, "I promise you and I promise myself: *No more garbage!*"

Cy had him repeat this mantra, and turned with him so Josh could make eye contact with each person as he tearfully affirmed his promise. I recalled my Gollum session, where I'd been helpless except for Cy at my side, channeling the acceptance that flowed from the sea of loving faces.

Index cards poured toward Cy, and he called on some of the writers to share their observations. Men wept over their failures, and women grieved because they'd driven their husbands into empty careers. My parents whispered together until I wanted to club them.

CY GRANTED THE CROWD A "COMFORT BREAK" AND EXPLAINED, "Unlike some personal growth seminars, ours won't challenge your bladder. It's enough to challenge your mind, heart and spirit."

I knelt before my parents. "Do you see? I was afraid I'd end up like Josh if I didn't get help."

Susi stroked my hair. Alex smiled and replied, "I can't imagine you hanging from a garbage truck, but we understand you're afraid of not living up to your potential."

They glanced around awkwardly a moment, then Susi rose and headed for the restroom. I endured Alex's silent scrutiny until she returned. I kissed her and stiffened at the musky-sweet smell of sherry, then sat near her on the floor, prepared for the worst.

The sinewy rodeo rider and his young tapestry-clad companion were up next, introduced as Leon and his son Gordon. They faced each other on pillows in the center of the room. "How many of you parents," Cy asked, "have worried about your children? Worried about the choices they made, the mistakes that might bring them suffering?"

Many hands rose. Cy slowly pivoted on his heels, acknowledging each worried parent with his eyes. I caught the pain in Vivian's face. Then I saw that Susi hadn't raised her hand, but Alex held his high. Cy stopped to look at them. "That's my son over there," Alex volunteered. "Steve."

"Mr. Susoyev," Cy said. "Even you? At Rancho Vista we have kids who were facing twenty-year prison sentences, punks who mugged old ladies and shot girls up with heroin to 'seduce' them, which really meant to rape them. Others burglarized pharmacies to get drugs. All their parents were scared to death for them. From what *he* tells us, Steve wasn't the kind of boy whose parents worried about him."

Susi shook her head, too vigorously for my comfort. Alex took advantage of her silence to quip, "Wouldn't you worry about a twelve-year-old who reads *The Fountainhead* twice in one goddamned summer?"

The crowd laughed quietly. Their appreciation of Alex's joke inspired another: "I used to pray for a sign my son was normal. Always hoped I'd find some stolen hubcaps in the garage." I laughed with the others, grateful my father was participating, though afraid of how my mother might try to upstage him. Seriously he added, "Steve avoided the draft by pretending to be a homosexual. I'm worried it will follow him."

I held my breath and watched my mother's face collapse into a bitter scowl. Cy nodded and went on to a woman who said she was frightened for her daughter, who frequently took LSD. Others spoke of their children marrying as an act of rebellion, dropping out of school to join the Army, choosing frivolous careers. Cy called on Vivian last. She looked at my parents before she said unsteadily, "My son. My beautiful son. Killed himself because no one understood him."

The crowd murmured sympathetically. I tried to nail each of my parents with a stare, but they were busy, politely averting their eyes from Vivian.

Cy turned to the leathery man who faced his son in the center of the room. "Sir, I think it's safe to say your son is afraid you'll think *he's* making a big mistake."

"Call me Leon," the father said. He offered his hand and Cy shook it with dignity.

"Your son has asked you here so he can share some very difficult secrets with you. Am I right, Gordon?"

Susi and Alex scrutinized me with stony expressions that seemed to say, *So you're planning to humiliate us with family secrets. Guess again!*

Gordon's deep tan had faded to pale green. He nodded, and Cy asked, "Is that a Yes?"

Gordon took a couple of deep breaths. "Dr. Aaron, I'm having a hard time following you, I'm so scared."

Cy stepped back. "What's the scariest part?"

"What is it, son?" Leon asked. "I seen a lot in this world. Just not sure I can talk about it in front a all these folks."

Cy was prepared for this objection, as he seemed prepared for everything. "The people in this room are here to cheer you on, like the spectators at a rodeo. It's a complex, powerful process to get two people communicating again who haven't said enough to each other for several years." He let his words sink in, then asked,

"Gordon, how long has it been since you had a real heart-to-heart with your dad?"

I looked with hope toward my own father, trying to remember if Alex and I had ever talked about anything meaningful. Still he avoided my eyes.

"We've never done that," Gordon answered. "I've never given him a chance."

Leon was nodding. His proud, sun-creased neck bowed with sadness. "I want to think it's never too late."

Cy's tone seemed to be letting the eighty spectators in on a private conversation. "Leon," he said, "your son is burdened by his secrets. We want to set him free." He placed a hand on Leon's shoulder. "We must take the garbage in our lives and compost it to nurture our growth. Otherwise it poisons us."

Leon held Cy's gaze, and Cy continued, "If we see no capacity for love behind the parent's eyes, we do a less dramatic process, only enough to show the kid there's nothing there."

"But if we see the *spark* of love behind the eyes," Zoë said, "then we know we can have the loving Breakthrough. Leon, you have that spark! Do *you* not agree, Cy?"

"Exactly, honey."

After an anxiety-amping pause, Cy asked, "How many folks here have sexual secrets?" The Vistans' hands shot up immediately along with a number of other people's. Cy raised his own hand. "We're talking about things nobody else knows, or that you've done your best to hide." My hand was up, but my parents may as well have been sitting on theirs.

"Gordon," Cy said, "it's time to show your dad you're sincere. Let's start with one of your smaller secrets to get the ball rolling." He shifted into an archbishop's voice. "My son, have you ever practiced the Solitary Sin?"

"I started masturbating when I was six," Gordon admitted. Cy repeated the question to the crowd. Nearly everyone except Susi and Alex raised their hands. Leon slowly raised his.

"Leon," Cy went on matter-of-factly, now sounding like a Fresno farmer. "Before Gordon tells you what he's here for, he'll need a sign from you that he's safe. We've all heard the legends about farm boys and their experiments with the livestock."

Alex and Susi glared at me like horses refusing to enter a burning barn.

Leon shrugged again. "I know what you're gettin' at, Doc," he said simply. "With me, it was a heifer. Name of Lona."

"So you lost your virginity to Lona," Cy said without losing his composure, though people around the room tittered. Leon nodded seriously. Gordon's face bore a look of relief that had been unimaginable thirty seconds before. "But," Cy went on, "can we be sure Lona lost her virginity to *you*?"

With this permission from Cy, the onlookers allowed themselves a hearty laugh. Even Alex chuckled, and Leon wore a serene smile—understanding, I believed, that the laughter of the Beverly Hills sophisticates was not at his expense.

"Dad," Gordon said abruptly, "I'm leaving Gloria."

The wrinkles around Leon's sharp blue eyes deepened. "Your mother left me," he replied gently. "People move on."

"Dad, I'm leaving Gloria for—someone named Timothy." Leon's expression froze and he shuddered as if he'd been shot. Gordon added, "I love him. I love him more than I thought I could love anybody."

I avoided my parents' faces and watched Leon, praying the sun-cured bronc buster could allow his love for his son to prevail over his prejudices and fears.

"This has got to be a shock," Cy said. "Don't try to be the perfect father, Leon. What do you feel like saying?"

"What's to say? I want to get my hands on this pervert Timothy so I can break his neck."

Cy nodded soberly. "Gordon?"

"He's here, Dad."

Alex whispered to Susi. She fiddled with her purse.

A handsome young black man walked to the center of the room. His dark skin had a sheen of health and his hair was in a close-cropped Afro. "Dad," Gordon said, "This is Timothy."

Leon stood to shake Timothy's hand, looking dazed.

Timothy smiled shyly and sat cross-legged beside Gordon. Cy stood aside while Gordon sat back down. After a silent moment Cy asked, "Timothy, how did you seduce this man away from his wife?"

"I asked *him* out!" Gordon nearly shouted.

Timothy said, "I'm an actor, Gordon's a photographer. We met at a photo shoot. I felt so open and free with him. We talked about our childhoods. He told me how much he missed his dad and—"

"Gloria even understands," Gordon cut in. "She says I look ten years younger."

Leon didn't take his eyes off his son, didn't smile and didn't frown. Who could know what was going on inside that weathered skull? At last Cy asked his simple question: "Leon, what do you feel like saying?"

The old man's shoulders rose and fell. When he spoke, his voice carried throughout the hushed room. "Son, God loves you and I love you, too."

He and Gordon fell into a tight embrace. The collective release of the Marathoners' tension sounded like cheering, though many people sobbed.

Susi clutched her purse. Alex was working his fists. Neither looked at me.

"Gordon," Cy said quietly, "how would it feel to see your dad give Timothy a hug?"

"That would mean so much."

"If my son cares about you," Leon exclaimed, "then you're okay." The old coot and his son's black lover embraced.

"I wonder," Cy said. "Leon, could you go out on a limb and really show your son this isn't an act? Could you kiss Timothy—closed-mouth, of course. In Christian communities it's called the Kiss of Peace."

Leon grasped Timothy by the scruff of the neck and, quickly but with feeling, kissed him on the lips. Gordon rolled into a weeping ball on the floor and Leon knelt to hold him.

Alex rose and took Susi's arm. I remained on the floor feeling stupid and helpless. "We've seen enough," Alex bellowed over the crying of dozens of Marathoners. "We were betrayed! We're not spending another dime on this 'therapy.'" He leveled an icy look at me. "You can come with us now or forget you ever had a family."

I glared back in defiance. My parents seemed to move away from me in slow motion, Alex steering Susi along by the elbow toward the exit. The champagne-colored carpet seemed to rise to meet each step they took out of my life. When they were about to disappear through the doorway, Susi turned back, straining against Alex's arm. My heart leaped when her eyes caught mine.

"You think your generation invented sodomy," she shouted. "Well, you didn't. You only invented *talking* about it all the goddamned time."

Alex propelled her from the room. The door slammed.

I longed to run after them, and wanted never to see them again. I laughed at their melodrama as tears stung my eyes.

Cy crossed the room and knelt beside me. "Time to let them

go," he said softly. On all sides, grieving Marathon members wailed for Leon and Gordon, for themselves and their lost parents. "At least until you can face them as an adult. You coined the term—they're your 'obligatory significant others.' But I'm your father now, and Zoë is your mother." He stood and pitched his voice above the sobs. "Within every human is a deep well of pain. Gordon, Leon, through your courage you shared a sacred moment with us, a moment of Unconditional Love."

Father and son rocked in each other's arms. The Vistans knelt with various crying Marathon participants, hugging and soothing, asking gentle questions. I got up and embraced Vivian. She stroked my hair and sobbed with me. Elsie distributed boxes of Kleenex. George Larkin, Professor Homer and the cashmere therapist circulated, ministering to bereft patients. Cy continued, "Pressures of life in the 'real world' cause you to avoid this pain and deny your own soul each day. With martinis and television and noise you distract yourselves for fear of falling into the well of pain and drowning in its cold depths. Here, among others who enjoy the freedom to feel, you can surrender to the waters of pain and be healed by the tears of everyone in this room."

That pathetic pair, Susi and Alex, had done me a favor by walking out.

FOR OVER TWELVE HOURS, Cy maintained the concentration of an air-traffic controller. When the Marathoners joined hands to sing "Amazing Grace," his shoulders sagged and his eyes were red. But later he and Zoë joined the rest of us in the Grunt Suite and he asked, "Anybody got shit?" A few people raised their hands. I wanted to crawl into my sleeping bag, but joined the other Vistans in their cross-legged circle.

Willow said she needed help because men in the city flirted with her and she couldn't say no. "If a guy's attracted," she admitted, "I feel obligated to ball him."

Zoë said a woman must determine whether she was horny or not. Cy agreed, and quickly devised Willow's process: "Have all the sex you want, honey, but only when you decide you want it. You can be a sexual predator if you want to, but not a victim."

"Sample *all* the flowers," Zoë advised. "The butterfly tastes all the nectar but stays away from the Venus fly*trap*."

Lucky had a predictable complaint about Rainbow. She defensively accused him, and both issues were dealt with quickly.

After a pause Elsie asked, "Are we finished? I've got something wonderful." She slid a stack of *Psychotherapy Currents* magazines from her bag and passed them around. "Wanda Richter left these for us at the front desk. Steve, she's the reporter who wrote the *Radical Therapist* article you sent to Rupert Seville's grandmother."

"You remember that?" I asked. "I'm impressed."

Willow winked at me. "*We* were impressed. That was your job interview."

Elsie read aloud: "*Like the Pied Piper, Cy Aaron promises to rid society of its rats but captures the hearts of its children.* Let's see—He has *a gift for reaching young people who have logged suicide attempts, psychiatric hospitalizations, or jail time. After a few months in his wilderness community these surly kids are respectful, articulate, communicative—*"

"Let's get Wanda in line," Cy said. "We're out of the 'troubled youth' business. We're focusing on couples, families, team-building in corporations. That article reinforces the image of Rancho Vista as a backwater reformatory for teenage misfits."

"She's covering the conference this week," Elsie said.

"Good. We'll talk to her every day."

"Time to promote some new summer programs," I ventured, feeling giddy. "How about '*Executive Trails*'? Ken could get corporate ladder-climbers into the rappel harness."

"Yes!" Cy enthused. "That's exactly the thinking we want." He sighed and took my hand. "Son, have you any regrets? You let go of your past today."

I didn't have to consider my reply. "My parents can't accept me. If I cling to them I'll never accept myself."

14

MY HEAD RESTED IN SUSI'S LAP, MY FEET IN ALEX'S. The Buick rocked gently, warm with her perfume. I nuzzled my face into her mink. She stroked my hair and sang my favorite sleepy song, *"Lie low, little doggies, lie low, lie low, the wind is a howlin', lie low . . ."* Going home late from somewhere special—
"Steve?"
Stay close to your mama, lie low, lie low—
"Steve, wake up!"
My mother's perfume evaporated and Elsie's voice cut through the howl of my hangover. A sob born deep in my chest rose and emerged as a sigh. I clung to the warm body spooned against me.
"Cy needs you."
I opened my encrusted eyes. The early sun glared through the vines. My head throbbed. Vivian moaned beside me. Vaguely I recalled that the Vistans had drained a five-gallon bottle of Joy Juice to toast my adoption. I had thrown up over the balcony. The saxophone-and-guitar jam session had triggered a visit from hotel security.
I yanked myself up and staggered past Elsie and over the sprawled bodies. Willow and Puck occupied a sleeping bag that blocked the bathroom door, and neither stirred when I lifted the foot-end and swung it out of the way. I flooded my head with cold water. When I emerged from the bathroom, Elsie had crawled back into her bag. I found my clothes and dully ignored a big yellowish stain on my shirt.
A room service cart outside Zoë and Cy's suite held breakfast plates smeared with congealed oatmeal and egg goo. The door was ajar. I tapped on it and walked in.
A man I had never seen waved from the menacing sunlight on the terrace and called in an unrecognizable accent, "You are Steef? Come, come." He held scissors and a comb and stood beside a barstool. "I cut the hair of movie stars and presidents but never have I made a house call so early on a Sunday. But Dr. Aaron saved the life of my dear wife. For him I do anything."
Warily I approached but stopped short of the terrace. "Cy just got his hair cut. I'm not even sure where he is, but he doesn't

need—"

"I know this. I cut his hair yesterday. You are Steef?"

"I'm—sick," I moaned, and ran for the wet bar. While I vomited into the little sink, I heard the bedroom door open behind me.

"Tempting to let him handle it alone," a woman was saying. "But he's barely twenty—a risk, no matter how intelligent . . ."

"Steve," Cy said brightly, "you've met Dimitri?" The strange woman's voice faded behind the closing door. I swished out my mouth and turned around. Cy was in briefs and socks. "Have you had breakfast?" he asked.

"I could use some aspirin."

"Dimitri, did you explain?"

The cobwebs around my head promptly dissolved. "He's not cutting my hair," I said in a metallic voice.

Cy re-opened the bedroom door and leaned in. "Zoë, Charley, I'm sorry to interrupt your important business discussion but we've got a therapy case on our hands."

I planted myself in a loveseat. Zoë entered the room dressed as when I'd first met her—in nothing but white panty hose, and her hair in the same whimsical topknot. With a sleepy little-girl look in her dark eyes she grasped my hands and kissed me on the cheek. The garbageman's wife from the Marathon appeared behind her, dressed for an executive conference in a sharp, raw-silk suit with pearl earrings and medium heels, perfect makeup and blonde chignon. "Hello, Steve," she said, not reaching for my hand. "So nice to see you again."

I grunted and attempted to smile. God, why hadn't I found a cleaner shirt?

I gratefully accepted a cup of coffee from Zoë and she sat beside me. "Because your parents have withdrawn financial support," Cy explained, "you'll have to earn your way at the Ranch." His voice softened. "You are absolutely equal to the task. I have nothing but respect, approaching awe, for your mind and ability. At the Ranch you can wear your hair down to your ass. But this is a week for the history books. The leaders of modern psychotherapy are holding high-level conferences in L.A. You'll be meeting people whose names you've read in textbooks. You personify the article you edited so brilliantly—*you* are the well-adjusted and self-accepting homosexual. But you've got to look like a professional, not one of the Furry Freak Brothers, or not even the love-beaded humanists will hear a single astute word you say. And the starchy psychiatrists will pillory you."

You'll have to earn your way. The magic phrase defined my future. If I hadn't been so hung over I would have jumped up and danced through the room. Zoë's smile reached me, full of love and playful reassurance.

Charley's sleek presence made my hair length suddenly seem a petty and childish thing to argue about. I slouched to the terrace and sat on the barstool. Cy and the others followed. While Dimitri hacked and clipped, Cy explained that Charley was a vice president of Universal Life & Casualty. She had offered her services to Rancho Vista as a consultant, to optimize insurance collections. After reviewing copies of my reports she had "some serious concerns." Cy stepped back and let her elaborate.

"The reports I've seen were—well-written," Charley said slowly, as if feeling she must choose each word carefully. She stepped onto the terrace and drummed her perfectly manicured fingers on the rail—the nails a peachy shade today, while yesterday they'd been pale violet. "But the subtleties could trip you up. And Steve, if—"

"Cy read those before he signed them," I told her. "I only drafted them. He changed some."

"If," she continued sharply, "an insurer conducts an audit, Dr. Aaron will be subjected to trick questions. I will be happy to review each month's reports before they're submitted."

"We'll have to get them to you pretty early, then." I tried to suppress the defensiveness in my voice. "Can you mail them back to us right away?"

"Actually, that—will not be necessary." She sounded both superior and vulnerable. "Josh and I have arranged to spend six months at Rancho Vista. I'm taking a leave of absence from work. The health of our marriage is more important than my career."

My shorn hair had been piling up on the terrace like wads of excelsior. How my father would enjoy seeing my newfound confidence hacked away while the blonde Delilah supervised!

Cy had watched the exchange with a bemused expression. "That's what I call a growth case," he said, then returned to the bedroom with the women. I was left wondering, Who's the growth case—me for accepting the haircut, or her for putting her marriage ahead of her job?

Finally the hacking stopped. Dimitri snipped near my ears and announced, "I am finished." I ran inside and checked myself the mirror over the wet bar. My sun-bleached, strawberry-blond hair rose off my forehead in two arched waves and barely covered my ears and collar. Trail had left me tan and, for the first time since puberty, free of blemishes.

Zoë stepped out of the bedroom and stood beside me, smiling at my reflection. "I look like a Mormon missionary," I whined.

She kissed my cheek. "Meet me *down*stairs in one hour. We will go shopping."

I FISHED MY PEPTO BISMOL OUT OF THE FERNS, finished it off and returned to the Grunt Suite, where the Vistans made a satisfying fuss over my haircut. Travis stood back with folded arms and said, "Looks like you got your head caught in a weed-whacker," and Teddy ran to Zoë and Cy's suite to collect the trimmings.

Wearing a clean shirt I borrowed from Ken, I met Zoë in the lobby and walked with her to the big Mercedes. She handed me the keys and stood at the passenger door until I caught on and did the gentlemanly thing.

"I'm pretty hung over," I said helplessly.

She giggled. "Good! The rest of the Sunday morning drivers have had their champagne breakfast. But you are *sober*."

The Mercedes felt as big as the dump truck, but handled smoothly and accelerated alarmingly. The traffic was light for my début at the wheel. Zoë directed me through side streets to Beverly Hills' legendary Rodeo Drive shopping district, and smiled indulgently while I pulled in and out of a parking spot until I felt I'd done it perfectly.

We breezed into several shops where the salespeople greeted Zoë with, "Good morning, Mrs. Aaron." Each time she announced, "My son Etienne needs a new image." She spent over four thousand dollars on what she called "basics"—trousers, dress shirts, luxurious sweaters, belts, black lace-up shoes for two hundred and fifty dollars, a second pair of slightly cheaper cordovan tassle loafers, knee-high socks, and something I hadn't worn since junior high, underwear. I was fitted for two sport coats and a double-breasted suit. Zoë picked out a sky-blue silk tie and complimented my taste when I chose a second, more conservative striped one. My hangover faded but still I moved in a haze of unreality. In the fitting-room mirrors I seemed to be watching a movie in which a character who looked vaguely like me was being outfitted for an undercover operation. Before we went to lunch Zoë bought me a crocodile-skin briefcase. I could hardly stop ogling the opulent thing. What would I put in it?

At a café I asked, "Do those salespeople really believe I'm your son?"

She purred, "Zay belief you are my young *lover*."

"And that your husband pays for my wardrobe because I can make you happy in ways he cannot?"

"You do not *beat* on the bush, Etienne. You are learning the ways of the world."

THAT EVENING, AGAIN AT THE WHEEL OF THE BIG MERCEDES, I drove Willow, Zoë and Cy to the Beverly Wilshire for a cocktail party. I wore my creamy vicuña V-neck and sky-blue tie. People who didn't know we were from Rancho Vista, and hadn't read about the place, would never have imagined we lived in tipis and used outhouses. Even anyone aware of Cy's wilderness outpost might not guess that the hem of Willow's cashmere skirt was secured with duct tape, or that on cold mornings her suntanned escort shat onto scraps of newspaper he threw into a wood stove, and pissed into a half-gallon thundermug labeled *Cribari Fine Red Wine*.

Cy introduced me to Carl Rogers, the father of modern psychotherapy . . . Arthur Janov, who had gotten the country doing the "Primal Scream" . . . Stan Standal, author of *The Need for Positive Regard*. On Willow's arm I met Werner Erhard, founder of est, and Zachary Bush of "Anger Lab" fame. Famous people who regarded Cy with the same deference he'd received from the therapists at the Marathon. I stood beside him as they asked questions and listened carefully to his answers. When they talked about their professional and personal problems, sipping martinis or scotch, Cy responded with intense, sober concentration. To a few he said, "This is Steve Susoyev, the young man I told you about," and I shook their hands, nodded and gave them my most mature smile.

Zoë and Willow circulated through the room. The hum of conversation surrounding Cy made clear he was at the heart of a political controversy. Psychiatrists, psychologists, social workers, body therapists, sex therapists—leaders of the mental health field, and trend-setters in something I had never heard of, the "human potential movement"—all jealously guarded their territories. Cy was one of a few who strove to bring the warring camps together. In work that I was only beginning to learn about, the strength of Cy's intellect and personality had earned the trust of everyone except the patriarchs of his own profession.

I listened while Cy spoke with a couple who'd spent thirty years cataloguing Freud's archives. Suddenly I stepped away and muttered, "Oh, shit." At Willow's side, Dr. Turner from Los Perdidos was approaching. He was towing along a woman I'd never seen by the elbow. Turner smiled weakly and introduced his soft-spoken wife to Cy. Was I hallucinating? I shook Turner's hand, mumbled, "I'm Etienne" and realized the bastard didn't recognize me. I excused myself with my heart thumping and pulled Zoë aside.

"You are a hit, Etienne," she said. "You were wise to accept the haircut."

From behind a potted palm we watched the Turners with Cy. Dr. Turner chewed his lips while his wife spoke with an expression of urgent distress. "I hate that man," I told Zoë. "He tortured my friend Rupert at the state hospital." I reached for a clump of hair to suck. My hand closed on nothing, and I nibbled a hangnail.

"He looks like a tortured soul himself," she observed.

Turner exchanged cards with Cy and earnestly shook his hand, then led his wife out of the party. I rushed over to Cy. "I know Nathan Turner," I said. "What'd he want?"

Cy eyed me with tactful annoyance. "If you know him why were you so abrupt? I need your help with public relations."

"He hates me. He didn't recognize me. What did he say?"

"His wife read about us. Their son's in jail on a drug charge. You and Ken go interview the kid. Write a report, refer him somewhere. Don't worry, we won't take the kid. I told them we're out of the drug-crazed youth business. People like Charley Thurgood are joining us."

I took Turner's card, flipped it and read in the hauntingly familiar tight blue script, *Tobias Turner, Orange County Jail*. Delighted to be in on this spectacular failure of a father-son relationship, I slid the card into a pocket.

Of the people crowding around to meet Cy, one particularly impressed me—a rakishly handsome psychiatrist named Nelson Christopher. Though gray at the temples and wearing a tuxedo, Dr. Christopher sported a boyish grin and bangs. He and I shared a look that confirmed we recognized something in each other even without having met.

Dr. Christopher told Cy, "You're making it safe for me to be myself in this profession," and enthusiastically described the group of gay psychiatrists who considered Cy a hero. I could barely contain my excitement. "No one will listen to *us* about this," Christopher said, "because we have a *personal* interest in seeing homosexuality declassified from the mental illness inventory. But you, Dr. Aaron, with your credentials, your international reputation, your beautiful wife and unassailable heterosexuality—the people in power listen to you."

A tall woman lugged a tape recorder over, accompanied by a photographer who'd shot pictures when Cy spoke with Rogers and Janov and now took close-ups of him with Nelson Christopher. Cy appeared not to notice the blazing flash, but I knew him well enough now to see that in his quiet way he was posing.

"Wanda," Cy told the reporter, "I want to say three words to you." He kept a hand on Christopher's shoulder. "Wall. Street. Journal."

Cy introduced her to Dr. Christopher and went on, "I appreciate the priceless publicity you've given Rancho Vista in your magazine pieces. But we're moving into a new realm—working with executives and their families, training therapists. Have you met Steve Susoyev?"

I blushed as if caught eavesdropping. She gushed, "The nineteen-year-old Columbia graduate!" and pumped my hand. "Wanda Richter. I'm thrilled to meet you."

I wouldn't challenge whatever Cy had told her, and certainly preferred the sound of "Columbia graduate" to "high-potential dropout," especially with the handsome Nelson Christopher beaming at me.

"Steve's latest brainchild," Cy went on, "is a wilderness program for corporate stress management. 'Executive Trails.' Wanda, you might come on our first Executive Trail and write about it for the Wall Street Journal. Steve helped enormously with the paper I'm distributing at this week's conference."

"Your secretary left a copy for me," she said. "It appears very controversial—"

"It's earth-shattering," Nelson Christopher interrupted. "My colleagues and I have already mailed copies to over a thousand gay therapists around the country."

She thrust her microphone at him. "A thousand others?"

Christopher nodded with a calm look of confidence. "Far

more, certainly. Only three of us at this week's conferences are openly gay, but eleven hundred responded to our recent notice in *Psychotherapy Currents*. Many identified themselves by initials and used post office addresses, they're so frightened. They're coming out of the closet one by one. With Dr. Aaron's article they'll be coming out by the dozens. The hundreds."

I caught a smile from Cy that said, *Jump in. This is why you're here*. I thought wildly of my parents and how I might explain any of this to them. "Do you fear a backlash?" I ventured. "The silent majority can't be taking this calmly. Cy, imagine talking about this at a town hall meeting in Rifle, Colorado."

"There's a revolution underway," Christopher replied. "Dr. Aaron is the generalissimo, you're his trusted lieutenant. I'm the standard-bearer and Miss Richter here is in charge of the war drums. You won't have to travel to Rifle to see the backlash. The antediluvian psychiatrists are beating *their* war drums tonight, in this room. Their livelihoods are at stake."

Nelson Christopher was older than anyone I had ever been attracted to, and so sophisticated in his tux, but his boyish enthusiasm was exciting. I cooked up a fantasy starring Nelson as my very own tipi-mate. Maybe I would add a wine rack and crystal glasses.

While Cy and Zoë posed for photographs, another man in a tuxedo approached. He squeezed Nelson's hand and kissed his lips, and I saw the gold bands on both men's ring fingers. The heat of jealousy scorched my insides. I shook hands with Donald, introduced as Nelson's "significant other," and forced myself to be polite.

AT MONDAY'S FIRST COMMITTEE MEETING I sat at the front table with Cy, facing the crowd. Many therapists appeared angry, some hopeful, none bored. I was glad to be clean-shaven and in my new suit like a mature professional.

In his opening comments Cy summarized his article and concluded, "In spite of the corrosive effect of society's contempt, there is a large population of well-adjusted gay men and women in this country." The audience began mumbling with a malicious undertone.

"Since when are inverts 'gay'?" yelled a man. "The ones I've worked with are profoundly *unhappy* specimens."

"How about equal rights for necrophiliacs?" jeered another.

"Let's give *them* an adorably misleading nickname."

I had always known the world hated people like me, but until this moment hadn't grasped that the hatred was institutionalized. The sudden viciousness of these well-dressed, urbane professionals shocked me. The proposal to remove homosexuality from the catalogue of mental disorders had sparked an insurrection. Cy raised his voice but couldn't be heard over the babble of the crowd, the words "queer" and "fag" ringing through the room along with "perversion" and "neurosis."

I glared at the mob in sudden fury and leaned toward the microphone. I found Zoë's shining face in the front row and spoke to her: "I have to say something."

The crowd refused to quiet down. "This is abominable." a red-faced little man kept bleating from a side wall. "Abominable!"

I stood up, clutching the microphone in my fist, and talked into the roar. "The day I discovered Dr. Aaron's work, at nineteen—"

A tiny, elderly woman stood in the front row and faced the crowd. "Let the young man talk," she declared, and raised her hands. "We've heard enough from all of you."

Whoever she was, she commanded immediate respect. The heckling died down. I remained standing and began slowly and softly, "Before I met Dr. Aaron I was preparing to kill myself." After a few soothing "shushes" the room was silent. "I could not face life as an outcast. I was what the gentleman over here called a 'profoundly unhappy specimen.' Many teenage suicides are gay kids traumatized by your profession. Unethical psychiatrists bank on our inability to accept ourselves. Playground thugs and brutal police use your words as weapons when they attack kids like me, sometimes killing us." I described the genital shock treatments my own psychiatrist had proposed. "At Nuremberg such torture was branded a war crime. To fit in we've submitted to psychic mutilation. But some day you and the world, and we ourselves, will accept who we are."

My tears blinded me so I couldn't see who cheered, who roared in anger. After the session ended, the diminutive woman who had quieted the throng introduced herself as Dr. Evelyn Hooker. Later, at the UCLA library, I learned that she had spent years leading the fight to which Cy and I were newcomers.

The press was barred from the meetings, and even Wanda Richter didn't manage to sneak in. But by Tuesday, Nelson Christopher and several other gay therapists held a press conference and tried to generate media attention for the revolution, which the American Psychiatric Association hoped to keep private. I didn't care whether it made the papers or not, satisfied that Cy had given me the chance to tell my story, and I had managed to speak articulately.

The only tarnish on the sterling week was Eric's frequent absence. Cy often referred to his "recruiting" activities, which I dimly understood involved following up with those Marathon participants who were interested in visiting the Ranch—or at least, as far as I could tell, the women. Eric also missed most of the Vistans' shared meals. He often came in looking tired and distracted, and remained distant from me and everyone else.

FOR THE JAIL INTERVIEW WITH DR. TURNER'S SON, Cy instructed me to wear my suit and drive the big Mercedes. Ken wore faded jeans and a sleeveless sweatshirt, and left his hair uncombed. At the Orange County Jail, as Cy had predicted, the guards ignored Ken but answered my questions with deference. Ken's appearance was calculated to win the young delinquent's trust, but Tobey Turner was a shy and surprisingly sweet sixteen-year-old who made direct, searching eye contact with both of us. He'd been held as an adult for more than a month, and appeared gaunt and ravaged. His dark, lovely eyes filled with tears when he explained, "My dad didn't bail me out of jail 'cause he wants to teach me a lesson. I guess that's why he didn't hire a lawyer. I've got a public defender."

I fought the urge to rant about his father's evil nature. "But he's worried about you," I assured the teenager, "or he wouldn't have come to us." Ken nodded in agreement.

Tobey came alive with the attention. He explained it was his mother's idea to contact Dr. Aaron, and cried when we asked about her and his young sister. Although my gut churned, I felt an odd pleasure. Tobey was the child of a monster but his gentle soul cried for help. My desire to exact revenge on the father dissolved into a deeper yearning to rescue the son. Alone, armed with good intentions, I had failed to help my friend Rupert. Now I could offer Rancho Vista, the greatest resource in the world.

Approaching the car after the interview, I decided it was time to kick over the stone Ken and I had been avoiding. I stood in the sun and gave him a pointed stare. "Why'd you come to my camp that night after Trail?"

He studied his hands. "You weren't asleep, huh?"

"Did you really believe I was?"

"I couldn't have done that otherwise."

"Was it to thank me for pulling you out of the river?"

"I wanted to try that for the longest time." Though no one was within fifty yards, he whispered, "Sucking a cock. You're the only guy I ever trusted enough to really do it."

Despite the urgent swelling in my silk-lined trousers, I said only, "Thank you." Ken had satisfied his curiosity, but the Great God Pan wasn't interested in falling in love with a man. And after my humiliation at Eric's feet, I wasn't going to chase someone who could only love me when I pretended to be asleep.

DURING THE WEEK CY SAW INDIVIDUAL CLIENTS AT HIS SUITE. Some were celebrities and politicians so concerned about privacy that they paid in cash and even Elsie didn't know many of their names. In addition, Cy and Zoë met with real estate lawyers, tax lawyers, copyright lawyers and accountants. Travis was called in for a meeting with a team of architects who were designing a futuristic lodge to replace the triple-wide trailer in Keystone as Cy and Zoë's home. Eric cornered them for help with his design of a geodesic dome to serve as a Group room at the Ranch. Money was flowing from sources I couldn't imagine.

At mid-week Elsie asked me to accompany her on an errand to the Department of Motor Vehicles. In the hotel lobby she whispered, "A man I only know as 'the Colonel' owes Cy over a hundred thousand bucks. *Owed*, actually. He just paid part of it by signing over the title to his Rolls Royce. The balance was in a briefcase full of hundred-dollar bills."

"A *Rolls Royce?*"

"Extravagant, huh?"

"Outrageous." I nodded to the doorman and silently calculated what the Ranch's operating costs must be for a month: food, several tanks of gas and a ton of coal. Vehicle insurance, but no payments, because the cars and trucks had been donated or taken in barter, like the Rolls. And no mortgage on the property. "That car could bankroll the Ranch for a year."

"Cy says it's a great car for traveling between Beverly Hills and the Ranch. He wants to register it in your name."

I stared at her. "A Rolls Royce is an obscene reminder of

who's winning the class war." If only Lydia could hear me!

"I think Cy sees it as a very well-built automobile."

"Why does he want it in *my* name?"

"To show his trust," she said with gentle admonition. "You just divorced your family."

The Rolls was a classic older model, creamy white, and stood out even among the Ferraris and Bentleys parked nearby. Elsie handed me the keys and added playfully, "The DMV in West LA, darling."

Hoping Nelson Christopher wasn't around to see us get into this chariot, I opened the passenger door for Elsie. It felt as if it weighed five hundred pounds, but was so well balanced I swung it out easily and clicked it shut with no effort.

While Elsie snuggled into the burgundy leather I adjusted the driver's seat and turned the key. The motor purred a moment, then was silent. The tachometer registered a thousand RPMs, telling me the engine hadn't died. I drove through the parking lot, concentrating intensely, testing the acceleration and the brakes. Then I laughed. "I want to see Dove MacKenzie's face when we drive this through Keystone. He'll think the Queen of England's picking up a load of irrigation pipes."

The car silently swooshed into the morning traffic on Sunset Boulevard. I wanted to enjoy the ride, but couldn't forget the car was worth as much as I would have earned in a lifetime at my Los Perdidos job. "Makes the Mercedes feel like my old Karmann Ghia."

Elsie read from the owner's manual. "This is a 1962 Austin Princess." She giggled. "Who's winning the class war now?"

"Good thing Satan didn't offer one of these to Jesus during his forty days in the desert."

THE HIGH-PROFILE ACQUISITIONS DIDN'T STOP WITH THE ROLLS. The same morning, Cy and Zoë attended a bankruptcy auction and bought a thirteen-bedroom mansion on Bedford Drive in Beverly Hills. Once Elsie obtained a key and had the power turned on, I brought over a Mercedes-load of Vistans. We parked in the driveway, beside an aging maroon Lincoln with a broken taillight. Who in this neighborhood would drive such a derelict car?

Because it hunched between a stucco Parthenon and an Italianate villa, the mansion appeared almost modest when viewed from the street—a Tudoresque gingerbread house of red brick with a slate roof and mullioned windows. Its flagstone driveway was the only one on the block that wasn't shaped like a great horseshoe. The brown lawn and ratty palm trees were the blight of the block. Inside, an ominously sagging banister had once curved majestically up a grand staircase. The former owners' neglect showed in the soiled draperies, stained carpets and broken plumbing fixtures. Furniture was piled everywhere—some broken, some garish, some serviceable.

Travis grilled Sonny Tornado, the nervous little real estate agent who owned the broken-down Lincoln in the driveway, and insisted on a tour that included every closet and out-building. He finally certified that the house was well-built and that fixing it up would be fun. Mr. Tornado frantically puffed a cigarette beside the pool, since he wasn't allowed to smoke in the house, and Zoë questioned him further. Travis pointed out the two-foot thick walls, window seats "each one big enough for an orgy," the magnificent art deco tile work, and heated towel racks in the numerous bathrooms. In the cathedral-ceilinged kitchen he became intimately involved with the twelve-burner stove.

"There's a torture chamber downstairs," Teddy announced.

Travis explained, "That big round room in the basement was a recording studio. Soundproof. Probably *would* make a good torture chamber."

We moved into the mansion for our last night in Beverly Hills. Travis outfitted the master bedroom and Cy's study with the best furniture, and dumped much of the rest in the alley. We put on our best attempt at swimming suits—cutoffs, halter tops, boxer shorts—but once Cy was satisfied that no neighbors could see into the yard, we skinny-dipped. The enormous pool was furry with emerald algae.

I felt I was being swept away by a great wind. I paced around the pool's edge. Fancy cars and grandiose houses didn't mean anything—but could I explain to Lydia the practicality of a thirteen-bedroom Beverly Hills mansion? Cy was already calling it the "Rancho Vista Administrative Center." Even the Rolls Royce and Mercedes Benz were practical—safe, reliable automobiles for long trips. Lydia would never buy that, but she'd chosen to live underground with a man who slapped her around whenever he felt like it. I leaped off the diving board and pretended I was splashing into the Mother River.

That evening we christened the house with a low-key party,

mindful of the presence of neighbors, and watched a late-night broadcast of the movie *Funny Girl* on television. Cy sipped lemon-lime soda while everyone else consumed cheap red wine and Joy Juice. The movie hadn't interested me when it was released. But with Cy's commentary, the story of Fanny Brice became a fascinating social phenomenon.

"Look at this," Cy said. "A woman who didn't hide when she became pregnant out of wedlock. A pioneer. You kids can't imagine what things were like before the sexual revolution."

While Streisand sang "My Man," Cy stood beside the television and wept. "Listen to her," he entreated us. When the song ended, Willow lowered the volume and he continued, "*Whatever my man is, I am his.* What does that say about the state of womankind? Girls, you've got to overcome four million years of socialization if you're going to exercise sovereignty over your own bodies, your own lives. Speaking of which—Willow, how are you doing with your process? Does everybody know Willow's becoming a sexual predator?"

"My process," Willow said, with what looked like a half-serious scowl, "is to decide for myself when I'm horny. It means I ball only when I initiate it, and sample all the flowers."

"And?" Cy asked.

Puck raised his hand. "She's a gentle predator."

Several women said they wanted to try Willow's process.

"Thank God," Cy said, "we have Rancho Vista. Where else could people do this?"

I said, "Thank God we have *you*, Cy. I've always thought of that movie as a schlocky romance. You could find something profound in a TV commercial."

Before the night was over, to our delight, Cy exploited the opportunity to do just that. "The key," he told us, while a woman on the television screen fretted over the unsightly stains in her toilet bowl, "is to be in the world but not of it. We can't avoid the culture we live in. But we can recognize when politicians and merchants are trying to manipulate us. We can thwart them by thinking for ourselves."

ON OUR LAST MORNING IN CALIFORNIA, the house echoed with the chaos I had become accustomed to. Vistans sat nude eating cereal on the diving board, or rushed through the rooms dragging duffel bags and looking for lost clothes and notebooks. The flagstone entryway was strewn with supplies Travis and Elsie had gathered, from cases of canned hominy to Army-surplus mosquito netting.

I'd heard nothing from my parents. They had the answering service number. Why they hadn't called? Why did I expect them to? They were on the opposite side of a widening chasm. Yet I couldn't stop hoping that they would have a change of heart and come through like the salty old cowboy had done for his flamboyant son.

I was scheduled to drive the Mercedes home. My passengers, Vivian and several kids, were already waiting in the car when I ducked out to the poolside phone and dialed the service. "This is Steve Susoyev, with Rancho Vista. Any messages for me?"

"Nothing since Thursday, Mr. Susoyev," the operator said. I learned that Nelson Christopher had called twice with dinner invitations, and that Elsie had taken the information.

I stormed into the house and shouted for her. She looked frightened when I found her. "Why didn't you tell me Nelson Christopher called?"

She would not look at me. "I—"

"He's an important associate of Cy's." I fumbled, realizing *He likes me* wasn't relevant.

"Cy said—." Her wavering voice trailed away.

"Cy said *what?*"

She always seemed to tremble slightly but now she was shaking hard, and tears came into her eyes. "Steve, you've got to talk to him about this. It wasn't up to me."

"*Cy* told you not to give me Nelson's messages?"

"I think Cy called him back. So everything's okay."

"Nelson left messages for *me*," I howled. "It's not okay!"

I ran outside, hopped into the Mercedes and slammed the door. As I was backing into the street Cy emerged from the house with a hand held high, and I lowered my window. "Why don't you and the kids go swimming," Cy suggested to Vivian. "We've got an emergency to handle. Steve'll come out for you when he's ready."

He led me into the study, where the staff was already gathered. I assumed the position in the center of the floor. "Elsie," I said, "I'm sorry I gave you a hard time."

Cy snorted. "The issue isn't you and Elsie, though I'm heartened by your offer of an apology. Willow, please relate your experience with young Dr. Bush."

Willow gave me a worried smile. "Cy's saying you're vulnerable right now. You just divorced your parents. Nelson Christopher seems like a nice guy but he lives by the world's standards. He can flirt with you, and kiss his lover in front of you. If a man like that invites you into his life it's not an honor. It's a threat."

"Young Dr. Bush," Cy reminded her.

With part of my mind I saw Cy's genius operating, as if I were watching a brain surgeon at work—I would accept this from Willow but I'd get defensive if he lectured me.

She shrugged. "You met Zachary Bush the other night, the Anger Lab guy. His son Myron asked me out last year. Cy told me what I'm telling you, but I didn't want to hear it. I went out with Myron Bush. He tried to recruit me away from the Ranch, to work in his father's clinic for five bucks an hour, letting his patients hit me with foam rubber bats. What an honor. Oh, and he wanted to ball me. A double honor."

I chuckled along with everyone else.

Cy explained, "I asked Elsie to hold Nelson's messages until we got home to the Ranch. Dr. Christopher could have invited several Vistans to dinner. Instead he's trying to separate the juiciest lamb from the herd. I can't let that carnivore sink his teeth into you."

I saw in the crinkles around Cy's eyes that he wasn't angry. Even Elsie smiled with concern. "So," I asked, "You guys really think Nelson's a carnivore?"

Cy chuckled. "The crocodile isn't evil, he's hungry. He doesn't care who plops into his pond. Ghandi? A platypus? Either is a tasty snack." He held out his arms rigidly and snapped them together—huge jaws closing on a meal. "Christopher could seduce you away without intending harm. But when Gollum popped out he'd make himself scarce, and where would you be?"

Eric, Ken, Willow and Elsie all nodded. Zoë winked when my eyes caught hers.

I had to admit Nelson Christopher belonged to the world that Cy had rescued me from in my darkest moment.

"Let's go home," I said.

15

DRIVING OUT OF LOS ANGELES, while Elizabeth read "Dear Abby" aloud from the morning paper, I tried to picture the bushy-haired kid who had hitchhiked to Rancho Vista, afraid of freezing to death by the roadside. So much more than the weather had changed in two months.

Over Nevada highways with no speed limits we cruised at a hundred forty miles an hour, escaping from the filth and noise, my intolerant parents, and all reminders of my failed life. I pulled in at the Blue Worm less than twelve hours after leaving the ramshackle mansion on Bedford Drive. The tiny high-desert outpost looked like paradise.

Instead of falling asleep to the song of the Mother River, I spent several nights in town working late on the following month's insurance reports. I intended to overwhelm the executive Charley with the efficiency of my system when she and her husband arrived for their six-month stay.

I WORKED IN THE BLUE WORM'S KITCHEN, typing color-coded labels for the insurance files. Elsie sat across from me paying bills. Willow, swathed in maroon silk, prepared a tangy lamb curry with basmati rice and mango chutney. Ken, Eric and Puck showered and did their laundry, flopping naked through the kitchen.

A Staff Group was scheduled at the triple-wide—a "time for informal sharing," Cy called it. For me the scene felt domestic, adolescent, suburban: hanging out doing homework surrounded by the brothers and sisters I'd never had, getting ready for dinner with Mom and Dad. Except Mom was still in California, and Cy was unlike any dad I'd ever heard of.

As soon as the food was ready we all carried it to the triple-wide. We settled on the floor with our plates in a semicircle around Cy. He sat naked in his Danish chair and used the ottoman as a table. "We've got some heavy shit to handle tonight," he said. "But before we start I want to share something very personal with you kids." He swallowed a mouthful of lamb and sipped from a blue mug rimmed in gold.

The angles of his handsome face softened in the pink glow of the sunset from the atrium skylight. With his white hair untamed and his crinkley eyes alert to the faces around the room, he looked like an inspired monk. He held his firm body like a much younger man. His foreskin covered all but the slit at the tip of his cock. I chuckled quietly. Cy looked like a *naked* inspired monk.

Willow and Eric stared into their food. They'd each drunk a few glasses of Cribari Red. Ken took huge bites and washed each down with a slug of wine, then chewed with his eyes shut. Elsie fluttered around. Only Puck seemed at peace. He ate and grinned. Zoë's dog Wolfie, still a clumsy puppy but bounding around in a large dog's body, was well-trained not to beg. When I said "Down," he lay flat and placed his head on my foot.

Elsie refilled Cy's plate and brought him a cup of coffee, but he sipped again from the gold-rimmed mug. Then abruptly he said, "You grunts are my C.S.O.," and opened his arms to encompass the staff. Those who were eating put down their plates and forks. "It's a miracle. Ken, look at you. Remember when I found you in that hospital bed?"

Ken's shapely lips tightened in a serious smile.

"All of you," Cy continued. "Even you, Steve, rat-faced when you followed Eric up here. But look at you now! So sweet and capable. You were a sensation in Beverly Hills." My face warmed. "You should have seen your darling Eric when he came into our world, the menacing leer on that handsome face. A purse-snatcher until he graduated to drug-dealing, the kind of sleazy criminal other inmates literally piss on in the joint. Lovely Willow, a groupie with that reptilian rock band, thinking she was so urbane while they used her like a toilet. Puck, living like a little monkey up on the mountain, a schizophrenic castaway. And Elsie! Plotting to shove her mother down the basement stairs.

"My point is, your reality and caring levels are so high, I'd rather share my time with you kids than with therapists my age, and I know the most brilliant ones in the world. In Beverly Hills I couldn't wait to escape the ass-kissers and ego cases to be with you. You kids are my fucking Composite Significant Other."

"It's an honor to be close to you, Cy," Willow said.

"Thank you, honey." He held out his open hands. "The thing I want to share. Zoë didn't come back with me from California for a special reason. You know that she and I have been working for years on something we call the Pure Relationship, and I've mentioned our new concept, 'Polysex.' Yesterday she flew to

Tahiti in a Lear jet. It's her childhood home but she's not visiting her family. She's balling a Swedish billionaire we call 'Samuel' on his yacht, and I'm affirming her."

If the others had a reaction to Cy's news, they sat on it. I was the only one who came close to revealing any anxiety when I asked, "She's balling him right *now?*"

Cy smiled and looked at his watch. "In Tahiti it's only two o'clock, so maybe not yet. We'll talk tomorrow. The point is, I'm actively enjoying her pleasure. Merely tolerating it isn't my goal. She called this morning from Samuel's yacht and told me what they did last night. The little darling said, 'His nine-inch cock isn't silky smooth like your fellah, Cy!' Wasn't that sweet?"

His eyebrows shot up, and I thought I understood that he expected, wanted, our approval. "When I affirm her, it clarifies my vision like a psychedelic potion. I see that when I was young I branded women like livestock to hold onto them. I called it 'love.'" He sipped from his mug. "I've certainly struggled with the desire to control Zoë. If I try to dominate her even once, that little butterfly will flutter away."

He took a deep gulp of his drink. For an instant his eyelids drooped and his smile slid sideways. He was drinking something other than lemon-lime soda. A bit alarmed, I explored the others' faces. Willow knelt as if ready to jump up, and hadn't touched her food. Ken bolted the last of his meal and rocked back and forth, studying Cy. Elsie and Eric sat with full plates before them. Only Puck appeared relaxed and unconcerned.

"And this," Cy said, "is the real beauty of the limited relationship Zoë's developing with this man. She didn't demand it from me or even request it. I *offered* it. That's the essence of Polysex. The world doesn't understand this, but Zoë and I are writing a book to explain it. Polysex is about *affirmation*. Adultery is a sin because it's based on dishonesty and selfishness. Polysex is a high-level spiritual exercise that allows a couple to enjoy each other's pleasure. It enhances commitment rather than eroding it."

His voice recalled the eloquence I had heard during Garth Elfinger's funeral. "Jesus taught that when two people marry, they stop being two and become 'one flesh.' But how many couples affirm each other's joy? Zoë and I are reviving such affirmation."

He paused with his eyes closed.

Willow said, "Now I feel *really* honored, Cy." We all nodded.

He drained his mug. "Good, because tonight's issue is you and

Puck. We left the process loose in Beverly Hills, to see what would emerge if you were free to become a sexual predator."

"I thought it was to help me learn to know when I was horny, instead of leaving it up to some man to decide for me."

"Look at Puck," Cy said. "The poor man hasn't slept in days."

"Puck's fine," Puck said contentedly. I've been happy to sacrifice for Willow's mental health."

Everyone laughed except Willow. She narrowed her eyes at Cy. "The sexually predatory female is *your* fantasy. And you know better than to do therapy when you're drunk."

"Honey, you're drunk too, so—"

Ken interrupted, "If we waited 'til we were all sober we'd never start."

"You're fucking well *right*," Cy said, in a bitter tone that jarred me. "If you people had to deal with the problems I'm responsible for, you wouldn't get out of bed without a drink and a joint and a shot of smack or whatever you got off on before I rescued you from the sewer your families had flushed you into."

Willow sat up straighter. "If any of us used those rationalizations, you'd pounce."

Cy roared, "Am I the only one who sees she's changed the subject?"

Wolfie barked and I put him outside, then leaned back against the wall, pulled my knees to my chin, and wrapped my arms around my shins. Ken appeared eager to speak but didn't. Eric and Elsie studied their uneaten food. Willow said, "We'll talk about my process when we're all in condition for therapy. We had a lovely dinner, if I do say so myself. Let's go home with a nice memory of it. I've had plenty of help with my horniness process for now."

"You've had *no* help," Cy shouted. "You've run this thing all along. That's why it's going haywire. There wasn't supposed to be a *relationship* between you. Puck's still a grunt." He gestured at the cheerful teenager. "Show everybody those fingernails."

Puck's smile faded and he held up both hands. Though he'd showered and scrubbed himself pink, each of his nails harbored a rind of garden dirt.

"Poor little guy," Cy said gently. "Look at that sweet face." He spoke as if reciting a nursery rhyme to a very small child. "He says, 'Gee, Ma, I warshed my hair, and a coupla days ago I brushed my teeth. Do I hafta clean my fingernails *too*?' And his Mama answers, 'No, son, not if you're playing with Willow's pussy. Most women respect themselves enough to demand clean fingernails, but not Willow!' "

I folded in on myself.

Cy pounded the ottoman. "You were supposed to 'sample all the flowers' but you got hung up on one that was easy! Did you approach Eric or Ken? Or even Steve? Guys who can hold their own with a powerful woman like you?"

"She's passed up chances to be with me," Ken said.

Willow snapped, "Don't start doing therapy on me. You're drunk, too. And yes, I'm drunk, we're all drunk, so please let's not do therapy tonight!"

I wished I could melt into the floor. As a child, when my parents fought, I dragged a blanket and pillow into the garage and slept in the back seat of the car. Tonight, if I got up even to go to the bathroom, I might join Willow on the hotseat.

"Ken," Cy said, "you can't reason with her right now. It's like Brer Rabbit and the Tar Baby. Your feedback just got swallowed up by the tar."

"Of course I want feedback," Willow said. "Just not when we're drunk. Let's put on some music. I got the new Moody Blues in L.A."

I smiled to show her I thought this was a good idea, but she didn't look at me.

Cy said, "Ken, can you let her punch you a few times? Just to vent this anger so we can get to something productive? She seems to be focused on you."

Ken shrugged and walked over to her. She stood up and slapped his face, hard.

"You'll have to slap her back," Cy said. "She's just showing us how afraid she is to relate to a real man."

I tried not to watch but couldn't help myself. Ken waited until Willow looked into his eyes, then slapped her with measured precision, matching the resonance of the blow he'd just endured.

Her fist flew at his face. He caught it with an open hand.

"Don't let her get away with that," Cy yelled, and sat back. "Are you going to help her, or will Eric have to step in?"

I looked at Eric's feet in their red socks, the ones he'd worn on the night Gollum first slithered into the light. I heard an open-handed smack and looked up. Ken's red face was tight with anger as Willow struck him back. He clutched a fistful of her hair close to the scalp, lifted her and flung her against the wall. She fell, screaming, "You fucker!" He wrestled her down, sat on her and held her wrists to the floor.

I jumped to my feet. "This is too much!"

"Christ," said Cy. "Somebody gives her honest feedback and we've got Nursie coming in with the Band-Aids. If Steve wants to talk he'll have to wear the cap. Elsie?"

While Willow squirmed under Ken, Elsie disappeared down the hallway and returned with the box of Marathon props. She handed me the Red Cross nurse's hat. "Put it on," Cy said.

The cap's elastic strap held it securely on my head. Against my will I looked at my ridiculous reflection in a floor-length mirror on the far wall.

"You meatball shithead," Willow fumed at Ken. "Keep a good grip." I sat down on the floor while she raged, "Let me up and I'll fucking turn you into cosmic dust!"

Ken laughed. "*Cosmic dust?* Them's fightin' wor—"

She hawked up a wad of phlegm and hooted it into his face.

He leaned over and slowly dribbled saliva into her eyes.

As she squirmed and thrashed, I sat on my hands, desperate to get up and kick Ken in the head. I would fling off the preposterous cap, stomp on Ken, grab Willow by the hand and lead her to some safe place.

Cy knelt beside her. "Honey," he asked gently, "what's really going on?"

Ken sat back, still holding Willow by the wrists. Her phlegm gleamed on his face.

Cy stroked her hair. She began to cry. "I'm not a predator," she sobbed, her voice empty of anger. "Just a lonely girl." Her tears mixed with Ken's spit and ran into her ears. Finally Ken released her hands and pulled at his own hair. He too was crying.

"We're all lonely children," Cy said. He went on stroking Willow and placed a hand on Ken's shoulder. "Yearning to be connected to other human beings."

Eric rose and knelt at Willow's side. Elsie followed, then Puck. With my own tears rising, I knelt among them. Willow smiled when she saw me, and reached to touch my hand. "Aw, Steve," she said, "you wanted to protect me from the process. Sometimes I forget what a short time you've been with us. Cy, can he take the cap off?"

I didn't wait for permission and tossed the cap into a corner.

She sat up and hugged Ken. "Thank you, sweet thing. I got trouble with men."

"How do you see the trouble, honey?" Cy asked.

"I've given my personal power to psychopaths. Now I'm afraid of all strong men, even compassionate, good men." She described her relationship with the lead singer of Cloud 9, who had given her LSD and then made her ball men she didn't know. "One of them *buttfucked* me."

The pain in her voice struck me. I reached for her at the same moment the others did. In one motion we lifted and cradled her while she continued to sob.

In a quavering voice Elsie began the melody I hadn't heard since the day Gollum emerged from his cavern, "Sometimes I feel like a motherless child . . ." The others joined in to finish the line, ". . . a long way from home." Willow seemed to drink in the love that held her aloft, and let her tears flow. The cradlers sang on while Elsie pressed a Kleenex to Willow's nose. She blew like a tiny child. Ken's handprint still blazed on her face.

Soon her tears subsided and the singing softened. Cy stroked her hair. "Honey, I never knew it was so bad with those rockers."

"It was terrible," she murmured. "This session woke me up."

The staff continued to sing while Willow sat facing us. Cy sat behind her in his chair and rubbed her shoulders. Softly he said, "Let's modify the process we started in L.A. Ken, can you step in for Puck and help Willow through the next phase of her exploration? She'll decide when she's horny, and approach you to act on it."

Ken nodded gravely.

Willow hugged and thanked Puck. Elsie began to pick up the dirty dishes.

I got myself to the bathroom, locked the door and vomited. On my knees I thought through everything that had occurred after Cy stopped eating. Out of what looked like drunken brutality, he had brought forth a new understanding of what it meant to be human.

Back in the main room the Moody Blues were on the stereo and I joined the others dancing by candlelight. Willow moved sensuously, her scant silk wraparound hanging off one shoulder so a nipple peeked out occasionally. Even in the soft light, bruises were showing on her face. Puck shimmied near her but didn't horn in on Ken, who danced close.

I sipped lemon-lime soda, amazed at how readily I had misjudged the situation. During my first weeks at the Ranch I had wanted to be in on staff sessions. Even now, months later, I could barely witness high-level therapy without freaking out.

IN THE MORNING I DROVE THE LAND ROVER TO THE RANCH. Willow and Ken cooed together in the back seat while Puck stared out the window. Eric talked about the drying racks that would be ready in plenty of time for the fruit harvest, and the amazing progress of his pet project, the geodesic dome whose enormous skeleton, a structure of triangles, commanded the view from the plateau above the cookshack. While I maneuvered through the swale Eric asked, "When's that Charley chick coming? You ready for her?"

I smiled, thankful for his understanding. "She has a lot of very *important* executive business to tie up in L.A., so she may be a while." My tone would constitute subgrouping if I were talking about a Vistan. "But I'm ready for her," I added benignly.

Over breakfast Willow and Ken announced that they were moving in together, to the foot-stomping cheers of the Vistans. After I washed my tray she followed me onto the porch. "I want to explain some things about last night," she said.

"Oh, that's history."

"Your face is so expressive. I always know when you're going through something."

I looked into her own expressive face, slightly lopsided with lilac bruises rimmed in dull yellow. The revulsion I had felt rushed back. "I'm afraid of Cy," I said flatly.

"When he drinks, which isn't often, his power is undiluted by niceties. But he was right last night. He thought it was time for you to be in on something more important that a session of 'Who stole the peanut butter?' We all think you're ready to handle some real therapy."

Yes, real therapy. Cy could approve of Zoë's affair—no, it was much more: he could *affirm her pleasure* with a sexually gifted billionaire. He could function as a brilliant therapist even on the rare occasion that he got drunk. Cy could handle violence and turn it into love.

16.

"THE PROBLEM," INTONED CY IN A VOICE OF DOOM, "is the imminent inspection by the eminent Dr. Folsom of the Six-County Department of Health. His visit will coincide with the midsummer burgeoning of our fly population."

I had stopped noticing flies months before, but now they buzzed in every corner of the cookshack. They ignored the limp strips of sticky paper, black with their comrades' corpses, that spiraled from the ceiling.

"The solution," Cy declared, "is the Slammer," and nodded toward the pantry. Travis returned the nod, brought out a blackboard and propped it on the serving counter.

I swallowed a yawn. For several nights I had worked late—in town, organizing insurance records, and in my snug tipi by lamplight, studying the Diagnostic and Statistical Manual—all in preparation for the arrival of the chignoned Charley and her garbage-collecting husband. A health inspector's visit seemed a minor event next to her victory ride into Rancho Vista.

Cy sketched with tan chalk and explained, "The Slammer is a classic *grunt catcher*—a simple device that short-circuits the efforts of even the most irresponsible member of society." He drew a side view of a slant-roofed shitter with its near wall cut away. "Here's a Rancho Vista comfort station. This is the vent pipe rising from behind the toilet seat and through the ceiling." Affecting a prudish grimace, he added in an Oxford don accent, "To whisk away offensive odours." He sketched green fumes wafting from the top of the vent pipe, then red flies gamboling through them.

I recalled that the impending inspection was the result of an anonymous complaint, which got me thinking. The Vistan way was to embrace challenges and eliminate defensiveness. How could this principle guide us in dealing with the potential inspection crisis?

Cy went on explaining his Slammer invention. "Remember when Travis risked his neck climbing a ladder, and capped these vent pipes with screens, to keep out the flies?" The Vistans nodded. Cy's eyes bugged out in mock astonishment. "Well! Certain members of the experimental community, whose identities are known only to themselves, left the toilet lids up so the flies got in anyway!"

Puck groaned. "Just when I think I'm high-level enough to make it onto the staff, I find out I'm still a pitiful grunt."

"Honey," Cy said to Zoë, "make a note for him on that T.I. The diagnosis is chronic preoccupation, otherwise known as Being In His Shit."

Zoë pretended to write furiously, then grinned at Puck. Since her Tahiti trip she was even more engaged with all of us and affectionate toward Cy. Polysex worked, I had to admit.

Cy became serious. "The health inspector serves an entrenched bureaucracy, and won't visit until after his five-week vacation. That gives us a reprieve. But we don't have time for everyone to learn to function at a high level even when you're in your shit. So we'll cut the Gordian knot and install Slammers in all six shitters."

I wrote an idea on a card, then looked up and smiled. Even the seven-year-olds were watching Cy with fascination. Thanks to the ongoing seminar that was life with Aaron, they understood "burgeoning," grasped the difference between "imminent" and "eminent," and knew something of how bureaucracies became entrenched. They recognized "T.I." as shorthand for Therapeutic Issue and could recite the story of King Gordius's complicated knot, which Alexander had sliced with his sword. From the wry smile on Elizabeth's face I felt she understood something further—that the ubiquitous flies were Cy's convenient device for whipping up community spirit in preparation for weeks of unpleasant work.

With white chalk Cy drew a wedge, wide at the top, attached to the base of the ventpipe. In a W.C. Fields voice he said, "This little wedge-shaped wooden wonder makes it impossible for anyone to leave the toilet lid up. As soon as the seat is vacated, gravity will slam the lid shut." He wiggled his eyebrows. "Theories are grand, but aeronautical engineers tell us the honeybee is incapable of flight. Let's watch this thing fly."

Like thirty goslings trailing after their mother, we followed him outside and up to the demonstration shitter. Lucky had built the prototype, and Cy allowed him the honor of showing it off. He had attached a wooden wedge to the vent with pipe clamps. He lifted the toilet lid as far as the wedge allowed, then turned it loose. It slammed shut.

While we cheered, I pictured Charley in her medium-heeled

pumps—hiking up her skirt, pulling down her pantyhose and trying to lift the toilet lid without dropping her Parisian handbag down the hole. Her husband Josh, the former garbageman, might not mind the odor. But the stench would flatten the insurance executive. Suddenly I realized she wouldn't last a weekend at Rancho Vista, and I retired one of my many anxieties.

Back in the cookshack I passed my card to Cy and chewed on my pen while Willow expounded on the need to scrub the coal-smoke stains off every tipi, and dispose of such incriminating items as wine bottles and beer-making equipment.

"Here's an idea," Cy said at last, and read aloud from my card: "Somebody who's only seen this place through binoculars filed an anonymous complaint. Let's call their bluff: scrub and paint like crazy, have an Open House and invite everybody we know, from Carl Rogers to the sheriff. People are gossiping anyway. Let's give 'em something to talk about."

Cy held up the card and shook his head. "Do we really need to discuss this?"

I reddened. "It was just an idea."

"Just a brilliant idea. Who wants to try designing Open House invitations?"

Mine was the only hand that rose.

Cy bowed slightly toward me. "That's one job assignment out of the way. Company coming is a great excuse to clean house." He erased his slammer sketch and installed Travis at the black-board to organize work teams. The children would scrub the shitter walls in preparation for fresh paint. Lucky agreed to whitewash the goat pens. Vivian volunteered to sew window curtains for the cookshack, and Eric offered to make a screen door. Within an hour every Vistan had at least two assignments.

Cy concluded that until the Open House, Group would be for handling work-related issues and emergencies. "Pack up your troubles in your old kit bag and give 'em a rest," he advised. "Our problems always get top billing around here. Let's put *work* first for a while. After the Open House we can have Group non-stop for a week. Then we'll fling off our clothes and dance 'til sunrise."

IN ADDITION TO ITS ENTERTAINMENT VALUE and simple, effective operation as a fly-obstructor, the Slammer had a ripple effect even Cy may not have anticipated. Suddenly people came up with their own "grunt catching" developments, such as Puck's color-coded rack at the front door of the cookshack, which kept all the tractor, truck, and gate keys organized and eliminated the constant frustration of mismatched and misplaced keys.

I packed my duffel bag for an indefinite stay at the Blue Worm. The Open House invitation began to take shape in my mind as a large postcard with a map on the back. Brown ink would give the rustic-but-professional look I wanted, but cost more than black. En route to town that evening I cautiously asked about the budget for the invitations.

Cy replied, "What's it worth to establish Vista as the world's foremost intentional community? Fuck the money. Make something beautiful."

That night I sketched the map, typed and retyped the text, and got three hours of sleep. In the morning I called print shops in Denver to order typestyle catalogues and paper samples that included exotic colors and textures.

When we met over breakfast at the triple-wide, Cy was far more concerned with the mailing list than the invitation itself. From the Abraham County phone book—the size of a hefty comic book—I had typed the names of Keystone's thirty heads-of-household. Elsie provided the names of a hundred people who had attended Beverly Hills Marathons. When we added Cy's close professional associates from her rolodex, the list felt unwieldy with two hundred and eighty names.

After lunch several thousand more entries were added when Cy decided to invite the members of the American Psychiatric and Psychological Associations, and the Association for Humanistic Psychology. Elsie recruited typists to prepare mailing labels. Elizabeth, bored with scrubbing shitter walls, set up a typewriter next to my desk in the Blue Worm.

In my daily meetings with Cy, the Open House invitation evolved from a postcard into a ten-page booklet. "Make this invitation a first-class brochure," Cy said, and explained that most people wouldn't attend the event, but the invitations would help reinforce the Ranch's growing reputation. He wanted descriptions of the *Executive Trails* program, a *Family Communications Marathon* and *Body Image Confrontation*. Willow would lead the *Yoga Institute*. The Open House, my idea, was now Cy's top priority. With each development my euphoric sense of purpose increased. The sixties had belonged to Timothy Leary. Cyrus Aaron and his young team were claiming the seventies.

I refined the rustic but precise map and purchased Keystone's first bulk-mail permit, and with a thrill I shipped the text and artwork to the printer in Denver who had come in with the highest bid but had the most impressive list of clients. Elizabeth mastered the Selectric with minimal instruction and typed most of the six thousand address labels. Moved by her eagerness to please, I saw myself in her. When her fingers swelled from typing, or my ear ached from talking on the phone, we whistled for Wolfie and went for long walks.

One afternoon she led me through the tumbleweeds of Keystone's tiny cemetery and stopped at the grave of a boy who'd died in Vietnam at nineteen—the age her brother Garth had been when he shot himself.

I put an arm around her shoulder, thinking of her father, who had died in the same jungles as this young soldier. "Imagine growing up here and dying half a world away."

"Imagine," she echoed, "dying in Orange County without ever seeing anything else."

Long ago Lydia had asked me, *What do you say to someone whose son has committed suicide?* "You miss your brother a lot?"

"Sure, but . . . Don't tell my mom, but I'm glad he's not suffering. Garth was miserable."

We talked of happiness and grief, life before Aaron, hopes and dreams. "Cy's the first grownup who understands I need to play and have fun," she said. "Sometimes fun means reading Spinoza, but sometimes it means playing jacks. I never want to leave the Ranch, except . . ."

"Except?"

"I want to go to art school some day."

"We'll have an art school here! The finest in the country."

"I want to go to the Royal Academy. In London."

"Huh. Just be sure to come back." I kicked a tumbleweed and it flew away. "Your turn," I shouted, and we raced off to play soccer with the dry ball of sticker-twigs while Wolfie bounded between us.

"DO WE REALLY WANT the local yokels and the Beverly Hills crowd in the same place at the same time?" Eric asked.

I sighed as silently as I could, and waited for Cy to stop scribbling in his tiny spiral notebook. It was after midnight. Since noon the staff had sat at the Triple-Wide's round fruitwood table, chewing on one issue after another related to the Open House. Hours earlier Elizabeth—newly welcome at meetings as the "staff pet"—had fallen asleep in a corner, wrapped in an afghan. Eric's question threatened to keep us up all night.

Dozens of details had to be coördinated at each meeting, and Cy supervised all decisions. Today he'd vetoed Travis's plan to have the children groom the horses on the morning of the big day, and instead designated Teddy. She owned three of the horses and would want them to look their best. He determined that Dr. Folsom, the health inspector, should drive his own vehicle onto the Ranch—but with Vistan passengers to recount the Ranch's history. He directed that just before the event, new holes should be dug for the shitters, and cottonwoods planted in the old holes. On top of everything else, Travis's crew would complete the geodesic dome.

I smiled when Cy turned to me and said, "This whole thing was your idea. What's your answer to Eric?"

"It's a good question," I conceded. "Let's do it in stages—a big buffet lunch for everybody, and a tour of the tipis. The locals, especially Dr. Folsom, will be impressed by the sophisticated professionals who send us clients. And the Beverly Hills people will see the salt-of-the-earth folks who—. Well, at least they'll see the rednecks we have to deal with. If the inspector's an asshole, we're fucked no matter who else is at the Ranch that day."

The others nodded.

"Around sundown the locals can head back to town and we'll fire up the sweatlodge for the folks with Ph.D.s. The Executive Trail can start the next day."

Cy agreed, and Eric let it rest.

"One last thing," Cy said. "Today, Steve, I received a call from an old friend of yours."

"Inscrutable even at midnight," I quipped, wondering with a thump in my heart if Lydia had called. "Do tell."

"Dr. Nathan Turner. Orange County Probation approved his son's transfer to Rancho Vista. He asked if we're going to accept the kid. Please help us make an informed decision."

I sat up straight and briefly explained my history with Dr. Turner. "The son of a bitch damn near electrocuted my friend Rupert. But his son Tobey is a growth case."

Cy's eyebrows rose high. "*Really?*"

"He reminds me of myself before I found you. Scared shitless, doesn't know he has any choice but to suffer."

Ken confirmed my impression that Tobey was a sincere, bright boy with a chance at rehabilitation. Cy snapped me a military salute. "Sign up Tobey and his parents for the Family Communications Marathon. Their session will christen the Group Dome."

The staff nodded in unison.

"We're like Congress," I observed. "If you want to get something passed, propose it at midnight. Everybody'll vote for it so they can go home."

EACH MORNING I CALLED the answering service in Beverly Hills and transcribed messages from all over the world. Many messages were from reporters eager to do interviews with Cy. "Could you get me in touch with the young man who was contemplating suicide?" one asked. Apparently, Nelson Christopher had been spreading the word.

My parents left no message. I began to believe my father meant what he'd said—*"You can forget you ever had a family."* Their twenty-fifth wedding anniversary was a week away. I'd planned to send them an Open House invitation with a congratulatory note inside. Instead I added the new callers to the invitation list, and removed Susi and Alex.

The invitations arrived from Denver by overland courier. I held my breath to open the first carton. Inside I found a marvel of woodsy sophistication, printed in turquoise and brown ink on leathery, butter-yellow card stock. The cover and matching envelope were graced by the Mother River waterfall rendered in muted sepiatone, from one of Ken's photos. Inside, pictures of life at the Ranch and on Trail—including one of me helping Teddy into her rappelling harness—spoke of people who deeply trusted one another.

Cy held a sample aloft in triumph and said, "You're an artist, my son. This is the first of many brochures you'll be designing." He grasped my shoulder. "You are Rancho Vista's scribe, destined to tell the world who we are."

I smiled over this bittersweet success. The more I proved my value at the typewriter and on the telephone, the less likely I was to become a Trail leader. But I started to believe I might always have a place at Cy's side.

Once the invitations were mailed, I stayed up all one night

finishing the month's insurance reports. Elizabeth, increasingly treated like a responsible adult, typed the finals.

For weeks the Vistans worked ten-hour days, stealing moments during the sweltering afternoons to swim in the river. The cookshack team whitewashed the walls inside and out, nailed plywood over the plank floor, and lay terra cotta tile. They installed window screens and Eric's beautiful hand-crafted door, and hung Vivian's gingham curtains. One crew dismantled the sweatlodge while another weeded the roadsides and scrubbed down the smoke-stained tipi canvases. Teams hauled broken bottles, sagging box springs and other junk to the Keystone dump. Eric hid the distillery equipment in the coal bin under his tipi floor, and supervised the construction of drying racks for the fruits and vegetables.

RSVPs began to arrive within a few days after the invitations were mailed. Nelson Christopher reached me at the Blue Worm. "I can't come to your event," he said, "but I have an important proposition for you."

What the hell, no one was listening, so I joked, "You're propositioning me?"

"Don't tease an older man. We're starting an intentional community down here. A group of gay therapists. We have ten acres in Topanga Canyon. Not like your wilderness, but it's beautiful. We'll be doing weekend workshops, encounter groups, sensitivity training. I'd like you to visit and help us get established. We can pay you a nice consultancy fee."

"Thank you," I said, imagining I heard the crocodile licking his chops. "But—"

"Surely Dr. Aaron could allow you a month's sabbatical. Rancho Vista's not a cult, is it?"

"I'll ask Cy," I lied.

I'D BEEN WORKING IN THE BLUE WORM for more days than I could count, sleeping on a foam pad I rolled out from under my desk. I ate bread, eggs and cheese and an occasional plate of leftover spaghetti or roast turkey from Travis. On a cloudy Friday, with only a few phone calls left to make, I was eagerly looking forward to a noisy dinner at the cookshack when Zoë phoned. She invited me next door to the triple-wide for a private meal, "So Cy and I may thank you for your *hard* work."

Not since my first day in Keystone had I been alone with her and Cy. I hoped to hold up my end of the conversation without becoming a therapy case. For the first time since Beverly Hills, I dressed in a silky shirt and nice trousers.

Inside the door of the triple-wide, a brew of exotic spices enticed me toward the kitchen. I called out, "Yum!" and Wolfie approached with his tail wagging fiercely. I knelt to scratch his ears and submitted to an enthusiastic face-licking.

Zoë greeted me wearing high heels with panty hose and a scanty apron, her large erect nipples having their way around the lacy straps. "Calamari, Etienne! I hope you like it." She handed me a steaming wooden spoon. "No *begging*, Wolfie," she laughed, and the dog obediently held himself back, though he could easily have wrenched away the spoon and my hand with it. "The sauce, it needs something. I think another dash of sherry?"

I sipped the sauce, glad I didn't taste any sherry, and pronounced it perfect, but another essence tantalized me. "Zoë, I smell—"

Cy padded down the hallway in red briefs and dress socks, and handed me a lighted joint. "You've worked hard, Steve. It's time to alter your state of consciousness."

I accepted the joint with overwhelming gratitude. I'd gone without for months, since the day I sneaked into Eric's tipi, and had wondered if I would ever be close enough to what Willow called the "inner circle" to enjoy the therapeutic pot sessions she'd mentioned. Getting stoned and relaxing with Cy and Zoë in their home was an even greater privilege.

"If you smoke the pot with Cy," Zoë said, accepting the joint from me, "your mind will *get* no rest."

The dining table was set with antique china and sterling. Tall candles burned in elaborate candelabra and the creamy linen napkins had been pressed. Zoë removed her sexy apron and sat at the table in her pantyhose and high heels. Cy remained in his briefs and socks.

The wine was a delicate Gewürztraminer. The calamari steaks were tender and rich with cilantro, lime and something Zoë called galanga. Cy continually refilled Zoë's and my wine glasses, but drank only club soda himself. As she'd promised, he challenged me to think throughout the meal, asking my opinion on the fundamental flaws in both capitalism and Marxism, the effect on society of Freud's cocaine addiction, and the inconsistencies between Old and New Testament teachings.

After a silent moment he asked me, "Do you think Machiavelli was a psychopath?"

I was feeling articulate, but didn't want to trip on something I only dimly understood. "Isn't that someone with no conscience?"

His lips tightened. "Some people believe psychopaths have *too much* conscience. It overwhelms them." His brows bunched over his eyes and he stared into the wine bottle.

Zoë gave me an "I told you so" wink. Even without pot, Cy would challenge my most cherished prejudices. Stoned, he made me question everything. Did he believe I was a psychopath? Or that *he* might be one?

"Nicolo is thoroughly misunderstood," I opined, eager to rescue our conversation. "He was like you, Cy. He didn't advocate the evil that men do, he merely observed and described it, like a botanist detailing the invasive habits of that passion-flower vine in your atrium. We've rewarded his honesty by calling every petty political intrigue 'Machiavellian.' In the same spirit we tag totalitarian regimes 'Orwellian' because poor George wrote *Nineteen Eighty-Four.*"

Delight shone in Cy's face. "I've longed for someone to talk with like this." He raised his glass. "Here's to the day you kicked over that pail of carburetors outside our bedroom window."

Zoë declined my help in cleaning up after dinner. She ignored the dishes and asked Cy, "Is the Jacuzzi heating up, darling?"

"It's ready."

I took this as my signal to leave. I sat on the floor to put on my shoes, scratched Wolfie's ears and said, "G'night, buddy."

"Etienne," Zoë said. "Will you not join us?"

Already overwhelmed by the honors I'd received this evening, I tried to answer casually. "I guess I could stay a few minutes." I followed her into the bedroom, undressed and folded my clothes, then splashed into the hot tub after her and Cy. The water was wonderfully soothing. I tried to think of a worthy follow-up to my comments on Machiavelli.

After a silent moment, Cy said, "This beats stealing herb from Eric's tipi, I hope."

"Thanks for reminding me of my most shameful moment."

Zoë giggled. "He is so helpful, not to let us forget our times of weakness." In a Garboesque purr she added, "So very helpful— *Meester M.*"

I felt as if an electric current had shot through the water. For an instant I was back in Eric's tipi, poring over journals in greedy astonishment, reading about his stud service for "Mr. M's" wife.

"Just doing my job, Mrs. M," Cy answered.

I ducked under the hot bubbling water and held my breath for as long as I could. This meant Eric had balled Zoë. Part of his sexual surrogate duties? I surged out of the water and hoisted myself onto the lip of the small pool. "I feel like a boiled lobster." Wolfie began licking me.

Cy crinkled his eyes at me. "You couldn't have spent all those hours reading Eric's journals without encountering references to Mr. and Mrs. M."

"You guys?"

"How does that make you feel?"

"It's not my business." The more casual I tried to sound, the tighter my voice became.

"It *ees* your business, Etienne," Zoë said.

Cy nodded. "Poor Eric. He's not cut out to be a sexual surrogate. Gets his own needs into things. A sexual surrogate is a professional who focuses entirely on the client's needs."

I nodded as if this made perfect sense, and suddenly it did. I had been a client, that long-ago night with Eric in Perdido Valley. The session had triggered mistaken hopes of love, but since then my understanding had ripened and matured. Eric had put his own needs aside to serve me.

"I'm not a whole man," Cy said with gravity, and climbed out of the tub. "You can see I have a penis, a rather nice one as they go. Thank God I wasn't mutilated at birth like many American boys of my generation. But it's been years since my stint in the Navy, where my nickname was Hatrack."

"Hatrack?" I repeated, at a loss for a snappy reply, and followed Zoë out of the tub.

"Because my cock was so hard before my first piss of the morning, I could hang my sailor's cap on it. No longer. It's become unreliable. A far more common problem than you might imagine. Oh, Zoë and I can still make love. I lay my poor floppy cock against her lovely box and press the vibrator on top of it. She has thunderous orgasms and tells me I'm the best lover in the world. But there's nothing like the real thing, and that's where you come in."

Nervously I realized that Eric, amazingly well-equipped for sex, had failed somehow at the job now being offered to me. My stomach tightened. Zoë was lovely, but I saw her as my adopted mother, or a sister. What if I couldn't get aroused?

She lit candles and incense in the bedroom. Should I watch or turn away while Cy kissed and stroked her? The two of them whispered and giggled together, then she held out a hand to me. I kissed it and knelt at her side. Cy suckled at her breasts, then nuzzled down to her furry mound, his body in the attitude of prayer.

I closed my eyes and pictured Eric in this role, imagined his swelling eagerness. Zoë clutched my hand and gasped. My cock began to stiffen. Cy lay at her side and she drew me nearer.

"I come up short beside Eric," I joked. Zoë laughed, and praised my springy cock.

"May I stroke your breasts?" I asked, with a feeling of reverence.

"*Mais oui*," she cooed. "You have a *gentle* touch. But I kiss only Cy."

She guided me closer, and I knelt before her as at a sacred altar. Cy reached to stroke my cock before it entered his wife. "I must work through you now," he said. "And don't suck around for sympathy because your cock isn't as big as Eric's. I'd trade twenty IQ points for a cock as hard as yours. Our Eric is a freak of nature."

Cy guided me. Zoë's soft, juicy labia slipped open, and I entered her slowly.

"Etienne!" she exclaimed. "Your cock feels *so* alive."

I slowly buried myself in her, waited until I felt Cy's hand pushing against my abdomen to pull out, and followed as Cy guided and timed my thrusts and withdrawals.

Cy moved away and I heard a sudden, loud electric hum. He had switched on an enormous vibrator, like a child's baseball bat. He stimulated his cock with it while he watched Zoë and me from every angle. Wolfie hopped onto the bed. Zoë giggled and sang out, "No *begging*, Wolfie," and he jumped back to the floor. The vibrator clicked off, and Cy's Polaroid flashed from one angle, then another.

Several times Cy kissed Zoë, deeply and slowly, and sucked at her nipples. I saw that my job was indeed to provide a reliably hard cock while they made love. What had Eric done to forfeit this place of honor?

Zoë moaned softly, giggled and babbled French baby-talk to Cy. I gave up trying to maintain eye contact with her. At times I felt they wouldn't notice if I left the room, except that her body danced with mine on the bed, and her slippery, silken pussy gripped my cock in spasms while she and Cy kissed and cooed.

She cried out and dug her fingers into my buttocks, then wept with Cy after the crescendo of what appeared to be her third orgasm.

When Cy pulled away slightly, I asked, "Shall I stop?"

"*No*, Etienne," Zoë answered. "Please have the *orgasm* inside me."

Free of concern about performing for her pleasure, I imagined Eric in my place. Riding the wave toward my own climax, I remained aware of Zoë, her need to be held and noticed, and gazed into her lovely face. I came in one long, slow, moaning thrust, careful not to collapse on her. Finally, gingerly, I withdrew with a deep sigh.

"Still hard as a rock," Cy observed. " 'If youth but knew, if old age but could.' "

"Estienne," I said, recognizing the quote, then sheepishly added, "Or Mark Twain?"

"It's Estienne and you know it. Zoë, the kid's a stud and an intellectual, but guilty of false modesty on both counts."

I smiled shyly, amazed that I'd succeeded as the sexual stand-in for the world's most brilliant therapist. Suddenly Wolfie planted his front paws on the bed and hungrily sniffed at my cock. "Wolfie, no!" I shouted.

"Steve," Cy admonished. "Wolfie hasn't studied Leviticus and doesn't understand about abominations. What you've got on your cock is far more interesting to him than the kibble in his bowl. Don't let your conditions of worth deny him a taste."

"Conditions of what?" Would the challenges ever stop? The dog tongued the semen residue that welled at the tip of my cock.

"You met Standal in L.A., the Positive Regard guy. His mentor, Carl Rogers, got all the credit for 'Positive Regard' because Stan never published his theory. So much for mentors." He gave me a crooked smile. "Anyway, your social training says you're *bad* if you have sexual contact with a beast. Thus your self-worth is conditional. The first step toward giving unconditional love to others is giving it to yourself. And you're *not* having a sexual encounter with Wolfie. This isn't bestiality."

I watched while the dog lapped away the sticky juices. My cock remained erect and this was starting to look very much like a sexual encounter. I fished for something else to say. "But isn't our conditioning the only thing that holds society together?"

"Could society be any worse off?" Cy countered. "The Inquisition and the Holocaust were fueled by conditions of worth.

Likewise the cataloguing of same-sex love as mental illness."

Zoë had been right. Cy would never let my mind rest.

Wolfie finally completed his cleanup project and Zoë led me to the guest bathroom. In the shower I wondered if people lived like this anywhere else in the world. And I knew I would never stop learning from Cy, whose ability to affirm the woman he loved was a goal worthy of the greatest growth case.

Yet I also knew I wouldn't tell anyone about my evening with Mr. and Mrs. M. Even more than the memory of having helped them, I would cherish their trust. They seemed to know they didn't need to ask for my discretion.

17

I HIKED FROM TOWN AT DAWN and sat outside my tipi. The gardens and fields were verdant, the vehicles parked in neat diagonal rows. The horses trotted through the pastures holding high their freshly-brushed tails. Even the goats looked respectable in the whitewashed paddock. There was no sign of a sweatlodge, and the early-morning bathers at the waterfall wore their best approximations of swimming suits. The new Group Dome, with its gleaming skylights and wild skin of shingled triangles, had landed like a spaceship on a plateau overlooking the orchard. The team designated by Travis as the "sanitation specialists" had painted the shitters snowy enamel inside and out, and installed slammers. Other workers had lined the floors with tile left over from the cookshack, and shingled the roofs.

RSVPs had poured in from prominent therapists, business leaders and the Nobel Prize-winning dean of Rutherford College. The health inspector and other locals would get in on a feast, then the executives would spend a night in the Pasha's domain before embarking into the wilderness for Trail. I smiled, thinking of ten acres in Topanga, Nelson Christopher's smoggy pretend wilderness fostering a pretend community.

Dr. Folsom of the Health Department arrived as scheduled at eight o'clock, bringing Cy and Zoë in his blue Dodge pickup. The other Vistans and I gathered on the cookshack porch and released the breath we'd been holding since dawn. The inspector was small and bespectacled, almost totally bald, with a sweet face and broad smile. A bureaucrat perhaps, but a good-natured and fair-looking man.

"That's some road you've got there," Folsom called out to the assembled Vistans.

Travis wore a new apron and had tucked his ponytail under an amazingly clean white cap. "Shoulda seen it before we filled in the potholes," he shouted back, then opened his arms. "Breakfast's still on. Lunch won't be 'til one, when the rest of our guests arrive." He introduced himself, led Folsom inside and asked pointedly, "Coffee?"

"Black, please."

Another near-silent sigh passed among us. Folsom's choice of beverage meant he wasn't a Mormon, at least not a strict one.

Most Vistans had already eaten and moved outside. Folsom ate with the staff. Travis served one unheard-of delicacy after another—sausages, French toast with Vista honey, hash browns with catsup. Cy prompted staff members to tell bits of their stories. Willow talked about her days as an exploited rock 'n roll groupie, Eric about his conviction for sale of controlled substances to an undercover officer. Ken skimmed over his father's brutal beatings and the eventual family breakthrough. Already introduced as "a nineteen-year-old Columbia grad," I mentioned my suicidal depression and a string of vague failures. Our guest asked respectful questions that revealed a gentle nature.

Teddy helped out as a waitress, having retired her usual indifference for the day. She had grumbled when Cy asked her not to wear her white leather miniskirt—"But it fits me now since I lost all that weight." In a shirtwaist dress borrowed from Elsie, and with the straw blonde cut out of her hair, she looked and spoke like a mature young woman. Indeed, she'd lost over twenty pounds since her body image. Only the teardrop tattoo reminded me of the overweight street kid she had been until so recently. She spooned Dr. Folsom more hash browns and teased, "You've got a healthy appetite."

While people scraped their trays over the compost barrel, Cy took me aside and assumed a confidential tone. "I asked Willow to accompany Dr. Folsom on his tour of the Ranch. But he's forty-three and never been married. I think he may be more up your alley. Why don't you join them?"

"You mean you think he's gay?"

"Son, you haven't rocketed to your position in this organization through naïveté. Use your wondrous intuition."

Folsom clutched a metal clipboard thick with forms. He asked to see the sanitary facilities first, and Willow and I led him to one of the shitters. After studying the interior for a moment he remarked, "That wedge wasn't in the original design. What is that thing?"

"We bought the outhouses second-hand from the Forest Service," Willow said, and nodded to me.

I explained, "Dr. Aaron designed the wedge to discourage flies." I smiled and added, "We call it the Aaron Slammer."

Folsom winked me. "Ingenious."

"I've got some pies to check in the oven," Willow lied. "No men may enter the kitchen until the pies are ready. Dr. Folsom,

Steve will show you the culinary system."

Hiking to the spring, I wondered if she'd acted on instructions from Cy when she contrived an excuse to leave me alone with the inspector, or had simply employed her own wondrous intuition. Was I supposed to snuggle up to Folsom at the cistern? This seemed to be carrying the sexual surrogate business too far.

I demonstrated the filtration valves while Folsom's fascination burned into me. Of course Cy was right. The inspector was a middle-aged gay guy, deeply closeted in a hick town.

Folsom's eyes gleamed. "You'll need to submit periodic water samples to my office," he said, then added almost apologetically, "As a formality. No reason to think this spring's not safe."

"Yes, we've thought of bottling our water as a cottage industry. But Dr. Aaron keeps reminding us we're here for personal growth and not to make money." Good thing the Rolls was parked in a windowless garage in town.

I led him toward the holding pond, understanding now that my job was to fascinate, perhaps to make myself available for seduction—Eric's job when he asked me to share the bathtub in Perdido Valley. I said smoothly, "I want to show you the irrigation system, but would you like to see the inside of a tipi? We'll be passing near mine."

"I thought you'd never ask."

Inside my high, round home Folsom sighed deeply. "Nothing here is as it appears." He fingered the ivy that cascaded from a hanging pot, as if to make sure it was real. "I'm ashamed to admit this. When I heard you lived in tipis, the word 'squalor' came to my mind. At best, I imagined a sleeping bag and a Coleman lantern." He sat on the double bed and stroked the velvet spread, took in with wide eyes the worn but exotic tribal rugs, the Victorian armoire and hurricane lamps, the shelves of hardback books.

I pushed the Play button on my cassette player. The voice of Maria Callas sailed into the "Sempre libera" aria from *La Traviata*—a shock, because I'd left *Rubber Soul* in the machine. Had someone planted classical tapes in the tipis where guests were scheduled to stay? "Willow," I said absently, answering my own unspoken question, then caught myself: "Willow has a Louis-the-Sixteenth desk in her tipi."

"Sempre libera," Folsom said slowly. "That could be your theme song here. *Always Free.*" He seemed to shake himself out of a trance and knelt before the stove, which served as a pedestal for a bushy fern. "This pot-belly keeps you warm during the winter?"

"With coal. It burns all night." I realized that this sensitive, educated man, trapped in a backwater, was starved for the freedom the Vistans took for granted. *You got him onto your bed,* I imagined Cy asking later. *And then?*

Callas continued singing while I escorted Folsom into the sunshine. From this elevation I indicated the holding pond below us, and the stream that fed it. Travis drove the gleaming dump truck on a shuttle run to the parking area at the bottom of the Ranch.

As Dr. Folsom and I hiked down the hill, I sidestepped a question about why the Ranch had no showers. "We only use biodegradable soap in the stream," I ad-libbed, then realized I must tell a direct lie to avoid tricky questions. "The new showers'll be built before fall. We'll hook them up to the two hundred-gallon water heater in the cookhouse." Folsom's face still seemed to hold an unasked question, and I tried to anticipate it with an even more imaginative fabrication: "We'll install the flush toilets then, too." This received a nod and satisfied smile.

Even before Cy met me, I thought, he knew I'd be good at this.

Above the river bank I bent low to demonstrate how a culvert funneled water into the sprinkler-intake valves. How wondrous did my intuition have to be to know the inspector was admiring my hairy legs and perky ass in my tight white shorts? I straightened up and turned to face the man.

His eyes fixed on the outline of my cock. Casually I leaned back against the culvert housing. This is innocent, I told myself. I'm not unzipping my pants, just letting him enjoy a look. But I genuinely liked this man, and presenting myself as an object of pornography unsettled me.

With a quick turn I led up the steep, uneven ridge beyond the culvert. Folsom stumbled and I grasped his forearms. The inspector gazed into my eyes, then righted himself, blushed, apologized and asked to see the compost pit and gardens.

While we continued past the beehives, he talked non-stop about the county politics that dominated his life. I gave him a few sympathetic grunts, then recalled that the ear was the most powerful organ in the human body. I began to chuckle as if appreciating the one-sided conversation. Folsom smiled, clearly believing his listener was entertained by a story about a Health Department secretary who mistook a colored condom for a child's balloon.

We walked through the immaculate gardens and past the compost pit, which usually out-stank the shitters but just last night had been aerated with fresh straw and saturated with perfumed fly spray. Finally approaching the cookshack, I showed Folsom the pristine goat pens.

I had saved the root cellar for the end of the tour. In the dim, cool space Dr. Folsom marveled at the pulley system that kept the bins of onions and potatoes hanging safe from rodents. "You're doing a wonderful thing here," he said, and grasped my shoulder. "You've more than met my agency's requirements for a residential facility license." His breath closed in on me. "You're a fine young man. I'm so glad you found Dr. Aaron, that he delivered you from—whatever made you to want to die." His hand relaxed and slowly slid toward my neck.

I could let him kiss me, I thought. But I felt touched by his sincerity and hoped I wouldn't have to adopt the sexual surrogate role. "Thank you," I said. "Dr. Aaron saved my life."

The door flew open, and Dr. Folsom recoiled from me. Framed by the harsh daylight, the eight-year-old Mikey burst in with Wolfie. The boy cried, "My mom's makin' more lemonade!" and began filling a basket with lemons. "Travis is almost back with the last load of people. Lots more locals than we expected."

"I believe I'll conduct a more personal inspection of that Slammer," Folsom said, and ducked outside.

"I'll meet you in the cookhouse," I called after him.

Travis parked near the holding pond among a number of unfamiliar vehicles, including an Army Jeep. Our men helped visiting women down from the back of the truck. Children leaped to the ground and ran toward the pond, where Lucky stood ready to act as lifeguard. He intervened gently when a small boy chucked a rock at the swans.

I was about to join the group for casual introductions when Travis walked toward me, muttering. We stepped together to one side of the cookshack porch. He asked, "Do you know that gal in the safari suit, lecturing everybody?"

I followed his gaze to a woman standing with her back to us. A large group gave her their full attention. She had shapely legs and wore hiking boots and a crisp khaki safari suit. A few wisps of blonde hair trailed from under her pith helmet.

I shook my head.

"At the Ranch gate she sounded like a tour guide," Travis said, "reciting things about Cy I'd never heard. Like he was a Fulbright scholar? I didn't know what that was, but she explained it for us."

I listened for her voice above the song of the river and the screaming of the visitors' children. She spoke slowly and seemed to choose each word carefully. From behind the Jeep appeared a muscular man I recognized: no-more-garbage Josh lugged several pieces of expensive-looking luggage that included two big hat boxes. He set these down, disappeared and came back with an enormous drum case, then returned with a few small ones.

"That woman wants my job," I said.

Travis scratched his chin. "Acts like she's after Zoë's."

Should I take control and welcome her, or let her make the first move? She and Josh hadn't RSVP'd for the Open House. Had they told Cy they were arriving this weekend for their six months of therapy? And had Cy declined to pass this information on, sensing how threatened I was by Charley? I would never ask. If I admitted disliking her, Cy would want to process that in Group. Then she would realize her power over me.

TRAVIS HAD PREPARED A BUFFET WORTHY OF A LAS VEGAS CASINO, with roast venison and fresh trout among the steaming meats. He hadn't counted on the good will of the Keystone housewives, who bore a bounty of casseroles and pastries. After a quick consultation with Cy, he had the kids stash some of his delicacies in the root cellar. I smiled at Cy's sensitive cunning: it was more important to let the locals feel their contribution was valued than for us to show off our own feast.

Dr. Folsom presided over the kitchen and showed visitors how well the propane refrigerators worked. "It's ninety-two degrees outside, but there's a layer of ice on this milk," he said. The Keystone grandmothers murmured approvingly.

Outside, Charley still had her mouth going. A woman I recognized from the Beverly Hills Marathon stood beside a mountain of matched leather luggage, fussing over a spot of pond mud a visitor's dog had spattered onto her fine high-heeled boots. Willow headed toward her, but Charley got there first—striding, I thought, as if she owned the place.

"You can get your boots polished back in the city, Dr. Fitzimmons," she said lightly. "Surely you won't waste your time in the wilderness trying to stay clean! Moments with Dr. Aaron are rare treasures."

From anyone else these words would have warmed my heart.

But they chilled me because I sensed Charley's fascination disguised ferocious ambition.

She turned and bee-lined toward me. "Steve, I wondered when I'd get to see you."

Wanting to ask how much she and her husband were going to pay for their therapy program, I managed a polite, "Wow, you're finally here" with a limp smile and matching hug. I endured her examination of my hair—"Overdue for a trim," she opined—and asked how her trip had been,. then gladly passed her off to Willow.

The visitors toured the grounds surrounding the cookshack. Local women commented on the rich soil in the terraced gardens, and applauded Eric's apple-sized radishes. Luke Buford, the crimson-necked sheriff of Abraham County, inspected the irrigation system with Travis.

Charley's husband Josh chatted with the ranchers as if he'd grown up among them. Before anyone could stop him, he made plans to bring Vistans on an elk-hunting party. "Bow season next week? Count us in," he told Dove MacKenzie's father.

Travis sounded the gong and a crowd gathered on the grassy patch in front of the cookshack for a question-and-answer session. Lucky responded to a rancher's curiosity about the irrigation system and explained that a Pontiac transmission had been rigged up to handle the pump's fluctuating demands.

Another rancher muttered to a buddy, "Pitiful."

Cy overheard, and turned to the men with a disarming smile. "Not too impressed by our alfalfa, fellahs?"

A woman's voice pierced the murmurs. "Some of us are plenty impressed, Dr. Aaron." This was Nina MacKenzie, whose son Dove had picked me up the night I hitchhiked into the wilderness. He nodded at her side.

Cy waved to her and went on. "Puck over there is in charge of maintaining the pump. Do any of you remember him from a few years back, when he wandered down off the mountain where he'd been looking for magic mushrooms?"

"Oh, we remember him, all right." Nina laughed, and several in the crowd joined her. Puck put on his sanest smile and appeared to enjoy the good-natured teasing.

Cy looked directly at the rancher who had ridiculed the irrigation system. "Puck had been diagnosed as a schizophrenic—a crazy person, useless and maybe dangerous. His family and a team of psychiatrists had given up on him. We found him living like a caveman on the mountain. Would you have put Puck in charge of irrigation two years ago?"

"It's a miracle, Dr. Aaron," Nina said. She was giving her blessing where it counted, among her people.

"It *is* a miracle," agreed Dr. Folsom, "that anything besides sagebrush grows here."

Cy now spoke softly. "We don't measure our success by counting up bushels of tomatoes or tons of hay. This is a people farm. Our success bears fruit in Puck and the other kids who came here from psych wards, kids who jammed needles into their arms, or who'd been left to rot in jail. Our primary purpose is not to grow hay, but we appreciate advice from neighbors who grow it better than we do."

Sheriff Buford removed his hat in an unmistakable gesture of respect. Tears welled in my eyes. I'd never believed in God, but surely something larger than myself had led me here.

The Vistans ate side-by-side with the guests, at picnic tables in the shade of a cottonwood grove. "I'd like to offer a toast," Dr. Folsom said, and raised his Mason jar of lemonade to the crowd. "This land was sacred to the ancient Anasazi. They left walls of picture-writing on cliffs throughout the Southwest, a few graves and grain-storage caves, and little else but stray arrowheads and pottery shards. Those ancients thrived in this fertile valley where the river divides, and disappeared nearly a thousand years ago. No one knows why they left. Getting along was hard then, and it's hard today. Dr. Aaron, your community has brought this land back to life. Long may you thrive here."

The Vistans and our visitors cheered. Cy gave me a smile that said, *Whatever you did to that guy, it worked.*

I WALKED WITH FOLSOM TO HIS PICKUP, carrying a box of specimen jars filled with water samples. The inspector clutched a bag of food Vivian had packed for him. He reached down with his free hand to pet Wolfie.

I handed him the jars. "Visit us any time."

"I wish I could live here." The glimmer was gone from his eyes. He was shutting down. In a businesslike manner he shook my hand, climbed into his truck and drove away.

Locals packed their picnic baskets for the trip back to town. Already the Vistan kids were gathering rocks for the sweatlodge.

A motorcycle appeared just past the swale and roared toward

the cookshack. When the bike passed the final turn, I saw the rider was a large man with long hair.

"Did we invite the Hell's Angels?" Cy asked me.

I shook my head, bewildered. The Harley pulled up beside the holding pond. The rider killed the engine and hopped off, combing back his hair with his fingers, which glinted with numerous rings.

"My God," I murmured. A ghost had come to life.

"Friend of yours?" asked Cy.

"Rupert!" I squealed, and ran to throw my arms around him. "I was afraid you were dead."

Rupe hoisted me high in the air as an uncle would do with a tiny child, then caught me and held me tight. I hung on with my legs around his waist, my eyes clenched shut. The scent of patchouli intoxicated me. "Rupe, how the hell—?"

"I'll tell you all about it by and by, li'l buddy."

His tone was firm, both promising and disappointing, but the joy of seeing him, holding him, smelling him, was enough for now. Something in the way he hung on said he wasn't leaving soon.

I slid to the ground as Zoë and Cy approached, and introduced them, adding, "These people saved my life."

Rupert mustered an attitude of elegance in his ratty jeans and sleeveless shirt, and bowed low to kiss Zoë's hand.

"Etienne is not the only *gen*tleman of his generation." She laughed while Rupert shook Cy's hand with the same dignity.

I grinned and looked heavenward, spied a high-flying hawk and muttered, "Thank you" to the sky. No one in the world could have surprised or pleased me more. I deeply missed Lydia but she was surely all right wherever she was. Rupert, though, had joined Dean on my list of people who had been martyred by my selfishness. I gazed into the big, cheerful face and was jarred to see that he had continued to scratch the welts left by his shock treatment. Dr. Turner's sadism had left permanent scars.

Charley stood at the edge of the cookshack porch with her arms folded, watching the scene with a sour expression, eyes hidden behind big Hollywood sunglasses, her perfect red nails like bloody talons. My gut tightened, but even she couldn't ruin this moment.

WEEKS OF LABOR unrelieved by music or joy juice had left the Vistans ready for a celebration. As soon as the truck carrying the last locals rolled beyond the swale, Travis's crew began reconstructing the sweatlodge.

The sunset made a promising start with vivid coral streaks across a ripple of high clouds. Willow gathered the women and led them to her tipi for the pre-party. Rupe slung an arm around my shoulder and watched them skip hand-in-hand up the road. He squeezed me and exclaimed, "Let's go with *them!*"

"We're not invited. The women'll listen to Vivaldi and drink champagne and put on sexy lingerie. We'll stay here and chisel the barnacles out of our armpits, and if we're lucky they'll dance with us later."

"There's dancing here?"

"You won't believe what's here."

CY AND ZOË'S TIPI WAS A SANCTUARY with a sprawling deck and the Ranch's best view of the round canyon. Even their new sexual surrogate had never been invited inside, but tonight they opened it to everyone. Travis's crew lugged up champagne and storebought liquor, homemade beer and Joy Juice, as well as Josh's complete drum set.

I hiked to the party with Eric and Rupert. Torches lined the final hundred feet of the path, as if lighting the way to a sultan's dwelling. Elizabeth rushed over. A garland of evening primroses cascaded through her curled hair, and she wore only a length of yellow batiked silk over her slight frame. Turquoise eye shadow, glitter blush and crimson lip gloss made her look playfully glamorous. She threw her arms out to Eric and me for hugs, then hesitated when Rupe loomed at my side.

"Don't be afraid," I said. "My buddy's a very gentle giant."

Shyly she reached for his hand. "You must be the tallest man in the world."

"You must be the tiniest lady," he answered.

She giggled. "I'm only twelve."

Through the filmy fabric I saw the buds of nubile breasts on her narrow chest. "You look like you're ready for the sacrifice of the vestal virgins," I remarked, trying to be funny, but her look of pubescent whorishness disturbed me.

Executives and other special guests sat in leather chairs inside the white-carpeted tipi, sipping martinis and scotch, while the dancing and serious drinking happened on the deck. Most women wore some version of Elizabeth's sari. Apparently Willow had brought out trunks full of exotic fabrics. Dr. Fitzimmons, a horsy woman who had arrived wearing a mannish suit, was transformed: in pink satin, with her hair curled and cheeks brightly rouged, she looked ten years younger. Pheasant feathers bloomed from her hair at erratic angles.

Out on the terraced deck, the musicians set up while Mason jars of yellow Joy Juice passed from hand to hand. Josh proved to be a surprisingly good drummer, maintaining rhythm for the other players without demanding attention as a soloist. Outside the luxurious tipi, the band created a hot cloud while they dug into each other's styles—rockabilly, Delta Blues, dirty bop, Streets of San Francisco, junk and acid rock. One song cascaded into the next as Eric and Rupert took turns playing lead and rhythm guitar. Ken's sax wailed, and Willow's clear soprano echoed through the canyon. Teddy shook a tambourine with wild, head-tossing glee.

By the time the half-moon rose over the far cliffs, Cy was the only person still sober. He led a circle dance and called repeatedly for his favorite dance number, "Rollin' on the River." The usually-dowdy Elsie wove among the guests to refill champagne glasses. She sported Cleopatra eye-makeup and a swath of sheer fabric that showed off her anything-but-dowdy breasts. Bodies gyrated in the tipi, around the deck and on the surrounding ledges of smooth rock. The women had worn little enough to begin with, and now many of the men shed their shirts.

While the party rocketed on, Cy and Zoë attended to each guest. They meandered through the gathering, and with alarm I recognized their strategy: they brought Willow together with the chairman of an architectural consortium, Vivian with the president of an airline, and, amazingly, Teddy with Lawrence Beckett, the dean of Rutherford College. Cy summoned Eric to Gertrude Fitzimmons' side. The equine psychiatrist's makeup gave her the mirthful radiance of an aging female impersonator. With blazing charm, Eric asked her to dance.

I knew too much simply to get drunk and let the evening pass. I had to watch myself slide into my shit, becoming depressed, preoccupied, pissed off. Even Teddy and Vivian were assigned to important guests, and Rupert was part of the entertainment, but I wandered, useless after the departure of my object of seduction, the health inspector. The reporter Wanda Richter, clothed in scarves, seemed eager to practice her Salome dance on me. I excused myself, walked off and whistled for Wolfie.

When the dog and I looked down from a ledge of the moonlit rock, I recognized Charley at the edge of the deck, sipping champagne alone. Among the women, only she, with her tasteful makeup and simple cocktail dress, would have fit in at a party beyond the pastures of Rancho Vista. She seemed to study the bonfire that raged near the sweatlodge, or perhaps her gaze followed the twin silver ribbons of the river. Did her remote expression reflect disdain for the women in their asinine getups, or dismay that she couldn't loosen up with them?

On a bench in the shadows, Teddy and Dr. Beckett were necking. "Snagged herself a Nobel Prize-winner," I muttered to Wolfie, and felt deeply lonely when the band played "Michelle" and couples slow-danced by torchlight.

Elizabeth shuffled the children off to bed. Soon after, Travis rang the gong. The sweatlodge rocks were ready. I dreaded the goings-on, but couldn't stay away. We Vistans and our amazed guests streamed down the hill toward the leaping bonfire, where silks and feathers dropped to the sand along with shirts and trousers.

Outside the sweatlodge, Eric was using his flopping dick to recruit Gertrude Fitzimmons, and she couldn't take her glitter-shadowed eyes off it. Teddy was recruiting Dr. Beckett with her womanly breasts. Willow and Vivian were recruiting two executives—not with body parts, but with well-honed listening skills. Both middle-aged men talked on about their problems, their fears and frustrations, the lack of fulfillment in their outwardly successful lives. The two Vistan women nodded and asked questions that began, "So you feel . . ."

"Are we ready?" Travis asked. Everyone roared in the affirmative. Puck closed the door flap and Travis trickled water onto the rocks, so a gust of steam filled the low space. We gasped. The rocks faded, then regained their glow. "More?"

I could barely breathe but I screamed, "*Yes!*" with the others, and Travis splashed on enough water to spew volumes of steam. The crowd squealed, howled and moaned. A bucket of cold water with a ladle was passed around, to be splashed over sweating heads. Jugs of frigid homemade beer went from hand to hand and were guzzled. Fingers caressed my chest, slithered over my nipples and tickled my abdomen, then moved to knead my swelling cock. I didn't reach to reciprocate. Imagining that Eric was teasing me was preferable to learning it was someone else.

Cy began to sing, "Rollin', rollin' . . ." Willow picked up the melody of *Proud Mary*. A cold bottle of beer pressed against my leg. I drained it. Next came a jug, and I gulped down all I could. A light beam shone through the pearly steam. We screamed, "No!" Puck was the offender, and quickly surrendered his flashlight to Travis. The light shone long enough for me to recognize Eric's engorged recruitment tool across the way. Darkness was essential for the anonymity of the slithering hands, the Vistans' rare opportunity for leaving any unturned stones.

Finally I was about to explode. I flung aside the tarp that sealed the entryway and leaped into the icy pond, followed by a whooping crowd. I swam to the far end and climbed out through the cattails, then stumbled off naked and drunk with Wolfie, careful to avoid kicking any prickly-pear with my bare feet. From the orchards I watched the group return to the steam with fresh shovelfuls of glowing rocks, heard the shrieks of hilarity, the sweatlodge version of "I Cain't Get No Sat-is-fac-tion." Everyone howled inside and cannonballed into the pond while the moon journeyed slow and sure across the sacred land.

Eventually couples spun off into the night, singing and laughing, and the bonfire and hilarity dwindled. I recognized Teddy hiking with Vivian to her tipi, and felt relieved that neither had gone off with a guest. Ken and Willow paired up, both swathed in silk. Travis led Wanda Richter to his tipi, then hiked to the cookshack for the night.

I planted myself in the moonshadow behind Eric's tipi and eavesdropped on his earnest grunting and the bellowing of Dr. Fitzimmons. Twice I had to shush Wolfie when he growled at the noisy revelry. Burning its way into me was a sensation even worse than jealousy: the knowledge that I was exactly like Gertrude Fitzimmons—a creature Eric had serviced only because servicing horsy women and needy queers was his job.

By the time Eric and his latest recruit fell silent, the bonfire had died to a glowing pit. I padded back down the path, amazed at how cold the sand was on such a warm night. I retrieved my clothes and stood facing the coals. Could walking across the firepit in my bare feet hurt any more than listening to Eric with Dr. Fitzimmons? I hiked to where Rupert and I had spread our sleeping bags. Rupe's bag was empty. Even he had found a better place for the night.

AT BREAKFAST, Dr. Beckett looked like a boy trapped in an aging man's body. A playful smile came easily to his lips. His newly-bright eyes followed Teddy. She strode about the dining room with poise, a scrap of orange silk tied behind one shoulder, and corrected anyone who failed to call her "Theodora."

Charley cornered Cy and whispered, her eyes full of steely self-importance—already, I was sure, planting the seeds of my obsolescence. Zoë complimented Josh and the other musicians on their performances, and poured coffee for the executives.

I hiked to the highest ridge above the valley, the lookout where just yesterday I'd surveyed the final preparations for Open House. The vehicles were parked in their familiar disarray, and with the sweatlodge back in place the Ranch again looked like home. People moved slowly, dawdling through hangovers. Eric and Rupert softly played their guitars.

The Executive Trail was getting a sendoff at today's Group. Dr. Fitzimmons would want to remain at the Ranch, to howl on Eric's bear skin for ten more nights, but she'd be dragged into the wilderness, along with Dr. Beckett. He would conduct himself more maturely, but would want to stay behind with Teddy. Cy might point out how needy the college dean was, to have kissed an underage girl. People would praise Josh for his contribution to the music. Charley would try to upstage the poor guy. I hoped to escape any mention of how in my shit I'd been during the party.

Even from the ridge I recognized the individual Vistans as they made their way around the dunes. Rupert emerged from Eric's tipi, took a leak, and ducked back in. Teddy and Dr. Beckett strolled around the pond and tossed bread to the swans. Vivian, her hair under a pink bandanna, hiked through the orchards and stopped outside my tipi.

I shouted to her and ran down the terraced cliff. She turned in a full circle with my voice echoing around her. I came to a panting halt and raised the door flap to invite her in.

I began making tea. "You caught me feeling unnecessary."

"Boy, are you out of touch. Cy wants you to go on Trail. And take Rupert."

"You're kidding!" I grinned open-mouthed, then lost my exhilaration to anxiety over what Charley might accomplish while I played mountain goat. She could take over all financial management, and demand payment from me instead of allowing me to trade my skills for therapy.

"But I wasn't looking for you about that," Vivian said. "I want to talk about Elizabeth."

A mother who's lost one child to suicide must always worry about the others. But Vivian didn't need to hear my theories. I asked, "Are you concerned about something?"

"Last night. It was great fun, all of us women getting dressed up. Willow boiled hot curlers in a coffee can and we drank champagne and did each other's makeup. My little girl fit right in. I want *so much* to let her grow up without me keeping her under surveillance. My mother monitored me like a parolee, and I still managed to get pregnant under her roof."

I nodded. Though she'd never told me this, I had figured out that Garth had been born when she was sixteen.

"Last night I acted like some kind of—harem girl. Cy had me talk to that airline executive, and when we left the sweatlodge the guy thought I was going to fuck him. Teddy's just turned sixteen, and Cy encouraged her to neck with a man over three times her age. I looked at my Elizabeth with that makeup, in that slinky flap of fabric, and saw how Cy looked at her. Like—."

"Like a woman?"

"Like a sexual being. She's not even thirteen."

I sat back and practiced empathic listening.

"I haven't talked to anyone else about this. Am I nuts?"

"Teddy used to screw ten speed freaks a night," I reminded her. "It's a growth step for her to kiss a college dean. Cy won't send Elizabeth down her path." I wanted to believe every word, though last night I'd felt Elizabeth looked like a creature out of Fellini.

Vivian's deep sigh told me she wasn't convinced but wouldn't harp on the subject. She sipped her tea. "She *is* a woman now. Last week she had her first period. She's going on Trail with you. Won't you talk to her out there? She trusts you."

Vivian's firstborn had shot himself, and her daughter was flowering into womanhood in the world's most sexually liberated community. "Of course," I promised, wondering what I could say to change Elizabeth's destiny as a child of Rancho Vista, and why I would want to.

18.

WHEN WE HIKED THROUGH THIS MEADOW ON MY FIRST TRAIL, in the spring, it had looked like a freshly-trimmed golf course. Now Indian paintbrush blazed in crimson shades, and the hikers waded through knee-deep horsetail and buffalo grass that shimmered in the wind. The tiny arrowhead-shaped leaves of the river birch rustled with a ghostly timbre. Had the trees' bark gleamed such a rich shade of purple in May? Had I been too seriously in my shit back then to notice? The country was like a place once seen in a dark dream, now revealed in sunlight.

But I was still in my shit and hiked at the end of the line with Wolfie at my side. What was my problem? Cy respected and relied on me, and even allowed me a generous share of the spotlight. I was learning from Ken how to lead Trails. Rupert, for whom I had grieved, was alive, radiant in his independence, and making friends. Even Eric was warming up. I began to think that if I wasn't happy now, I never would be.

Ken marched far ahead, appearing to savor his solitude as much as I loathed mine. Robins and jays, grubbing in the grass for insects, scattered in his wake. When Wolfie ran ahead and barked, I slowed my pace, not wanting to catch up with the other hikers.

I didn't have to worry about what Charley did in my absence. When she heard about "Executive Trail" she insisted on joining it. Her safari suit quickly lost its crisp sheen and was now soiled with grass stains and streaks of pink mud. She'd left the pith helmet at the Ranch, and wore a Chanel scarf over her champagne-colored hair. Soon her brand new Vasque boots blistered her feet. The ten pounds of leather rode in Rupert's backpack, and she hiked in the canvas high-tops Ken had recommended in the first place.

She had spent her first hour on Trail chatting with the others, then found her way to Rupert's side. Puck took charge of the executives, teaching them the basics of weight distribution in their packs, the need to sip water even when they weren't thirsty, the proper use of insect repellents and sunscreens. I kicked stones and subgrouped to Wolfie about the sharp tone of

Charley's voice.

Willow tended to the troublesome Dr. Fitzimmons—who dithered, as I had predicted, that she should have stayed at the Ranch. Wanda Richter kept her tape recorder running and interviewed each participant.

I would take my turn with the executives after dinner, to get them started in their journals. But my main assignment from Cy, even while on Trail, was to work with Charley on the insurance system. I had prepared myself with an outline sealed in a ziplock bag. When she fell behind Rupe to re-tie her shoe, I trotted to her side and offered, "If you put your foot up on that rock you won't have to bend so far, and it'll be easier to stand back up. Your pack can really throw you off balance."

"Steve! You surprised me," she said in her careful way. I doubted anything ever surprised her. She managed to kneel and tie her shoe without taking my advice. When she wobbled to her feet, the strain showed in her face, although her pack weighed only fifty pounds. I didn't offer my hand.

"Didn't mean to scare you," I said.

"You didn't. I just thought you'd been—avoiding me."

I established piercing, non-defensive Vistan eye-contact, and resumed hiking. "My own first Trail was so overwhelming, I like to let other people spend the time they need getting acclimated."

She fell in at my side. "Trail," she said, hesitating, then chose her words even more slowly than usual. "It sounds—pastoral. Like the simple life. But surviving on one's own isn't exactly simple, is it?"

I seized the chance to compliment her. "You're learning fast. Listen, let's not get caught up in dinner preparations tonight. I want to get your input on my insurance outline."

"Great, but I won't shirk potato duties. I intend to pull my own weight."

You could start by carrying your own boots, I thought.

She went on, "Ken tells me you saved his life out here."

I shrugged off my surprise. "I helped."

She released a deliberate-sounding sigh, and turned to look straight into my eyes. "I hope somebody can save *me*."

Startled, I stepped into a bog, then sloshed my muddy shoe in the stream. "From what? I thought you were just here to help Josh." My shoe squished as we walked on.

"Josh is fine, actually. While we're on Trail he's going to Denver to take the Colorado teachers' exam. He wants to develop the school program at the Ranch. Suddenly he's the picture of motivation and I'm the one at loose ends."

You? I wanted to hoot, but managed to say, "Cy and I are counting on your guidance with the insurance project." To comfort myself I added, "And it's only for six months."

Her voice went flat. "I haven't told Cy, but I quit my job. I'm here for as long as you guys will have me."

So there would be no time limit on my anxiety. "I came here without all the facts in the open, too," I confessed. "Actually I'd been *fired* from my job. Cy figured that out before I hitchhiked into Keystone. Like he figures everything out." I lifted my wet shoe onto a boulder and pulled up my sock. I had revealed far more to her than I meant to.

Ahead on the path, Rupe bowed low to present Elizabeth with a little bouquet of wildflowers. She curtsied in thanks. I felt a strange mixture of joy and envy. My two favorite people were becoming close—and I was stuck with the person I liked the least.

"Can I tell you a funny secret?" Charley asked. "My parents— God, nobody but Josh knows this. My real name is Charlette. I changed it in high school."

And your real haircolor? I wanted to ask.

WE MET OVER THE INSURANCE PAPERS while the others gathered firewood and began preparing dinner. To my surprise and relief, Charley praised my outline. "You're a mature writer," she said, speaking without her usual halting rhythm. "The reports sound as if an experienced psychiatrist wrote them. The adjuster's job is to deny coverage. Never make it easy by submitting exotic claims." She shuffled through my recent reports. "You have an instinctive feel for establishing suitable therapy goals. This one's excellent: 'An important objective for Harvey is to learn appropriate social skills with women of his age.' You'll want to narrow that next month, and keep drawing out specific goals and objectives to last for several months' worth of reports."

I needed this information, and took notes as she continued, "You've wisely left out any reference to sex—isn't Harvey the fellow everyone calls 'Lucky'?"

I nodded. "Attached at the loins to 'Rainbow,' whose real name is Sarah."

A cheer went up around the fire. Puck and Elizabeth pranced into camp, swinging five large rainbow trout from a cord. Charley smiled as if indulging the foolishness. "Each month," she told me, "set a therapeutic goal for each patient. The next month show some progress, and introduce a new goal. As long as any goals are unmet, the patient still needs therapy."

"So it's Scheherazade and the Thousand and One Nights. Keep the adjusters coming back to see what happens next."

Her calm reserve cracked and she laughed delightedly. "Something tells me you won't need much supervision."

And something told me she had bigger trout to fry than taking over the insurance project.

After dinner I met with each of the executives. They amazed me with their trust as they discussed the hidden failures of their outwardly successful lives. "My wife will leave me if I don't learn to communicate more openly," confided the airline official. "I'll do anything to keep her, but I have no idea what she means." After more discussion, I got him started on a Relationship Workbook—not concerning his wife, but his dead mother.

The architect was a widower with a different problem: at fifty-one, he was in love with a woman less than half his age. "I don't know if she loves me or if she's only after my money. How can a beautiful young woman love *this?*" He gestured at his sagging, lumbering body as if it were a bloated carcass that had washed up on a beach. I helped him begin a Relationship Workbook on his ideal self.

Dr. Beckett, the Rutherford College dean, said his kisses with Teddy had been his first with anyone in twenty years. "My wife is full of anger," he explained. "Many men my age are in this situation, and use prostitutes. But I'm not after *sex.* I want love."

"So the sexual revolution doesn't comfort you," I said, feeling I could say the same for myself, "because the world hasn't had a love revolution."

Dr. Beckett smiled broadly. "Not for me. Not until Theodora."

I marveled that a street-wise, shoplifting car thief with a tear-drop tattoo had somehow satisfied this Nobel Prize-winner's need for love. The man was quietly weeping, and I took his hand. "Of all the therapists in the world, I think Cy can best understand and accept your experience."

"I believe you understand it, too."

At the campfire, over marshmallows, Puck shared a few secrets of bare-handed "trout hunting." Ken played his harmonica, and Elizabeth brushed each of the women's hair. I sat against a log and wrote in my journal. Not long ago I'd planned to die a miserable failure. Today I was calling a Nobel Prize-winner "Larry." Was I staring happiness right in the face and failing to recognize it?

In the coming days the rappelling and solos went smoothly, but with enough terror for the participants that when it was over they felt they'd accomplished something tremendous. Assisting Ken, speaking the language of top businessmen and coming up with journal assignments for them, I felt I had found my true calling. At the same time I yearned for love as much as these people overwhelmed by personal problems.

Rupert spent more time with Charley each day and became more vociferous. He ranted one afternoon about "Henry fucking Kissinger, the Antichrist." Both Charley and Elizabeth were able to calm him, yet with me he just grunted and said he needed to take a dump, or shuffled over to help Charley with her pack or her shoes. When anyone approached her for any purpose, Rupert planted himself beside her like a bodyguard.

After dinner one evening, Charley asked me to go for a walk, and left Rupe at the campfire looking helpless. "I've got some good news," she said. In meetings with Dr. Beckett, she'd pursued a suggestion from Ken—that Rancho Vista host a satellite campus of Rutherford College. Beckett was enthusiastic, and had promised to approach the school's governing board. If everything worked out, Rutherford College/West at Rancho Vista would be fully accredited, part of a nationwide group of old-guard schools granting credit for life experience.

"Also," she went on, "Rupert told me he found Rancho Vista thanks to a letter you wrote to his grandma." I was pleased to know this, but would have preferred to hear it from Rupe.

"ELIZABETH, YOU'RE BECOMING A WOMAN," I said, and shrugged over my clumsy words. We hiked behind the others over an ancient lava floe.

"My mom asked you to talk to me, huh?" With her petulant expression she looked like a full-fledged teenager.

"Don't you think *I'm* interested in what happens to you?"

"Oh, please. I can just hear her—'Talk to Elizabeth! She won't listen to me because I was pregnant at sixteen and she knows I'm projecting and she thinks I'm an old nag.'"

"That about covers it," I admitted, realizing I couldn't fool this wise child. "Your big brother's gone and you're stuck with me. What do you want to know about men?"

She yawned elaborately. "Since you asked, are they all obsessed with the size of their genitals, like Eric? Women don't seem interested except to laugh. Behind the guys' backs."

"Eric is—gifted. If I had his equipment I'd strut it too." This wasn't at all what Vivian had asked me to say, and I took a deep breath. "The important thing is, you can't trust men." I watched Wolfie trot from hiker to hiker, begging for bites of cheese. "We're dogs. We'll tell a woman anything to get her to—you know."

"To get her to iron your shirts and cook three meals a day? What are you saying?"

"That I'm here if you ever want to talk. I want you to know you can trust me."

"One of the hounds is assuring me he won't bite?"

I put a hand on her shoulder. "I'll help you protect yourself."

"Tell my mom you've done your duty." She squeezed my fingers, then bounded over the rough rocks as lightly as a butterfly, making me remember what it was like to be almost a teenager, fearless and free.

THE LAST GUEST LEFT soon after the end of Trail. Ten days of life in the wilderness had worked a variety of changes in all of them, and closure was reached in final personal sessions with Cy. The next day the breakfast gong rang just before noon. I yawned in bed and closed my journal. Eric and Rupert were playing a blues progression on their guitars, the music carrying on the breeze. Life moved at its own pace again, now that we were living for ourselves and not a Health Department inspection or executive guests. On a pristine shitter wall someone had penned, "How many different kinds of butts are there?" Already the Vistans had sketched five. My favorite, the delicately-shaded "Tightwad Butt," looked like Elizabeth's handiwork.

Tobey Turner had arrived during Trail and was staying with Lucky. Monosyllabic, exhibiting classic symptoms of depression, he brightened when I appeared at the cookshack for breakfast. "Thanks for getting me out of jail."

I looked into his lovely dark eyes, wondering how this sensitive kid had survived sixteen years as Dr. Turner's son. "Thank God they let you come," I said, and didn't mention that I knew his father.

Charley left the entire insurance project to me, and spent her time developing the Rutherford college program. Between phone calls in the Blue Worm, she updated me on her negotiations with Dr. Beckett. His board had approved our proposal. Adjunct faculty members would conduct seminars and supervise each student's practicum. Vistans could do accredited work with periodic visits to a college library.

She organized thesis committees and appointed herself the chair of each. Privately I begrudged her the gratitude she deserved. *I'm a five-time loser,* I wrote in my journal. *Thanks to her I'll finish college.*

I went to work immediately on my thesis concerning wilderness therapy. I lived in a pair of overalls and added a tee-shirt when I hiked to town, and always returned to the Ranch for dinner. Each morning back in town brought more mail and phone messages. The Open House brochures, and Wanda Richter's *Wall Street Journal* article about the Executive Trail, were generating referrals of the type Cy was eager for, highly-functional people seeking enrichment and meaning in life. More executives were coming, many with their spouses and children. We confirmed arrival dates for the "Family Communications Marathon."

At Cy's invitation, Charley came to a staff meeting and spread her materials across the triple-wide's dining table. With a red marker on butcher paper she sketched a diagram of the administrative structure of Rutherford College/West at Rancho Vista. Dr. Beckett was to be the Dean, Cy the Academic Director. Dr. Fitzimmons, Nelson Christopher and other therapists were among the adjunct faculty. "We'll need an administrative director," Charley said slowly.

I feared Cy would take the bait and offer her the job. Yes, her work would enable me to finish college and even earn a Master's degree, but my resentment and distrust of her didn't ease. To my relief she left without being invited to join the staff in any capacity.

Cy shuffled through the confirmations for the Family Marathon and asked me, "How about inviting your buddy Dr. Turner? His son's here. It's a case of no time like the present."

In a sudden panic, I quipped, "How unlike you to employ

banal clichés."

"And how unlike *you* to sidestep a direct question. This may be your greatest challenge yet. Tobey's father—the man who tortured your friend Rupert." Cy raised an eyebrow. "You planned this, Mr. Susoyev. I heard the well-oiled machinery clicking in your brain the night Turner accosted me in Beverly Hills. You'll be tempted to abuse your power over him."

"I don't have any power to abuse."

Willow whistled. "Get real. You know Turner's character. That's power."

"I'll go on Trail when he comes," I offered.

"Oh, no," Cy said. "At the Beverly Hills cocktail party he didn't recognize you as the surly hippie he'd fired from the snake pit. We can use that to help his son. We'll let him be very impressed with you, and *then* reveal who you are."

I shrugged to conceal my sudden excitement, but couldn't help pointing out, "Plus we've got an ace named Rupert up our sleeve."

"FATE IS DRAGGING US FORWARD," Cy announced. His hair shone like a halo under the skylights of the new Group Dome. "Thanks to Charley's hard work, this dust bowl is now the satellite campus of a top-drawer New England college. How many people want to earn a degree based on your life experience?"

I wasn't the only dropout in the room. Most of the Vistans raised their hands.

Josh groaned to Charley, "No matter what I accomplish, it pales next to you, babe."

"That's a suck," Elizabeth called out. "What are you saying, Josh?"

He conceded her point with a nod. "I was going to announce I passed the Colorado state exam. I'm a certified teacher. Not a garbageman or a janitor. I'm starting a school program out here for you kids. I was excited about sharing my good news in Group."

Vivian gave her daughter a stern look. "Josh, that's wonderful. You've inspired me to get certified in Colorado too."

"It *is* wonderful," Cy said. "Josh, you and Charley are both competent adults. She's simply had more practice being herself. This is new to you. I'll expect you to enroll in the Rutherford

Master's program."

The door creaked open. Lucky stuck in his head, then his body, and Rainbow followed. They grimaced with exaggerated stealth, hunching their shoulders while they tiptoed toward opposite corners of the room.

"It's time to prepare everybody's parents," Cy went on. "Rutherford is a private college, not cheap. Charley will let us know soon how much the tuition will be." He watched the latecomers with a sly smile.

Even after Dr. Beckett left, Teddy had insisted on being known as "Theodora." The name alone seemed to give her new poise. She now said, "If you two are trying to call attention to yourselves, you're doing a bang-up job." Lucky and Rainbow froze in their furtive poses.

I nodded vigorously, wishing I'd said it first.

"A profound observation," Cy told Theodora, giving her his full attention. "When people try to look unobtrusive, why do they make themselves more noticeable?"

"I'm not a theorist," she answered, with the maturity I was beginning to take for granted from her. "But I got arrested at K-Mart the first time I tried shoplifting because I started running before I was even out of the store."

Cy munched a cashew and offered the bag to Zoë. She shook her head and kept her smiling eyes on Theodora. "So," he gently teased, "guess that was the last time you tried *shop*lifting!"

"Fuck, no." Theodora thrust out her magnificent breasts. "But it was the last time I ran, and the only time I got caught."

"Until your arrest for Grand Theft Auto."

She shrugged off everyone's giggles. "Different situation."

"Some day, when we're not doing a seminar, we'll explore why a girl who could buy the entire K-Mart chain with her lunch money was stealing bathing suits. For now, Theodora, can you show us the difference between your successful and unsuccessful shoplifting techniques? In case anybody's taking notes"—and, as always, several Vistans were writing in their fat spiral books— "this is not a course on criminal behavior, okay? It's a Rutherford College/West seminar on body language. The young woman before you has been thoroughly rehabilitated."

Theodora adjusted her halter top, and with ladylike grace smoothed the hem of her white leather miniskirt, back in action since being shelved for the Open House. First she pantomimed taking two bathing suits into a fitting room, putting one on under her clothing, furtively hanging the other back on the rack, then racing out to the parking lot. "I was in handcuffs before I knew what hit me."

Next, at Cy's prompting, she explained what she'd learned from the experience: "Always buy something. Don't act sneaky." While Willow role-played a store clerk, Theodora looked into her eyes and said, "Wow, I love your nail polish. What color is that? Sorry, all I have is a twenty. I hate to ask you to make change for this gum. Oh, thanks." She scuffed away in her rubber sandals, lazily counting her change. At the door she mimed pulling a packet from her waistband. "Cigarettes," she stage-whispered. "Shermans."

I stared in bewilderment at her sophisticated, convincing reënactment. Had making out with a Nobel Prize-winner raised her to a new level of poise and maturity? Or was she simply growing up?

"Observe this young woman's mind at work," Cy said. "Body language is a profound form of communication, often much more so than the spoken word. Who else wants to demonstrate how body language has or has not worked for you?"

Eric showed how he'd stolen purses from cars, standing at crosswalks and watching for unlocked passenger doors when women stopped at red lights. I shuddered at his reptilian glance and predatory posture, but reminded myself that Eric had stolen money for drugs and hadn't *hurt* anyone. Ken demonstrated the businesslike way he'd learned to walk into an alley while casing a pharmacy's alarm system. Lucky acted out raising the hood of his mother's car in a parking lot, as if making a mechanical adjustment, while he urinated against the fender without being noticed. "People walk right by," he explained, "and think there's water leaking out of your car. They look away 'cause they don't want you to ask 'em for help."

Next Josh showed how, as a garbageman, he'd pocketed a Rolex watch someone had discarded with wads of Christmas wrap. Anxiously Charley clarified that he later found the owner, returned the watch and received a reward. In her clipped tone she drained the juice from his presentation. Josh sat back looking deflated. How strange that she could castrate her husband even by pointing out what a good man he was.

After more demonstrations I swaggered to the center of the Dome and announced, "I'm a nurse who's gonna get fired for stealing drugs." Shifty-eyed, with shoulders hunched, I played out the conspicuous furtiveness of stuffing pills into the pockets of my uniform. "But here's how I collected my suicide meds and never got caught." I turned to Rupert and said smoothly, "Mr. Seville, I know those pills don't make you feel good. Doctor Mengele has prescribed them for you, but if you'd feel better without them, notify me. I'll dispose of them appropriately."

After all volunteers had taken a turn Cy asked, "If we had to hire someone for a top-secret assignment, sleuthing among the agents of a hostile power, who would get the job?"

Lucky's urination trick earned several votes. Theodora had impressed everyone by admiring the cashier's nail polish. But the Vistans agreed I deserved the espionage assignment.

"Just remember," Cy reminded us all, "we're using these skills in pursuit of truth, justice, and the Vistan way."

"Speak for yourself," I said. "I'm coming back from our next trip to Denver with a new bathing suit."

ON TOP OF EVERYTHING ELSE WE DID, thirteen students commuted to Boulder twice a month to use the University of Colorado library, meet with faculty sponsors, sit in on seminars and soak up the collegiate atmosphere. For the first time I was glad to be a five-time dropout. My earlier college experiences had been disconnected and irrelevant to anything that mattered in my life. Now everything I had ever done felt exquisitely significant—even my years at Los Perdidos—because every event of my life had prepared me for Rancho Vista.

19.

TOBEY TURNER WASN'T "SHY AND WITHDRAWN,"
as I had described him in my report to Orange County Probation
& Parole. "Catatonic" was more like it. Cy had assigned Ken to
work with the kid to prepare him for his family session. As the
staff member who had suffered the most severe abuse as a child,
Ken seemed to be in the best position to help him with his Relationship Workbook.

I hiked to Ken's tipi to see if any progress had been made.
"So," Ken was saying when I ducked in through the canvas door,
"this item is simple. At what times have you felt let down by your
father?"

I added some sketches to Ken's pile of Trail-brochure materials, poured myself a mug of tea and settled into a bean-bag.
Tobey whimpered like a mouse dying in a trap.

"Hi," I said gently. "Mind if I sit in?"

Tobey grunted without lifting his dark eyes.

"How's that again?" I thought I might at least annoy the kid
into speaking a full sentence.

Tobey squeaked, "Yeah. I mean no. I don't mind."

Ken's nostrils flared in a well-suppressed yawn. "We're moving at the speed of a runaway glacier. Tobey's one of those rare
people who has no resentments against his parents. His father's
never made him feel sad, ashamed, hopeless, or hurt. But he's
also never made him feel happy, alive, hopeful, or valued. His
mother's made even less of an impression. Dr. and Mrs. Turner
will be here next week and I guess Tobey won't have much to
say, except to apologize for embarrassing them when he got
busted for pot possession."

I took a risk. "Tobey, are you afraid of your father?"

A sullen silence hung around the teenager. "No," he said
finally, with a defensive twang I would have detected even before
my Vistan training.

"Do you think if you confronted him—you know, just called
him a vicious bastard—he'd find a way to hurt you?" While
Tobey stared at me, I went on, "Are you afraid we wouldn't
protect you?"

"Why *should* you? You don't even know me, and he's paying

for my therapy."

With a sad smile I acknowledged the wisdom of his reasoning. "Ken," I said, "have you told Tobey about your relationship with your dad?"

In grim detail Ken recounted the routine lashings of his bare ass with the buckle end of his father's belt. He tugged down his shorts to show the scars. I had always avoided looking at them close-up, but now forced myself to study the ghostly crescent ridges while Ken described the voluntary beating he'd undergone to reach his father. "I took a whipping in Group as a therapy process, to show my dad the pain he'd given me."

Tobey hugged himself and stared at the lightning bolts woven into Ken's Navajo rug.

Ken pulled up his pants. "And Dad came through. He screamed, 'Stop!' and cried and held me. I got to see he loved me after all. But even if he hadn't stopped the beating, I still couldn't have gone on hating him. I would have accepted he was a monster, and moved on."

Tobey seemed to be stirring to life. "My dad's never laid a hand on me," he said with more animation, "unless you count pinching me real hard a few times." He looked wonderingly into my face. "But you called him a vicious bastard. He *is*. I can't explain."

I improvised a question that wasn't in the Workbook. "At what times have you hated your father, Tobey?"

"Every minute since I was six years old."

While Ken transcribed the particulars, I filled the kettle for a fresh pot of tea.

"I PROMISED WE'D HAVE GROUP EVERY DAY after the Open House," Cy said. "I guess you're holding me to my word."

Elizabeth wanted to confront her mother, Josh asked for time with Charley, Rainbow and Lucky needed help with their relationship. Would I ever have a relationship to work on? I was lonely, but didn't envy couples their constant troubles.

Tobey was beginning to look alert. He arrived at Group late, in a tank top and cutoff jeans, and sat on the floor holding his journal close to his chest. He'd been swimming with Elizabeth and working in the garden with Eric, and had lost his mushroom pallor. His dark suggestive beauty hid behind eyelashes longer than any girl's. I looked sideways at his flushed cheeks and long, tanned legs, the bare feet oversized like a St. Bernard puppy's paws, unsure why I didn't want Cy to know I was appreciating his beauty.

Vista's problem couple took the hotseat. "All right, people," Cy said, "let's plug up this energy drain."

Rainbow had her usual complaint against Lucky: "When we're alone together you act like I'm not even there, but when people are around you stick to me like a fly on shit."

"What's that say about *you?*" Lucky demanded. "You—"

"Cool it," Cy said. "How many people have had their fill of this?"

Tobey's hand rose after mine. Of everyone in the room, only Rupert, busy fashioning a cat's cradle from a string of glass beads, failed to vote in the affirmative.

"Any ideas how we can cut the Gordian knot?" Cy asked.

Lucky's face darkened. "I think Rainbow needs—"

"Sorry, Lucky," Cy interrupted. "Anybody else?"

Many people raised their hands. Elsie distributed index cards and we Vistans scribbled. Cy read through several cards, then smiled and announced with sudden buoyancy, "I think Steve's got it. *Maybe they need time off from each other. A month? They could live in separate tipis and do Relationship Workbooks on each other. But no communication between them.*"

Cy noted the approving smiles around the room and avoided the two stricken faces in the center of the circle. "Your Month-Off starts right now," he said. "No—in the morning, so you can separate your belongings and have one last dynamite fuck. A month from today we'll re-evaluate. Until then you don't exist to each other."

"Maybe Charley and I need the same thing," Josh said. "I'm having a hell of a time."

He and Charley took the hotseat and faced each other in the center of the floor. "I'm living in your shadow," he said. "I'll try not to suck about it. But when I start to feel like I've done something that matters, you accomplish something much grander. I graduated with decent grades. You were *summa cum laude.* I've barely got my teaching certificate and you've started a branch campus of Rutherford College." His voice cracked. "I love you, babe. But if we did this Month-Off, maybe I'd get a taste of life outside your luminous shadow."

He wept with his head in his hands. The Vistans, so accus-

tomed to tears, stared awkwardly at the floor when a man with
twenty-four-inch biceps shed them.

I scrutinized Charley's enigmatic smile. Her eyes remained on
Cy as they had during Josh's "No More Garbage" breakthrough
in Beverly Hills. She said haltingly, "Josh, I'm—shocked. I've
always thought I was helping you. Now you say I've held you
back. I hope someday we'll—support each other's growth." Her
placid face showed none of the confused sadness in her voice.
Josh had asked for a month apart, but she talked as if they'd
agreed to an amicable divorce.

As soon as they worked out the details of their process, Elizabeth asked, "Can mothers and daughters go on Month-Off? I
think my mom and I need it too."

Vivian stared into the skylight and I pictured Garth's casket.
One child commits suicide, another divorces you. At least little
Mikey wasn't abandoning her.

"Steve," Cy said, "you'd better patent this process."

**KEN AND WILLOW WORKED FOR TWO DAYS AT
THE MOTEL IN KEYSTONE,** guiding Dr. and Mrs. Turner
through Relationship Workbooks in preparation for their session
with Tobey. I stayed at the Ranch to avoid being recognized by
Turner. Early on the morning of the session I hiked upstream
with Tobey.

The teenager's improved confidence shone from his tanned
face, yet couldn't disguise his troubled state of mind. "Since you
got me out of jail I think of you as my savior," he confessed.
"Can you save me from my dad?"

"Something tells me you won't need saving." Like Ken's brutal father, Turner might be reached by his son's pain and come
through with a moment of unconditional love. But, in case he
didn't, we had Plan B. When Rupert learned who Tobey's father
was, he had agreed to participate in the session.

The Turners arrived at the Ranch with Cy and Zoë in time for
breakfast. I stayed away and staged the session in the Dome. In
the center of the floor I set two oak chairs side-by-side for the
parents, with their backs toward the door, and a lonely-looking
chair facing theirs, for Tobey. While the Vistans gathered, I sat
near the door where I could watch Dr. Turner without presenting
myself for scrutiny. The family entered last, just as warm rain
began to fall.

Turner was wearing a dark suit and tie, a ridiculous costume a hundred miles beyond the pavement, and he chewed at his lower lip. When he removed the jacket and sat, his body collapsed into itself. The waistband of his trousers rose to his shirt-pocket, swallowing his entire ribcage. He slumped like an old man beside his fair, pleasant-looking wife. I had never imagined Turner could appear vulnerable, but now he looked tired, defeated, pathetic. My heart stirred with hope for Tobey. Maybe Turner had been humbled by the questions in the Relationship Journal, and would be able to demonstrate his love for his son without much of a struggle. Then, perhaps, he could even apologize to Rupert.

Mrs. Turner sat calmly in a pastel skirt and sweater with pearls, hands twisting a handkerchief, the only outlet for her anxiety. Physically Tobey favored his father, but without the etched-in meanness—the dark passionate eyes and shapely lips, the high intelligent forehead. Until the session in Ken's tipi, he'd had the posture of a concentration-camp inmate. Today he sat with his feet firmly planted before him, shoulders back, eyes flashing.

Cy established the standard ground rules—no physical violence, no walking out "until the process is complete." He then opened with his favorite question, addressed as usual to the youngest participant: "Tobey, what do you feel like saying?"

In previous Family Marathons—between Puck and his mother, Rainbow and her sisters, Lucky and his father—the kids had responded with some version of, "I feel like saying thanks for coming." The fanged resentments, terrifying Withholds and finally the long-buried love had flowed only after Cy prompted them.

But Tobey's jaw tightened immediately. "Dad," he said, "I feel like saying I think you've always hated me. Tell me why."

Even Cy looked astonished. "Apparently we won't waste time on pleasantries," he joked, then became as serious as Tobey. "Nathan, what do *you* feel like saying?"

Turner chewed his lower lip and spoke to his son. "A question in that Relationship Workbook puts it perfectly: 'When have I felt hopeless?' I'm hopeless right now. I've shown you my love in every way I know, and *you* act as if you hate *me*. Have you heard of projection?"

In the week since my return from Trail, the boy had filled several notebooks with resentments against his father, and grown a set of balls. If Tobey could confront Nathan Turner, was it really too late for me and my father to face off?

Tobey picked up his stack of journals, flipped through one, then slammed them onto the floor. "Fuck it. I don't need to check my notes. You're a cruel bastard." He gave me a quick glance. "Vicious! You've humiliated me my whole life."

His father appeared to be near tears. "You know I could never hurt you," he said in a pleading tone. "Please tell me you know that, son."

Tobey glared at him.

"Are *you* hurt, Nathan," Cy asked, "that your son calls you vicious?"

"Of course," Turner replied, and pulled his lips tight. "My only comfort is the knowledge that his mind is addled by the chemicals he's abused." He turned to his wife. "This isn't our son. He is his own LSD hallucination. His life is a nightmare of his own creation."

Mrs. Turner patted her husband's arm and spoke in a tiny voice like the one Tobey had used until recently. "Nathan—"

He recoiled and cut her off in a steely tone, "I had to pull strings to get him out of jail so he could come here for treatment." He appealed to Cy. "What humiliation he brought us. 'Possession of a controlled substance' by a psychiatrist's son! His mother is the president of our Junior League."

"You kids don't realize how your actions reflect on your parents," Cy said. "They've worked hard to give you good lives." I avoided looking at him, afraid I would laugh. Tobey's crooked smile showed he understood that his father was being baited.

Turner began to catalogue the many problems associated with raising a difficult child. As a toddler Tobey had "fussed about being carried and fussed about being allowed to walk."

I rose and quietly left the Dome. Outside I waved to Elizabeth and Rupert at the pond. Rupert was coöperating with the session, but remained distant and continued hanging onto Charley. I hoped that as a fringe benefit of exposing Turner I could earn back some of Rupe's trust.

Elizabeth waved back and took Rupert's hand. He crushed out his cigarette, dutifully put the butt into his shirt pocket, and walked with her toward the Dome. When they reached me she crossed her fingers, kissed me on the cheek and dashed inside.

"Here's our chance," I whispered to Rupert. "Don't let me do all the talking." I pulled open the heavy door. Rupert and I knelt behind the Turners.

Tobey's father was still lecturing us on the burden of raising a vexatious son. "I tried to coax him out of his shyness. When he was six I took him to the dentist. In the waiting room I encouraged him to sign in at the window. He refused."

I recalled Tobey's side of this story in his Relationship Workbook. I glanced at Cy, received the nod I hoped for, and asked, "Tobey, do you remember that incident?"

Tobey looked into his father's face without fear. "You 'encouraged' me by pinching my leg so hard it left a bruise."

Turner snorted. "That's ridiculous. I patted your thigh."

Cued by another nod from Cy, I asked, "You don't have it in you to be cruel, do you, Nathan? Tobey's entire childhood must be one protracted hallucination."

Turner twisted in his chair. "Yes, I really believe—" He caught his breath. Rupert rose to his full height, crossed the room and sat on the floor beside Tobey. "What the hell—" Turner's eyes burned with recognition as they leaped from Rupert to me. He grasped his wife's arm. "We've been entrapped! Those two belong in prison."

"The issue is cruelty," I said, and walked to Rupe's side. "Rupert, can you show Tobey the scars on your temples?"

"This is outrageous!" Turner stood and backed away. "We're leaving."

Alice Turner had spoken only once during the session, to say her husband's name. Now, still in her mouse voice, she asserted, "I'm not going anywhere."

Turner stalked around the room while the silent Vistans studied him. When he stood still, the only sound was the spatter of rain on the skylights.

"The issue," I repeated as smoothly as I could, "is whether Dr. Nathan Turner is capable of cruelty. Rupert?"

Rupe pulled back his hair to display the patch of scar tissue at each temple. "Tobey," he said, "I knew your dear old dad at Perdido Valley State Hospital. He gave me a shock treatment at about twenty times the lethal voltage."

"The *legal* voltage, you pathetic—." Turner caught himself. By correcting Rupe, he had confessed.

Tobey reached out and stroked the scars with gentle fingers.

"If we examine your dad's scalp," Rupert continued, "I believe we'll find he carries the Mark of the Beast."

I smiled like a proud parent.

Turner roared, "Alice, Tobias, we're leaving! If they won't give us a ride to our car we'll walk in the rain."

"I said," his wife replied slowly, "I'm not going anywhere. I'm here for Tobey. And as painful as it sounds, I want to hear more about Rupert's shock treatment." She shook her head as if tearing herself free from a suffocating mesh of cobwebs.

Cy asked, "Alice, what else do *you* feel like saying?"

"My son is a sensitive boy." She clenched her hands in her lap. "He just spent six months in jail." She turned on her husband. "What 'strings' did you pull? You wanted him tried as an *adult* at sixteen. You made sure he was represented by a public defender because you wanted to teach him a lesson. The lesson was, 'Don't you dare embarrass me at the country club.'" She knelt before Tobey and held his hands. "Forgive me for leaving you in jail."

"My wife has joined the lynch mob!" Turner shouted.

Tobey reminded him, "When you got busted for drunk driving you didn't have a public fucking defender."

Turner looked out at the storm and chewed his lip. I said softly, "Nathan, I have copies of the records you backdated in Rupert's chart. I'm not the only former state hospital employee prepared to testify against you." Turner's gaze didn't leave the window. I continued, "You don't see yourself as a cruel man, do you?"

"What I see," Turner sputtered, "is that you're still a sociopath, Mr. Susoyev, but a much more successful one with that haircut. Now at least you *look* like a human being."

Alice Turner beat her thighs with her fists. Cy knelt beside her and asked, "What have you been holding inside? This is the place to say it."

She wailed, "Years of cruelty toward our children, toward me, with no hope of freedom!"

Turner stood over Tobey with a look of menace. I put a hand on Tobey's shoulder and stared his father down.

"You've humiliated me for the last time, you little bastard," Turner told his son. "I hope you rot in prison, because I'm certainly not paying for you to stay here." With a final look at his wife, he strode to the door and muscled it open.

Alice Turner stayed and wept with her head in Tobey's lap. He absently stroked her hair and smiled at me through his own tears. In his eyes I saw love as pure as the hatred I'd seen in his father's face moments before.

"I'll drive him to his car," Cy said, "to patch up the manly pride. Alice, it was great to see the doormat stand up and kick her abuser in the ass. But are you sure you want to stay with us?

You're welcome here. Only you know the bridge you're burning."
Kneeling before her son, she gripped his hands and nodded. I
volunteered to let them stay in my tipi. Everyone remained in the
Dome while Cy went out alone.

After Cy's Rover had groaned past the swale and the other
Vistans dispersed, Ken and I stood side-by-side peeing in the
sand. The storm had moved west, toward town and beyond, and
the scent of sagebrush was strong in the air. "You nailed him,"
Ken said. "Is revenge as sweet as they say?"

"I'd still like to give the fucker a shock treatment." I aimed my
stream and let out a final blast of piss that drilled a deep hole in
the sand.

**OTHER CLIENTS CAME FOR FAMILY MARATHON
SESSIONS** but I excused myself and attacked my pile of work at
the Blue Worm. I had submitted four proposals for the fall conference of the Association for Humanistic Psychology, in Santa
Barbara. All had been accepted, and now my job was to outline
workshops on *Wilderness Therapy, Body Image Confrontation, The
Relationship Journal,* and the topic that promised to be the hottest
of the year, *Polysex,* "A revolution that allows couples to affirm
each other's sexual involvement with guests by following the
Biblical one-flesh model."

Each day's mail was full of requests for information about
Rancho Vista. I designed new brochures with a limitless budget.
To get by until these were finished, Elsie mimeographed a form
letter on beautiful sandstone-textured paper with matching
envelopes. When she handed me a personal message, *Your mom
called the service,* I crumpled it. After months of waiting to hear
from my parents, I'd be damned if I would respond to a phone
call. They could at least write.

Travis's crew finished framing Cy and Zoë's new house in
town, a chalet poised on the sunny side of a verdant private
canyon, a quarter mile from the triple-wide. Once the chalet was
complete, the triple-wide would become the office, and I would
take the trailer's master bedroom for myself—unless Charley
grabbed it first. The new place was hidden down a half-mile
gravel road where few locals would ever see it. With cathedral
ceilings, panoramic windows, a greenhouse, four bathrooms and
a wrap-around deck, it would be the most sophisticated building
within a hundred miles. The master bathroom at the north end

was to feature a bathing pool of pink marble. Ceiling-high hardwood bookcases were on order from Denver for Cy's study—finally enough room to store the heaps of books, tape recording equipment and journals that spilled everywhere in the triple-wide.

While Tobey and his mother occupied my tipi, Ken and I spread our sleeping bags in the sand near the river. Each night I watched the stars through slitted eyes, feigning sleep and awaiting Ken's furtive approach. He was getting better with practice, and kept his teeth out of it. I began to feel we were lovers after all, but my silent partner always returned to his own sleeping bag, leaving me with an emptiness that never seemed to be filled.

Rupert withdrew further after his brief coöperation. I couldn't help envying the time my friend spent with Eric and Charley. All those hours playing guitar, the protectiveness toward a woman who didn't need it.

THE BRONZE GONG ON THE COOKSHACK PORCH NEVER SOUNDED except to summon the Vistans to meals or Group. When it rang two hours after breakfast, a few days after the Turner family session, Ken and I looked at each other in confusion. We folded our Trail brochure mock-up and ducked outside his tipi. Someone continued to hammer on the gong while Vistans ran toward the cookshack.

When we approached the porch, Elsie called out, "Sheriff Buford wants equipment for a rescue operation, over at the Razorback. And a crew of climbers." She looked anxiously from face to face.

Travis and Ken ran to the root cellar to collect ropes and a stretcher. "Can I go?" Tobey asked.

Elsie avoided his eager face. "I don't think you're covered on the insurance," she said unevenly, then gave him a full dose of Vistan eye contact, with a smile. "When you're eighteen you can join the rescue squad."

This sounded like a lame excuse—Puck and Lucky were both younger than eighteen and had found places among Travis, Josh and the other men in the back of the truck. I shrugged it off and got in behind the wheel with Ken and Elsie in the cab. Once past the main gate she explained, "Dove MacKenzie spied fresh tire tracks going over the cliff, but couldn't see anything below. It's at that sharp curve where the road's so narrow. Sheriff Buford came out with binoculars and spotted a yellow car at the bottom. He thinks it's a Cadillac."

"A yellow Caddy was in town this weekend," Ken said.

"Yeah," Elsie confirmed. "Dr. Turner's."

I groaned. "That's a joke, right?"

She fiddled with her hairpins. "I wish."

I clutched the wheel, feeling sick. "That's a two-thousand-foot cliff. How can anybody see what make of car is down there?"

Ken scribbled in his pocket notebook a moment. "How about this for the Trail brochure?" he asked. "The Rancho Vista Wilderness Survival Staff is honored to serve on the Abraham County Search and Rescue Posse."

"Shut up," I said quietly. "Jesus."

Sheriff Buford was at the curve with three civilian deputies. While he and Ken set up for the climb down, Elsie whispered to me, "Notice anything funny about those tracks?"

I looked across the narrow dirt road to the shoulder, where the mud of the recent storm had dried into hard ridges. "They're at right angles to the road," I murmured.

"That car didn't just slide over the cliff."

"It dove straight off," I agreed, unable to understand what had happened. I grabbed Ken's binoculars, stepped to the cliff's edge and looked down. Pointing heavenward were the unmistakable tailfins of a canary-yellow 1971 Coupe de Ville. My vision blurred. I passed the binoculars to Elsie, stumbled behind the Vistan truck and retched.

When I returned to the edge of the cliff, the sheriff was explaining, "From the angle a them tire marks, looks like the driver was turnin' around in the middle a the narrowest section a road. Hadda been drunk to do that."

Ken, three other Vistans and the two deputies went over the side. I stayed on the road to help lower a stretcher. Through the binoculars I watched them slowly descend. Eventually they touched down and opened the car, then Ken photographed whatever was inside. I handed Elsie the binoculars after I watched them wrap a bloated, purple body in a blanket and strap it onto the stretcher.

Slowly Ken and the others hauled their cargo up one section of the cliff at a time. The stretcher bounced, snagged on a tree, and finally swung free. The tedious process of raising it didn't get easier until the thing flopped onto level ground, just after sunset.

I stood back dizzily and marveled at Ken's composure, thankful that the job of telling Tobey and his mother would fall to Cy. I tried to imagine their faces. Would Tobey even cry? Would Alice scream and tear her hair? Maybe they'd both fall on their knees and thank God.

The sheriff and the posse left for Gentile with Turner's body, and the Vistan rescue squad picked up Cy at the triple-wide. During the ride to the Ranch he asked Ken and me dozens of questions. When we arrived, he strode into the cookshack and called Group just as Vivian was serving dinner. "Alice, Tobey," he said, once they had settled, "the sheriff called us because there was an accident. Nathan's car went off a cliff after he left here."

"But?" Tobey asked, with a tone of dull resignation, as if he hadn't quite heard.

"He drove off a curve where the drop is two thousand feet. He died of shock before the car hit the canyon floor."

Mother and son stared back in silence. Ken said, "There was an empty vodka bottle in the car."

Tobey came to sudden life. He jumped up and embraced me. "Thank you," he cried.

Several Vistans eyed him with looks of shock. "Exactly what," Cy asked gently, "are you thanking Steve *for?*"

"He made it possible for me to tell my dad how I felt before he died."

Alice clutched her knees and rocked herself. "He wasn't the strong man he pretended to be," she said in a strained whisper. "Just a frightened child."

"A frightened bully," her son corrected.

Rupert shot out of his seat and thumped his head against the wall behind him. His eyes blazed and he roared at the ceiling, *"I smote you with blasting and with mildew and with hail in all the labors of your hands, yet ye turned not to me, saith the Lord."* He glared around the room. "The beast is dead! Steve and I smote him."

The other Vistans, including Cy, sat frozen. Tobey clutched my arm. Suddenly Theodora barked out a lusty laugh and asked, "Rupe, did you say *mildew?*"

"The horses and their riders shall come down," he hissed, "every one by the sword of his brother!"

Charley rose and took his hand, acknowledging he wouldn't be teased into sanity. "This sounds very interesting," she said, and led him outside. "I'd like to hear more about it."

I wanted to scream. Rupe was lost to me. Only Charley could comfort and subdue him.

Group broke up quickly. Elsie drove Tobey and Alice to Gentile, where Turner's body had been taken. I spent a fitful night under my desk at the Blue Worm. When the phone rang at seven a.m. I leaped at it, and grabbed a pen.

"Sheriff Buford here," the caller said. "The coroner done his autopsy. That feller contained enough alcohol to render him intoxicated under state law. Actually enough to render two, three people. Also had a tranquilizer in him, and a mood elevator, whatever that is."

"Does that make it suicide?" I asked, and immediately regretted the question.

"Oh, hell no. City folks have a hard enough time driving the Razorback sober, much less impaired. The coroner's ruled it a accidental death. Hope that's a comfort to the family."

"I'm sure it will be."

"Crazy, huh? You've got them kids out there offa drugs, but their parents are drivin' around loaded to the gills, makin' U-turns off cliffs."

I agreed the irony was remarkable, and thanked the sheriff for the information. *Accidental death*, I wrote on a message pad, recalling Cy's warning that I would be tempted to abuse my power over Turner. Tobey and Rupert believed my forced confrontation scheme had caused the fucker's death, and in their own ways they seemed satisfied about it. I told myself I hadn't wished the man dead, that I'd only wanted him to suffer enough to come through with love for his son.

Yes, and a week before I'd insisted I had no power to abuse.

PART THREE

You do your thing and I do my thing.
I am not in this world to live up to
your expectations, and you are not in
this world to live up to mine.
You are you and I am I, and if by
chance we meet it's beautiful. But if
we do not, it can't be helped.

> Frederick S. "Fritz" Perls
> *Gestalt Therapy Verbatim*

> How bleak this world would be if
> we all just 'did our thing' and
> didn't shoulder one another's pain.
>
> Cyrus Aaron

20

WHEN THE LIGHT OF CY'S LOVE and attention shone
on me, Rancho Vista's glassy puddles thawed and the alabaster
skies cleared as if forever. I came to believe I would be able to
sprawl in an open sleeping bag under the Milky Way any time I
felt like it. But one morning I emerged naked from my tipi and
emptied my thundermug over the cliff's edge, and the slab of
frosty sandstone I walked on threatened to grip my feet and hold
me until May. The blustery wind ripped through me and rattled
the scrub oak, which appeared to have lost its leaves overnight.
No sparrows chirped. A lone hawk patrolled the sky.

Far below me, Josh and Travis organized a hunting party
around the cookshack. They spread tents and tarps everywhere,

and weighted them against the wind with rifles and ammo boxes. Deer season would open the next day, and the work crew was heading for the mountain to bag its legal limit. As I often did when others prepared for an adventure, I allowed myself to wallow in envy. I couldn't go hunting because I had to write brochures and conference proposals and insurance reports. I would even have to sacrifice Ken's autumn Trail, which would embark after the close of hunting season.

In my tipi I put on thick socks and built a quick fire of cardboard, then smashed a broomstick and tossed in the pieces. For a true fire I would have to axe my bookshelves. I settled for the heat that radiated from the single burner of my little propane stove, and dug in a drawer for thermal underwear while the kettle warmed my tea water. Tatters of last night's dream came together: Eric's mother had written me, saying, *You must kill my son and eat his penis.* Going longer than three days without pot to suppress such weirdness felt dangerous.

My nights sleeping beside Ken, and his still-furtive blowjobs, had left me longing more than ever to be with someone I could hold and kiss and love. In the soft, dark eyes that followed me through the meal lines, I saw that Tobey Turner, whom I thought of as a boy, loved me—or maybe those eyes simply shone with gratitude for my role in liberating him from his father.

Each morning I hiked to town. Charley drove in and spent the day on the phone, drumming up support for Rutherford College/West at Rancho Vista, inviting Cy's colleagues to serve as faculty members. She approved my latest insurance reports with few changes, and praised my Open House success backhandedly: "Surprised when Cy told me *you* designed the invitations, they were so professional." Next she asked me to draft a brochure for the college program, which told me she had greater ambitions than usurping my trivial duties.

My own ambitions began with documenting my experiences for college credit. Working in a mental institution, learning wilderness therapy, addressing a psychiatric conference, my ongoing projects—all would contribute toward a bachelor's degree in applied psychology. One day, I promised myself, I would muster the humility to thank Charley for making it possible.

For the autumn conference of the Association for Humanistic Psychology in Santa Barbara, Cy chose me to lead the workshop on the Relationship Workbook. My hair had finally grown out so it almost made a ponytail, and since the humanists were a long-hair crowd I figured Cy would let me keep it. Ken was in charge of the seminar on Wilderness Therapy, Willow would facilitate the sample Body Image session, and Eric was moderator for the Polysex workshop. "Your star keeps rising," Cy told me. The young Vistans were a team, each articulate and dynamic. But only I was invited to drive with Cy to Santa Barbara.

Zoë announced to the staff she was going to Tahiti and would return to meet Cy in Southern California for the conference. I understood that "spending a week on a friend's yacht off Bora Bora" meant fucking the well-endowed Swedish billionaire she called Samuel. Cautious not to subgroup, I silently wondered how Cy expected to hold onto her against such competition, and what would happen if she left him. But when she rested her head in Cy's lap at a party, or he braided her hair during Group, I realized nothing could come between them.

Cy planned to make our five-day trip to Santa Barbara in the big Mercedes. He had scheduled sessions with private clients in each city along the way, and I would be his valet and personal secretary—and to whatever extent I could manage, his friend. The rest of the staff would travel in the Land Rovers.

"I'm trying hard not to be envious," Ken confessed, and Willow enthused, "You'll soak up so much *juice!*"

I knew that being chosen to make the trip was both an honor and a test. If I sucked or tried covertly to get therapy, Cy would never spend another moment alone with me.

I HEARD THE TRUCK DOOR SLAM before the engine stopped roaring, but didn't look up from the typewriter until someone stomped up the Blue Worm's front steps, two at a time. Eric suddenly loomed glassy-eyed at my tiny alcove office, his chest heaving. "Where's Charley? We need an emergency meeting with Cy. She's got to be there."

"Back room. But she's not on staff. Not yet. What's going on?"

Willow raced in and asked, "Charley?" Eric gestured down the hall with his chin. While she ran toward the rear of the trailer, Eric picked up the phone.

I explained helplessly, "Cy and Zoë are having a quiet day. She's leaving for Tahiti tomorrow."

Eric dialed, then closed his eyes as if in prayer. He apologized into the phone for calling and said there'd been an emergency. I insisted, "*Tell me what's happening!*" Eric slammed down the phone and stalked out of the Blue Worm. Charley trotted past my office ahead of Willow, adjusting the scarf that held back her hair and looking self-important. Ken was nowhere around. I put on my shoes and followed Elsie to the triple-wide.

Cy and Zoë came to the dining table with wet hair and in bathrobes. The rest of us gathered but didn't sit down.

"Charley," Willow began gently, "Josh has been injured. Rupert stabbed him in the leg. Three times."

Charley's eyes grew huge. Weakly she asked, "Where is he?"

"Vivian's driving him to Gentile. I put on a tourniquet. His femoral artery's nicked."

My stomach rippled in panic. Rupert had been agitated for several days. He'd ranted at Travis one morning about serving goat-milk pancakes with ham, "an abomination since the ancient of days." But that morning and every morning since, I had rushed to town to draft the brochure that would put my stamp on the Rutherford College program. In my zeal to keep up with Charley, I'd ignored Rupert's distinct warnings.

"After breakfast he talked crazy," Willow said, "working his jaws and pacing around."

Charley slapped the table. "Why didn't you people *talk* to him?"

"I did," Eric said, not bothering to suppress his defensive tone. "He was pissed off—his usual rap, 'People gonna find out the will of God.' We talked about playing guitars today."

"Why didn't you play right then?" Cy asked.

Willow cleared her throat. "When Josh rolls into emergency, the hospital will call Sheriff Buford. Let's worry later about who's responsible for what."

I asked, "Where's Rupert now?"

"In my bed," Eric answered, "chained to the new septic tank. Good thing it wasn't in the hole yet. Puck towed it up there with the tractor."

"Several guys sat on Rupe while I gave him a Benadryl shot," Willow said. "The closest thing we had to a sedative. A hundred milligrams. Ken found forty milligrams of Valium and cooked it up in a spoon, and I injected Rupe with that. Then he let the guys restrain him."

Zoë said softly, "Someone must call Rupert's grand*mother*."

"Of course," Cy snapped. "But first we've got to decide what to tell the sheriff."

"*Etienne* should call them both."

I bit my lip. Luke Buford would be easy. But I dreaded telling Irma Seville we hadn't protected her grandson from himself.

Charley said calmly, "We will tell Sheriff Buford that one of our sicker patients stabbed a teacher. The teacher is en route to the hospital. The patient is sedated, in restraints. Steve, does the mental hospital expect a patient to be hauled off to jail when there's an assault?"

For a moment I couldn't reply. Charley was so composed, I half expected Cy to ask her to make any necessary calls. "No," I answered. "They just report it to security."

"Not even the police," Cy said. "A report goes in some file."

"Stabbing a *person* is a *crime*," said Zoë. "We are not a hospital and have no security de*part*ment. An ex-junkie prepares Valium in a *spoon* because we lack the proper drugs to handle a violent psychotic. The sheriff will probably *take* Rupert to jail. We must let him go. We can*not* beat on the bush with the sheriff."

Her words chilled me, but I knew she was right.

"Charley," Cy said, "under the circumstances I'm amazed at your ability to think so clearly. But does everyone recognize Zoë's grasp on the deep structure of the situation?"

"It was my idea to call the sheriff," Charley replied sharply, "but for an entirely different reason. To avoid appearing defensive we should notify him before the hospital does. And Dr. Aaron is the one to call."

"Good," Cy said. "Now."

I scrambled to find the number in the tiny Abraham County phone book, dialed and handed over the phone.

Cy explained the situation briefly, then listened and repeated bits of what the Sheriff said. "Medication, of course . . . observation at the state hospital . . . no criminal charges. Well, we wouldn't have expected . . . Yes."

Charley watched him with what I saw as a self-satisfied smile. While her husband bled she'd issued commands as if she had a decisive stake in Rancho Vista's future. Her pet, Rupert, would go back on Thorazine and maybe enter Colorado's version of Los Perdidos.

When Cy hung up the phone it rang immediately. I answered, "Dr. Aaron's office."

"Josh lost a lot of blood," Vivian said. "He's getting a transfusion. I'll stay at the White Aspen Motel." She hesitated. "Has Charley left yet?"

Charley was gazing at Cy with no apparent intention of going anywhere. When I passed her the phone she reached for it as if accepting a bothersome business call. "How is he?" she asked. Her eyes followed Cy while he left the room. She listened a while, then said slowly, "Oh, thank you, Vivian. But we *are* on Month-Off, which he requested, so we're not supposed to exist to each other. Thank God he's got you there for support. Under the circumstances, though—would you let him know I wish him well?"

Cy returned with ampoules and syringes and instructed Willow, "Give Rupert two of these a day. The stuff's past the expiration date but it'll work. I never thought we'd need Thorazine at Rancho Vista." His eyes met mine and he sighed. "You go, too. I'll call Rupe's Grandma. You're his best friend. Charley should stay here in case something serious happens to Josh."

I hated to leave her in town with my files. "Will you be okay?" I asked her.

"I'll feel better being close to the phone. Thanks for your concern, but you should get out to Rupert. Like Cy says, you're his best friend."

I heard the accusation in her sugary words: *If you'd been doing your job he wouldn't have stabbed Josh.* And though I hated to admit it, I knew this was true.

No one spoke during the drive to the Ranch, and I tried to prepare myself. I'd seen Rupert truly crazy only once, after his shock treatment, but I would never forget the horror of looking into the beloved face and seeing the contortion of madness. I jumped out of the truck and ran to Eric's tipi, then stopped when I heard Elizabeth's soothing voice. "Entreat me not to leave thee," she was reading, "or to return from following after thee." I poked my head inside. "For whither thou goest I will—Steve!" She closed Eric's tattered Bible.

Rupert was propped up with pillows atop the bear rug, and surrounded by children. Over flannel pajamas he wore a contraption like a chastity belt with suspenders, all fashioned from chains and connected to the septic tank outside. On his feet were the bejeweled slippers Hermione Pitt had made for him in my art therapy group at Los Perdidos. He looked at me, then stared down at his hands. "Did I hurt him bad, li'l buddy?"

"Is Josh mad?" Mikey asked.

"A simple punch in the nose would have conveyed your idea, Rupe," I said. "He'll be fine." I looked into Mikey's worried little face. "Josh isn't mad," I said, oddly sure this was true. "He knows Rupe wasn't himself."

Rupert blew his nose on a wad of toilet paper. "It's back to Los Perdidos with me, huh? Or the big house. Funny they're not gonna fry you and me for killing Doc Burner."

"Turner was killed by his own meanness," I said. "And the sheriff says the worst thing that can happen is you'll have go to the Colorado State Hospital for observation."

Rupert's eyes froze in panic, and I added weakly, "It's in Pueblo, a pretty little town. A month at the most, then back here. It's not as bad as Los Perdidos. Nothing is."

THE STABBING DIDN'T DISRUPT Zoë's travel plans. When the staff arrived in town early the next day, the Rolls stood with its trunk yawning open. In the triple-wide Charley was making omelets. I reported that Rupert was calm and remorseful, snowed on Thorazine, sane enough to be scared. Cy said Josh was in stable condition with a normal temperature, so his wounds weren't infected.

Willow joined Charley in serving breakfast. Zoë poured orange juice. She wore a suit and a little veiled hat, and her luggage was lined up at the front door.

"By the way," Cy said, "Charley spent the night here. She and Zoë sat up chatting. The next thing I knew they were slurping on each other's pussies and then they dragged *me* into the filth."

Charley dropped a spatula on the floor and busied herself wiping up the bits of omelet.

Zoë waved him away like a deerfly. "Aaron, you *set* it up." She laughed. "*Everyone* knows you always start the orgy." She took Charley's hand. "What does not always happen is that Cy got a *hard*on. I thank *you* for that, Charley."

I knew this wasn't a joke only because of my own experience with Mr. and Mrs. M. I tried to read the faces at the table, but everyone seemed deeply involved with their food. Could I be the only one who was appalled that Cy had made moves on Charley, or that she'd made herself available? And amazed that Zoë had coöperated and was now celebrating?

After breakfast Eric and I fell over each other carrying Zoë's bags to the Rolls. She kissed us each, spent a moment with Cy, and drove off with a wave of one gloved hand. On the way back to the Ranch, Willow, Eric, Ken and I discussed Rupe's future and Josh's prognosis, the state of the drying apricots and the ripening pumpkins—but we were too well-trained to subgroup, and no one mentioned the three-way.

I spent part of the afternoon reading to Rupe from Lydia's *Rubáiyát*, then returned to town and slept under my desk. At seven the next morning Sheriff Buford called. "That Seville boy's got a mental history long as a mule's pecker," he said, and explained that he would drive Josh to the Ranch, then take Rupert to the Colorado State Hospital.

"But Rupert's on medication," I protested. "He's remorseful."

"Scramble him back up a little before I come get him."

Buford and Josh arrived at the Ranch in the sheriff's white Ford pickup. They climbed out laughing. Cy had arranged a confrontation session between attacker and victim, and the sheriff's attendance was the best kind of PR. Before he transported Rupert to the state hospital, he would see us at our loving best.

A short way up the path from the cookshack, Rupert stood barefoot in his harness of chains and squinted into the sun. Travis and Eric held him back by ropes, and Josh limped through the sand to face him. The sheriff joined the great circle of Vistans surrounding the two men.

"Somebody better truss me up too, so we're fair and square," Josh said. "I'm movin' a little slow but I'm mad as hell." Ken and Puck improvised a harness of climbing straps, and held him about eight feet from Rupert.

"Let's try this with Rainbow and Lucky," Theodora suggested. I chuckled for the sheriff's sake, but knew she wasn't joking.

Rupe worked his fists and called out, "Looks like time to get all the cards on the table."

"But let's leave the cutlery in the drawer," Josh replied.

The sheriff laughed, eyes sparkling, and the Vistans joined in.

"Vivian was moaning in your tipi that morning," Rupert said. "I thought you were breaking the Seventh Commandment."

"I was giving her a shoulder rub. We were fully dressed."

"When I stormed in, the flaming sword of the archangel showed me where to bury the knife. If Vivian hadn't grabbed my arm, I would have planted it in your cheatin' heart."

I watched Sheriff Buford's bemused face as the dispute went on, and wondered if Rupert sounded crazy enough. No, he sounded perfectly sane. And Josh may as well remain in his harness. Only a few days remained until the end of his Month-

Off from Charley. He would want to kill her, and probably Cy, when he heard her Withhold about the three-way.

Finally the accusations and justifications died down. "You love my wife," Josh said. "You thought I was cheating on her. Your methods were extreme, and you're a strong S.O.B. But thanks for defending her honor."

The two men reached out their arms to each other, and the guys holding the restraints allowed them to embrace. "I'm sure glad you're alive," Rupe said.

Josh held him. "Hurry home and we'll make lovely music."

We cheered. The children ran to Rupe and hugged his legs. Suddenly Mikey charged the sheriff and kicked him in the shin. "Don't put Rupe in the crusty bed!" he yelled.

Buford placed a hand on Mikey's head and held him beyond kicking range. "The crusty what, little feller?"

I hoisted Mikey into my arms. "He means the Procrustean bed." The creases between the sheriff's eyebrows deepened. "He's worried about Rupe at the state hospital."

"Naw, they got nice soft beds there," Buford said gently. "Probably even one big enough for your friend."

Buford tossed his handcuffs onto the floor of the pickup, offered Rupe a cigarette and opened the passenger door for him.

Rupe reached for me. "Sorry I let you down, li'l buddy."

I managed a dim smile. "Just get back in one piece."

WHEN THE MONTH-OFF ENDED I expected Charley to express her Withhold and reveal her three-way with Cy and Zoë. But Group opened with a fight between Elizabeth and her mother, and ended with Rainbow and Lucky growling and pawing the air while members of the work crew held them in restraints. Nothing passed between Charley and Josh beyond a sterile acknowledgment that they again existed to each other. Cy announced she would be traveling with the staff to the Santa Barbara conference—news that knotted my gut. I searched the faces of Willow, Eric and Ken. Charley was moving in on Zoë and Cy. Could everyone feel as indifferent as they acted?

21

"**WE'LL KEEP HAVING GROUP EVERY DAY,**" Cy promised, "before the staff and I take off for Santa Barbara. That way I can douse any smoldering brushfires before we leave you grunts in Travis's hands, to be sold into slavery to the local ranchers."

But in spite of his daily attention, a few flare-ups required additional, impromptu Groups. The morning before the trip, half-way through breakfast, Theodora marched into the cook-shack and raged, "I'll kill the fucker that stole my Oreos!"

Cy gulped his last bite of French toast. "Honey, fuckers are people too."

She slitted her eyes at him. "I'm gonna wring the scrawny neck of the motherfucker *who* stole my cookies."

"Magnificent! Travis, kindly raise the drawbridge before any suspects can escape."

The gong summoned the Vistans who had already left the cookshack. Those of us still eating gobbled what we could, scraped our scraps into the compost bucket, dutifully dumped our trays into the soapy-water barrel and headed for the Dome.

I wearily imagined a replay of the purloined peanut butter Group. I had piles of work to do in town before Cy and I hit the road. How long would the criminal wait to fess up this time?

Cy began before all of us had found seats. "Theodora and I talked on our way from the cookshack. Honey, if I understand, you're not upset over the loss of the cookies, but because the thief rifled through your drawers to find them. Am I right?"

"Fuckin' A." She moved to the center of the round room. "Before my Body Image, when I weighed six hundred pounds, I ate a case of cookies every day. Now I eat one cookie a *week*. Did you think I wouldn't *notice*? There were sixteen before breakfast, twelve when I got back." She crossed her arms. "And we can stop talking about 'the thief.' Mikey, I saw you slither out of my tipi. Drag your sorry ass over here."

Vivian's tired eyes studied the patchwork of pine triangles surrounding the skylights, while her son stalked to the center of the Dome.

"Don't even bother to sit down, Mikey," Eric said. "We're not going through another all-day ordeal. Did you eat Theodora's cookies?"

Mikey put his small, coal-stained hands on his hips and glared at Eric. "No. I'm saving 'em for later. Travis won't give us anything between—"

"You little rodent," Theodora snarled. "If you asked me for a cookie I'd give you one. But I saw the look on your face. You got off on going through my stuff."

"Is that true?" Cy asked. "Mikey, did you get a thrill looking in Theodora's drawers?"

His hands remained on his hips. "It was fun."

"My fucking *under*wear drawer."

"I'm missing a jar of jam my mom sent me," said Rainbow. "Mikey, did you take it?"

His defiant posture didn't change. "Yes."

Others asked if goodies they thought they'd misplaced—candy, soda, bags of nuts and dried fruit—had been among his plunder. My impatience dissolved into fascination. Despite his insolent stance, the boy confirmed each theft. Over many months he'd stolen cashews from Willow's tipi, candy bars from Lucky's, root beer as well as the preserves from Rainbow's. He usually took a single soda or candy bar, a few cookies or a handful of nuts, not enough to be missed.

"What shall we do?" Cy asked.

"I think—" Vivian began.

"And you," he interrupted, "don't have to carry the burden of your son's sins. Mikey, in Tahiti, where Zoë grew up, you'd be tending your own grove of coconuts by now. You're a responsible member of this community."

Theodora calmly addressed Mikey. "I did time in Juvie for car theft. I wouldn't have gotten in so much trouble if somebody'd taken a big shit in my mouth the first time I stole something."

Cy clapped his hands. "The classic defecation-in-the-mouth process as the natural consequence of light-fingered practices. Other suggestions?"

"Seriously," Eric said. "Public humiliation is the most natural consequence. I was a lowlife purse-snatcher. First time, if they'd put me in stocks in the mall instead of treating me like a disadvantaged youth, I wouldn't have ended up with a twenty-year prison sentence hanging over my head."

"Keep talking, folks," Cy said. "I don't run this place, I just earn the money that buys the lentils. Ken? You led a life of crime.

Do you agree with Theodora and Eric?"

Ken agreed, as did each of Mikey's other victims, including his sister Elizabeth, from whom he admitted he'd stolen fifty cents.

"How about," Vivian said with tight lips, "if Mikey does something more constructive than stand in stocks and eat feces? Like replace what he stole. And he could haul coal for people."

"I love you," Theodora told her, "but have you ever stolen anything?"

Vivian stared blankly at her.   .

"I didn't think so. See, he's not stealing 'cause he's hungry, but for the *fun* of it. Like I did. In ten years your little angel could end up in prison for burglary. You'll beg the judge to let you wash his victims' windows as restitution."

Cy held his hands before his face is a prayerful gesture. "I haven't shared this with most of you," he said, in a suddenly serious tone. The note-taking stopped. "But it's important for Mikey, so here goes. When I was sixteen I went to jail for siphoning gas. There was no 'juvenile hall' in those days. Just buttfucking by angry men three times my size. They'd get together and hold me down."

The room fell silent. In the other Vistans' faces I saw horror like my own. The image of the youthful Cy being raped cut into my heart.

"Of course I couldn't understand at the time," he continued softly, "but they did me a favor by convincing me I never wanted to return to jail. So I do believe appropriate punishment can serve as a life-changing deterrent." He closed his eyes and seemed to swallow back the memory he had invoked for the sake of Mikey's mental health. "So," he asked, "what's the process?"

Led by Theodora, the group reached a quick consensus that the compost pit, "where scavengers hang out," was the appropriate location to deliver consequences. The thought of putting Mikey in the compost pit appalled me. But if a few minutes among the reeking, maggoty vegetables could circumvent a boy's criminal career, it wasn't extreme at all. I raised my hand and joined the vote. Only Vivian and Josh dissented.

Theodora led Mikey to the pit and helped him into the rough, wood-lined trough. His canvas shoes sank through the top crust of chicken skin, fish heads, scabby oatmeal and brown lettuce. The rank, effervescent muck below foamed up and swallowed the hem of his blue jeans. Flies buzzed all around him and settled in his hair. For the first time all morning he cried.

"It does stink pretty bad," Theodora said, "but I want to throw some on him."

Vivian cried, "He's eight years old!"

"Nice try, Mom," Elizabeth jibed. "Why don't you get in there with him? After he stole the peanut butter, everybody was nice to him. He didn't stop, he just got sneakier."

Tears and snot ran down Mikey's face. He shifted his weight, and the pit belched a putrid bubble.

Holding Josh's hand for support, Vivian descended into the slop to stand beside her son. "Maybe he needs this but he's not going through it alone."

Theodora folded her arms. "I still want to throw something at him."

"Throw it at me, too," Vivian urged.

Theodora reached into the morning's compost bucket and flung a handful of banana peels. They hit Mikey's shoulder and fell onto one shoe. Rainbow pelted him with eggshells. Lucky threw cantaloupe rinds. Willow splattered French toast, soaked in rancid milk, over his denim jacket. Stray coffee grounds sprayed in Vivian's hair.

Cy knelt at the edge of the pit and spoke softly. "Mikey, do you see that people are trying to help you? Look at your mother, standing in the garbage with you. If that isn't love, I've never seen it. Look at the tears in Theodora's eyes." Mikey nodded and sniffled, and Cy continued, "You've copped to all the thefts people asked you about. Now reach further inside yourself. Tell us about the thefts no one mentioned."

Without hesitation Mikey sobbed, "Steve, I took a box of matches and some flashlight batteries from your tipi. Travis, I swiped a bottle of beer from under your bed. Tobey, I ate one of your Butterfingers . . ."

Cy motioned to each newly-identified victim to stand at the end of the pit and face Mikey during his confession. "Ken, I raided your coal box," the boy admitted, then fell silent.

I scooped a handful of soggy bread encrusted with coffee grounds. My gut lurched. I flung the mess without watching its path, then stepped aside. Travis reached deep. Omelet chunks and cottage cheese thwacked Mikey's face and ricocheted onto Vivian.

"Baptism by garbage," Cy intoned when the last handful had been flung. Covered in slop, Mikey sobbed violently with his mother holding him at her side.

Theodora lifted Mikey from the pit and hugged him tight. The Vistans surrounded them, then lifted and cradled the little stinking bundle, singing, "Sometimes I feel like a motherless child . . ."

Tobey Turner, witnessing his first Vista cradle, fell into my arms and wept.

Vivian stood with Josh, her gaze fixed somewhere far away. I squeezed Tobey, wishing to hell Vivian's eyes would meet mine.

AFTER LUNCH I BEGAN A RELATIONSHIP WORK-BOOK DEVOTED TO CY. I was riddled with thought-Withholds. At the head of the list: *I've subgrouped in my head that you were a shit for fucking Charley while Josh was in the hospital.* I had been the shit—a jealously judging him for enjoying some pleasure with Charley, pleasure even Zoë affirmed. Many of the Workbook's pages remained blank. I couldn't come up with anything about myself that might have given Cy comfort, joy or hope.

That afternoon in town, after gassing up the big Mercedes, I called the Colorado State Hospital to arrange to visit Rupert at the start of Cy's and my trip trip. After an hour of bureaucratic shuffling, an official informed me that Mr. Seville was on a locked criminal ward and couldn't have visitors. A routine check had revealed he was a California escapee and would soon be transferred back to Perdido Valley State Hospital.

Reeling with helplessless, I left an urgent message for Rupert's grandmother. Her lawyers had once obtained an injunction to prevent shock treatments. I went to sleep praying they could block the transfer to Los Perdidos.

"I GUESS YOU'VE NOTICED HOW BEAUTIFUL Tobey Turner is," Cy said a few miles out of Keystone. He drove carefully, with both hands firmly on the wheel.

I shrugged, then admitted, "Those eyes! He's prettier than most girls."

"He follows you like a puppy. He may give you a unique opportunity."

"Really?" I was distracted as we approached the spot where Tobey's father had driven to his death.

"Through him you could contact your own innocence. Overcome the guilt you've lugged around all these years over your first love. You could give him his first sexual experience—"

"Tobey's sixteen!"

"Aw, shucks, I fergawt," Cy drawled. "Kids don't have sexual needs. And to think I'm being reminded by someone who was cornholing his best friend in the hay loft at thirteen."

I pretended to drink in the scenery I'd seen on countless trips to Gentile. Only fifteen miles into the journey, I'd managed to irritate Cy with my limitations.

"Ever wondered," he asked, "why a confirmed old heterosexual like me is working to make the psychiatric world safe for gay people?"

Relieved that he was still engaging with me, I ventured, "As a kid you had a homosexual experience? You weren't gay but realized gay people deserve humane treatment." I chewed at the inside of my cheek. "Not sure where those convicts who raped you fit into my theory."

"Your theory is sound." Cy sighed deeply and suggested I dig out a certain large pickle jar from one of the ice chests Elsie had packed in the back seat. Baffled, I turned around and opened the smallest of three ice chests, then fumbled through jars of protein drink and yogurt. Finally I found the pickle jar. Inside it, floating in soya sauce, was a narrow olive jar, and inside that I found a baggie packed with fat joints.

"You're giving me a therapy session," Cy said, while I wiped soya sauce off my hands with a paper towel. "A few hits will loosen the essential neural pathways."

"Is this ingenious jar system meant to fool drug-sniffing dogs?"

"How would you have asked that question before coming to Rancho Vista?"

" 'What the fuck's this soya sauce for?' "

He smiled.

The joints were perfectly uniform, straight and thin as pencils, and twisted tightly at each end. After two hits I stared out the window and imagined I could see the spirits of coyotes lurking in the sage. Cy suggested I snuff the joint and re-pack the jars. This task took on complex dimensions almost beyond my grasp.

"I'm hammered," I admitted. "I can't give you any therapy."

"When I was five, as I think you know, my mother was killed by a hit-and-run driver."

I scrambled for the only phrase I could remember. "How'd that make you feel?"

"See? You can do this. My mother's death devastated me. My grandmother took me and my baby sister in. Every day I waited

at the end of our road for Mama to come back from town. I
prayed and cried. I felt completely alone without her. My father
had abandoned us before my sister was born."

What would Cy say if our positions were reversed? "So you
became an orphan," I ventured.

"'Orphan' is a loaded word." In Cy's tone I heard no censure,
only instruction. "A therapist wants to leave the charged language
for the patient, and then follow it down the path of the emotions.
But yes, I did feel like an orphan. My grandmother was uncom-
fortable around me, and desperately needed money." He looked
straight at me as if checking to be sure his young protégé could
handle what he was about to say.

I was ready with eye contact and a loving smile.

"So my grandmother sold me to an old homosexual."

"She *what?*"

"He adopted me informally and gave her money."

"Did you understand what was happening?"

Cy chuckled. "And you thought you couldn't handle doing
therapy with me. No, I didn't understand she'd sold me. I just
knew I'd left the home of a bitter, harsh woman whose only
books were a Bible and a Sears catalogue, and moved in with a
gentle man who had more books than I could count, and taught
me to read and appreciate them."

"What was his name?"

"Wilson. Know why it was astute of you to ask me that?"

"Because it makes him more real, which invites you into the
emotional realm?"

"Excellent! Wilson and I read together every night—Sinbad,
Robert Lewis Stevenson, later Dickens and Twain, eventually
Plato and Kant. After our reading he gave me a blow job and
tucked me into bed. 'Suck and tuck,' we called it."

"He molested you!"

"More loaded language. Don't call Child Protective Services
on the poor man. He's long dead. He *loved* me. Without him I
wouldn't have gone to high school. And I would have jerked off
furtively every night anyway. He gave me a better orgasm, with
affection. And he obviously didn't make me a homosexual. He
just made me appreciate a good blow job. When I started dating
girls, I was appalled by how terrible they were at cocksucking."

Worse than Ken? I was tempted to joke, but this wasn't my
therapy session.

Cy followed the speed limit precisely. When I suggested he

could probably drive a bit faster on a straight-away, he quoted Christ: "*Render therefore unto Caesar the things which are Caesar's.* Do you see how that applies here?"

I giggled and gave the riddle a try. "If we follow the rules on the trivial stuff, Big Brother will ignore the important things."

Cy beamed. "That mind of yours! I assume you realize I wanted you at Rancho Vista the first time we spoke. I knew you were a kid posing as a bureaucrat—but a brilliant, resourceful kid. And that you had compassion, trying to rescue your friend from the snake pit."

Overwhelmed, I managed to say, "Thank you, Cy."

"I'm a typically bad father. I've never told you I loved you. God, even that's indirect. I love you, Steve."

"Then I've been a bad son. I love *you*, Cy."

I cherished the silence that followed.

When he finally spoke again he sounded sad. "I was afraid you would run screaming if the Vistans came after you. I had to accept that you might reject our way of life, knowing you would thrive among us if you gave yourself the chance."

I had feared this trip, feared sucking or turning Cy off in some other way. Now my only fear was that I was so stoned I wouldn't recall later what we'd said to each other.

"I'll never forget your pinched face at Garth Elfinger's funeral," Cy went on, "or the morning you showed up in Keystone so full of fear. But you had hope or you wouldn't have hitchhiked beyond civilization in a blizzard."

The crystalline moment passed with the scenery. Cy loved me. Nothing else mattered.

HE DROPPED ME AT THE DENVER MARRIOTT and drove off to do a therapy session with a local politician. When I registered, I learned we had a room with only one bed. The clerk pointed out that this had been specified in the reservation, and explained that because of a cattlemen's convention no other rooms were available. I ordered a cot, wondering how Elsie could have screwed up, and fearing Cy would think the one bed was my idea.

Upstairs I unpacked Cy's shoulder bag and felt strangely embarrassed when I grasped the big Hitachi vibrator. I'd never really looked at the thing before—like an ivory cudgel, about eighteen inches long with a tapered plastic handle, a great head of white rubber, the electric cord a long tail. A three-speed switch. I returned it to the bag with the Polaroid, since Cy wouldn't be needing either until Zoë joined him in Santa Barbara.

Cy had prepared me to spend the evening alone, and encouraged me to have a nice dinner. I dressed in a pair of Beverly Hills trousers and the vicuña sweater, and slipped into my Italian loafers. In the hotel restaurant I ordered a glass of good wine with dinner and thought of Rupert in a cold seclusion room. If we were together we would find a barbecue joint where we'd be the only white patrons. Rupe would play his guitar to pay for our meal. I promised myself we would do just that as soon as he got out of the hospital.

Back in the room I resisted the novelty of television. I undressed and pulled out my Relationship Workbook on Cy. So much to write! So many Withholds, so much gratitude. Under the covers of the cot I propped myself on an elbow and recounted on pages of lilac, pink and blue the ways that Cy had enriched my life. Within a few minutes I filled the page headed, *AT THESE TIMES YOU HAVE MADE ME FEEL HOPEFUL.*

Sometime later I awoke to the swoosh of the toilet, the Workbook wrinkled under me. Cy emerged naked from the bathroom carrying his shoulder bag.

"I unpacked that already," I said.

"Look at your feet, hanging off that silly cot. I'm planning to have you drive tomorrow, so you'll need a good night's sleep. This bed's big enough for six people. Get in. Just don't try to cornhole me in the middle of the night."

I smiled, moved to the bed, said goodnight and rolled away from Cy. Quickly I drifted back to sleep.

The droning vibrator woke me. I lay still, confused and frightened. The contraption clicked off. Cy slid out of bed and padded around to my side. Through one slitted eye I saw that he sported a semi-erection and carried a towel, a jar of Vaseline, and the vibrator, which trailed a long extension cord. Mortified, I squeezed my eyes shut and remained still.

Cy perched on the edge of the bed. A greased hand reached for my cock and stroked it until it became hard. Then he slid under the covers, lay on his side facing away, and slowly worked the head into his ass.

I lay motionless. The vibrator clicked back on, and through Cy's muscles and membranes I felt the motorized buzz. He had the machine pressed against his cock. His ass slowly relaxed to take more, and I ludicrously feigned sleep while the hot, slick butt bore down on my cock until there was no more to take. Though Cy used his ass and not his mouth, his approach was as silent and strange as Ken's. My cock was of interest only as a disembodied organ. I was a human dildo! With Ken I'd learned to stifle my need for affection and cuddling. Now I shoved away revulsion, fear, even anger. What if I thrust hard, like the inmates who victimized Cy in his youth? Like my own soap-bar rapists in the gym shower?

There was no in-out motion, only the full length of my cock gripped inside a hot, slick sheath of muscle. I breathed as evenly as I could. Eventually the surprisingly supple ass grasped and milked at me in the spasms of Cy's orgasm. The vibrator went quiet. Cy pulled away, wiped my cock with a towel and headed for the bathroom. My erection subsided immediately. Long after he returned and began snoring beside me, I lay there wondering how we would talk about what we had done. No—what Cy had done, what I had allowed.

THE NEXT MORNING NEITHER OF US MEN-TIONED THE FUCKING. We took turns driving, and wrote down ideas for books and workshops. We talked about history and philosophy and the Vistans' role in the future of therapy.

In every hotel room over the coming days, I lay with my back to Cy and pretended to fall asleep. After I breathed steadily for ten minutes or so, the vibrator clicked on and Cy came to my side of the bed. Never during the penetration or Cy's climax did either of us speak. On our last night of traveling, in the Claremont Hotel above Berkeley, I met his motions half way, taking the lead and plunging myself in, so that by the time he underwent his orgasmic spasms I had already shot my seed into my mentor. And after Cy did his own cleanup routine, I got up and showered. But still neither of us spoke.

Driving through Berkeley in the morning, Cy said, "You've developed into a superb sexual surrogate. You intuitively under-stand all the important principles."

Giddily relieved to be discussing this at last, I asked, "Like knowing I should pretend to be asleep?"

"That did help, but it's certainly not always necessary. You were rather vigorously awake for Zoë and me. And this morn-ing."

"Does my job include asking how you feel about the experience?"

"Ordinarily, no. But—how many of those joints are left?"

I dug out one of the two that remained. After we paid the toll and drove onto the Bay Bridge, I lit it.

He took a deep hit. "Most of the men who raped me in jail were brutal. But one guy was kind. He smuggled bacon grease out of the kitchen to use as a lubricant, and stroked my cock while he fucked me. It was wonderfully pleasurable. I had super-intense orgasms with him inside me. Your generation would say the discovery 'freaked me out.'"

He took another long, slow hit. "I tried to suppress the memory once I got out of jail. Years later, in medical school, I learned that the prostate gland is a pleasure center, and its stimulation can greatly enhance orgasm. But until I tried it with you, this knowledge was academic, and my adolescent memory remained buried under layers of shame and fear." He rested a hand on my knee. "You will be one of the world's great sex surrogates."

Ahead of us the San Francisco skyline disappeared behind a mountain of fog. I knew I would sound ungrateful if I confessed to feeling like an exotic jellyfish, poked at by curious boys.

OUTSIDE SAN JOSE THE CAR BEGAN TO SPUTTER.
I blew out the fuel line at a gas station, and we enjoyed a smooth ride for several hours. But in front of the Hotel Santa Barbara the Mercedes lurched forward and stalled.

"You'll want to see Rupert down south anyway," Cy said. "Take the car to Euro Motors on Sunset. We have an account."

I borrowed his shoulder bag and stuffed in a few toiletries with a change of clothes. I got the car moving again. In Encino I pulled off the freeway to find a pay phone. The admissions office at Los Perdidos had no record of Rupert Seville, except as an Unauthorized Absence. I next dialed Irma Seville's number, thrilled with the certainty that her lawyers had prevented the transfer after all.

A man answered. No, Mrs. Seville was not available.

"Do you know if she's blocked her grandson's transfer—"

"Who is calling, please?"

"Forgive me. This is Steve Susoyev, from Rancho Vista."

The man sighed. "Mr. Susoyev, she's in Colorado, arranging her grandson's burial. He hanged himself last night."

22

RUPE'S PATH THROUGH LIFE HAD BEEN FULL OF PAIN AND HUMILIATION. Years in the back wards, torture by Turner and others almost as cruel. Finally he'd known a few months of peace and hope, and now this.

I dug my fingernails into the heels of my hands to keep from crying. Once I started I wouldn't be able to stop. Cy liked to say, "When you're in your shit so deep you think you can't function, move the body." Numb and stupid with grief, I climbed back into the car and sputtered over surface streets to the palatial Euro Motors garage. Lining the inside walls were Jaguars, Ferraris, an even larger Mercedes than the one I drove—and near the door, a Rolls Austin Princess of the same vintage and creamy shade as Zoë's. The luxury was a bitter reminder that the Seville wealth hadn't helped keep Rupert alive.

In the office I wrote Cy's name on the service order. The chic cashier read it and asked, "Same phone number as the Rolls?"

I grunted without digesting the question.

She raised her perfect eyebrows and pulled a clipboard from the wall. Her expression implied, *We charge top dollar and even grunting morons receive respect.* "Mrs. Aaron brought her car in this morning. You didn't put down a phone number for Dr. Aaron's Mercedes."

I gave her a pinched frown. "*Who* brought the Rolls in? Mrs. Aaron won't be back in the country for two more days."

"Sir, Zoë Aaron dropped off her Rolls at eight this morning."

"That's imposs—. Did she leave a phone number?"

The cashier replied with the same smile Los Perdidos nurses often used on patients. "Let's start at the beginning. I just asked you—"

"*I'm* asking for the number she left here. I need to get in touch with her."

"You're driving the Aarons' car and you don't know their phone number?"

I reminded myself to breathe. *My best friend just killed himself,* I wanted to say. *Could you please just help me?* I recited the number of the answering service, but the cashier consulted her clip-board and shook her head. Finally I stalked over to the Rolls, grabbed the paperwork from the glove box, then with trembling hands lay the registration slip on the counter beside my driver's license. "See? Her car is in my name."

She scrutinized the photo, taken when my hair looked like a pyramid of straw, then produced the repair ticket for the Rolls. The sight of Zoë's handwriting made me ache to see her. Whatever her reason for coming home early, she would know how to comfort me about Rupert. I copied the phone number and the words "Room 20," then grabbed Cy's shoulder bag, left Euro Motors and called from a pay phone across the street.

A woman answered, "Gateway Motel."

"Mrs. Aaron's room, please."

Pause. "No Aaron, sir."

"Room twenty."

Why was Zoë in a motel when the house was furnished? And why hadn't she called the service to let Cy know she was home early from Tahiti? Maybe Samuel had rejected her, and she was embarrassed. I would find strength to comfort her, too.

After five rings a man answered. I held my breath. The man repeated, "Hello?" then hung up.

I found the address of the Gateway Motel in the white pages, ran for a Sunset Boulevard bus going west, jumped on, paid and sat down. Tears spilled down my cheeks and I faced the window, clutching Cy's shoulder bag. Rupert had known what lay ahead. At Los Perdidos he would have been locked up with psychopathic murderers, and treated like one.

UCLA and the enormous houses of Bel Aire and Brentwood rolled by, then the relative modesty of Santa Monica. I suppressed my tears when a group of noisy kids clamored aboard and stared at me. I climbed off the bus near the beach. A few blocks south, on the only depressed real estate in view, squatted the Gateway Motel. I approached it feeling confused.

In the parking lot between a stairway and an ice machine, a maroon Lincoln with a broken taillight listed toward the Pacific. I was sure I'd seen the same car months before. It belonged to the agent who'd handled the foreclosure sale of the fixer-upper mansion on Bedford Drive—a pot-bellied little chain-smoker, Sonny somebody. Sonny Tornado.

Obviously Zoë had borrowed Mr. Tornado's car and was staying here for some legitimate reason. A gas leak at the house. Workmen tearing up the kitchen. Why spend money on a hotel when this quaint place was so close to the beach?

This quaint, weed-infested dump with peeling paint. And the strange man answering her phone. I could get on a bus back to Beverly Hills, pick up a gallon of cheap wine and guzzle it while I soaked in a tub at the ramshackle mansion. And forget everything.

But I spotted room twenty—downstairs, in a corner. Casually I walked behind the motel and slipped into an unruly stand of oleanders that hid me from the street. Each downstairs room had a tiny patio, enclosed in chain-link fencing run through with slats of weathered wood. From the corner room a television blared. Above the howls of a game-show audience, I heard the unmistakable, giddy laugh of Zoë Aaron.

I peered between two warped boards. On the patio table lay a few slices of pizza in an open take-out box. An ashtray overflowed with butts. The sliding glass door into the room was open but I couldn't see beyond it.

"Shakespeare for six hundred," a contestant called out.

"No, not Shake*speare!*" Zoë squealed. "You will be sorry, you foolish woman."

"The answer," said the master of ceremonies, "is *'Even so quickly may one catch this plague.'* For six hundred dollars, state the question."

Zoë's laughter drowned out the show and she exclaimed, "What is *love?*" Abruptly the television went silent and she purred, "I know that one because *I* have caught this plague."

"Not quickly, though," Sonny Tornado said sadly. "I've waited so long."

"Oh, *Samuel,*" she answered. "I have waited, too. So many flights in your *Lear* Jet."

"Thank God the waiting is over."

I bowed my head against the fence. Cy couldn't affirm her being with a man who drove around with a broken taillight. To make him happy she'd conjured the Billionaire "Samuel," then fallen for a simple man with whom she could watch game shows and eat junk food.

And she couldn't comfort me about Rupert because she was with this outsider.

Move the body. I felt I should call Cy, but to say what? *Here's the latest on Polysex and the Pure Relationship.* What would happen to Cy without Zoë at his side? My grief for Rupe mingled with anger at Zoë. My hot tears splattered onto my shoes.

I remembered that Cy's shoulder bag still held the Polaroid. I crouched in the shadows across the street from the motel and checked to see if the camera had film.

THE NEXT AFTERNOON, the historic Hotel Santa Barbara was crowded with the people Cy called "the love bead crowd." Their burlap and denim luggage spilled over the colonial Spanish tile floors. Through my exhaustion and grief, I recognized faces from the Beverly Hills conference, where people had dressed more conservatively.

Cy wasn't at the center of any of the clusters of people, but when I entered the cocktail lounge I saw that a pack of men had gathered around Charley. In a pastel suit, with her roots freshly dyed and her hair billowed in a wheat-blonde version of Zoë's Gibson Girl, she looked like a movie star. She sipped a glass of white wine. Zachary Bush, the creator of the "Anger Lab," sat beside her at the bar. He tilted precariously toward her while she sat erect. The other Vistans hunched around a table in the corner, looking adolescent even in their grown-up outfits.

As I approached, Willow was remarking to the others, "If Zack Bush comes to our presentations the camera crews will follow him. He's the hottest thing on the growth circuit."

"He seems to be leaning in that direction," Eric quipped.

They all laughed, then rose gravely when they saw me. "Elsie told us about Rupe," Willow said. "Cy feels terrible."

"Listen," Eric offered, "thanks to you, Rupert had some freedom. Rancho Vista was paradise after where he'd been."

Ken and Puck both volunteered to help me to the Grunt Suite with my luggage.

"It's just this bag," I said. "What I really need is to see Cy—"

Charley's voice sliced into me from behind. "Steve, I'm glad you're here. But Cy's resting. Of course you're upset about Rupert. We all are." Her voice shifted into her best imitation of good-natured teasing. "But I don't think you should try to corner Cy for therapy after a whole week alone with him."

I wanted to spit in her face. "Something's going on with Zoë," I said, implying *Something that's none of your fucking business*. I walked off and called from a house phone near the bar.

Cy answered after several rings, in a tone of irritation: "What's the matter?"

My heart thumped. "An emergency."

"Elsie already told me about Ru—"

"No, it's Zoë."

"Oh, my God."

"She's not hurt, don't worry, but I have to see you right away." Charley eyed me from the bar while she smiled for Zachary Bush.

"You'd better get up here."

Seconds later I stepped into an elevator and knew there was no question I would betray Zoë. She had made my life more colorful, but Cy had rescued me.

In his suite, I spread out Polaroids of Zoë and Sonny leaving the motel room together, getting into the broken-down Lincoln, driving away. They had returned an hour or so later, when it was too dark to photograph them without the flash. So I'd rented a room at the motel, and caught them again in the morning as they walked to breakfast in fresh clothes.

"When did you take these?" Cy asked.

I had never heard him sound so confused. "Those, yesterday afternoon. These, this morning."

"She's back from Tahiti?"

"She never went, Cy. This is the guy she calls 'Samuel.'"

He recoiled from me. "Preposterous! Rupert's tragedy has distorted your thinking."

"I hid outside their motel room and listened. She told him she loves him. They ate pizza and watched 'Jeopardy.'"

"Zoë does not eat pizza." He studied a morning photo of her holding Sonny's arm, head tilted toward him, appearing relaxed and well-fucked. "That's the chain-smoking grunt who sold us the house. My poor sweetheart." He shuffled through the other photos. "What did you do, stake her out?"

"I found her by accident."

"She deserves the benefit of the doubt." His voice cracked. "Is she coming tomorrow?"

I had never imagined Cy crying, but now tears shimmered at the corners of his eyes. "She didn't see me. I assume she'll do whatever the two of you planned."

Cy slumped into a wing-back chair, suddenly looking very old. "I'm devastated. But thank you. I won't shoot the carrier pigeon who delivered the bad news."

"Do you want me to stay? I can tell everyone you're resting."

"I have to practice what I preach. You just learned your dear friend is dead, but you tracked down my cheating wife. To survive this, I've got to move the body."

For me the phrase entered a new dimension. Cy dunked his head in cold water and dressed with care. During dinner with us he didn't mention Zoë, and calmly focused on work. He prompted me and others who were scheduled to make presentations to run through our outlines without notes. He attended a late-night cocktail reception and electrified the crowds as always. No one except me knew he was running on enough Valium to sedate a walrus.

When Cy made his conspicuous departure for the night he had Charley on his arm. Well-trained to avoid subgrouping, I followed the others to the Grunt Suite silently, but had found one more reason to dislike her: She'd robbed me of the opportunity to comfort Cy.

MY MORNING WORKSHOP ON THE RELATION-SHIP WORKBOOK drew about forty people. Cy beamed at me as I walked to the podium. "You're scheduled opposite Werner Erhard," he whispered. "Having more than two people show up is a coup."

Thrilled to be in direct competition with the father of est, I addressed the crowd without notes, and began by describing my dead childhood friend. "He went to reform school because of our childhood sex play. He was murdered there. My guilt pushed me near suicide. Using the Relationship Workbook, I reclaimed my will to live." With confidence I elaborated on the steps of relationship analysis the Workbook made possible.

The audience responded warmly and shared examples of unresolved relationships from their own lives. I separated these into categories and listed them on a large flip chart as people murmured with enthusiasm.

Afterward, a group of well-dressed men asked me whether we had considered licensing the Relationship Workbook for use in a corporate setting. "Of course," I ad-libbed, and summoned Cy. He invited the men to visit Rancho Vista. Over lunch with the Vistans he explained, "They're industrial psychologists. If they come and prove to be growth cases, we'll consider inviting them to join the community and train them. But we won't be 'licensing' the Relationship Workbook. Imagine licensing the Lord's Prayer."

Willow said, "A few years ago I almost went to work for Zack Bush. I should be at his workshop, but I don't want to go alone."

"We'll all go," Cy suggested brightly. "Charley, I understand Zack's rather fond of you."

"He's fond of scotch," she said, "and making people do ridiculous exercises like hitting each other with foam-rubber bats. But *Inside the Anger Lab* has been a best-seller for eight months."

Cy scribbled on the schedule of the remaining sessions, crossing off presenters who offered neither competition nor possible referrals. Those who offered both, like Zachary Bush, would find all the Vistans in their audiences.

WE SAT IN THE FRONT ROW AT THE ANGER LAB WORKSHOP. When Zack Bush called for pairs of volunteers to participate in an improvisation, Cy jumped up. Anxious to preempt Charley, I sprang to his side.

Cy didn't wait for direction from Bush. He announced, "I'm role-playing a modern psychological sophisticate, getting in touch with his nasty feelings. And this is my son."

I bowed my head contritely for my role. "Dad," I said, "I borrowed your favorite tie without asking, and I sort of spilled gravy all over it, and it shrank when I washed it, and—"

Cy pursed his lips, threw back his head and moaned. "Oh! Oh! I *feel* something rising up within me . . ." His hands traced the phantom emotion as it ascended through his body, and he added in sweet bewilderment, "Why, it feels like—oh *my*." Then he roared, "Like, like—*anger*. Anger toward *YOU!*" He lunged, and I hopped out of his path. The audience howled.

"If I can't strangle you," Cy screamed, "I'll whack you with a foam-rubber cudgel!" He grabbed one from the playpen where Bush kept the Anger Lab props, and pummeled me with it.

Bush's face remained impassive while the audience cheered, but the creases tightened around his lips. Smoothly he moved on to other material. When his workshop ended, the larger crowd, and the reporters, gathered around Cy.

Suddenly Cy was popping up at seminars he hadn't planned to attend, embarrassing other presenters with the same incisive glee he'd used against Zack Bush. After a workshop by the author of a popular self-help book, he held the attention to several reporters. "For pure entertainment you can't beat the pop psychologies," he said. "My favorite is '*I'm OK, You're Full of Shit*.' The problem is these authors give desperate people the illusion of control over their lives. A lonely guy who wouldn't dream of fixing a leaky faucet tries to straighten out his warped personality with the help of a dollar-and-ninety-five-cent paperback." The reporters hung on every word. He zeroed in on pop psychology's most sacred cow: "That lonely guy doesn't have to work on himself in isolation. How bleak this world would be if we all just 'did our thing,' as Fritz Perls recommended, and didn't shoulder one another's pain."

At Ken's Wilderness Therapy seminar that afternoon, over a hundred people signed up for Rancho Vista's mailing list. The next day's Body Image presentation would feature a nude volunteer from the audience. And Polysex—listed as "A system to deepen the marriage vows through sex with trusted guests"—was sure to lure a standing-room-only crowd.

THE VISTANS INVITED TWENTY PEOPLE to a party in Cy's suite, expecting Zoë to drive up from L.A. and join us early in the evening. Guests brought uninvited friends. I had counted sixty-six people when the phone rang. Zoë's voice sang out, "Etienne!" and I froze. Cy took the phone, talked a moment, then excused himself and disappeared. While the party raged on, the rest of us managed to keep the crowd entertained.

At midnight Charley helped clean up. Finally everyone headed for the Grunt Suite. In the elevator she asked me, "What's going on with Cy and Zoë?"

Ken's eyes snapped from her to me. "Maybe you're not comfortable talking about it," he said.

Relishing her anxiety, I shrugged at Ken and replied knowingly, "They're working some things out."

At one in the morning we had just settled into our sleeping bags, and several of us were snoring. The phone rang and I leaped for it.

"This is Zack Bush," said a leonine voice. "I've just posted bail to get Dr. Aaron out of the city jail. I'll drive him back to the hotel shortly."

My heart raced while Bush explained that Cy had been arrested in the hotel parking lot, where he'd screamed at Zoë as she drove away in the Rolls, then kicked the door of what turned out to be the bartender's car—while the bartender was watching. The police arrived almost immediately. Bush had observed the entire incident and followed the squad car downtown. By explaining Cy's unique situation, Dr. Bush persuaded the desk sergeant not to charge him with drunk and disorderly conduct, but the lesser offense of disturbing the peace.

Horrified, I thanked Dr. Anger Lab.

"Here's what my work has come to," Cy said, once we had gathered in his suite. "I'm affirming Zoë for being with a high-level man and she's fucking some rodent."

On the coffee table he displayed my Polaroids like icons on an altar. Everyone silently studied them. He drank vodka from a coffee cup and talked about their relationship—how he had met her in the South Seas while traveling with missionaries, and petitioned her family for the chance to court her. He'd accompanied her brother on a treacherous river journey to prove himself. "I got drunk at a village wedding and she refused to marry me unless I quit drinking. I didn't have a drink for twelve years."

"Except when she was out of town," Eric observed.

"Except when she was fucking that piece of shit Steve caught her with."

I had never imagined such bitterness in him, and tried to move past it. "Zack Bush was sure helpful," I offered.

"That prick calls you kids as my 'bisexual harem.' He loved exposing me as a cuckold to those tin badges."

He returned to his story, describing the marriage feast and his first night with Zoë. We listened, honoring his grief. Finally when he fell quiet I said, "Cy, it's four o'clock. You need to get some sleep. We've got a lot of moving the body to do tomorrow."

"You think I can sleep after this? Everything I believe in has just been flushed down the toilet. In a jail cell."

Charley poured more vodka. He gulped it and she poured still more, over Willow's protest that he'd had enough. "Stay with me," he said to Charley. "You kids go beddie-bye."

"BODY IMAGE ALIGNMENT" was scheduled for ten in the morning, in one of the hotel's meeting rooms. At eight, Ken and Puck carried in a huge plate-glass mirror they had lifted from the walls of the triple-wide.

They borrowed a ladder, and from a Ranch tool kit took out a power drill, molly bolts, a level and steel brackets. Within minutes the mirror hung square in the center of one wall. I positioned a small table beneath it, covered with a linen cloth from a room-service cart. The other Vistans moved chairs into concentric semicircles around it.

"Who is ready enough for growth," I asked, "to stand naked in a room full of strangers?"

"I had a Body Image," Puck said. "Theodora did too."

"Yeah, in the cookshack," Ken reminded him, "with thirty grunts. We're gambling that some sane person will volunteer to do it in front of three hundred people."

A camera crew arrived before nine, followed by early audience members. Zachary Bush took a seat near the front. By nine-thirty people were hauling in extra chairs. Just before ten, Cy and Charley took seats in the front row, as striking a couple as he and Zoë had been. I smiled weakly, sick with feelings I couldn't identify. Had Charley been planning this since the night of the three-way, while her husband lay bleeding in the hospital?

Willow welcomed the crowd and introduced Cy and the other Vistans. She briefly described our work "in the human relations laboratory in the Colorado canyons." I had resented her assignment to this high-profile workshop, but now I understood why Cy had let me cut my teeth on the relatively dry Relationship Workbook session. She had addressed large groups, and I could learn from watching her. After describing the Composite Significant Other, and explaining that a loving group could "impart feedback, reality-checks and *caring* far deeper than an individual therapist can provide," she added, "We form our self-concepts based on our warped body images, which we take to the grave—if we don't have heavy-duty intervention."

The table in front of the mirror stood empty, like an altar. Or a scaffold. Willow asked for a volunteer, "Someone ready to take a small risk in exchange for a huge growth opportunity."

The room hummed. I looked back and saw people elbowing each other and laughing uncomfortably. Some clutched the open necks of their shirts and blouses in parodies of modesty. When I faced forward again, my heart thudded with amazed rage. Charley was on the table, shedding her clothes.

She ad-libbed to the audience, "There's a waiting list at Rancho Vista for this process. I'm getting up here while I have the chance." She unhooked her pink satin bra and stepped out of the matching slip. With a final wriggle she dropped her pantyhose. "I'm ready, Willow."

Ready for what, I couldn't tell. Her left hip bore a purple discoloration the size of a flank steak. Murmurs of concern filled the room. "It's hard enough just getting up here," she said endearingly, "but I'm embarrassed about this bruise. I fell by the pool this morning."

I raised a brow at Ken, a gesture that bordered on subgrouping. When had she managed to go to the pool? The rest of us had worked the entire morning after three hours of sleep. Already she was taking unfair advantage of her new closeness to Cy.

She appeared small out of her clothes, almost adolescent, with girlish, perky breasts and delicate feet. Only her full hips looked like they belonged to a woman on the far side of thirty. Her face and neck flushed crimson as she began the process so familiar to us Vistans, but so unlike anything known in the "real world," listing all the things she didn't like about her body. "I tint my mousy hair to this shade of blonde . . . . My thighs take on a life of their own when I even smell chocolate." She wished for bigger breasts and hated her appendectomy scar. Genuinely vulnerable and charming, she finally asked the crowd, "What don't *you* like about my body?"

A man in a poncho disliked her sleek jewelry. A tweedy woman said, "You're so pretty. You don't need the blondina job." Willow observed, "Your hips could lose a few pounds."

I calmed myself with deep breaths. My tone would betray animosity if I offered even mild, friendly feedback—which wasn't what I wanted to give. I imagined saying, *Willow means your ass is the size of Wyoming.*

The crowd exhausted its modest negative comments. Charley smiled with apparent relief, and thanked everyone.

"You're one brave woman," a man called out. "We should be thanking *you!*"

To me it was obvious she wanted to impress Cy as a growth case. This desire, not courage, had driven her onto the table.

"Everyone," Cy said, "before we move on, you need to know this. Some of you probably noticed Charley here at the conference even before this morning."

A man confirmed loudly, "You bet we did."

"She lives at Rancho Vista but is not a shill. Willow expected someone less familiar with our work to step forward."

Brilliant. *Someone less familiar* implied that everyone was already somewhat familiar with the Aaron philosophy.

"Can I brag about you for a moment, honey?" Cy asked.

Charley's slow nod was like a regal bow. She blushed and stood with her shoulders back, so her breasts perked.

"Charley came to us desperate to save her marriage, and took a sabbatical from a distinguished executive position. She and her husband have decided to divorce, but they're doing it with mutual respect, like the high-level growth cases they both are."

I started to feel sick.

Cy sat down and nodded to Willow. She continued, "Charley, please tell us what you *do* like about your body."

Modestly she listed her small ears, even white teeth, and the color and texture of her pubic hair. "Though my breasts are small, I like their shape," she allowed. Several men, including Zachary Bush, made yummy sounds of appreciation.

When she finished, the group took over with a seemingly endless list of Charley's admirable traits—she was praised for her skin tone, posture, dainty hands, and on and on. Finally I joined in: "Your hair's gorgeous, no matter what color it is."

POLYSEX WAS THE ONLY WORKSHOP of the conference with no competing session in the same time slot. The hotel's largest ballroom filled early, but Zachary Bush beat the crowd to land a front-row seat. I sat near him and whispered to Ken, "Polysex just destroyed Cy's marriage. How can we promote it?"

His lip curled at one corner. "Zoë couldn't maintain the honesty," he whispered back. "*She* destroyed the marriage."

As Willow had done in the morning, Eric introduced Cy and the Vistans, then explained the theoretical underpinnings of the process. I admired his smooth discussion of the "One-Flesh model of marriage" set forth by Christ in Matthew 19:6. But how would Eric handle Zack Bush if he revealed what he knew about Cy's Polysex disaster with Zoë?

Bush smirked but Cy's expression remained proud.

"Let's have a show of hands," Eric said, just as our mentor would have suggested. "How many of you have jeopardized your marriage or an important relationship through sexual behavior with someone outside?" More than half the people in the room, including Cy, Charley and Dr. Bush, raised their hands. Eric's further, probing questions engaged the audience. He explained the theoretical foundation of Polysex, and fielded comments about how a couple could handle such problems as jealousy, or a "guest" falling in love with one of them.

Cy maintained his fatherly smile, and I saw that even though his desire to affirm Zoë had exploded, he still believed in the process. And Dr. Bush seemed unable to get beyond his smirk, like a man who lacked the courage for a public battle.

"The people who promote 'Open Marriage' don't advocate true openness," Eric explained. "They discourage telling your partner the details of outside sexual encounters. But in Polysex there are no 'outside' encounters. Everything takes place *within* the relationship. This requires scrupulous honesty."

Honesty beyond Zoë's ability, as Ken had said.

RANCHO VISTA PLUNGED STILL DEEPER into the public consciousness. Even people who hadn't attended the Body Image session murmured when Charley entered that evening's cocktail party on Cy's arm. She wore a new dress—peach-colored silk with a slit skirt and plunging back.

Later, in Cy's suite, she behaved like a hostess toward me and the other Vistans. She poured wine and herb tea, summoned room service for pastries and fruit, and gave each of us a shoulder rub. Cy called her "a gifted administrator" and praised her many ideas for improving our business affairs.

"My children," he said, "you hold psychotherapy's future in your hands. Rancho Vista was born at a unique time in history. Twenty years from now, the world will look back in awe on what we're doing today." He let us absorb this, then continued darkly, "Zachary Bush is our greatest threat. People clobbering each other with foam rubber bats! It's pathetic, but the world is desperate to channel its rage. He was itching to tell that crowd about my recent difficulties with Polysex. I'm sure he's saving his chips to play in a bigger game. Steve, for the spring conference, develop our proposal for Vesuvius."

"For—I'm sorry?"

"The process we initiated with Rupert and Josh, and refined with Mikey. Charley has named it 'Vesuvius.' Two people in conflict are restrained in harnesses so they can't hurt each other, then they vent their rage. When appropriate, each receives a supply of 'ammunition.' Even if Zack Bush invents a new kind of bat, where will he find people so highly motivated for growth that they're willing to have garbage thrown at them?"

I scribbled notes. How in hell would I translate this latest brainchild of Cy's into words the world would understand? But I'd wondered the same thing about Polysex and Body Image. Somehow Cy would pull this one off, too.

23

CY READ VIVIAN'S NOTE ALOUD THREE TIMES, adding theatrical flourishes with each run-through. *"I will return for Elizabeth. I cannot allow my children to be tortured."*

Back from the conference, the staff was meeting in his new chalet for the first time. A late-fall storm raged outside but we all sprawled on silken rugs that had been moved from the triple-wide. Pine logs crackled in the rock fireplace, warming my bare feet. Wolfie lay asleep at my side, his head propped on my leg.

"The poor sick cunt," Cy said finally. "Elizabeth, how did you prevent her from kidnapping you?"

Sick cunt, I scrawled in my notebook, and added, *or just scared?* I looked out through the floor-to-ceiling windows that faced a little private canyon. The blizzard obliterated everything but the trunks of three ponderosas just beyond the deck.

Elizabeth huddled in an afghan, looking very small. "Mom told me she was leaving the Ranch. I said, 'We're on Month-Off, so you shouldn't even be talking to me.' But I'm glad I got to say goodbye to my little brother."

Goodbye, I wrote. I'd never imagined anyone could voluntarily forsake Rancho Vista and embrace the "real world" of noise, filth and incongruities. At least I'd said goodbye to Rupert. But not to Zoë or Vivian, who had made this choice within a few days of each other. My sorrow for them was nearly as heavy as for Rupe.

"Mom couldn't handle it when we put Mikey in the compost pit," Elizabeth said. "She still doesn't understand he needed it. But I intend to grow. I want to stay if you'll let me."

I wrote, *I intend to grow.*

Cy said, "Your older brother's suicide didn't come out of nowhere. Your mother could have sent him to the Ranch two years ago, but chose to let him rot in her attic. Thank God you're free of that diseased family system. We're your family now."

Elizabeth knelt at his knee. He embraced her and stroked her hair while she wept.

I wrote, *Garth rotted in attic. Diseased family system.*

"But," Cy continued, "a young girl needs a mother. A role-model with an understanding ear, a pair of loving arms. Charley, are you ready to be Elizabeth's surrogate mother?"

I swallowed my nausea while Charley acknowledged how well-prepared she was to accept this new role. *Surrogate mother*, I scrawled. Why didn't Cy ask Willow, who actually cared for the girl?

Elizabeth knelt with her head in Charley's lap. I closed my eyes, haunted by the memory of a photograph from a psychology text: a wraithlike infant monkey clung to a wire robot, his ghoulish artificial mother.

Next on the agenda was a session for Charley concerning what, if anything, to tell Josh. Cy argued she didn't need to express any Withholds. But Willow insisted, "Charley's moved in with you. We've got to tell Josh what's going on so he doesn't speculate with the grunts."

Charley readily agreed. I brought Josh in from the greenhouse, where he and Travis were digging a trench. She opened her session of *What Do You Feel Like Saying?* with her explosive Withhold: "Josh, I spent the night with Cy and Zoë while you and I were on Month-Off. One thing led to another, and we all made love."

Beneath her creased brow I thought I saw that she enjoyed this.

"It was very special," she added, "and I wanted you to know."

"When?" Josh moaned.

"Monday, let's see—six weeks ago."

His usually lively face was ashen. "Monday?"

His sharp tone of anguish stirred Wolfie. The dog looked up at him and barked.

"That's the day Rupert stabbed me. Jesus, Char, you must really want whatever Aaron is offering you."

She held her expression of canned concern.

"You'll need someone to talk to," Cy told him. "Who are you closest to here?"

"I've always trusted Steve," Josh replied. "Since his parents marched out of that Group in Beverly Hills. And he was so gentle with Rupert after—what happened."

I looked into the rugged, drawn face and wondered how I could absorb the anger and pain Charley had caused this good man. *She's hurt me too*, I wanted to say. She'd elbowed Zoë away from Cy, and now she was elbowing away the rest of us.

Josh returned to trench duty, and the staff discussed what to tell the Vistans, and the world, about Zoë's disappearance. Opinions flew around without any conclusions. "It's simple," I offered finally. "Just say she and Cy have grown in different directions. Leave the options open. They're not getting divorced. It's more like Month-Off."

Charley's narrow eyes told me what she thought of this idea. But emboldened by the hopeful expressions of Eric, Ken and Willow, I went on, "People have memorized the Polysex seminars. This situation could look like Lifeboat-itis to them."

"Do *you* think I have Lifeboat-itis?" Cy asked, stone-faced.

I caught Eric's eyes before I answered. "With most people I'd say yeah—"

Cy roared, "I'm not some grunt, leaping from one failed relationship to another! Zoë and I shared a life for twelve years. She abandoned the principles of that life. She wants to watch game shows and eat pizza in a rowboat." I dared to glance around. The others appeared as confused as I was by the "rowboat" reference. Cy rose and stared into the blizzard. "Charley is here, now that I'm ready for a woman who can help me operate a luxury liner."

I couldn't look at her, dreading the triumph on her face. "That really helps," I said with strained optimism. Eventually Cy would free himself from her spell, but until then I would support him completely. "If anyone mentions Lifeboat-itis, we'll just explain about the luxury liner."

THE NEXT MORNING CY ANNOUNCED IN GROUP that the breakup of his marriage had been inevitable, because he and Zoë had grown in different directions. Charley sat beside him in Zoë's lawn chair. He took her hand and added that he couldn't have survived without her support.

I maintained a stoic smile, despising the permanent sound of this.

He continued brightly, "Charley wants to ask for your help with something that—"

"Let *me* explain, Cy," she interrupted in a sharp tone. "Everyone, I want to change my name. My parents burdened me with Char*lette*. It's always embarrassed me, a hillbilly name. 'Charley' worked as a perky nickname for a college girl heading toward the corporate ladder."

"But now," Cy said, "you're ready for a further step—"

"A more sophisticated variant," she said coldly, then seemed to catch herself, and spoke with the endearing vulnerability she'd employed during her Body Image in Santa Barbara. "I'm not getting any younger."

I wanted to scream. Before anyone could ask about Zoë's whereabouts or well-being, much less grieve her leaving, this creature had commandeered Group to rename herself.

Theodora called out, "Carlotta" and got the other Vistans going. Puck, Rainbow and Lucky made suggestions that Cy wrote on the blackboard. My entry, "Charla," earned a sour look from Charley and only one vote, from Tobey—who, I realized, might vote for "Hortense" if I suggested it.

Charley's own suggestion, which she pronounced "Shar-*lay*" and wrote as "Charlée" on the blackboard, won a unanimous vote. Even Josh, with a distant expression, raised his hand for it.

WHILE THE CHALET WAS UNDER CONSTRUCTION WE HAD CALLED IT "ZOË'S NEW HOUSE." The pink marble master bathroom had been designed as a sanctuary for her, with an atrium for her Zen garden. But the house was Cy's domain and he quickly dubbed it "the Center." The enormous main room could accommodate all the Vistans for Groups and parties. A twenty-foot serving counter separated this room from the ultra-modern kitchen. Cy's study commanded a view of the mountain. Floor-to-ceiling mahogany shelves held his collection of books and recording devices.

But I was still painfully reminded of Zoë, and held out hope that somehow she would return and be a part of our lives again. In the meantime, I enjoyed feeling I was keeping Wolfie safe until her return. Quietly, without consulting Cy or Charlée, I moved his bowl and bag of kibble from the Center to my tipi. On cold nights he snuggled against me, and I loved the look of bliss that came over his face when I scratched both his ears at once.

When Elsie received a call from Zoë, with a phone number and an address in the San Fernando Valley, I demanded more information.

"If you want to know whether she's living with Sonny Tornado, you'll have to call her," Elsie said. "All she told me was where to forward her mail. It's a P.O. box."

Though tempted to accept the challenge, I knew I wouldn't call. Cy was the one who should try to reconcile before Charlée put down roots in the new house.

I took over the huge former bedroom in the triple-wide as my private office—a booby prize made possible by Charlée's move to the chalet. Wolfie often accompanied me to town and sniffed the rooms, whimpering. He missed Zoë as much as I did.

At once I dove into designing a full-page ad for the Christmas issue of *Psychotherapy Currents*, highlighting Rancho Vista's training intensives for mental health professionals. As committed as I was to this project, each night I headed out to the Ranch in time for dinner. I'd spent more than enough time away.

One evening Josh politely requested an appointment for an after-dinner visit at my tipi. He brought half a gallon of frothy home-made beer. A little clumsily he stroked Wolfie while I filled two mugs with Travis's dark brew.

Josh turned to stare at me with frank curiosity. "How did you get to know Rupert, anyway?"

The question unleashed my first tears since I'd waited in the shadows to photograph Zoë with her paramour. I described Rupe at his best, correcting Dr. Turner on the fine points of psychiatric diagnosis. "My God," I said, after chuckling over the memory. "Now they're both dead."

We drank and talked for hours. Josh recounted the bewitching attraction he'd felt for Charlée the morning she first sat across the aisle from him in a UCLA lecture hall, and his amazement when she invited him to join a study group. "I pinched myself the day she married me. I guess I've just been waiting 'til somebody in her own league spirited her away. Little did I suspect it would be the author of the world-renowned Theory of Unconditional Lust."

I allowed myself a laugh at Cy's expense. But subgrouping with Josh could earn me a place on the trench crew, far from the master's ear. After my guest waded into the snow, I confined my catty commentary to Wolfie.

ELIZABETH AND TOBEY RODE WITH ME TO TOWN EACH MORNING. She helped Charlée set up her boudoir while Tobey catalogued Cy's books and journals. Together the two kids scrubbed vegetables and made lunch for the new Vistan First Couple. When Elizabeth received letters from her mother, she handed them unopened to Charlée. On the drive back to the Ranch she sometimes wore cast-off blouses of Charlée's, or jewelry and other gifts. She and Tobey shared private jokes whose meaning I didn't want to know because they hinted at intimacies between Cy and Charlée.

Winter arrived early and hit hard. The cookshack's water pipes burst, requiring a two-day repair job. The Vistans' letters to their parents, which they'd worked on in Group as the holidays approached, traveled with Travis to the Gentile post office on his coal runs. The mail truck, like the county snow plow it followed, came to Keystone only once a week. The bookmobile suspended service entirely. The temperature on the cookshack porch hit twenty-eight one morning and seven below zero the next. Fortunately, snow blanketed the tipis with natural insulation, so on snowy nights we were warmer than on clear ones. But occasionally a demon wind blasted down my stovepipe and fouled my sleep with coal smoke.

Thanksgiving dinner was a feast of venison and trout like nothing since the summer's Open House. Wine and Joy Juice flowed. After her first mug of cheap Chablis, Elizabeth announced, "I am under the spell of Bacchus and will sacrifice the blossom of my girlhood to the man who first proves himself worthy!"

She proclaimed that Tobey was a virgin as well, and he denied it too strenuously to be believed. She gave him a playful swat and he stalked toward her like Godzilla. As the two kids fell over each other I watched them with delight and envy. Had I ever enjoyed such freedom? The few moments of ecstasy I'd shared with my boyhood friend Dean had been steeped in fear. My first and only love had been murdered as a teenager in the concrete hell of reform school. Only at Rancho Vista did children have access to unconditional happiness.

"Tobey's ready to become a man tonight," Elizabeth declared. "He's been saving himself for someone special." She arched a brow at me and I felt myself blushing. "But," she went on, "me first." She swooned into Travis's arms. He propped her in a chair and poured her a glass of warm milk with honey.

Later Tobey stood beside me in the dessert line and whispered thickly into my ear, "I love you." His flushed face remained inches away. When I turned toward him our lips met briefly but warmly. I caught Elizabeth's glance. She gave me a lurid wink, and I squeezed Tobey's hand, then we all took servings of Vistaberry pie.

While the cookshack crew scrubbed pots, Cy persuaded Puck to play his harmonica then hoisted Charlée onto the serving counter. She began a sensual dance. He clapped a slow rhythm and the Vistans joined in. Only Josh and I stood apart, watching together from a corner. Theodora led a dance in a semi-circle around the serving counter. Everyone whooped when Charlée peeled off her pearl-buttoned sweater.

Cy and Zoë had always stood back while the Vistans entertained them. Now he sipped Joy Juice and contributed to the show. The community loved it. He didn't stagger or slur when he drank. If anything, he strode more surely and spoke with greater-than-usual eloquence. The only change took place in his eyes: they pierced but did not warm.

When Charlée unhooked her bra I retreated outside. I pulled a biscuit from my pocket and tossed it to Wolfie. The dog caught it in his teeth and trotted with me to my tipi. I banked the fire and bundled into bed, and Wolfie curled up on my feet. After a few minutes I heard Ken warming up his sax in the Dome. What if Tobey arrived for a follow-up kiss? Cy had virtually told me to do far more than kiss Tobey. But I could think of nothing I'd rather do than kiss and snuggle the boy who loved me.

I dozed and woke hours later. The belly of my stove still glowed red. Somewhere a truck roared, and a noise like the smashing of a thousand bottles crashed through the night. Wolfie woofed half-heartedly and stayed on the bed. Far away a woman screamed. Men yelled. The truck roared again, then the engine died.

"Let's go back to sleep," I mumbled, and pulled a pillow over my head. Some drunk had run a vehicle into the sprinkler-pipe rack. Probably poor Josh.

The excited voices outside gained momentum. I knew I wouldn't sleep, but neither would I join the chaos.

DURING BREAKFAST THE VISTANS WERE MORE SILENT THAN I'D EVER IMAGINED POSSIBLE. When I left the cookshack I still didn't know who had driven into the pipe rack. Near the coal bin, Josh stepped out of the shadows and asked to hike with me.

"The sonofabitch is out of control," he said. "Charley—" He muttered something. "Shar-*lay* hugs me. Next thing I know Aaron calls me 'that pathetic grunt,' then he's careening around the garden in a Land Rover. He smashes two thousand dollars' worth of sprinkler pipes and does at least that much damage to the truck. If you or I drove a Ranch vehicle drunk, we wouldn't be allowed to chop onions, much less tell other people how to live their lives!"

My smile felt insipid.

He held out his open hands as if begging for understanding. "If you don't check the tire pressure on the tractor before you plow a field, you do two years of Hail Cy's before you can drive the goddamned thing again. He got away with fucking my wife while I was lying on what I thought might be my deathbed."

Cy isn't in his right mind, I wanted to say. *She's destroying him.* But I knew my job and tried to steer the conversation back to the damaged vehicle: "So you feel there's a double standard."

"Where I come from it's called a mindfuck. You watch. He'll get one of you staff saps to drive the Rover to Denver for the body work, so the folks in Gentile don't ask any embarrassing questions. The midnight ride of Cyrus Aaron'll never be on the Group agenda. The grunts are shivering in fear that if they mention it they'll be shot for subgrouping."

I shook my head and tried to sound reasonable. "*You* can bring it up in Group, Josh. Anybody can."

He spat. "Nobody's said a word about it since she drove him to town last night. Way before breakfast Travis took the Rover to the bottom pasture, out of sight. The day this gets brought up in Group, please make sure Elsie's got her tape recorder going. Send me a transcript. I'll be at Vivian's."

Before the lunch gong sounded, he packed his Jeep and became the third person to leave Rancho Vista voluntarily.

"Josh needed perspective," I explained at Group that afternoon. I was grateful no one asked what that meant, because I had no idea. Many eyes studied the pattern of knotholes in the ceiling, but I saw no furtive glances to suggest the grunts had subgrouped.

The day's agenda included Rainbow and Lucky, choosing which species of squash to plant in the spring, and Charlée's update on the college program. She asked to go first, and Cy granted her request without discussion. Briskly she announced that Rutherford would honor most transfer credits—good news for me, since I'd attended five colleges and accumulated sixty semester units. "Some professors," she said, "will require students to audit core classes, like science and math, at the University of Colorado. We'll work out the details."

We covered other mundane topics, and Group broke up an hour later. No one mentioned the smashed sprinkler pipes or Cy's midnight ride.

A FEW AFTERNOONS LATER, SHERIFF BUFORD drove up to the triple-wide with legal documents that required Cy's signature. I called ahead to the Center to be sure everyone would be dressed, then walked with the Sheriff down the short road. Cy signed for the envelope and shook Buford's hand, but appeared relieved when the sheriff declined an invitation to come in for coffee. From a bathroom window, Tobey and Elizabeth watched with wide eyes.

I went in and stood beside Cy while he sliced the envelope open. A legalistic-looking document slid onto the kitchen counter. "Zoë Aaron, Petitioner," he read aloud, then left the papers where they fell and opened a half-gallon bottle of vodka. "We need a staff meeting."

I drove Tobey and Elizabeth to the Ranch and returned with Willow, Eric and Ken. Elsie was in the Center's main room, fussing with cassette tapes. Everyone waited while Charlée finished a call on the kitchen phone, harassing an insurance company clerk about twenty-some thousand dollars past due. Yes, we're all impressed, I thought. That saber-toothed voice does come in handy.

She joined the circle, and Cy began to read the divorce petition aloud. His voice cracked when he reached an allegation of "mental cruelty." He read the entire document to us, including the date of Zoë's signature, then stood and gazed out at the pale sunset, appearing as lost as the five-year-old boy he'd once been, waiting for his dead mother to come home.

Charlée took his hand. He kissed her absent-mindedly, then said, "Time to move on."

Very softly, I began to hum the melody of "Sometimes I feel like a motherless child . . .," to suggest we give Cy a cradle. Abruptly he withdrew from Charlée and lumbered to the kitchen. Ice rattled and soda cans popped, and he lined up drinks for everyone. "I need a new lawyer," he said. "Steve, phone Zoë. Arrange to get the Rolls."

"Well, okay," I replied, faking a pensive look to hide my enthusiasm. "Elsie, have you got the number?"

Charlée sat in Cy's Swedish chair and wrote in a leather-bound notebook. I hoisted myself onto the buffet counter, shoving aside her paperwork, and dialed the kitchen phone. I imagined I might persuade Zoë to apologize to Cy and stop this divorce nightmare.

"Hi, Zoë!" I gushed when she answered. Cy stalked into his study.

"Etienne, c'est toi?" She giggled, sounding happy to hear from me. It wasn't too late for her and Cy to reconcile.

"C'est moi. Allez-tu bien? Tu me manques."

Cy appeared in the doorway and nailed me with vodka-sharp eyes. "In English, for Christ's sake," he snapped, and turned back to his study. Seconds later Eric handed me an index card that bore Cy's squarish printing: *Rolls is millionaire's car, should be sold.* A moment later Willow brought another card: *Zoë, car not yours.*

I told her I had enrolled in the Rutherford College program, and answered questions about her beloved Wolfie. "He misses you almost as much as I do," I assured her.

Cy stormed out of his study. Willow flattened herself against a hall-closet door to let him pass, then followed him into the kitchen where he straight-armed Ken and Eric out of his way. On a sheet of legal-sized paper he'd printed in fat black letters: *When I'm in L.A. for my school program, I can pick up the car.*

Zoë was describing an avant-garde play she'd seen that featured a watermelon in the role of a small child. I laughed. Cy wrenched the phone from me and told her in an oily voice, "The kids have to go to the Ranch. I want to talk to you about the car . . ."

I ran to Cy's study, where the phone lay in pieces. He had unscrewed the mouthpiece, removed a mechanism and listened undetected to our conversation. A suction cup attached to the handset led to a tape recorder whose red light glowed. I lifted the mangled receiver and heard Zoë say, "I need only enough to establish myself."

"That weasel can establish you," Cy barked. "I have a community to run. What happened to your billionaire with the nine-inch—"

"I too have given my life to Rancho Vista. The billionaire was *your* fantasy. I manufactured him because it gave you pleasure to think of me with such a man. Sonny Tornado lives with his sick mother. Oh, *why* do I tell you this?" She made a sound between a groan and a whimper. "I do not *want* the car, but I must keep it until we reach the settlement."

"Splendid," Cy snarled. "I must keep the wolf-dog on the same terms." He hung up and flew into the study, where I was still holding the disabled handset. "My God," he raged, "you're still under the spell of that deceitful cunt."

I dashed past him toward the kitchen. I'd never imagined raising my voice to Cy, or feeling like it. But now I turned and yelled, "You're too drunk to tell anybody what to do. As fucking usual."

He lunged and slammed me against the kitchen counter. I felt something inside me snap and I dropped to the floor. Eric screamed, "No!" and ran forward, but Cy rammed him into the corner and stood over him as he slumped. Ken, Elsie and Willow grabbed Cy to restrain him. I pulled myself up and seized handfuls of his hair. Eric raised his fists. Cy elbowed me in the gut and I collapsed again, nauseated with pain.

Charlée remained in Cy's chair, feet tucked under her, writing. I managed to rise, and limped past her to the far corner of the room. Cy shook himself free of the others, ignoring Eric's fists, and shouted, "I've failed! I thought Steve had become human, but Gollum is alive and well. And Eric, you steaming psychopathic turd, you should have bled to death from the asshole in jail, but I accepted the challenge of creating something worthy. Both experiments are failures."

Eric cried, "Yes, I'm an incurable psychopath! Don't let me fuck up your statistics."

Cy charged him. Eric lunged aside, grabbed the empty vodka bottle from the counter and wielded it like a club while he whipped a dish towel around his fist. He smashed the bottle on the floor and shoved the jagged remnant at Cy.

I shouted, "Eric, that's enough!"

He brandished the primitive weapon, looking wild and stricken, and backed away, reaching behind him with his free hand. When he found the knob he slipped outside the door and slammed it, leaving a dark silence. Moments later a rock smashed through a high kitchen window and struck the stove. Outside, the green VW cranked to life and spun away.

"Cy needs rest," Charlée said. She walked into the kitchen and began picking up shards of glass. "Eric will calm down." She looked up at the broken window. "It's freezing outside. Will you guys cover the hole before you leave? We'll work through this in the morning."

"Somebody's got to make sure that psychopath doesn't come back and kill me," Cy said. "His bottle is a street-fighter's weapon. He's regressed to where he was the day I rescued him."

"I'll check on him," I replied. Ken placed a step-stool on the counter and climbed up to seal the gaping window with card-

board. Elsie tore strips of duct tape for him. A few minutes later
we all trooped outside in silence.

When I tried to climb into the truck, a wave of pain in my side
nearly knocked me over. Willow heard me grunt and gently
pressed the painful spot, put an ear to my chest while I attempted
a deep breath, and said, "A few broken ribs." She took the wheel
of the truck but couldn't do much else except prescribe aspirin
and a large shot of Joy Juice. Ken ran back into the Center for the
duct tape, and encircled my tee shirt with it to bind my ribs.

We rode silently to the Ranch. I wanted to cry and scream, to
denounce Charlée's evil influence and describe how delightfully
soft Zoë's voice had sounded. Instead I stared out the window.
The snowbound sagebrush crouched in heaps beside the road,
awaiting the warmth of spring just as I awaited the return of Cy's
sanity.

At the Ranch I limped over to Eric's tipi. The place was
strewn with clothes and half-packed duffel bags. "I have to
leave," Eric said. "I can probably stay with my sister in Boulder."
He stuffed shirts and socks and jeans into bags. "You're welcome
to come."

"I *would*," I assured him, "but Cy's in some kind of trance. I've
gotta be here when he snaps out of it." Through my own pain
and confusion, I remembered that Eric was on a reprieve from a
prison sentence. "You're not going back to jail."

He yanked on the rope of a duffel bag. "Gotta take that
chance."

"I wasn't asking a question. Call and let me know where you
are. If Charlée answers, make static noises and hang up. Get
settled and register for classes. Don't get high. If you piss-test
positive for pot or anything else, it'll be a probation violation and
you *will* end up in jail."

He removed a baggie from his coat pocket. "You just want my
stash," he joked, and tossed it over. Our eyes met and he moved
close enough to place his hands on my shoulders. He looked
deeply into my eyes for the first time since our night in Perdido
Valley, a lifetime ago. "I brought you here and now I'm leaving.
Cy wanted you—have you figured this out? He wanted you here
the minute you called him pretending to be a hospital administrator, to save Rupert. He thought you were an audacious little
genius, and sent Willow and me to seduce you. I thought bringing
you here was the greatest gift I could give anyone. Now I'm not
sure."

Of course I had accepted that our "lovemaking" was a setup, though at the time I'd believed Eric really would love me some day. I didn't look away from his gleaming eyes as he continued, "Willow was supposed to go to California alone to meet you. But Cy picked up something in the way you talked about Rupert. 'Susoyev might be gay,' he said. If you'd turned out not to be, Willow would have been the one in your bed that night. But *one* of us was going to get you to the Ranch. I hadn't been with a guy that way before—except Cy, which is how I learned to do what I did with you."

I kept my eyes on Eric, though it hurt to hear my worst suspicions confirmed. He finally broke the eye contact and looked at the floor to add, "I freaked out when you actually showed up here, because I thought Cy was going to make me marry you or something. Sorry I never explained."

We hugged carefully—Eric also seemed to have suffered some cracked ribs—then we loaded the VW together. It took less than five minutes for our lives to split apart. I watched the tiny taillights disappear into the clear night.

Each time Eric hit the brakes, the snowy road glowed red. The road to hell. One more person I loved was gone. I dragged myself back to my tipi and got stoned for the first time in weeks, eager to shut out any evil dreams that might torture me.

AT THE CENTER IN THE MORNING, Cy and Charlée remained in the bedroom until Elizabeth and Tobey served breakfast. Ken, Elsie, Willow and I shuffled around trying to help. Rancho Vista's First Couple came in when everyone was seated. Nobody looked at the one empty chair. Eggs and toast were passed around, then I announced, "Eric left last night."

Charlée whacked the table. "He stole the VW?"

I stared her down. "He borrowed it. Travis is gonna pick it up in Denver tomorrow, when he drives the Rover in for body work." If Josh could hear me now! "We should get it fixed there, so people in Gentile don't ask any funny questions."

"You're starting to think like me," Cy said sunnily. "We don't want the local grunts going wild with I've-Got-A-Secret-Itis." He sipped his coffee and spoke in a low tone. "This is my fault. I gave Eric more power than he could handle. Jesus, I hope he can survive out there." .

Charlée shook her head. "*I* hope our credibility with the Probation Department can survive. We have to let them know he's left treatment."

I stared into the goo of my omelet, the bright bits of pimento like splats of blood.

Cy said gently, "Eric may return to prison over this. Steve, can you handle writing to his probation officer?"

"It's my job," I replied smoothly. I braved a look into Cy's eyes and began to eat, knowing I would write two letters. The first, bearing Cy's signature, I would copy for the Ranch file. But I would burn the original. The other letter, with a signature very much like Cy's, I would mail to the probation office. *Eric Swensen will remain in treatment while attending classes at the University of Colorado,* the second letter would say. *He will voluntarily submit to unscheduled drug tests.* By the time I mopped up the last bite of egg with a wedge of toast, the letter had completed itself in my head, including the closing paragraph: *Please feel free to contact our social services director, Steve Susoyev, with any questions.*

24

CY AND CHARLÉE WORKED TOGETHER EACH DAY
and spent weekends in Denver—engrossed, as far as I could tell,
in shopping for expensive dresses. At every Ranch party she wore
a new beaded or diaphanous gown.

The divorce case was referred to a tax lawyer, and Cy appointed me the main Rancho Vista contact. I didn't understand
the relevance of taxes until I saw the complexities involved in the
real estate, stock and other investments Cy owned with Zoë. A
fifty-fifty split seemed fair to me, but the lawyer and Cy, and of
course Charlée, had other ideas.

Much of the marital property, including the luxury automobiles, had been signed over by patients in lieu of payment. Many
items were in Zoë's name. I contacted lawyers in California, New
York and even Tahiti for documents, and gave up on sorting out
the sources of several pieces of property. I copied deeds, stock
certificates and limited partnership agreements as well as hand-
written promissory notes, and sent them to the lawyer with
copies of the Polaroids of Zoë with Sonny Tornado. As I sealed
each envelope I suffered a fresh betrayal of the woman who had
stroked my soggy head on my first morning at Rancho Vista.

Just before Christmas Josh filed for divorce from Charlée. The
same week a certified letter for Cy arrived from Vivian. *I've hired a
lawyer*, she wrote. *If Elizabeth isn't home for the holidays I'll have to sue.*

Cy instructed me to respond, with a promise that Elizabeth
would visit as soon as she felt ready. *"Your daughter is finally dealing
with her grief over the suicide of her older brother,"* he dictated. "Yes.
Nail her with that."

I didn't want to nail Vivian with anything, but I transcribed
this word-for-word. I had bigger concerns. Cy had begun to talk
about marrying Charlée. I feared he would see the Withholds in
my eyes and grill me in Staff Group. Before Eric left, his willingness to challenge Cy had egged Willow on, and allowed me to
crouch behind their courage. But Willow had kept to herself since
the night of the broken ribs, and I cringed when Charlée opposed
Cy in her venomous tone.

Cy said his main concern was replacing Eric with another
counselor for Theodora. "She needs a lot of attention," he

reminded everyone, without bothering to mention the size of her trust fund. "I think it's time to invite her onto the staff."

"Ridiculous," Charlée declared. "As I remember correctly, she's still on probation."

Her threatened to strangle me like a noxious gas.

"Darling," Cy said gently, catching the flash in my eyes. "The expression is '*If* I remember correctly.' It sounds more humble."

She refused to be humbled. "What can Theodora contribute?"

"Her IQ is one-fifty-nine, so a brilliant young woman is hiding behind that bluster. And she's the most honest person in this community. She doesn't give a shit what anybody thinks."

No one could argue with that. I pointed out she was a growth case. After her Body Image she had shed thirty pounds, and she'd cut off the last of her bleached blonde hair to look presentable for the Open House. I gave her induction my full support, thrilled to see Cy prevail in any way against Charlée's will.

EACH MORNING, TOBEY AND ELIZABETH walked the quarter mile from the center to the post office for the mail. One Saturday while Cy and Charlée were in Denver, Tobey brought a letter to the triple-wide, addressed to *Steve Susoyev, Keystone, Colo.* It bore a Boulder postmark and no return address. "Charlée told me to give her anything that came from Eric or Zoë, no matter who it's addressed to," Tobey said. "I know that's Eric's handwriting." He shrugged. "Charlée won't be back 'til Monday, so I thought—you know."

"Oh, sure," I said smoothly. "I'll copy it for her." I avoided Tobey's eyes and their offer of complicity.

Eric wrote of depression and loneliness, but also his determination to succeed in school. He was taking psychology classes at the University of Colorado. He'd counted three ridges of scar tissue where Cy had broken his ribs. He worked a newspaper route and delivered pizzas. He'd dated a girl for a few weeks but she complained he always talked about "such weird stuff," and dumped him. His letter ended, *I feel like a misfit.*

Because you are, I thought. The world isn't made for us. Outsiders don't know how to communicate or work through their problems. I wrote back a newsy letter and mentioned that I, too, had counted three broken ribs.

The days before Christmas blurred past. I walked upstream every morning with Wolfie and smoked some of Eric's pot. I sewed beads on a pair of suede gloves for Travis and framed a dreamy photo of Elsie's tipi for her. I wrapped my twin-volume *Oxford English Dictionary* in rice paper to give to Cy. For Tobey I wrapped my worn volume of Cavafy poems, for Willow the copy of the *Rubáiyát* Lydia had given me the day I left her grove. I struggled with myself over a gift for Charlée. Finally, when Travis and Elsie were leaving for Denver to pick up the repaired Rover, I gave them twenty bucks for a bottle of perfume.

At the Center party on Christmas morning, Charlée praised my offering and the other tributes she received. But her face shone with the greatest pleasure when she opened one of Cy's many gifts, an encyclopedic "World Traveler Guide."

I allowed myself a moment to enjoy a vision of her in her safari suit, falling from a boat into the piranha-infested Amazon. She passed out extravagant presents to each staff member. Willow had already put on her genuine pearl earrings when I opened a set of Rapidograph pens that I knew had cost several hundred dollars, a dream gift for a graphic artist. Stoned and a little drunk on champagne, I nearly blurted, *If you're shopping for my friendship you're definitely in the right department!* But I silently embraced her and winked over her shoulder at Tobey.

In response he gave me a subtle nod. A minute later we paired up beside the fireplace. Just standing together at a slight distance from everyone else created a little corner of privacy. When I gave him the Cavafy, Tobey turned to a dog-eared page and read aloud:

> *"From all I did and all I said, let no one try to find out who I was. An obstacle was there that changed the pattern of my actions and the manner of my life. An obstacle was often there to stop me when I'd begin to speak. From my most unnoticed actions, my most veiled writing— from these alone will I be understood. But maybe it isn't worth so much concern, so much effort to discover who I really am. Later, in a more perfect society someone else made just like me is certain to appear and act freely."*

Tobey closed his eyes a moment, then looked into my face. "It's about us, huh?"

"He wrote that in 1908."

The others seemed to melt away while Tobey and I fell into each other's arms, understanding ourselves as men who had known since childhood that we were destined to love other men. Tobey's body trembled against mine and he whispered, "I'm so lucky you found me and brought me to this perfect society."

He brought out his gift, a necklace of juniper berries he'd strung, and said Willow had told him they were called *ghost beads* by the Arapaho.

While he fastened it around my neck Cy asked, "Have you two fellows something to share with the rest of us?"

"Yes," Tobey answered. "I love Steve, and I'm willing to wait for him."

I laughed with the others and admired my necklace in the mirror, avoiding Tobey's eyes.

The Ranch-wide party began early in the afternoon, fueled by a special batch of Joy Juice that Travis had concocted with honey and orange rinds. Everyone got loose in the name of the joyful season, and mixed carols with delta blues. During dinner Elizabeth made a show of giving me a little pillow she had hand-sewn from tapestry scraps and stuffed with my hair, which she and Theodora had rescued off the balcony in Beverly Hills when I allowed it to be cut.

The party roared on past midnight. Travis did his best as percussionist, playing an old drum set Josh had left behind. Without a sure timekeeper, Ken's sax and Lucky's guitar battled to set the rhythm, but the Vistans danced with their usual gleeful frenzy and whooped in a great circle when I paired up with Tobey. Everyone shuffled through fresh snow to the sweatlodge. In the hot, close darkness, I recognized the giggles of Elizabeth and Tobey first on my left and then on my right, but could never tell whose hands were stroking me. I rolled naked in the snow between steam sessions, always aware of Tobey's smiling eyes and floppy, swollen cock.

While the die-hards built up the fire for a fifth go-round in the steam, I got dressed and sat down to pull on my boots. Tobey appeared at my side wrapped in a blanket and asked, "Can I walk you home?"

"Your place or mine?"

He narrowed his eyes at me. "That's some kind of homosexual jargon, isn't it?"

"I don't think gay people invented the one-night stand. It must be in the Old Testament somewhere."

"I'm only interested in a lifetime stand with you."

Tobey wanted to be with me openly and freely, with vulnerability. It terrified me.

Wolfie bounded along behind us as we walked together up the

hill. In a clearing beside the orchard, each with an arm around the other's waist, we collapsed in the snow. For a long moment neither moved, then Tobey rolled on top of me.

"Wait," I began.

"Cy warned me you'd say I'm too young. All I want is a kiss. Please don't ruin Christmas for me."

I lay still and closed my eyes. Tobey's breath was warm with honey and oranges. I felt his lips on my cheek. He nibbled at my chin and gently sucked my lower lip. Wolfie licked our faces, then lunged to sniff at our crotches.

"I've never kissed anyone," Tobey said. "Not the way I want to kiss you."

I raised my lips to his and whispered, "Merry Christmas." Our mouths met. I tingled at the tentative exploration of his soft tongue. We kissed with growing passion, and his cock throbbed against my thigh. As my own cock strained in my trousers, I found with Tobey the affection I'd craved during Ken's torturous blow jobs and Eric's wordless seduction.

How easily we could become lovers. But not yet. I didn't hold back because of Tobey's age or the law. Cy had made clear these were trivial technicalities. I knew of sex as a destroyer of all it touched. Sex had killed my first love and nearly wrecked my friendship with Eric by awakening Gollum's insatiable craving. It had created strange silences between Ken and me, and even caused me awkwardness with Cy. It had opened Rancho Vista's inner circle to Charlée and banished Zoë from paradise.

In the wonderful here and now, Tobey's love was generous and exuberant. Sex would arouse jealousy and rage. But kissing! Kissing and snuggling, and giggling—this delicious warmth we shared in the snow, this was what I'd wanted whenever my cock was sucked, when Cy's vibrator hummed, when Cy and Zoë shared their bed with me. Tobey and I tasted deeply of each other's innocence, moaning softly until Wolfie whined and nudged us with his frozen nose.

Finally we tramped up to my tipi. I rolled out a sleeping bag for myself on the bed and threw back my comforter for Tobey. We jumped in and molded our bodies together through layers of goose down and wool, snuggling spoon-style. *"Never let me go,"* he whispered.

I wrapped myself around him. Some day, I thought, we will not fuck or ball or screw or blow each other. "Some day," I promised softly, "we'll make love."

WINTER BLASTED THROUGH THE CANYONS and dumped snow in record heaps. After the county plow came through, many Vistans left to spend New Year's Eve with their "original" families. Tobey's mother was among the few parents invited to visit. She arrived with his kid sister a few days after Christmas.

Following breakfast one morning, Alice Turner walked with me around the glassy pond. "He idolizes you," she said. "He always wanted a brother. His relationship with his dad was——."

Torment, I thought, but I said, "Strained. Tobey's doing really well." I gave her my gloves and she took my arm. With a giddy rush I imagined saying, *I love him, you know*, and almost believed she would accept this. I did say, "It means so much to him that you're here."

I continued to work many nights at my office in the triple-wide. I sadly resigned myself to living in an orbit that spun ever further from Cy. One day, I trusted, he would emerge from his trance and ship Charlée back to L.A.

Tobey was my comfort and hope. We stole an afternoon to go snowshoeing. Wolfie, his white fur rendering him nearly invisible, pranced through the drifts. "I've always wanted a brother," I told Tobey. Later over hot chocolate we drew plans for a two-story dome and imagined the life we would share in our perfect society, where two men could love each other with the affirmation of their neighbors.

New articles by Wanda Richter in psychology and business publications brought a fresh wave of inquiries. By March I had a stack of four hundred letters to answer. I got a thousand "Summer Growth Spurt" flyers printed, each with a discount coupon—one of Charlée's many marketing ideas. Among her other innovations were staff salaries and a group insurance policy. "We've finally arrived," Cy announced, and agreed with her plan to rename the operation "Rancho Vista Institute."

I would not challenge her ideas. The Ranch was making more money than ever, expenses were down, and the staff was getting paid. But—except for Tobey and Elizabeth, who laughed in the Land Rover to and from town—no one seemed very happy.

As soon as the ground thawed enough for planting, Puck and Lucky stepped into Eric's job as chief gardener. Travis's crew began construction on five small, well-insulated domes, the first to replace the quaint but freezing tipis. When the gardens started to sprout, a wave of new Vistans arrived—including a stockbroker, his wife and their three children. The wife was a certified teacher and took over the school program that Vivian and Josh had abandoned. The days of rescuing suicidal, drug-addled teenagers had ended forever.

I had the summer brochure ready on schedule for the printer, because I ignored tipi parties and chances to watch the sunset with Tobey or Elizabeth. Virtually living at the triple-wide, I produced a full-color booklet with deckled edges and twenty photographs. The custom-made, oversized envelopes were in a color and texture close to Rancho Vista's sandstone. No one seemed to mind that the project was a thousand dollars over budget. I knew I had accomplished my goal when Charlée called it "alluring."

Her words proved prophetic. The brochure lured over six hundred people—many psychotherapists among them—into sending two-hundred-dollar deposits to experience wilderness trails, summer massage and yoga workshops, communication intensives and human relations weekends.

Cy was realizing his dream at last. "Rancho Vista," he announced at a staff meeting, "is no longer a muddy devil's island for the halt, the lame, the sociopathic and the psychotic. We have become a world-renowned growth center, attracting high-level professionals disillusioned with their lives but still in command of their faculties and resources."

With all these high-level folks around, would there be room for Eric again?

LATER I WOULD REMEMBER THAT VALHALLA THUNDERHEADS ROILED when I left the triple-wide, that the tulips screamed as I approached the Center and that Wolfie growled at them. In my memory the kitchen door's brass knob crackled with sparks when I reached for it, and the stewpot seethed with a noxious stench.

In fact, I received no warning beyond the now-familiar twist in my gut, where I stored my Withholds. The morning was sunny. The flowers nodded in the breeze. Wolfie rolled in a horse-pie. The doorknob yielded readily to my grip, and a savory soup simmered on the stove. But when Tobey failed to look up from scrubbing the kitchen floor I knew something was wrong. He finally glanced up, with red eyes and a pinched smile, and seemed to study my knees.

You've betrayed me, I thought, and twin pits of panic and sorrow opened within me. *She tricked you into it.*

I'd arrived early for the staff meeting, expecting to grab a few moments to laugh with him and Elizabeth. She was scrubbing the shower in the hall bathroom and grunting with effort. Elsie and the others were due from the Ranch soon. Tobey sullenly told me that Cy had gone for a walk with Charlée.

I sat on the Chinese rug near the fireplace and spread out my materials, pretending I was ready to discuss brochure colors and septic-line specifications. *Letters from Eric?* I might ask casually, when Charlée brought it up—and she would be the one. *Yeah, the poor fucker, they're so depressing. Didn't I put them in your file?*

Eventually she and Cy entered and wordlessly went to their separate quarters. Elsie came in and fluttered around the kitchen until Cy emerged from his office and asked her about cassette tapes. Willow and Ken arrived last. They carried in a case of eggs from the truck and had barely set it down when Charlée walked out of the bedroom and started the staff meeting without bothering to sit. "Steve," she declared, "Eric's been pulling you away from us. And you've drawn Tobey into an pernicious subgroup by forcing him to keep your Withhold."

"You mean Eric's pathetic letters? Didn't I put—"

"Don't dig yourself a hole you can't crawl out of," Cy warned. "Eric has *poisoned* you!" He paced in a tight circle around me. "He's sabotaging your sanity and you're coöperating. And Charlée's right. Tobey, you might not have supported this scheme if you'd seen Gollum clinging to Eric's foot a few months before you came here."

My skin burned. "Eric's trying to survive," I protested. "And I haven't asked Tobey to do anything."

"Eric is a psychopath," Cy said. "When his game stopped working on us, he ran away. You're so needy for the sick fuck you probably feel honored that he's using you as his lifeline. If he *does* survive, it'll be by coming back here and facing who he is."

Charlée assumed a mollifying tone. "You probably meant to help Eric. But you're reinforcing his delusions. And what you've done to Tobey is unforgivable. For reasons Cy and I can't fathom, he sees you as a role model. You've done your best to alienate him from his community. This morning he was distraught, trying to hide *this* from Cy and me." Between thumb and index finger she raised a hand-addressed envelope.

I held my breath. I'd never asked Tobey to hide Eric's letters, but the two of us had forged an implicit agreement. And anyway, a growth case would be thankful for the feedback, and request a process to learn the necessary lessons. A growth case would name all crimes, including those still undisclosed, and end this anxiety at last. A growth case—

"A process is premature," Willow offered, "since Steve hasn't been reached. But maybe he should go and live with Eric. That might reach him."

"Great fucking idea," Cy said.

Ken studied his hands. "But if Steve stays, Month-Off from Tobey, for sure."

A sound like the buzz of a broken neon fixture began inside my head, a noise I hadn't heard since Gollum slithered out from the underworld of my soul, when I'd dragged myself around the cookshack to expose my raw craving for Eric, then fainted in shame. The day I realized I couldn't survive outside Rancho Vista.

"You guys've reached me," I said. "I think I was waiting to get caught." I shivered though the room was warm. Tobey finally looked into my face.

I spoke to Cy and avoided Charlée's probing eyes. "I need to tell you what else I did." I felt a rush like stepping off the cliff the first time I rappelled. "I didn't send the letter you signed to the Probation Department."

"Enough games," Charlée demanded. "What *did* you send?"

"A different letter, to keep Eric out of prison. I forged Cy's signature."

"Sounds like some kind of felony," she said.

Cy looked as if he might cry. "Jesus, what were you thinking?"

"I wasn't. I was reacting." I breathed slowly. My skin no longer burned, and my stomach felt calm. "I was hurting. You broke three of my ribs that night."

"Cy was in crisis!" Charlée shouted. "How do you think I got that huge bruise on my hip the night Zoë left him? He threw me against the dresser while the rest of you got your beauty sleep. But I didn't use that as an excuse to commit treason. I understood he was grieving."

I didn't try to hide my shock. For the first time since she'd come into our lives, I wanted to hold Charlée because of her heroic suffering on Cy's behalf. For months she had kept this to herself. She wasn't the thorough monster I'd always imagined. I pictured myself crawling on my knees and reaching to comfort her, to apologize for my brutal thoughts. If I could bring myself to do that, she would kiss my hands, stroke my hair while I cried with my head in her lap. But my own treachery overwhelmed me. I cried only in my heart, for myself, and agreed when she said I must write to Probation and correct the wrong.

She slid Eric's letter from its envelope and cleared her throat. *"Dear Steve,"* she read softly, *"I've finished my second semester at the U. with straight A's. I got a win out here, and I'm ready to come home."*

I had imagined Eric's eventual return as a triumph. Cy and the others would recognize his humility and devotion. Hope drained out of me when the steel edge returned to Charlée's voice and she read, *"Has Charley still got Cy by the balls?"*

I squeezed my eyes shut. Everyone seemed to be holding their breath. Finally Cy said, "Eric needs a profound, dramatic opportunity for growth. He needs Grand Silence. The process *I* would do if I didn't have to run this place."

The staff regarded him with perplexed looks.

"It's a spiritual process," Charlée explained. "The Trappists practice Grand Silence."

I couldn't pretend I understood something this important. The only clear thing was that this was her idea, but I faced Cy to ask, "He won't be able to talk?"

"He will communicate only with his God," Charlée replied. He will write in his journal and explore what his life has become, and what it can become."

"And it's mandatory?" asked Willow.

Cy nodded gravely. "If Eric chooses to reënter the Rancho Vista community, he will come with humility and in silence. The process will continue indefinitely."

I tried to imagine Eric silent while around him the community laughed and sang.

If he accepted the process, Cy pointed out, he would put away his gregarious self. "A new, humble being will emerge. How many people ever have such opportunities, particularly in an environment of caring and reality?"

If Eric knew about this tremendous opportunity, I felt sure, he wouldn't return unless the alternative was prison.

Cy wasn't finished. "Item Two," he intoned. "Elizabeth. She's got to start answering her mother's letters. Maybe we should have her declared an emancipated minor. Steve, please work on that."

That night, in my tipi, I pictured Eric's return. The staff would greet him at the Center with limp hugs. No one would look him in the eye. Anxiety would grip his handsome features. Cy would explain the theory behind Grand Silence, then slowly the meaning of the process would pull Eric's face into a grimace of shock and betrayal.

Dear Eric, I wrote in my journal, *there's something you should know before you come home . . .* Was I going to commit treason again?

I opened the stove door, tossed in the journal page, and scratched Wolfie behind both ears at the same time, something he couldn't do for himself.

MONTH-OFF MEANT MORE THAN NOT TALKING TO TOBEY and avoiding eye contact with him. We were never alone together. I hiked to and from town each day, and missed his giggling with Elizabeth in the Rover—but knew I was blessed still to have my home and responsibilities.

By mid-June the Ranch buzzed with visitors attending family workshops, yoga retreats and various training programs. Rainbow and Lucky still flipped between Month-On and Month-Off, setting an example of willingness and self-discipline for the visitors. With Eric gone, Puck had more than garden responsibilities to live up to. Cy often assigned him to act as a "surrogate escort" for visiting women.

Was Cy's logic as blunt as it appeared? The guy with the biggest penis leaves the Ranch, so the guy with the next-biggest penis inherits his job servicing women. Though Puck and Theodora still slept together when he had no other assignments, she never acted jealous, and bragged to me that her personal concubine was establishing a career with "high-class broads."

Still, Rancho Vista refused to validate its critics who tried to give it a reputation as a sex farm. Single men arrived for a weekend, expecting to get laid, but ended up in the middle of the Dome floor, weeping for their lost mothers, embracing their loneliness and planning career changes. Families came for week-long workshops and stayed for the rest of the summer. I moved the body to and from my office, clinging to my belief that some day Cy would be released from Charlée's enchantment.

25

"I WANTED THIS PROFESSIONALLY DONE," Cy told me, "but Charlée reminded me, '*Steve* is a professional.' My son, make a wedding invitation worthy of Rancho Vista."

"She really wants me to design it?"

"Don't misjudge her. Of course you miss Zoë, but I can grow with Charlée. Rancho Vista can grow with her. And so can you."

I found myself bowing to the destiny I had set in motion when I photographed Zoë with Sonny Tornado.

The date was set for early fall, after the wave of summer visitors and before the huge job of harvest. The guest list included the journalist Wanda Richter, who could be counted on to provide colorful coverage of the wedding. But Cy didn't expect her to publicize the event before it took place. A week after the invitations went out, Elsie opened a staff meeting by passing around a clipping from the Los Angeles *Times* under the headline, *Innovative Therapist to Marry Protégée.*

"Let's hope we don't get any uninvited guests," Cy said. "Now, let's discuss those corporate clients."

Who was he afraid would show up? Zoë and Josh wouldn't humiliate themselves or embarrass Cy and Charlée by coming.

For the ceremony, Charlée chose a stone alcove where ancient Anasazi petroglyphs overlooked the gardens. I made a rubbing of my favorite glyph—two figures who appeared to be holding hands—and designed the invitation around this image, with the caption *Wherefore they are no more twain, but one flesh. Matthew 19:6.* I inscribed the same quotation in my childhood Bible and wrapped it as a wedding gift in a square of silk.

The industrial psychologists from the Santa Barbara conference had participated in Ken's third Trail of the summer. Before returning to civilization they arranged for Cy to conduct consultations with managers of Hilton Hotels and the personnel department of Los Angeles International Airport. "Either of these contracts," Cy told the staff, "could pay the Ranch's expenses for a year. We've arrived."

Cy seemed to consider each new blast of recognition from the "real world" to be such an arrival. Would we ever stop arriving, and just enjoy life?

TOBEY CANNONBALLED INTO THE POND and frog-kicked to the rock at the far end. I cherished the view of his agile body shooting through the clear water—dark, billowing hair reminiscent of Zoë's, his well-defined torso, perfect ass and strong legs. This was the first day of our Month-On. Cy and Charlée were in Denver for the weekend, and the Vistans were taking a day off. Upstream at the waterfall, the big swimming hole was crowded. Tobey had suggested we hike to this isolated little pond.

Wolfie trotted up the narrow path, snapping his jaws at butterflies. When Tobey hoisted himself onto a ledge at the far end of the pond I fumbled with my towel, then propped the Cavafy poems in my lap to hide my growing erection.

He lay prone on the rock and munched a sprig of watercress. Across the water he called, "Know whose birthday is next month?"

I closed the book and tried a casual tone. "You'll be seventeen, right?"

"Age of consent in Colorado." This didn't provoke the expected response and he added, "No more jailbait!"

"It's illegal for *adults* to make love if they're the same gender." I put down the book and dove in. The cold water didn't discourage my cock as I swam toward Tobey. I popped my head out of the pond and stood in the sand below the rock, reaching for his hands. "When we make love, I want it to be really special. No anxiety, no sneaky stuff. There are worse things than being a virgin."

Tobey's gaze darted past me into the cold shadows where the trout slept. A Withhold flickered in his eyes.

I felt a twitch in my gut. "What's that?" I asked, trying not to sound like an interrogating therapist.

"It's too late for me to worry about being a virgin. Technically, anyway." He didn't bother to push the hair out of his eyes. "Don't pretend you don't know about Mr. and Mrs. M. I think you know them pretty well."

I tried to keep my voice free of the horror I felt. Until this moment I hadn't realized how much I wanted to be Tobey's first love. "You mean with Charlée?"

"It's an honor, I know. But she's—not *you*."

Rage and betrayal shook my insides. I kissed each of Tobey's fingers. "Look at me," I pleaded.

His dark eyes shone behind dripping hair. I pulled myself up onto the rock and stroked his sad face. "You probably weren't supposed to tell me."

He shook his head.

"Are you afraid I won't want to be with you now?"

"Everybody knows you hate her."

"Can I kiss you?"

Tobey's face brightened. "You mean it's already time for our semi-annual smooch?"

I stroked his hair and drew his soft lips toward mine. "One kiss. Then you and me and that big towel are movin' over into tall-grass country."

Tobey's mouth tasted sweet, and his tongue and lips were at once soft and insistent, yielding and hungry. The kiss flooded me with a powerful knowledge of who we were together. I took his hand and we climbed away from the pond. Each of us had performed for someone else's pleasure. Once, sloshed on Joy Juice, we'd rolled in a snow bank and kissed furiously until our mouths went numb. Today, sober and naked in the shade of the willows, we explored the magic of slow, deep kissing that heightened every sensation. Columbine and horsetail reeds danced in the breeze while we stroked each other with tentative fingers and spoke only with our eyes, our silence borne not of shame but reverence. How wonderfully strange I felt to be with someone who *wanted* me awake and reciprocating. After the weird, mute ministrations of Eric, Ken and even Cy, I'd begun to believe my sexual life might never include these simple pleasures.

I ached to please Tobey, but was afraid of being detached. My mouth moved down his smooth, firm body, teasing his nipples and even his armpits, then tickling his navel, and I discovered unimagined freedom.

We went from grunting fever to giggling joy, from obsession with each other's cocks to fascination with each other's earlobes. We melted together like two candles burning side-by-side. As the shadows deepened into evening we held each other and wept. Once I had promised, "Some day we'll make love," without knowing what this meant. Now I knew. It meant giving all of myself to a man who wanted to share my life.

"I'VE ALWAYS HOPED ERIC WOULD RETURN TO HIS PLACE in this community," Cy said. "He could be a leader of modern psychotherapy."

"A leader of psycho*pathology* is more like it," Charlée rejoined. "Aren't you interested in hearing from tomorrow's true leaders?" She was heading for a grandstand play. My newfound affection for her had withered in only two days. "I could have left with Eric that night," I said, eager to get the jump on her. "While he drove away, I realized this is my home. I want to spend my life carrying on your work, Cy."

"Me, too," said Willow.

"Count me in," said Ken.

Elsie, then Elizabeth and Tobey, and finally Theodora affirmed their lifelong commitments.

Charlée spoke last, holding Cy's hand. "Until death do us part," she said with blatant theatricality.

Lady, I thought, don't give me any ideas.

Eric coördinated his return in phone calls with her. I was careful not to answer when the phone rang at the office. How could I hear his voice without screaming out a warning that Grand Silence was awaiting him? Words like "betrayal" and "inhuman" haunted me, and I kept busy with my projects. The day he was scheduled to return, the staff met for hours—talking almost exclusively about his process. Cy repeated what an honor and a privilege we were about to bestow upon our "prodigal brother." I said little, anxious about facing the man who had brought me into this family, and about the future that awaited him after he ran back into the unreal world outside.

Just as I had imagined a thousand times, when Eric strode into the Center's big room, looking freshly scrubbed and more handsome than ever, I couldn't look into his eyes. I hugged him feebly, and watched Willow and the others do the same. I wanted to warn him not to drink the wine that Charlée offered. I hadn't drunk any myself, yet I felt numb when he sat in our circle with his frightened half-smile. Yes, he could see something was terribly wrong. I listened to Cy's explanation of the extraordinary growth opportunity that was available to him as if I had never heard of it before.

As the nature of this opportunity was made clear to him, Eric reacted with shock, then anger. He leveled one accusatory look at me, and asked, "You knew about this, huh, Steve?" I shrugged.

Shortly after this his tears came. He wept as he explained that he did have a choice now, because his probation had been terminated—thanks to publicity generated by Vivian, who had written to state officials complaining about events at the Ranch. Prison was no longer hanging over his head. But he wanted to try the process. "I don't fit in out there," he cried. "This is my home."

Could I possibly defend a process that I thought was inhuman? Could I enforce it?

I could, and I did. In Group, Cy introduced Eric as if none of us knew him, and defined Grand Silence. "No communication of any kind, with anyone, while Eric develops his relationship with the realm of the spirit." In medical emergencies he would go to Willow. He would eat among us in the cookshack, write in his journals, work in the gardens—without speaking to anyone, without eye contact, without hugs or any touch of any kind.

By the second day I realized this wasn't going to be as difficult for me as I had imagined. After all, Eric had freely chosen to stay. And his clear gray eyes never focused on me—in fact, by the third day, because he had attempted to make eye contact with other people, the process was modified to include very dark glasses, which he wore at all times when in the presence of others, even indoors. The first time he walked past me with no acknowledgment, my heart ached. But the next time it was easier, and soon I found myself leaving the cookshack after a meal, unable to remember whether he had been in the room.

WHILE THE COMMUNITY GEARED UP for the wedding, I finalized the coming month's insurance reports, prepared the fall brochure for the printer, and drafted Cy's proposals for the winter and spring conferences. "I'm taking a vacation as soon as they leave on their honeymoon," I told Tobey one morning on our hike to town. "A week on the mountain before it gets too cold up there."

I paused to give him a chance to ask, *Can I come?* But he merely sighed, so I continued, "Wanna join me?"

"Sure I do. But Elizabeth and I are going along on the honeymoon—you know, to help."

I nodded as if I should have suggested this myself, but my heart pounded. As the new sexual surrogate-in-training, what kind of "help" might Tobey have to provide? *At least with Elizabeth there*, I wanted to say, *Charlée'll have to keep her claws out of you.*

GLEEFULLY THE VISTAN WOMEN PLANNED a wedding party none of us would ever forget. Rainbow organized a crew to string festoons of fiery oak leaves and dried flowers in the cookshack, the Dome, Charlée's tipi, and the Center. Theodora's wedding gift was a set of antique sterling flatware. Others also brought out family treasures to give. Willow handstitched a pair of kimonos from her grandmother's silk. Elizabeth wrapped an 1888 edition of Grimm's Fairy Tales.

The men got into the mood and still I hung back. Travis ordered cases of good champagne, and caviar, escargot and pâté, from a shop in Denver with a European connection. Ken carved a mandala in sharp relief from a sandstone block, and composed a bluesy ballad about a king who shared his riches with his subjects. Finally Tobey persuaded me to collaborate with him on a gift—he painted a watercolor of the petroglyph grotto where the wedding would take place, and I constructed a frame for it from cottonwood.

In the midst of the wedding preparations, Elizabeth and I made sure Tobey's seventeenth birthday didn't get ignored. Travis decorated a chocolate cake with *No More Jailbait* in pink script. My lover and I made much of trundling off arm-in-arm, as if for our first night together.

The wedding RSVPs landed in daily stacks on my desk. One batch of mail included a typed envelope bearing my name and no return address. Inside, unsigned, was my mother's idea of direct communication: *Your father needs to talk to you.*

How typical this seemed of Alex and Susi—a cryptic note with no explanation, no please or thank you, just *Your father needs . . .* My father had breakfast with me this morning, I reflected. And if the guy who publicly disowned me needed me so much, he could tell me himself.

Each day one of the women hosted an intimate shower for Charlée, with champagne and lacy boudoir gifts. Cy was the guest of honor at a continuing stag party. The men brought him offerings—cigars ordered from Denver, bottles of scotch and tattered back issues of *Playboy*. For the bachelor party at the Center, Travis rented a projector and an eight-millimeter print of "Deep Throat." I started things off by imitating a stand-up comedian: "The locals are excited about the wedding. Dove MacKenzie goes around Keystone asking everybody, 'How many

times does fifty go into thirty-two?'" Cy chuckled with the men
at the feeble joke, clearly flattered that the locals were honoring
his virility.

The night before the wedding, at a staff party in her tipi,
Charlée up-ended her fourth glass of champagne, flipped tendrils
of hair from her face, and announced, "I have a special wedding
gift for Cy."

I groaned inside, wondering what extravagance she'd purchased with Ranch money to present as a tribute from herself.
She went on in her maddeningly slow way, "I vow to do anything
necessary to become—worthy of my betrothed." She smiled
coyly and Cy blushed. I shared a quietly incredulous look with
Willow, itching to ask if she had any idea what Charlée was
talking about. Was "becoming worthy" her special gift?

Ken ended the awkward silence with a toast to the One Flesh
Marriage, and everyone joined in.

Cy said, "Please look inside yourselves for signs you're envying Charlée, or tempted to subgroup against her." He gave
Willow and then me pointed looks. "If so, come and talk to us.
Honey, you want your relationships with everyone to grow, don't
you?"

Charlée nodded slowly with tears in her eyes. "You all mean
so much to me, and I don't want to lose your friendship just
because I've become—Mrs. Dr. Cyrus Aaron!"

I knew I should say something conciliatory—*I'm the jealous one,
and I'll work extra hard.* Instead I simply replenished Charlée's
champagne and clicked glasses with her.

Cy confirmed his plan to take Tobey and Elizabeth on a honeymoon cruise through the Caribbean. "This will be a family
affair," he said, "not a selfish indulgence of two lovers. The kids'll
share a magical time with us. Through them, the entire Composite Significant Other will be present." Tobey and Elizabeth's faces
shone with exhilaration.

Many Vistans never made it to bed that night. Travis drove
shuttle runs to town to bring in late-arriving guests, including the
journalist Wanda Richter and Father Ben, a Jesuit client of Cy's
who would perform the ceremony. Theodora took over the
kitchen with help from Rainbow and some of the children. I
spent the evening in town at the triple-wide, helping Tobey pack
his little suitcase. "All you really need is shorts and tee-shirts," I
told him.

"Be excited for me," he insisted. "You knew my father. He

went to conventions in Vienna but I've never 'traveled' further than Tijuana."

I kissed him. "Okay, I'm a little envious." I gave him two pairs of dress socks, a Gucci belt and my vicuña sweater, but worried: was the anguish in my gut really just envy?

BREAKFAST BEGAN SHORTLY AFTER DAWN as dinner had ended—with champagne. Ken serenaded the diners on his saxophone. The Vista women and their guests emerged from tipis in lace and satin, festooned in flowers, their faces luminous.

Just before noon we stood at the base of the Ranch's highest cliff, before mysterious inscriptions that had been ancient when the conquistadors arrived on the continent. While Ken picked his guitar, I faced fifty Vistans and a hundred visitors, stoned on Cy's best pot, knowing I looked great in a suit Zoë had bought for me a lifetime before. I'd practiced my song dozens of times and wasn't nervous. But my voice broke when I sang, "In my life, I've loved you more . . ." From Charlée's smile I knew she was misreading my emotions.

Father Ben's robes billowed majestically, and his purple velvet stole complemented the bride's plum-colored silk gown. The dress looked to me like a négligée as she approached the slab of sandstone that served as the altar. Cy wore a white tie and morning coat. He offered her his arm with the bearing of a senior diplomat.

I rarely noticed Eric, but today he was hard to miss. He sat in the back row of makeshift benches, dressed in a black suit as if for a funeral.

The couple exchanged vows that I had inscribed on a parchment scroll, cementing the wall that forever would exclude Zoë from her spiritual home. She was gone and I had helped banish her. When Willow led the guests in singing "Amazing Grace," everyone stepped closer to form concentric circles around the new couple. The familiar melody rose like an ecstatic shout. I wept—wondering if even Tobey, gripping my hand, understood that my tears were of grief, rage and resignation, not joy.

TWO DAYS AFTER THE WEDDING, I was preparing my backpack for a sojourn on the mountain when the whine of an unfamiliar engine reached me from the swale. I ran outside my tipi and watched Sheriff Buford's white Ford pickup ascend out of the garden.

I ran toward the cookshack and stopped short. The sheriff's sun-worn face had none of its familiar drollery. Vivian, wearing dark glasses, stood close to his truck. I approached her for a hug but she held up a hand. "Don't drag this out," she said. "We're here for my daughter."

Several Vistans came into the road and stood at a distance. Willow reached with open arms, then looked as if she'd been kicked when Vivian shoved out a hand like a stop sign.

"Elizabeth isn't here," I said. "They left for L.A. yesterday morning."

"They?" asked the sheriff.

"Elizabeth's going to St. Croix with Dr. Aaron and—his wife. It's their honeymoon." I avoided Vivian's eyes.

"Why in blazes would anybody take a twelve-year-old on their honeymoon?" Buford asked.

Vivian yanked off her sunglasses and glared at me. "He took her out of the *country*?"

I shrugged, trying to appear casual. No point mentioning that Elizabeth was almost thirteen, or that Tobey had also gone. Couldn't Vivian see that Cy had opened the world to her daughter? He had honored Elizabeth by including her.

"Sheriff," Vivian said, climbing back into the pickup, "I'm charging Dr. Aaron and his wife with kidnapping."

I canceled my camping trip and stayed close to the office phones. The day after the unexpected visit I received a call from Buford. Vivian had failed to persuade the prosecutor to file criminal charges, but the sheriff said, "That woman aims to get her girl back."

TRAVIS HAD HOARDED CAVIAR and French champagne to welcome the honeymoon party home. He prepared a dinner at the Center for the staff and a few other Vistans who could be counted on not to get too drunk or go into their shit.

We left the champagne on ice and kept the music soft. An air of sacred anticipation prevailed.

The big Mercedes rolled up as expected at seven p.m. Inside the Center we shushed one another as if for a surprise party. The honeymooners crossed the deck to the sliding glass door, silhouetted by a scarlet sunset. Charlée entered first, in her plum silk wedding dress and with her hair up, to the howling applause of the assembled greeting committee. I clapped, but refused to whistle like Ken and the other men. Cy walked in behind her, in a cashmere turtleneck, and a whistling roar rose among the crowd.

I expected Elizabeth and Tobey to trail in next with luggage, but Cy stood back and held out a hand. Elizabeth stepped into the room like a princess, with a demure half-smile. She wore a filmy dress and a garland of wildflowers in her burnished-copper hair. Tobey followed her, wearing black trousers, slick new shoes and my vicuña sweater. He had a fresh haircut that made him look like a Young Republican version of himself. I wanted to run to him for a hug, but he seemed to avoid my eyes, and I stood back with mounting distress until other greetings were complete. When we finally hugged, he still didn't look me in the eyes.

As everyone sat down to dinner, Cy stood and offered a toast. Instead of one more reminder of how he couldn't live without Charlée, and what a role-model for humankind she was, he said, "Everyone, please look at Elizabeth."

Her dress emphasized her budding breasts and trim waist. With her dramatic eye makeup she looked much older than the girl I had grown to love as a kid sister.

"With this magical party," Cy went on, "you're welcoming Charlée and me home to a new life. But I want to share with you that Elizabeth also is beginning a new life." He raised his glass to her. "Elizabeth is now a woman."

I looked at her carefully. She'd been menstruating since her second month at the Ranch, so that couldn't be the big news. What had happened to her precocious charm? She now appeared dignified, almost haughty.

Cy bent toward her, not for the peck on the cheek I expected, but to share a deep, open-mouthed kiss. Charlée raised her glass and dipped her head in a humble gesture like nothing I had ever witnessed from her. The other Vistans were all completely silent. With alarm I recalled Charlée's cryptic reference to her "special wedding gift" for Cy.

Platters of food were passed. I felt sick and couldn't join the conversation that started up. I mooshed food around and ate nothing. Tobey looked tired and remained withdrawn. Could he have been in on Elizabeth's welcome to womanhood? Willow and Ken and Elsie avoided the small talk at the table as I did. We spoke in monosyllables and stared into our food. Any exchange of glances right now could constitute subgrouping.

While Tobey and Theodora cleared the table, Puck put on a Cat Stevens album and the dancing began. Willow pulled me close and whispered in my ear, "Are you as freaked out about this thing with Elizabeth as I am?"

"God, yes. Let's tell him."

"Maybe tomorrow? He's pretty drunk."

"He's got to stop crowing about it *now*. He Frenched her in front of everybody."

She lay her head on my shoulder. "Staff meeting in five minutes in his study?"

"I'll spread the word."

When I told Elsie, she looked as if she might faint. But she entered Cy's study at the appointed time. Even the usually stoic Ken appeared rattled. Cy and Charlée entered last while Tower of Power blasted from the stereo out in the big room.

"This honeymoon development concerns me," I began, with a glance at Willow. "Cy, I know you trust Elizabeth. I trust her, too. But you can't just tell everybody you—God, I don't even want to know what you've done."

He backed away. "How can you people let him corner me like this? I need bodyguards."

"Steve's right," Willow said evenly. "Vivian showed up here with the sheriff while you were away. This is just what she needs to put us out of business."

"When the woman anointed Jesus with her fine oil," Cy said, "his apostles were *jealous of her gift* because they had taken their master for granted."

I stared at him, astonished by the comparison.

Cy met my gaze. "This is particularly interesting coming from *you*, who had Tobey down at the swimming hole sucking your cock before his sixteenth birthday."

I felt all power drain from my body. "His seventeenth," I lamely corrected him.

"You were committing infamous crimes against nature with an underage boy. My point is, both kids are safe. Tobey isn't going to confide in his mother, who silently watched his father torture him. And Elizabeth isn't going to share anything personal with her pathetic mother. *Elizabeth* is the mother in that fucking family." His voice turned soft. "You were there the day that poor woman staggered into her son's funeral, dragging Elizabeth and Mikey behind her."

In a businesslike tone Charlée asked me, "Didn't you get Elizabeth declared an emancipated minor?"

"The petition is ready to file," I replied, "but we have to go to court unless Vivian gives consent, and she's bound to fight it."

"You never told me that," Cy said. "I thought it was taken care of."

I looked to Willow. She nodded in support, and I continued more gently, "Having her declared an emancipated minor can't protect you from a statutory rape charge. It just means she can live where she wants. Besides, she's a *child* and we're her *family*."

Charlée thanked me and Willow for expressing our concern. With a stern look at Cy she agreed it was best not to openly discuss Elizabeth's entry into womanhood. He shrugged with a surly expression. The staff meeting adjourned to the dance floor. Elizabeth ran over and asked me to dance. Holding her, I remembered the promise I had made to her mother, to protect her like brother.

Later, as I drove to the Ranch with Ken, Willow and Elsie, I looked straight ahead. Elizabeth and Tobey had stayed in town to help with unpacking, but what else were they helping with?

"Remember the 'special wedding gift' Charlée said she was giving Cy?" I said. No one answered. "She got him to marry her in exchange for helping him take Elizabeth's virginity. Now it makes sense."

Beside me Willow patted my knee. "Yes, it does."

"She's a child," I went on, encouraged. "She's mature, but did you see the look in her eyes? She's in love with him. And if Vivian found out about this we could lose everything." I stopped short of saying, *Sex with a minor is a felony*, acutely aware that everyone present knew I'd been with Tobey before he reached the age of consent.

"It's a powerful male fantasy, huh?" Willow said. "To deflower a virgin."

I steered the Rover with extra care over the rutted road I knew so well. "Cy thinks he needed a bodyguard. I say he needs a goddamned keeper." Willow and I exchanged a look in the dim lights of the dashboard, the two who had confronted Cy, and our shared understanding forged a bond of seductive intensity. In the back seat, Elsie and Ken were silent.

In the moonlit sagebrush stretched possibilities that until now had lain in darkness.

26

THE DAYS OF RIVER-SWIMMING PASSED QUICKLY,
and one morning a membrane of ice floated on the holding pond.
The swans disappeared after breakfast, the hawks and sparrows
within a week, then the crows and finally the owls. We stockpiled
wood and hauled coal in preparation for winter—which, Travis's
almanac predicted, would be uncommonly dry and cold.

Tobey's anguished expression across the cookshack, and in
the Land Rover's rear-view mirror, spoke of his loneliness and
fear. *Give him a chance to talk*, I told myself, and considered a
dozen ruses involving the sharing of a wheelbarrow or an axe.
Finally, after trying throughout dinner one evening to get him to
look at me, I hiked with Wolfie to his tipi and whistled. "Hey, it's
me. Can I come in?"

"Sure." He was smearing waterproofer on his hiking boots,
and didn't look up when the dog and I entered.

"Listen," I began. "I know you're avoiding me and you still
love me and I'm sorry I've been too stupid to tell you but I love
you too. Now what's going on? By the way, if you hold your boot
over the lantern, the heat'll melt the wax into the leather."

"It's not wax," came the sullen reply. "This stuff is made of
mink oil."

"Whatever it is it'll soak in better if—." I caught my breath
and sat beside him on the narrow bed. My gaze traveled around
the tidy little round home, decorated with Tobey's colorful
artwork. Above the door in a driftwood frame hung a watercolor
portrait of me. "I miss you," I said. "I know things happened
during the honeymoon that you don't want to talk about. It's
okay. But I'm lonely and scared right now. I need you."

The boot thumped onto the floor. Tobey wiped his hands on
his overalls and pulled me close. "Just don't ask me anything.
Don't make me lie to you."

I kissed his forehead. When he began to cry in my arms I
wanted to demand, *What did they do to you?* but I waited.

Soon he revealed, "In L.A. Charlée took Elizabeth to get birth
control pills. I was scared to say anything. I kept wishing you
were there, because you could reason with Cy. Charlée started a
fight because he can't get a hardon with her any more. I couldn't

talk to Elizabeth, she was so *honored* that *he* was going to welcome her to womanhood. And maybe it's a silly legality, but they didn't wait 'til we left the country. It happened in Beverly Hills."

I listened silently and cradled him. "Everything's going to be okay," I promised, and we undressed each other for bed.

Having tapped the truth, Tobey needed to spill it all. He hadn't watched Cy with Elizabeth, or been asked to participate. "That would have been awful enough."

"But?"

"Don't ask me things you don't want to know."

Poor Tobey, even now trying to protect me from pain. "You were with Charlée while Cy and Elizabeth—"

"He pulled me aside and said I had to take care of Charlée, so she wouldn't get jealous. Please don't hate me."

I kissed each of his mink oil-scented fingers. "Just get the whole story out."

"Later that night the four of us shared a bottle of champagne, so I thought it was over. But it happened again the next day. And every night."

I held him, hating Charlée as I'd never thought possible. To get Cy to marry her she had betrayed her "surrogate daughter" and traumatized Tobey.

AS LONG AS I COULD CRANK OUT LOVELY BRO-CHURES that attracted high-level people, I felt assured of a place near Cy. At the start of the spring thaw, the cookshack was expanded to accommodate eighty people, our top summer population, and adorable pod-like cabins sprouted here and there, tiny versions of the Group Dome. Cy and Charlée outlined books and articles together, but little was published. He lived on the edge of constant fear about what Vivian might do to get her daughter back. With each change of seasons he seemed to be drinking earlier in the day. Charlée appeared at meals and staff meetings with bruises that she explained away as the result of her "clumsiness" when navigating icy stairs or slick-rock creekbeds. Ken's Trail program and Willow's Yoga Institute prospered. We traveled to conferences, recruiting the brightest attendees, and hosted ever more famous people at the Ranch, but eventually the cold weather always returned and chased away all but the most stalwart Vistans—who, as I entered my fifth year in the wilderness, numbered almost fifty.

Willow and I never discussed our night of subgrouping, and she withdrew into her yoga workshops like a Tibetan nun. Even Tobey, after relieving himself of the burden of the honeymoon particulars, became silent about what, if anything, was continuing between Cy and Elizabeth. He and I talked late many nights about exotic travel plans for the distant future, and drew sketches of the dome we wanted to build together. But we discussed nothing of the past and little about the present.

Eric's process ended up lasting exactly nine months—his "gestation period," Cy called it. But until the day he removed his sunglasses, Eric didn't know when, or if, it would end. Even now that he was back in communication with most of the community, Cy determined that Eric and I should remain "nonpersons" to each other. I was too vulnerable to him, had risked the Ranch's reputation to write fraudulent letters on his behalf, and might be tempted to help him gain power he couldn't yet handle. To foster the humility that had been the goal of Grand Silence, Eric was assigned to Travis's work crew.

The staff met less and less frequently, and Cy and Charlée spent days on end sequestered at the Center. During her first Group appearance in over a month, she made an announcement that earned her a standing ovation: The Rutherford College/West students had steadily mailed in documentation of real-life experiences toward college credit, and twelve of us were ready to graduate. We ordered caps and gowns, organized a ritual at the stone alcove where Cy and Charlée had been married, and made the graduation ceremony into a weekend-long party.

"VIVIAN ELFINGER HAS DONE US ALL A FAVOR," Cy declared to the staff. He had summoned us to town in the middle of the busiest day of the pumpkin harvest. "She's demonstrated what people are capable of." He unfolded a copy of the Abraham County Star-Union and exhibited the headline: *DRUG FARM LEADER ACCUSED OF KIDNAPPING.* "Life as we know it has ceased to exist."

I studied the article while Cy spoke. The anonymous mother of a resident of the "Rancho Vista drug treatment facility" had written to the editor. The first sentence screamed in bold type: *My twelve-year-old daughter was taken out of the country against her will.*

"This is silly," I said. "Elizabeth has been back in Abraham County for over a year, and she's fourteen now. She could go to

Gentile today and let the paper interview her. They make it sound like legal charges were filed, but the D.A. wouldn't touch it." I felt hurt by the tone of the article. "And we're not a 'drug farm,' we're a growth center. A college! This is a smear campaign."

"Oh, to have your innocence," Cy said. "This is the hottest story since that coal truck flipped on the interstate and the driver turned out to have a joint in his pocket. Our years of good work in this county are down the drain." He put his hands together prayerfully. "Charlée and I have discussed all the options. This community is moving to Beverly Hills, where we have clients and a referral base. Oh, and a house big enough for everybody."

I let out a sharp laugh of shock and pain. "But that's the scene of the crime."

Cy thundered, "There was no crime! Get that through your fucking heads." His voice abruptly softened and he spoke as if reading a press release: "Rancho Vista has reached a plateau in its growth. Our Rutherford graduate program requires that we relocate to an urban environment. We will continue to use the Ranch as a base for Trails, but the community is moving to Southern California."

Ken, Elsie, Willow and I traded stares of amazement. Charlée watched us, her lips in a tight line.

Cy told the staff to remain seated, then launched into a series of phone calls that began with the same incantation, "We're moving our main operation to Beverly Hills so Rutherford College/West can accomplish its objectives." The rest of us listened to him explain the move to the real estate lawyer in Denver, and the Los Angeles tax lawyer, then to Wanda Richter, who would tell the world. The staff was then excused. We filed outside the Center and went our separate ways.

Numbly I walked to the triple-wide to make my own phone calls, and began reciting the announcement to the parents and guardians of Vistans. With each call, the story made more sense, sounded more inevitable, more *true*.

I enjoyed one call. "I think you'll be pleased," I told Alice Turner, "to know the college program must be brought into an urban environment. Tobey has decided he wants to stay with the community." And, I thought, with me. Quickly I added, "And he's so glad he'll be closer to you."

She replied with a weak, hopeful murmur. The poor woman had never recovered. Dr. Turner's hateful influence seemed to reach from the grave.

Cy made the announcement to the entire community over dinner. "People," he said expansively, "this will be a challenge beyond anything we have faced so far. But it's a necessary one. We've become so comfortable in our backwoods home that we don't know how to talk to people in society. It's time to take what has been learned here and apply it in the larger human relations laboratory, the one that calls itself the 'Real World.'"

A number of Vistans sobbed. Several, including Eric, whom I watched furtively, sat with stunned expressions. A few even protested. "How could you decide this without talking to us first?" Puck demanded. "I won't live in L.A. I'm staying here."

PUCK DIDN'T STAY. No one stayed. A few peripheral members of the community simply returned to their former lives in Denver and beyond. The youngest children were placed with relatives. We abandoned the pumpkin harvest. We slaughtered and ate the turkeys, boarded the horses with the MacKenzies in Keystone, and donated the goats to Gentile High School's 4-H program. Travis's crew nailed boards over the cookshack windows, packed what they could into the trucks, and stashed everything else, from Victorian armoires to crates full of notebooks, in the root cellar. Travis planned to make several return trips for people's valuables.

The caravan left at five a.m., intending to make it to Beverly Hills by dawn the next day. Before we pulled out, Cy instructed me, "Once we're settled, be sure everyone has a valid passport. But don't wait 'til we're too settled."

I laughed. "It does feel like we're moving to another country."

"This is serious. We all need passports."

"We?"

"The paying patients, staff, everyone. Vivian can make things very difficult for us in this reactionary society."

I nodded, but felt I was being swept away by a powerful wind that kept shifting directions.

AT THREE A.M. ON A MOONLESS FRIDAY, after twenty-two hours on the road, the caravan pulled into the twelve hundred block of Bedford Drive in Beverly Hills: a red dump truck, a big black stakeside truck, two white Land Rovers, a green VW bug, a red Mercedes convertible and a red Mercedes sedan, all caked with dried mud. Dozens of young people crawled out of the vehicles to unload pot-belly stoves and a hobby-sized brewery into the corners of the four-car garage. These were followed by an assortment of farm implements including home-made fifty-gallon wheelbarrows, shovels and pitchforks, seed-spreaders and tractor parts that spilled out of the garage onto the ratty lawn.

The house was larger than I remembered, and in worse repair. The guest house behind the pool, in better shape than the rest of the place, became Cy and Charlée's private suite. In the main house, six of the upstairs bedrooms had fireplaces, but only two chimneys worked. Every room had at least one broken window. Leaky plumbing in two third-floor bathrooms had warped the subfloors, shattering the tiles. The large, round room in the basement, once a recording studio, reeked of mildew. Cracks ran the length and breadth of the Olympic-sized pool, which bordered a garden of dead roses and thriving weeds. The exhausted Vistans swam in the green water before falling into bed.

After breakfast Cy convened Group in the mansion's great hall—a space that could have served as a movie set for a medieval costume drama, with a cavernous fireplace that featured an ornate coat-of-arms. As we had done when Group met in the plank-floored cookshack, we dropped our parkas on the flagstones to use as seat cushions.

"We have a lot of exciting challenges ahead of us," Cy said with a buoyant tone.

"I hate this fucking town," Lucky muttered.

"Me too," whined Rainbow, while others grumbled.

"Okay, everybody." Cy looked at his watch. "Five minutes to say everything you hate about this city. And contrary to our usual procedure, you can all talk at once."

We did. "The water tastes like Clorox . . . I can't see the stars at night . . . if you cross the street anywhere but the crosswalk you get a ticket, and *in* the crosswalk they try to run you over . . ."

"Doesn't '*Beverly Hills*' sound glamorous?" Theodora shouted above the clamor. "But we breathe the same filthy air as the bums on skid row."

"Fucking A!" yelled Puck.

Travis never complained about anything, but now raised his hand and waited for Cy to call on him. "I've never seen the moon in L.A. At the Ranch I always know when the moon is full. Here I'll have to look at the almanac to make sure she's still up there. That gives me the creeps." He had everyone's attention and added slowly, "Plus, I don't know how long I can live in a place where people take their poodles in for acupuncture."

The Vistans shouted agreement. When we had exhausted our complaints, the faces around me were twisted with anger and pain. I saw annoyance in Charlée's expression, distress in Cy's. "Everybody," I said, "I'm as lonely as anyone for the Mother River. But we're home now. This morning, when I was putting gas in the truck, a man panhandled me. I asked him where he lived, and he pointed to a cardboard box under some oleanders. I thought, thank God I have a home and a family. Under the Colorado Milky Way I never appreciated all of you. Here, now, I really appreciate you."

The Vistans gazed at me with startled, loving faces. I stepped behind Cy's chair and continued, "The ideals of Rancho Vista will triumph in our lives. We are ahead of every therapy organization on the planet. If we do this right, we can get the Rutherford graduate program underway and go home to Rancho Vista any time we want. We'll have the best of *both* worlds. Today I'm getting my hair cut, so the neighbors don't call animal control to pick me up like a stray raccoon. Who's coming with me?"

I had one of my rare, unbidden thoughts of Eric—would he submit his long blond hair to be citified? Only now did I realize I hadn't seen him since we drove out of Keystone. He wasn't supposed to exist to me, and I said nothing. But eventually Theodora asked, "Where the hell is Eric?" and the group realized he hadn't made the trip with us. I felt frightened for him and relieved for myself. In a quiet place I still loved him, and ached each time he spoke and I couldn't look into his sunny face. But there was envy, too: wherever he was, he wouldn't have to go through this latest "growth opportunity."

We descended on a discount hair salon in Santa Monica and emerged two hours later looking "civilized." Afterward Travis treated everyone to ice cream cones. He still sported his ponytail, but had sacrificed several inches of it to the cause of urban living. That evening, as if resigned to a long stay, he installed the beer-making apparatus in the ramshackle mansion's basement.

Everyone wore smiles and worked hard at their assigned tasks. Tobey and Elizabeth served breakfast each day to the Vistan First Couple in the guest house. Travis organized crews that replaced broken windows, built long dining tables and repaired the leaky plumbing and the broken banister. Left for eager volunteers were re-seeding the lawns and patching the swimming pool. Charlée took Willow and me along to choose office space in Westwood, and included us in scheduling consultation meetings with the LAX and Hilton personnel departments. I drove a truckload of Vistans to UCLA, where we registered to audit courses that would satisfy Rutherford College's classroom requirements. Tobey and I signed up at a gym and scheduled games of racquet-ball with Cy to help him stay in shape. For Christmas Travis prepared a feast reminiscent of the Ranch—but, with no sweat-lodge or bonfire, we were in bed by midnight.

Through the following weeks I smiled along with everyone, although I hadn't been so unhappy since the days I hoarded pills. Dreams of being chased through a dark forest hounded me. The neighborhood boasted broad paved lanes called "alleys" behind the houses, landscaped as nicely as the streets in most neighbor-hoods, where Tobey and I took Wolfie for walks—the only private space we could find. We talked about the dome we still intended to build at the Ranch, and made other plans that didn't involve Los Angeles.

Occasionally I wondered if Cy was still . . . I didn't even know what words to use in my mind. Making love to Elizabeth? Balling her? Molesting her? And was Tobey still servicing Charlée? If that was going on in the guest house, they were the only Vistans enjoying any sexual release, because everyone else was acting like cloistered monks and nuns. Even Rainbow and Lucky—who'd once balled in the back of a Land Rover while I drove it through Denver traffic—now revealed in Group that they held each other and cried themselves to sleep each night, and hadn't gotten it on since they packed their tipi for the move to California. Since the caravan's arrival, Tobey and I hadn't even exchanged a kiss.

Finally we discovered we could carry on the tradition of Vis-tan parties in the recording studio. The work crew peeled up the scrofulous carpet, leaving a gray concrete floor streaked with old yellow glue. The round room had been carved out of the rock beneath the house. When the studio's big insulated door was closed, not even the cacophony of drums, saxophones, guitars, tambourines and voices escaped into the neighborhood.

The newly-leased Westwood suite featured a conference room with a massive table Charlée adopted as her desk, making her office four times the size of anyone else's. Willow decorated her office with peacock feathers and leather chairs. For mine, I built a desk of mahogany and smoked glass. Cy cranked out a dozen ideas every day for books and journal articles he instructed me to outline. Elsie resisted his decision to hire a bookkeeping service, and enrolled in an accounting program at Santa Monica College. "We don't need outsiders monkeying in our books," she said, and Cy applauded her spunk.

Soon *Psychotherapy Currents* reported that *Cyrus Aaron's therapeutic community Rancho Vista, long spread out between the Colorado wilderness and a Southern California campus, has concentrated all resources in its urban center in Beverly Hills.* Wanda Richter came for a visit and planned a series of stories on the relocation, focusing on Rutherford College/West and the Vistans' consultation work. Puck was assigned to spend evenings with her, in a bedroom with a functioning fireplace.

The move from the wilderness changed nothing for outsiders except that Cy and his retinue became more accessible. The Marathons at the Beverly Hills Hotel drew burgeoning crowds, and Cy continued seminars among the Vistans—with a new focus, "City Living." In one he likened Beverly Hills to "A *nouveau riche* socialite who doesn't know which fork to use for her lobster, but doesn't give a damn because the forks are all solid gold, by God."

We spent hours at the UCLA libraries. Rutherford College/West had eschewed the concept of grades, but we diligently evaluated one another's work. Theodora's impassioned presentation, *The Vagina Dentata*, won high praise. "In 1487, Pope Innocent the Eighth, a total moron, announced that women were eating an herb called 'cleavers' that grew teeth in their pussies, so they could bite off men's dicks. Women were burned at the stake for growing cleavers in their gardens."

"We did need to come to the city," Cy commented. "You might not have found that in the Abraham County Bookmobile."

In a field-trip spirit I took small groups of Vistans to the federal building, near the UCLA campus, where we applied for passports or renewed expired ones. "Who knows where we'll be traveling for Rutherford college," I explained each time. "We want to be ready."

There had been a time when I could ask Cy anything, and looked forward to the answer because a thoughtful question was appreciated. Now any inquiry seemed to imply a threat. I had committed myself to Cy and Rancho Vista for life. But with Charlée in charge, was the commitment reciprocal?

CY STEPPED UP THE STUDY OF TELEVISION COM-MERCIALS and their role in teaching a generation of Americans how to think, feel and behave. He persuaded us to follow the news. Weekday mornings began with "The Today Show," Sundays ended with "60 Minutes." On the morning Richard Nixon abdicated the U.S. presidency, Cy canceled everything on the day's calendar and sat before the television with us. "My generation came of age believing everything our government told us," he said. "Yours has learned to assume it's all a pack of lies. Is the Watergate generation better off?"

"My God, look at this," he said one Saturday morning, and asked Travis to gather everyone before breakfast. "A lawyer with ethics." When his students were assembled he read from the Los Angeles *Times,* "Attorney Felix Thornton entered Los Angeles County Jail this morning. He was found in contempt of court for refusing to reveal the source of information that exonerated his client, Ralph 'the Roach' Ryan, from several charges related to the murder of witnesses in a federal trial." Cy showed everyone the photos of the silver-haired lawyer and his chinless client, the accused assassin Ralph the Roach. Thornton had refused bail, saying he intended to use his prosecution as a test case, even though several charges remained against his client.

"If I ever get in trouble with the law," Cy said, "if Vivian and her Coalition for Decency mount a persecution campaign, I want a guy with guts like that to represent *me.*"

I nodded along with the others, but wondered: Was this a seminar, or should I be looking up Thornton's phone number?

LIFE WENT ON LIKE THIS FOR ENDLESS MONTHS. When the time came to "celebrate" our first year in the urban center, I wanted to scream. Ken took executives to Colorado for Trails, and I stayed behind. Tobey and I stole a half hour here and there to smooch in the alley behind the Bedford house.

Cy's private clients had always made the California trips worth his while, and now filled many of his days with hundred-dollar-an-hour sessions. The same "Colonel" who had paid part of his bill with the Rolls now signed over the deed to a house in Malibu—a wedge-shaped glass showplace called "Seabird" that hugged a rock cliff overlooking the Pacific. The place was about an hour from Bedford Drive.

"Charlée and I need privacy," Cy explained, an assertion even

I couldn't refute, because at least ten Vistans sat outside the guest house at any given time, hoping to grab Cy for impromptu therapy whenever the door opened. He and Charlée moved to Seabird and took Tobey and Elizabeth with them.

Any space Cy occupied lost its original character once he moved in, and the dramatic Seabird soon succumbed. In spite of ceiling-high bookcases, his study at the Center in Keystone had looked much like his and Zoë's old bedroom at the triple-wide, with books stacked against the walls, cardboard trays spilling over with cassette tapes and index cards, and bundles of his little spiral notebooks, each bursting with enough ideas to keep the staff working for ten years. Any hotel room where he stayed longer than two days took on the same look of disheveled brilliance, and soon the glass walls of Seabird were blocked by stacks of books, journals, and recording equipment.

In addition to seeing private clients, Cy lectured two days a week at Pepperdine and served as a UCLA research consultant. He appeared on a weekly public television show that was taped in Studio City. His time had always been divided—at the Ranch he had belonged to the Vistans, and on the road other people got to share him. Now he ran from one appointment to another, from the Seabird house in Malibu to Westwood, from Beverly Hills to the Valley. His individual sessions for the insured Vistans took place in the car between other appointments.

I could have stayed alone with Wolfie in the bedroom I'd shared with Tobey, but the hallway echoed with laughter from the other rooms, and I gratefully accepted an offer from Ken and Travis to move in with them. They even welcomed Wolfie.

With bitterness I accepted more distance from Cy and even Tobey. My work began to assume a kind of hectic loneliness that was strangely, dangerously familiar. Like my job at Los Perdidos, my current situation felt endless and hopeless.

Occasionally I thought with yearning about my parents. Might they be willing to try another Group? A smaller one maybe. But one day when the answering service relayed a message Isabel Susoyev had left at two a.m., I snapped my pencil. If she wanted me, let her call before Happy Hour.

27

"WE COULD USE A COUPLE TONS OF HORSE MA-NURE," Cy said, and I knew where to get it wholesale. As a boy I'd spent many Sundays tagging along behind my father at Santa Anita. I grabbed Lucky, gassed up the truck and drove to Arcadia.

The race track's John Deere tractor shuddered and groaned, drowning out the shouts from the loudspeakers in the public areas beyond the stables. The driver finessed the hydraulic levers and coaxed the front-loader bucket up high enough to drop its cargo into our dump truck. "Usually fill little nursery trailers," he called to Lucky and me. "Your rig's awful high."

I replied, "We got a big yard to fertilize."

"Fertilize the county with that much shit," the fellow hollered, but I had shown him a wad of twenties and he backed around for another load. The tractor's bucket gouged deep into the manure.

The truck accepted thirty loads, about two tons. I couldn't imagine Cy's new project would use a thousandth of this, particularly when it had nothing to do with gardening. I paid the man eighty dollars while Lucky checked the latches on the rear gate, then we climbed in and headed for the freeway.

"I'd trade with you if I could," I told Lucky. "You'll get to run the movie camera. I'll duck."

"And fling. You'll do your share of flinging."

At the house I left the manure to the work crew, and went upstairs to my new room. Ken was diligently at work on a Relationship Workbook. I sat down and scrawled, *Charlée, if it weren't for you we'd still have our home*, knowing I would never mutter this to anyone. I began listing my resentments toward people I felt safe confronting. "There'll be no holds barred during the Staff Vesuvius," Cy had said, calling the upcoming session "the most advanced therapy in the world today." But if I told Charlée what I really thought of her, I wouldn't be able to stop until I'd killed her. And holding back while others gave her hell could be the hardest thing I had ever done.

After an eerily silent breakfast, the staff paced downstairs to the recording studio. Over the weekend, Travis and Puck had drilled holes in the walls and attached eyebolts brawny enough to tether elephants. This was looking serious. My insides felt like a block of cold granite as I stepped up to my harness—climbing ropes and nylon webbing, tied elaborately around my waist and attached to two wall bolts. Willow, Ken, Charlée, Elsie and Cy were already strapped in.

Travis climbed into a harness and snorted as Tobey adjusted his straps. Theodora raised her arms high while Lucky secured hers. She looked like a biker chick in black sunglasses and her beloved white leather miniskirt. "First time I saw this room I thought it was a torture chamber," she said. "Guess I was right. I'm ready to do some torturing."

The truckload of manure had been dumped on the lawn outside the round room, and Puck had plopped several wheelbarrow-loads in the center of the floor. Lucky now dug into the mound with a pail and emptied it in front of Cy. He returned with another bucketful for Charlée, and methodically went around the room to supply each participant with manure. Near each heap Elizabeth placed several Styrofoam cups, and filled them with water from a plastic pitcher.

I chuckled in my harness, privately vowing to treat the session as entertainment, an operation designed by Cy to upstage the Anger Lab man, Zack Bush. Like everyone but Theodora, I was in long pants and a sweatshirt, but unlike most I wore nothing over my hair. "It'll be like a snowball fight," I joked, while Puck cinched me in.

No one laughed. I looked up and saw that someone had hung the microphones from the ceiling in gauze bags, with cords leading to the control room. "The equipment's protected but we're not," I called out.

Around the studio stood the people who shared responsibility for the future of psychotherapy. Ken lunged forward in his harness as if making sure he couldn't get loose when he lost control of his anger. Willow stared at the acoustic-tile ceiling in an attitude of beatific contemplation. Elsie silently tugged at the loose ends of her nylon harness. Charlée wrote in a small spiral notebook while Tobey adjusted her straps.

Cy tied a bandanna around his hair and asked Lucky, "Is there plenty of plastic wrap for the camera?"

Lucky zipped his green Trail poncho, pulled up the hood, and gave Cy a thumbs-up.

"What if somebody has to take a dump?" asked Theodora.

I watched Cy closely. I hadn't been able to defecate in two days. Cy's eyes crinkled. "If you need to pee, use your little cups, and Puck will carry them out. If you must move your bowels, Puck will remove the result with his shovel. Are we recording?"

Puck's disembodied voice answered through a ceiling speaker, "All systems go."

The movie camera began to whir on its tripod, and Lucky aimed it at Cy, who spoke warmly. "The people you see here understand academically what the Vesuvius straps are for. But until today none of us has worn them." While he gave a brief history of the Rancho Vista human relations laboratory, Lucky scanned the room with the camera. Wondering how wide the film's intended audience might be, I raised two fingers in a peace sign as the lens panned past me.

Cy now addressed the participants. "As each of you has noticed, our harnesses are rigged so we can't release ourselves. We would need three hands to get free. No matter how angry we become, we can't hurt anyone. If we are successful today, we will let go of the fear of anger—our own and one another's."

Tobey and Elizabeth moved to the control room where they could listen on earphones.

"Well," Cy said, once the kids were safely out of the way. He opened his arms wide and winked. "Who's got shit?"

"Charlée," Willow said, "you can put away your little notebook now."

"Thank you," Charlée said, but kept writing.

Condescending bitch, I itched to say. Trembling, I watched Ken squat at his manure pile. He separated out a small amount, dribbled water into it and made four baseball-sized clods, then started on a new batch. I knelt and did the same.

"What are you two doing?" Willow demanded. "Hoarding your shit-balls to ambush the rest of us? Stand up and say something for yourselves, you pathetic cocksuckers."

Ken hurled one of his balls at her and yelled, "Fuck you!" She ducked but it grazed her white bandanna and spatted a brown Rorschach blot onto the wall behind her. She knelt to mix up a batch, and flung a messy handful that sprayed his tee-shirt.

"You're just mad because I got tired of eating your stinking pussy," he hollered.

She lobbed a wad into his face. He spat, filled his cheeks with water, and spewed a mouthload at her.

Cy watched with an expression of amused contentment.

Theodora dumped her water into her manure pile and stomped in the mess with her bare feet. "You're all pathetic.

We've got the chance of a lifetime and you waste it insulting each other's twats. Well, I've got shit on every one of you and I ain't wasting any." She scooped a handful of sloppy manure and slung it at Travis, screaming, "Fucking Nazi!" He jumped aside but a second wad flew from her other hand and splatted in his face. "Why couldn't we wash our hair in the cookshack? And were you ever *really* gonna build showers?" Her next volley caught Cy mid-chest. "Which was up to you, since none of these ass-lickers'll pick their nose without your approval."

His face lit up with joy, as if confirming he'd been right to bring her onto the staff.

She slammed a handful of wet shit at Willow's crotch. "Mooch! You borrowed twenty bucks from me on a trip to Gentile and never paid it back. Just 'cause I've got a trust fund doesn't mean you can use me."

She continued around the circle, spewing shit and invective. When she reached me she lost her street-wise tone. "You let Eric leave the Ranch. It's because of you he went on that monstrous process."

Stunned, I didn't duck. Theodora's shit-ball struck me in the neck and dribbled under my tee-shirt. I squirmed and the tight harness reminded me I was restrained. My skin itched where the rank manure stuck to me.

Her voice rose steadily as she moved on around the room. When she returned to Cy she wailed, "How did Zoë get away? Do you really think that bitch over there—" and with this she lobbed a fistful of manure at Charlée— "has the heart to be a mother to us? She's *cold!*"

I shivered. If Theodora could say these things why couldn't I?

"Brat!" Charlée howled. She flung a shit-ball that splattered on Theodora's miniskirt and dribbled down her bare thigh. *"Spoiled-rotten-never-worked-a-day-in-your-life-how-dare-you-talk-that-way-to-Cy-wash-your-filthy-hair-in-the-river!"*

Theodora screamed that there was no river, only bullshit excuses for abandoning paradise. Travis caught her in the side of the head with a tight manure-ball. "Spoiled rotten," he said.

Theodora spat and spat, having dumped all her water into her manure pile. "Puck," she called, "please bring me more shit. And I need my own water bucket."

He trotted in and replenished her supplies, but explained that a thrown bucket could hurt someone. He barely made it back into the control room before the shitstorm resumed.

Several people pelted Theodora, but Elsie pitched a wad of manure at me. "You're easy so I'm starting with you," she announced. "I resent you for having sex with Eric. He isn't even gay, but you had him and *I never will*."

"Me neither!" Theodora beaned me on the side of the head. I felt shakier with each barrage that struck me or someone else. But I wasn't angry at anyone except Charlée. My breathing slowed while Willow and Elsie, Theodora and Ken, Travis and Willow scooped up the last of their piles, and called for more. Soon the studio's walls glistened with wet manure. Brown stalactites dripped from the ceiling. The putrid air hung close. Theodora was often airborne in her dance of rage, and ripped her gauzy blouse into tatters.

I shouted as I heaved shit-balls at Ken ("Every fucking morning you use my razor without asking"), and Willow ("Just once I'd like to see you pay for something when we go out"), and mugged for the camera when Travis thwacked me for stealing a bottle of beer from the cookshack the previous winter.

Cy appeared serene and thoughtful. Eventually everyone else was plastered with shit, and even he wore a few battle-stains. The room fell silent. I slumped against the wall, relieved that I'd made it through without trumpeting my hatred of Charlée. I watched with grim pleasure as she chipped drying manure from her face and yanked a mat of half-digested straw from her hair. She rinsed her hands with water from a cup, waved them dry, and retrieved the little notebook from her pocket.

"Writing something you'd like to share with us?" Willow sneered.

"Bitch," Charlée answered.

"Sometimes your head looks like it's made of glass and I see snakes writhing inside. When you open your mouth to talk, a tiny forked tongue flits out."

Willow's words jolted me and I folded my arms. Ken hollered, "Wish I'd said that!"

"Sounds like projection," Charlée said, and tucked the notebook back into her jeans. Then she howled, "Jealous! Not just Willow and Ken, but everyone here. Go ahead, why don't you *all* throw your shit at me and get it over with? You do it a thousand times a day in your snide ways. You, Ken . . ."

I didn't hear the rest of the rant. A mighty weight was crushing my chest, and I fought to draw a breath of the fetid air. I ached to throw shit at Charlée, but there wasn't enough in my pile, in the garden, in California to slake my hatred. My stomach lurched and I bent over with my hands on my knees to relieve the pressure in my gut.

"What do you feel like saying, Steve?" Cy asked.

I straightened up and turned on him with no idea what I would say until I opened my mouth. "Are you the world's greatest therapist or the neediest jerk?"

"I'm a participant in this—"

"You're a buffoon!" I slopped him with two fistfuls of manure. "You traded in a compassionate woman for that bottle-blonde tramp." I trembled but the words rose to my mouth with crystalline clarity. "I'd pity you if you hadn't inflicted that bitch on us."

"I agree," declared Willow. "Everything went downhill after Zoë—"

I thwacked her with a horse-pie. "Shut up I'm not finished." I breathed deeply and gathered my hatred for the one who deserved it. Coldly I said, "Char-*lette*." I aimed a ball of shit at her midsection. It splattered on target, clinging to the pink cotton of her Ship 'N Shore blouse. "It wasn't enough for you to elbow Zoë out of the way. You had to get your filthy claws into *Tobey*."

"Steve Susoyev," she proclaimed, "you are the sickest person in this community, too smart for your own good. You need a heavy process to break through it." She hurled fistfuls of dry manure. "*You-need-Grand-Silence!*"

The powdery explosions stung my eyes and flew into my lungs when I gasped for air. I gagged and gestured at Puck for water. As soon as I could speak, I rasped, "No holds barred, right, Cy?"

"Just be sure Lucky's got film," he answered. "We don't want to miss any of this."

"You won't." I pulled down my pants, squatted, grunted and produced a gleaming, foot-long turd.

"Puck!" Charlée commanded, "get that out of here before we expire from the stench." He trotted in from the control room with a shovel.

"Come near my turd," I told him, "and I'll slam it into *your* face instead of hers."

Puck hesitated a moment too long. I catapulted double handfuls of dry manure at Charlée. She gagged on the storm of powder while I continued the onslaught, raging, "You wanted Cy the minute you spotted him and you didn't care who you destroyed! We lost Zoë and Josh and Vivian and Eric because of you. Decent people." I stood and fastened my pants and began to cry. "And then we lost our home."

She gasped for breath, purple-faced. Her tongue, coated with dry manure, protruded over her lower lip. Before Puck could reach her with the water bucket, I scooped up my turd and slammed it across the room into her gaping mouth. I charged toward her and clawed at my harness. "Your 'special wedding gift' to Cy was setting him up to fuck a little girl."

My shit oozed from the corners of her mouth and her face shone with terror. Then she retched.

I lunged against my restraints and shrieked, "She won't even deny it! Cut me loose so I can stomp her evil brains out!" I screamed myself hoarse, stamped my feet in the manure, turned and pounded my head against the wall. Blood squirted from my scalp and I thrashed and ripped at my clothes. Puck approached and held out his arms as if to embrace me, but kept a safe distance.

Tobey ran out of the control room and stood helpless beside Puck. "Stop, Steve," he said softly. "It's okay."

I fell back and slid to the floor, sobbing. "It's not okay." Tobey knelt, peeled off his tee-shirt and wadded it against the pulsing wound.

"Are you paying attention, Cy?" I screamed. "Do you understand what you created when you married that monster?" I wept in great convulsing sobs, my snot and blood trickling into the manure.

Cy knelt in his harness, weeping also. "Thank God you've finally got this out of your system," he said, while Lucky drew close to him with the camera. Tobey and Puck released me from my straps and carried me out of the stinking, sweltering room.

THE GASH ON MY SCALP REQUIRED FIVE STITCHES AT THE UCLA EMERGENCY ROOM. Like the other participants I suffered from diarrhea for several days, a result of inadvertently ingesting untold amounts of horse manure. The recording studio sustained the only permanent damage, with stains in the pegged walls and ceiling tiles that bled through Travis's repeated coats of fresh paint. A lingering stench reached the mansion's upper floors but faded with the passing weeks. Or maybe we just got used to it.

Though Cy referred to Vesuvius as "just another Group, with

special effects," we treated one another with a strange new deference. Travis no longer called, "Soo-eee!" at mealtimes. During
staff meetings Charlée asked my opinion, and Theodora's, and
stopped introducing her own pronouncements with, "As I remember correctly . . ." The LAX and Hilton projects continued.
No one missed a single Rutherford College/West class.

A week after the session Cy took me for a walk on the beach
below Seabird. "Your loyalty reached me," he said. "I understand
what you see in Charlée. She's a very sick woman, but tremendously talented, and devoted to me and our way of life. She needs
an intensive therapy program. You can help because you know
her so well."

This was a surprise. I warily agreed to render any assistance I
could. No details were forthcoming. We strolled on, talking of
other things, and I had to be satisfied that Cy had tentatively
acknowledged my vision of her.

Yet before any intensive therapy could begin for Charlée, the
staff had to deal with a far more pressing matter. "Vivian Elfinger
is obviously suffering," Cy said one morning, opening an emergency meeting at Seabird. Spread before him were a summons
and complaint served at six a.m. "Her children either have to kill
themselves or run away to be free of her. My curse is that she can
attack me, and I am left understanding her pain."

Elizabeth held her head high. "I won't live with my mother.
I'm a member of this community."

Cy beamed. "I'm glad to hear you say that, honey. But your
mother has filed a lawsuit. Steve, you've been on the phone with
lawyers all morning. Can you untangle this?"

Tensely I explained as much as I understood about Vivian's
allegations, which a partner of Cy's tax lawyer said was a scatter-
gun strategy to get Cy into court. "*Alienation of Affection* is
obvious—Elizabeth would rather be with us, so we've supposedly alienated her from her mom. *Breach of Contract* is about how
Vivian never got paid for teaching at the Ranch. Our defense is
that she never expected payment because her work covered room
and board for her and the kids. We could countersue on that one
because *she* breached the contract by leaving before the end of
the school year."

"My, yes, let's countersue," Cy sneered. "We want years of
protracted litigation with that poor sick woman. Let's rack up
tens of thousands in legal fees so she can tell her story to a jury of
her peers, a dozen frigid Orange County housewives."

Charlée sighed. "What would it take for this just to go away?"

Such pragmatism was among the few things I appreciated about her. "Elizabeth goes to her mom," I answered. "Just for a while, to calm Vivian down. And we pay her lawyer's fees."

"I'm not going," Elizabeth repeated.

"Good girl," said Cy.

"But some things have to change," I persisted, and focused on her. "To show you're being cared for properly we have to send you to school. You should register tomorrow."

Cy agreed, and Elizabeth nodded. Willow volunteered to help her put together an outfit that included a blouse with a Peter Pan collar, a pleated skirt, and knee-socks.

In the morning a green Plymouth followed Charlée and Elizabeth from Seabird to Malibu Park Junior High. When she returned from registering Elizabeth, Charlée gave the car's license number to Cy's tax lawyer. He called back to report it was registered to a private investigator.

"This can't go on," Cy said after Elizabeth's first day at school. "They'll snatch you the first time you're out of our sight."

"She's got to go to her mom for a few months," I insisted.

Elizabeth skewered me with a glare.

"Honey," Cy asked her, "did you mean it when you said you want to spend the rest of your life in this community?"

"You know I did."

"Then you must rise to a difficult challenge. The only choice is for you to spend a short time in juvenile detention."

I let out a yelp. Willow and Ken both cried, "Jesus!" Tobey and even Charlée stared at Cy as if he'd proposed putting her out as a streetwalker.

Theodora folded her arms and said, "No fucking way."

Only Elizabeth appeared calm. She nodded slowly. "I can go to school in there. I'll be safe from Mom and her goons, and it'll show the court how much I *don't* want to live with her."

Theodora spoke softly. "I was a badass car thief and I still had a hard time in Juvie. I'd be afraid for you in there."

I tried to keep the exasperation out of my voice and stick to the facts: "Anyway, you can't just check yourself into Juvie."

"I'll turn myself in as a runaway," Elizabeth said.

"We could all learn something about commitment from this young woman," Cy said. "Honey, we'll get you through this."

Elizabeth filled a bag with books. Travis packed her a lunch and she walked to a pay phone up the highway. Within two hours she called to say she'd been admitted to the county Juvenile Detention facility in downtown L.A.

I took Tobey with me to visit her the next morning. A buxom guard, motherly but armed with a huge pistol, searched our clothes. She then escorted us to a game room equipped with ping pong tables and soda machines, and chaperoned our visit.

Elizabeth had dark crescents under her eyes. "I'm really glad to see you guys," she said. "But is Cy coming today?"

"I think," I ad-libbed, "he's waiting for your mom to drop her lawsuit. The lawyer says if he came it would strengthen her case."

She knew me so well—well enough to know I was making this up. That morning Cy had downed two shots of vodka and a few Valiums before he crawled out of bed. He could barely make it downstairs, much less downtown.

She stared out a window grate. "This place is tougher than I expected. I'm used to a lot of love and reality, you know? The girls in here are high on their own version of reality, but they're high on a lot of other stuff, too."

I visited her each day for two weeks, often with Theodora or Tobey in tow. I brought treats from Travis, notes from other Vistans, a pressed flower from Charlée, books from Cy's library. Each time, she asked when Cy would be coming, and I recited a prepared response. The truth was that the sight of a newspaper gave Cy a panic attack. If uniformed guards frisked him he might have heart failure.

When I brought a rambling, six-page letter from him, she opened it eagerly, then her expression became confused. She read a few paragraphs and handed it back. "He's in worse shape than I am," she said, and cut the visit short.

28

AT THE DECEMBER CONFERENCE of the Association for Humanistic Psychology, highlights of the Vesuvius film were shown—minus my bowel movement and the incriminating dialogue. With over two hundred people jammed into a San Diego hotel ballroom, the film attracted twice the crowd of its only serious competition, Nude Bioenergetics.

Cy's image flickered onto the screen and the audience fell into an awed silence. In his harness he explained the process and praised the Vistans' commitment. Everyone was silent even as the screaming and manure-flinging reached their vicious crescendo. Zachary Bush quietly took notes in the front row. I watched myself on the screen, caked with manure, levitating with fury and spewing froth. Amazed that I had revealed my hatred of Charlée, I feared when and how she would take revenge. In the closing scene Cy knelt and spoke softly in closeup, expressing relief that such rage had finally been released. The few manure stains on his sage-colored sweatshirt looked like dried blood on the uniform of a wounded but triumphant warrior.

When the lights came up, Bush launched the question-and-answer period by bellowing, "Dr. Aaron, therapists tread a fine line between therapy and abuse, eh?"

Cy acknowledged him with a nod and a vague smile, then took a question from the back of the room. Bush's attack was lost in the overall sensation the Vesuvius had created. People leaped out of their seats to speak. But after the crowd dispersed, Cy instructed me, "Invite Bush out for a drink. You're the star of our film. If people see you together it'll defuse his 'abuse' gibberish."

"He likes Charlée," I demurred. "She has a starring role, too."

Cy pondered this for a long moment, then broke into a grin and exclaimed, "Brilliant!"

Charlée went for drinks with Bush, and later they shared dinner and more drinks. She met him the next day, and again made dinner plans. Cy ate with the rest of the staff, enthusing about the Vesuvius book and other manuscripts that needed development. I sensed he was orchestrating something with Bush that took more of Charlée's attention than it deserved. What was he after? There were surely enough furious people in the world that poor

Zack could corral a few of them in his Anger Lab and leave plenty for the Vesuvius harness.

"YOU SET ME UP!" Charlée barked from the dark entryway of the Grunt Suite.

"Just a needy pussy," Cy seethed. "Where's the light switch, for Christ's sake?" He pounded on the wall.

I bolted out of my sleeping bag and turned on a table lamp. Tobey sat up, rubbing his eyes. Elsie and Willow stepped in from the adjoining bedroom and Ken rolled over on the loveseat. Theodora, bundled on the couch, clutched a pillow over her head.

I pulled on a tee-shirt and moaned, "What's going on?" The alarm clock said four a.m.

Charlée sat at Ken's feet. "He entrapped me," she said with a glare at Cy. "I'm supposed to be doing a sexual surrogacy session for Zachary Bush and next thing I know—"

"The next thing *I* know," he roared, "she's an hour late coming back from Bush's room. I thought you were a professional. You're a giggling, needy teenager."

"Zack was *talking* to me."

"A professional knows when to stop the session."

"I know what this is about," she snarled, in a voice that could etch glass. " 'His cock is probably on the small side,' you said. 'Let him work through his anxiety.' Ha!" She turned to Willow, who was on the floor wrapped in a blanket. "Zack Bush has a *huge* cock, hard as a rock, and he knows how to use it."

Cy slapped her. "You pathetic little tramp. You went there to provide therapy, not to get your twat filled up."

She stared at him a moment, then said softly, "My God, Cy, you're right."

They left without a glance at the rest of us, whispering to each other.

I almost danced down the hall after them. I had worried about when she would announce I needed "Grand Silence." But with the Zack Bush assignment she'd revealed herself as the manipulative woman I had raved at in a manure-filled basement.

IN *PSYCHOTHERAPY CURRENTS,* Wanda Richter described the Vesuvius as "cutting-edge therapy." She reported in the *Radical Therapist,* "Zachary Bush still has people acting out their anger in juvenile exercises, while the Rancho Vistans prove they're not afraid to eat a little shit for growth."

The publicity prompted letters from all over the world. Two accused Cy of scatological perversions, but scores came from therapists who requested information about Vesuvius training. *Repressed anger causes disease*, wrote an Australian psychiatrist. *You've managed to un-repress it. And then some!*

I fashioned a form response to the mail that poured in, and ordered an IBM memory typewriter that stored text on magnetic cards. The five-thousand-dollar machine enabled Elsie to personalize each letter without retyping anything. Even the mailing list could be revised on its own set of "mag cards" for future promotions. Our next project was a series of brochures whose budget exceeded the cost of the new typewriter, and I proudly began sketching elegant designs. Body images would be realigned, families would undergo breakthroughs, Trails would even embark for the wilderness—all from Rancho Vista's urban headquarters. In the face of such far-reaching progress, the organization's internal problems seemed petty and exaggerated.

I often worked through the night at the Westwood office, free of distractions. When the phone rang at two a.m. on a weekend, I thought a moment before answering. It could be my mother. I picked up the receiver warily.

"Cy's in the hospital," Tobey said in a rough whisper. "I rolled the car. He's okay but he wants to see you tonight."

"Are *you* okay?"

"I will be once you get here."

I reached Santa Monica Hospital at two-forty and found Cy's dim private room without alerting the nurses to my presence. Charlée saw me and waved a splinted wrist. "We could make a Mercedes commercial," she quipped softly. "The car's demolished but we're fine."

When I bent to hug her she clung to me, and I gently kissed her cheek.

Cy groaned in the bed and rolled his bandaged head. He said in a voice like gargling, "The gods are watching over us. Remember when I broke your ribs, my son? Tonight I broke a few of my own. Goose for the gander. Sauce for the—oh, hell." Even in this fucked-up state, on word-slurring drugs, he brandished his eyebrows and made me want to laugh.

Tobey was standing beside the door as if ready to bolt. I cuffed him playfully on the arm. "How'd *you* come out in one piece?"

"I had my seat belt on." The lovely dark eyes met mine. "I swerved—"

"Look at that loyalty," Cy said. "But Steve needs the truth. The old man was at the wheel. I thought Vivian was following us and I got scared."

Charlée snapped, "I think the word is *paranoid*," then moderated her tone. "Tobey thought fast. He told the police he'd been driving and swerved to miss a dog in the road." In a barbed voice she added, "To protect Cy from a *drunk driving* charge."

The hospital released Cy the next day with a large bandage on his forehead, and tape securing his cracked ribs. I perpetuated Tobey's fiction with the other Vistans, eager to equal his devotion. Each morning I left the Bedford house for Malibu, usually bringing Wolfie with me for comfort, and let the others believe I was on my way to a nurturing visit with the Vistan First Couple. In truth I dreaded each day at Seabird more than the last.

Cy spoke of almost nothing other than Vivian and Elizabeth. He spun schemes that Charlée swept away like cobwebs. "Let's invite Vivian over for a day at the beach, just to talk," he offered one morning, but Charlée pointed out that Josh surely would accompany Vivian, "and I'm afraid he could trigger your temper." Cy suggested hiring a private detective and Charlée groaned. "To record every word Vivian says on the phone to her lawyer? *That* sounds practical."

The two of them followed each other through the split-level beach house and argued about everything from the relative nutritional value of various breakfast cereals to the appropriate composition of the LAX consultation team. Often when I arrived at Seabird and hugged Tobey, I felt I was pulling him from a trance.

"They're getting worse," he whispered one foggy morning. "Cy's sure the phones are tapped. He listens in on every call, even if I'm ordering groceries. Which is another story. She's living on pretzels and he only eats organic macaroons. We go through a case of vodka a week. She screams about his drinking but she drinks just as much."

"Have you talked to your mom?"

"I only call when Cy writes a script, about the college classes I'm supposedly taking."

With increasingly exotic excuses, Charlée canceled Cy's lecture and research commitments. He often neglected to shave and rarely left the house except to walk on the beach. He began hunching his shoulders like an eighty-year-old man. Something fundamental had to change, and I felt it was up to me to take the initiative. Ken and Puck had to prepare an Executive Trail for the Hilton management team. Willow and Elsie were interviewing airport administrators for a team-building intensive. In the spirit of "moving the body," I continued preparing insurance reports as if Cy were conducting therapy as usual.

He managed to get to the monthly Marathon at the Beverly Hills Hotel, which still attracted newcomers, but he needed days to recuperate. He made it to the Bedford house on most Saturdays to run Group, but dealt only with emergencies. I drove paying patients to Seabird for individual walking-therapy sessions with him on the beach. Afterward Cy needed a triple shot of vodka and a nap.

One afternoon in April, he returned from a two-hour walk arm-in-arm with Theodora. Charlée attacked before he could close the front door. "Where have you *been?*" she shrieked.

I clapped my hands over my ears. She seemed to catch herself and went on in a more rational tone, "We're trying to have a staff meeting here. Cy, *you're* the one who told *me*, professionalism requires keeping a session on schedule."

"Beneath your insanely possessive jealousy crouches classic projection," he shot back. "You're threatened by my walk with Theodora because you're so needy for other men! The way you humiliated yourself with Zack Bush when you were supposed to be giving him therapy."

"When you pushed me into working with a brilliant, handsome man who turned out to have a big cock, then punished me for enjoying—"

"Okay, okay. We're into this now." Cy instructed everyone present to cancel their plans for the remainder of the day—even me, and I was scheduled to visit Elizabeth at Juvie. Puck, who had come to Seabird to prune the fruit trees, smiled, clearly pleased to be included in something special.

Charlée carried on for hours about the betrayal she had suffered as Cy's mate. "I'm the one whose needs always come last," she insisted. Cy stood straight and regained some of his old energy, and remained engaged. I thought everyone else managed to *appear* engaged. Tobey and Ken kept notebooks open in their laps. Willow sat in the lotus position with spine erect, turning from Cy to Charlée and back like a spectator at a cartoon tennis match. Theodora stared out at the sea, apparently as dazed as I felt. Elsie sipped her drink—lemon-lime soda, I knew from watching her pour it, though for effect she'd made a pass with the vodka bottle. Puck's face glowed with the honor of being included among the staff. When the session dragged on beyond dinner, his eyes remained bright, though he smoked more pot than anyone and drank a mason jar of vodka. I lay on the floor using Wolfie as a pillow.

Cy led Charlée through a chronicle of every sexual exploration, flirtation and interest she'd had since age six. Her story conveyed unfamiliar vulnerability. In tears she revealed that her uncle and brother had molested her—but she'd enjoyed learning she had something men wanted, even when they humiliated her. She recalled Josh's obsequious proposal and admitted, "I married him because I knew I could control him." I heard this as the story of a lonely, insecure woman who had given up on love—until Cy aroused hope in her tired heart.

In the morning she appeared at breakfast in full armor: heels, navy-blue silk dress, wheat-blonde hair puffed up in the Gibson Girl style long ago copied from Zoë, and makeup that showed effort—heavy eyeliner, blush, plum lipstick, violet nail polish. Cy continued the previous night's theme of loneliness and control. The rest of us were present mainly as observers, but sometimes he directed us to give feedback. When my first turn came I recalled, "The day you and Josh showed up at the Ranch, Travis said, 'That gal wants Zoë's job.' He knew what he was saying."

Charlée maintained eye contact with anyone who spoke, and after each comment wrote in her notebook. Acting like a growth case, I thought, but controlling us with all that scribbling. Still, after attacking her during Vesuvius I couldn't enjoy watching her squirm on the hotseat in the way I had once imagined.

All day the tough, hammering questions continued. I perked up when Cy asked, "Did you come to the Ranch intending to elbow Zoë out of the way?" She admitted this and much more. By dinnertime she'd given up on note-taking. Her hair hung limp and her makeup was smeared from crying. When she again claimed that her needs always came last, I ran upstairs to her closet and returned to confront her with a new two-thousand-dollar beaded dress.

In the morning Cy rose before dawn and typed notes for the ongoing therapy, then took Wolfie for a run on the beach. Afterwards he strode about the house, purposeful and focused, and with something like his old vigor. Charlée came downstairs looking as if she hadn't slept or bathed.

For several more days her process began before breakfast and ended after midnight. She ate little. Puck stayed, good-naturedly helping Tobey with meals, never questioning why he was in on staff therapy. Unlike the rest of us, he never seemed tired or grumpy, and Cy often praised his ability to stay out of his shit.

Late on the fifth night I gazed wearily out through the ceiling-high west windows. A trio of nighthawks cruised past in tight formation, the first birds other than seagulls I had recognized since leaving Rancho Vista. The surf below the house gleamed in the moonlight. I yearned to stroll on the beach before heading for bed. Even Ken, whose late-night walks were a Trail tradition, didn't seem to notice the moon's approach. *Let's slip away*, I imagined writing on a card, and passing it around to the staff. *The moon's out of the trees.* When had walking in the moonlight become such a distant goal?

When Charlée promised, "*I'll do anything to become—worthy of my betrothed.*"

"Poor needy pussy," Cy said, grabbing my attention. "You're trapped and I'm your hostage. We could accomplish great things. My God, the Pure Relationship!"

"The Pure Relationship is a fantasy," she sneered. "Zoë Fuckhead the Tahitian whore couldn't live up to it and you're taking it out on me."

Cy rose and slapped her. "Don't bring Zoë into this! And stop changing the sub—"

She bolted out the front door wearing only panties. Willow had on more than anyone else, and ran after her. I felt shocked and thrilled. How dare this bleached-blonde slut call Zoë dirty names? Had the time come for her to learn true humility?

When Willow led the fugitive back inside Cy said, "I've got it. You need to experience fully the needy pussy who lives inside you. You can let that part of yourself run free, with this loving group to accept and support you. The needy pussy is getting a treat tonight. Rancho Vista's biggest cock! Puck, let's go upstairs and advance your career as a sexual surrogate."

Puck nodded eagerly. I hoped that while the young stud serviced her in the master bedroom the rest of the staff might go home or at least take a walk. I smiled at Tobey and he waved to me from across the room.

Cy placed a hand on Charlée's shoulder. "Honey," he asked

softly, "are you ready to take a big growth step?"

"I'm ready for a man who can get a hardon." She scowled at Tobey. "And who wants to be with me."

The cloven crown of Puck's cock popped out of his boxers, ready to serve. Wolfie, always alert to the aromas of sex, stretched and shook himself.

"Kids, don't make Elsie carry all the equipment," Cy said. "Have you got plenty of Polaroid film, Steve?"

"You want *us* up there?"

"Of course. Remember how the group supported you when Gollum came out? Charlée needs your understanding, acceptance and compassion."

I stiffened but went to the closet where the cameras and sound equipment were kept, thinking how ridiculous it had been to expect a free evening. Ken carried the tape recorder. Everyone dutifully filed upstairs and sat on the edges of the low bed.

Early in the session Charlée let the needy pussy emerge. She bucked and bellowed in pleasure while Puck rode her. He proved an enthusiastic and enduring surrogate. I looked out through the steamy window at the moonglow until Cy remarked that by refusing to watch I was withholding my acceptance of Charlée. Willow wiped sweat from Puck's face, and Elsie held the microphone near Charlée's mouth. Cy photographed the session from every angle, then handed me the camera.

I studied the onlookers through the viewfinder. Their foreheads gleamed with sweat. The scene and the situation appalled me, as heavy as anything the sophisticated Vistans had ever witnessed, yet I couldn't bring myself to protest.

"Whoa, big fellah," Cy said to Puck. "Slow up now, but don't pull out." He knelt over Charlée. "Honey, have you been enjoying this?"

She nodded.

"Puck is going to pull away now." Cy beckoned to Theodora. "Here comes his old flame." While Puck withdrew his glistening cock, Theodora knelt beside him and Cy continued, "Puck, you still care for Theodora, don't you?"

He grinned.

"Theodora, how do you feel about giving your old pal a kiss?"

Theodora and Puck kissed quickly but sweetly.

"A real kiss," Cy said, "like your first time."

Theodora looked at Charlée, then at Cy. She closed her eyes and offered her open mouth to Puck. They shared a sloppy, lingering kiss and his rigid cock bounced.

Still naked on her back, Charlée crossed her arms. Cy asked softly, "How's that make you feel?"

She answered in a little girl's voice, "I feel—abandoned."

"Abandoned," he echoed, and while we listened, he followed a trail of memories of abandonment that had haunted her since childhood. Her busy father, incestuous uncle and brother, her distant mother, boyfriends and jealous girlfriends—even Josh, when he left the Ranch and later filed for divorce—all had made her feel inadequate, unlovable.

Finally Cy decided she'd gone through enough for one night. After the session, Tobey and I whispered together in his little bed in the servant's room off the kitchen. We agreed Puck's performance had been exciting but scary, and that if Cy asked us to participate we would decline. "Anyway," Tobey said, "the way you carried on at the Vesuvius, he'll never ask you to ball her."

Over breakfast on the sunlit deck I saw that what I had assumed were smears of mascara under Charlée's eyes were dark pouches of swollen skin. Her hair was flat and dirty, and the mousy brown roots were growing out. Her nails were ragged, and the polish badly chipped. While she stared into her untouched food Cy asked the rest of us if we admired her.

Willow told her, "You've inspired me."

"I'm awestruck," I said, meaning it. "What you went through makes my Gollum session look like a party game."

Charlée smiled timidly and looked at each person who praised her courage. Cy spoke last. "You are exceeding my expectations, darling."

That evening's session began in the master bedroom before sunset. This time Ken provided the cock. Charlée let herself moan and writhe with pleasure. The window quickly steamed up, and the fetid air of fucking and observing hung thick. But the sight of her surrounded by an audience had lost its shocking power. In the last rich light of the sun I found myself watching with clinical interest—Ken's cock projected at a higher angle than Puck's did, and curved slightly downward, and he held his body very differently, propping his torso on extended arms, with knees and elbows locked.

At Cy's direction, Willow stepped to the side of the bed, tossed off her scrap of fabric and began a sensual dance. Ken remained focused on Charlée until Willow opened her labia an inch from his face. He lost his rhythm and his cock flopped out.

"How humiliating," Charlée said. She sat up and reached for a blanket.

"Darling," Cy said patiently, "this is *exactly* where we need to go. The only way to become who you really are is to let the neediness come to the surface. Share it with us."

She clutched the blanket and ran to the bathroom. The lock clicked behind her.

Willow talked softly through the door. Everyone waited quietly, and I avoided looking into any of their faces. At last she persuaded Charlée to return to the bed.

"Honey," Cy said, "do you want to grow or stay trapped by your pain?"

Charlée grasped the blanket around her shoulders. "I came back, didn't I?"

"Good." He asked Ken to retrieve a bag of mountain-climbing supplies from the garage, and explained to Charlée that she must stay with the process even when it felt unbearable. Ken returned and Cy deftly fashioned a Vesuvius harness of soft ropes to fit around Charlée's hips. Puck and Ken tied it to the bed frame with turquoise nylon webbing. This restraint allowed her considerable freedom of movement, but when Ken entered her, she screamed. He pulled out. She continued screaming until Tobey and I untied her.

Moments later the doorbell rang six times. Elsie threw on a bathrobe and ran downstairs. She returned to announce, "The neighbors want us to turn down the TV." After a silent moment Charlée laughed, and the others joined her. Cy adjourned the session for the evening, but kept everyone up for hours praising Charlée's courage.

Over breakfast he said, "We can't handle the noise," then addressed Charlée gently. "I know it's important for your process that you discharge your rage. But this isn't Rancho Vista, where therapy could drown out the Mother River and nobody called the cops. This is civilization, where people sleep at night."

Some people, I thought.

"Later we'll look back on this the way people remember their first driving lesson. You'll laugh about the time you drove up on the curb and hit the tree." He reached for Charlée's hand and added with reverence, "We all recognize you're going through something extraordinary."

"I'll keep trying," she promised.

That evening, after she was in her harness, Cy fashioned a soft gag by tucking a racquetball into a nylon stocking. He punctured the ball with a syringe, drew out air until the ball folded in on itself, and fitted it in her mouth. He tied the stocking around her head.

"Is that comfortable?" he asked.

She nodded with tenderness in her eyes that made me want to comfort her.

"Try screaming, honey," Cy said.

Her muffled howl filled the bedroom.

"Steve, please go out into the street and see if you can hear her."

I heard her in the hallway and downstairs, but not on the front porch or beyond. Back inside I realized how much I had grown to admire her. Could I submit to therapy that required me to be restrained and gagged? Yes, if Cy thought it was the right process—but I would give him no reason to think so.

Upstairs Ken fucked Charlée with measured thrusts. On Cy's cue Willow again stood at the side of the bed and began a slow, gyrating dance with her pussy near Ken's face. I photographed the scene. Ken concentrated on Charlée, whose harness allowed her the freedom to move with him. Through the gag she moaned with each thrust.

"Hold onto him as long as you can, honey," Cy encouraged. Ken diligently ignored Willow's pussy as it danced an inch from his face.

"I know what'll distract Ken," Cy said abruptly. "Steve, give the camera to Tobey and come over here."

I took Willow's place and tried to catch my lover's eyes. Tobey was fumbling with the camera, his face deeply flushed.

"Tobey doesn't have to give you permission," Cy said softly. "If this were your process, how would you feel if people got their needy shit into it? You're here to help Charlée. Please take off your shorts."

Reluctantly I complied. My cock dangled before Ken's face.

"Ken," Cy asked, "how long's it been since you slurped on that bad boy?"

I stifled a wince, and Tobey's startled eyes met mine. I had never told him about Ken's long-ago midnight visits.

"Couple years," Ken replied without losing his rhythm.

"Do you miss it?"

Ken seemed to freeze. I recalled the toothy blow jobs as painful, but they had betrayed his hunger, and that memory excited me. My cock swelled.

"Steve's cock seems to miss *you*," Cy said. "How about a slurp for old times' sake?"

Ken took it in his mouth. It stiffened and he broke stride with Charlée to grasp my buttocks, gobbling. His cock slipped out of her. She grunted loudly in protest.

Cy asked, "What's that, honey?" and removed the gag.

"Will I ever just get to fuck somebody?"

"Can you say, 'Will somebody please just fuck me?'"

She asked the question softly. Puck raised his hand like a schoolboy eager to recite the names of the fifty states. My eyes caught Tobey's. I backed away from Ken, but Ken grasped my buttocks tight in his hands and swallowed my cock once more, deliciously.

"How about you, Tobey?" Cy said. "You care for Charlée, don't you? And your darling Steve is busy over here. Can you give her what she needs right now?" He re-fitted her with the gag.

Tobey yanked off his briefs, crawled across the bed and buried his face between her legs. When he rose and entered her, he stared straight ahead and thrust mechanically, with none of the sweet sensuality I had known with him.

I lost my erection and held my breath until I was dizzy. I felt capable of separating my professional duties from my lust, anger and disgust, and of detaching these from my admiration of Charlée's courage. But did Tobey have the maturity to compartmentalize the complex aspects of this experience? If Charlée's process damaged my relationship with Tobey I would never forgive myself. Or her. I pulled away from Ken and knelt beside Tobey and touched his hand. He plunged into Charlée with his eyes shut for what seemed like an hour. She bellowed through her gag as if to make sure I knew how much pleasure Tobey was giving her. Finally he finished and fell into my arms.

Cy put a hand on my shoulder. "Honey, here comes Steve," he told her gently. "You can let the needy pussy deep inside you take over while you fuck this beautiful young man."

I let go of Tobey and knelt over her, disturbed by my ready arousal. I'd never imagined having sex with anyone who was tied and gagged. I rarely made eye contact with Charlée but did so now. Through her vulnerability I saw that she didn't like me, but was willing to do this because it was her process. I closed my eyes, recalling the rise and fall of Tobey's perfect buttocks, and entered her. Cy photographed us while Elsie monitored the tape recorder. As I had done for him, Tobey knelt beside me and held me after I finished.

"That's good for tonight," Cy said.

Out of the straps and free of her gag, Charlée hugged and thanked us all.

Tobey wept quietly that night. "Don't tell Cy I got over-whelmed," he implored me. "I don't want him to think I'm too low-level to handle sophisticated therapy."

I stroked him and muttered, "Don't be ashamed of your sen-sitivity." I too felt overwhelmed. Sometimes Charlée seemed to be submitting to gang rape. But admitting my doubts right now could only add to Tobey's confusion. And to question the wisdom of a process she accepted, and even embraced, would be the most insidious kind of subgrouping. During my Gollum session I would have felt betrayed to learn people were critiquing it behind my back.

Over breakfast Cy spoke with sacramental awe. "Personal growth is a journey reserved for the devoted. Look at Charlée. This is the bravest woman I've ever had the honor of knowing." His eyes shone. "Like a goddess. A goddess of growth."

Without makeup Charlée looked young and exposed. She had washed her hair but not bothered to dye the roots or poof it up, and it hung dull and straight past her shoulders.

We said that in her smile we saw the beginnings of humility.

TRAVIS AND THE OTHERS AT BEDFORD DRIVE seemed to believe the staff was in Malibu "on retreat." Ken and Willow commuted to Beverly Hills each day to see paying patients, and I envied them their mobility. My workplace was always at Cy's side. On my visits to Elizabeth in Juvie I struggled to sound upbeat but knew she noticed my exhaustion, my jumpy eyes and evasions. I often promised that Cy would be coming "real soon." She cut many of my visits short.

In spite of everything Charlée had endured, her process was still not complete. Each night a couple of us restrained her as Cy instructed. Sometimes she began screaming immediately and was fitted with the gag. But before the end of each session Cy led her through memories triggered by the fucking—of the uncle who fondled her and forced her to give him oral sex, of sexual exploration with childhood playmates.

After each session I expected her to break down completely. How much humiliation could one person take? Often she did cry softly once the restraints were removed, but always composed herself to thank everyone.

On trips outside, I walked in fear that someone would guess what I was participating in every evening. Then, afraid I had caught my mentor's paranoia, I reminded myself that no one but Cy could read my mind.

One day Elizabeth told me I could stay only ten minutes instead of the usual half hour. She seemed petulant but I didn't confront her. On my way out I passed Vivian in the facility's lobby. Startled, I faced her with an unexpected rush of warmth—someone who had befriended and comforted me in my early days at Rancho Vista.

She made fists and refused to look at me. I wanted to cry out, After all we've been through together can't we at least smile at each other?

As she marched on I imagined her response: *Yes, let's smile and pretend you haven't helped turn my daughter against me!*

In desolation I drove to Seabird, intending to mention the encounter to the staff. But at the house everyone was busy. I walked into the heaviest phase of Charlée's process—she was fucking all the men in sequence and allowing the needy pussy to beg, "Don't leave me!"

I stripped to my boxers and dutifully awaited my turn. The sessions provided my only sexual release in months, yet I dreaded them. How many twenty-five-year-olds went so long without even masturbating? Although Tobey and I clung to each other every night, and sometimes kissed, we hadn't made love since our last night at the Ranch. It was as if we had reached an unspoken agreement that lovemaking would wait until Cy was again himself.

On my next visit to Juvie, the guard recognized me and smiled sadly. "Sorry you come for nothin'," she said. "Your girl left with her mama yesterday."

I squinted at her in disbelief. "With—did her mother have a court order?"

The guard laughed. "No, sugar, she had a puppy. Little floppy-eared thing."

I pictured a moist-eyed spaniel straight off a greeting card, so trite I almost laughed. Without another word I stalked out, and a full minute passed before reality sank in. If she hadn't done so already, Elizabeth would tell Vivian about her "introduction to womanhood."

"Cy, don't shoot me," I whispered as I ran through the parking lot, wondering where I could have left the car. "I'm only the carrier pigeon."

Of course Cy wouldn't hold me responsible for Elizabeth's defection. But even if no one accused me of anything, as a growth case I must search my soul for my true motivations: had I *wanted* Elizabeth with her mother, to spare her the horror show that had become the staff's daily life? Even worse, did I want to see Cy punished?

Finally I found the car and slumped behind the wheel. I had entered Cy Aaron's world in search of understanding and acceptance. During my quest I'd been trained rigorously to anticipate other people's feelings. How then could I have failed to understand that Vivian wanted to protect her daughter, and that Elizabeth loved and missed her mother?

Well, no matter what I understood, I was agonizingly sure where my gratitude, devotion and loyalty lay.

PART FOUR

If I let myself really understand another
person, I might be changed by that
understanding. And we all fear change.

>   Carl R. Rogers
>   *On Becoming a Person*

>   If you understood me, you could
>   not judge me.
>
>   Cyrus Aaron

29

I FLEXED A CRAMP OUT OF MY LEFT HAND and
steered with my right. Since five a.m. I had driven a rented van in
an enormous loop from freeway to freeway across the valley,
down through Studio City past Hollywood and the heart of L.A.,
west on 10 almost to Santa Monica and up the 405 back through
Sherman Oaks. Beside me in shorts, Charlée straddled the
console with a notebook open in her lap. Cy slouched away from
the passenger window and glared at the world through wrap-
around mirrored sunglasses he'd bought at a convenience store.

The van was loaded to the roof with luggage, typewriter cases,
and cartons stuffed with books, cassette recorders and cameras.
Cy and Charlée's suitcases were packed with clothes for every
climate, his-and-hers vibrators and blow dryers, and essentials
including what looked to me like a ten-year supply of toothpaste.

When we passed the Holiday Inn at Mulholland for the sixth
time I checked the gas gauge. I'd nearly emptied the tank without
going anywhere.

"Maybe we should just go on Trail," Cy said.

Insane. But, with no better proposal, I clutched the wheel and stayed quiet.

"To Rancho Vista," he persisted. "The last place anyone would expect to find us." He pulled up his collar and hunched like a cartoon gangster.

"Investigators might question people in Keystone," Charlée said in a tinny voice, "and if we were living out there—"

"Okay, okay," he snapped. "Let's face it. We have to get the hell out of the country."

I peered around him into the right-side mirror. I signaled and changed lanes, and heard something fall with a crash to the floor of the van. The idea of re-packing the mess made me want to cry.

"You guys don't have to leave," I said with false cheer. "Elizabeth probably won't tell her mom anything, and this'll blow over. You could rent a little bungalow in Ohio or someplace where nobody'd recognize you. But if you're more comfortable leaving the country, we've got enough cash to send you anywhere in the world for a few months."

Cy shouted, "Months! Is that what I saved your fucking lives for, working like a donkey all these years? To enjoy a few months of charity until my benevolent conservators deign to return me from exile? Or 'til I rot in the Akron Greyhound station? You neglected Elizabeth and she defected to her mother. The two of them have sentenced me to death. You and the other vultures are gathering to strip the flesh off my carcass. Charlée is the only loyal one."

I bit my lip to keep from screaming, *Who* neglected Elizabeth? Traffic had steadily thickened since noon and was now slowing to claustrophobic sludge. I ignored my earlier route toward Hollywood and continued north into the valley.

Charlée took out her dog-eared World Traveler Guide, a treasured Christmas gift from Cy, and flipped through it. "Several countries lack extradition treaties with the U.S. We can drive to San Francisco tonight and get visas in the morning. When we stop for gas let's swing by a drug store for hair dye. I think I'll go raven black."

I patted her bare thigh in gratitude. Her even tone and pragmatic ideas would calm Cy.

"Jesus!" the old guy wailed, and I slammed on the brakes. The car behind blasted its horn. "Our passports!"

I took a deep breath and sped up. "If you want me to turn around you don't have to scare the shit—"

"No," Cy said in his most reasonable voice. "We *have* our

passports, but they're worthless. When we apply for visas the authorities'll run us through some computer."

"We can travel," Charlée said in a lilting tone. "No one's looking for us."

He flubbered his lips like a horse. "Not *yet*, maybe! But when that cunt tells her sad story they'll hand her a box of Kleenex and an indictment."

"Kleenex," Charlée echoed, and began writing. "And we'll need strapping tape to seal those boxes. The hair dye. What else?"

"Vodka," said Cy, pacified. "Soda. O.J."

She squeezed my arm. "I'll drive when you get tired," she offered, and I marveled at her solicitous tone. Had the nights of tied-and-gagged fucking softened her? Or was she merely holding herself back to keep Cy calm? I wanted to trust the change, the one barrier between me and the tornado of his paranoia.

After an hour in a Simi Valley shopping mall, I drove toward Interstate 5, the boring but efficient inland route. Near the Buttonwillow exit Charlée rested her head on my shoulder, and the gesture grabbed at my heart. I'd shared no affection with this woman in the years I'd known her. Now, after her horrendous process, I was glad she could sleep. I had learned more than I wanted to know from my old friend Lydia when she harbored Chilean refugees. If Cy left the country to escape indictment, my presence in the driver's seat right now would constitute a felony, an act in furtherance of a flight to avoid prosecution. But Charlée was willing to become a fugitive with him, incurring her own legal problems. I could certainly prove myself equally loyal.

At one a.m. we drove into downtown San Francisco and I rented a suite at the Hilton. Afraid of being seen with them, I insisted they go up separately and hide in the bathroom when the bellhops rolled in three huge luggage carts. I argued, "Do you really need *two* electric typewriters?" and Charlée reminded me in her new calm voice that she and Cy didn't know how long they'd be away, that Cy was *comfortable* with familiar things, that "working on creative projects is the best way to pass anxious hours."

I filled a small bag with the few stray items they weren't taking—some ski clothes, a silver candlestick—and double-taped the cartons shut. How many fugitives traveled with the sixteen-pound, two-volume Oxford English Dictionary? I felt both annoyed and touched: it had been my gift to Cy on our last Christmas at the Ranch.

Charlée and Cy did a dress rehearsal, strapping on money belts and camouflaging them under bulky sweaters. I applauded their performance, and didn't say they resembled obese American tourists with strangely narrow faces. When they stripped and stepped into the shower together, I sneaked three blue Valiums from Charlée's purse and slipped one under my tongue. It tasted bitter but soon melted into a spot of numbing paste that disappeared into my saliva.

I unzipped one of their twelve money belts and caught my breath. It was jammed with hundred-dollar bills. I opened another, and another. Cy and Charlée were taking at least a hundred thousand dollars.

Cy emerged from the bathroom humming. He trussed himself back into his money belts and said, suddenly casual, "Think about visiting us soon."

"This thing could blow over within a week," I reminded him for at least the tenth time. "And if you *are* indicted, the best thing to do is come back and deal with it."

"Easy for you to say. The mother of your underage lover hasn't gone to the police. Yet."

My face flushed, then went cold.

"Don't try to scare Steve," Charlée said blithely. "If he gets caught helping someone under warrant, he'll be out of commission and we'll be on our own."

Cy ignored her and nailed me with his eyes. "As soon as you get to L.A. I want you to rent a post-office box. We need to be able to send you certain things. When we reach our destination we'll change our appearance and send you photographs of our new selves. Use the photographs for a set of passports."

The edge returned to Charlée's voice. "That's a felony."

"There's a reason these places don't have extradition treaties with the U.S.," he continued cheerily. "We'll have no trouble getting *into* some banana republic where school-crossing guards carry machine guns, but we'll be trapped there when they stage their next coup. We need the kind of mobility that only top-quality counterfeit passports can buy. Money is no object."

The sky was the color of abalone shell when Charlée picked up the phone to confirm flight schedules. I ducked into the shower to avoid hearing her. If the police questioned me, I had to be able to say *I don't know where they are.*

But unless I knew, how could I help if they got into trouble? I took what felt like the longest shower of my life and waited for the Valium to quiet my stomach. The hoped-for calm never came. When I finally stepped out of the bathroom the sun was blazing in through the windows. A room service cart had been wheeled in, and the smell of coffee and bacon sickened me.

Cy chewed a slice of toast and named the manuscripts he would complete while away from the distractions of city living. *"The Pure Relationship Revealed! The Relationship Workbook Method! The Executive Trail! Vesuvius!"*

I transcribed this on a card as enthusiastically as I could.

"If anyone asks, we're on sabbatical. Completing this series of books."

I wanted to yell, *If* anyone asks? But I nodded and quietly suggested Cy and Charlée leave the hotel ahead of me and walk around the block so no one would see us all together. Charlée agreed, and led Cy out, reminding him it was important to trust their young helper's instincts. With a sudden, profound sadness I watched them enter the elevator. She faced the task of containing Cy's paranoia while forcing him not to jeopardize anyone else.

I rolled a load of boxes and luggage to the garage, declining a bellhop's assistance. Then, as I packed the van and returned to the suite for more cargo, I fretted that my refusal of help might make me even more conspicuous. But there was no way to do this without worrying about something. I pulled a ski cap low over my forehead and drove the loaded van into the street.

A block from the hotel, Charlée and Cy climbed in, arguing about whether to abort the plan if the consulate entered their names into a computer. She sat down and snapped to me, "I refuse to absorb one ounce of his persecution complex." Minutes later she hopped out on Market Street near the ancient, wedge-shaped Flood Building that housed various foreign consulates.

I plowed the van through the traffic and Cy growled, "She talks to me as if I were retarded. I'll have to turn myself in if someone doesn't join us as a buffer. Her process helped, but it's tragic we had to cut it short."

I nodded to conceal my panic. Could I refuse to join the "sabbatical" if he asked me directly?

"You're the only one who really sees her shit," he said.

"We'd start fighting and make things harder for you."

"No! If she's discharging the bile onto you, there's less for me to absorb."

This felt like a sickening truth. Cy studied himself in the rearview mirror while I circled the block with the deadly feeling that my world was disintegrating. The man who had saved my life needed me to be strong, to commit bold felonies. And I couldn't wait to get rid of him.

On our third trip around the block I spotted Charlée at the curb, calmly reading a travel brochure. She hopped in, looking refreshed. "They don't have anything like a police computer up there," she reported. "Just a museum-quality typewriter and an impressive collection of antique rubber stamps." She grinned, spoofing her profound relief. "Your turn, Cy! We'll meet you at the corner in front of that quick-lunch stand. Now take off those silly sunglasses."

Cy kissed each of us on the cheek, as if saying a last goodbye before facing the firing squad. He approached the old building and smoothed his hair with trembling hands. I drove away slowly but couldn't shake my greatest fear—that he would next demand I also go upstairs to have my passport stamped, and that I'd end up on a plane with them.

Ten minutes later Cy was standing behind a sandwich board across Market Street. He climbed into the van, poured vodka into a Dixie cup and said, "I got the visa, but Jesus! I thought I'd pass out up there." He rifled through Charlée's bags, opened a jar of Tang and added a large splash of the orange powder to his drink. He took a long gulp, then assumed a solemn tone. "We're flying into the unknown, like lost birds. We'll call you in a week or so."

"I'll hang up." I gunned through a yellow light onto the freeway ramp south, toward the airport. Straining to speak softly, I explained, "If you're indicted our phones will be tapped."

Charlée took over in her new, modulated voice. "I'll leave messages at the answering service after hours. Call us from a pay phone when you know you haven't been followed. Let's figure out a code for the messages I'll leave you." She printed neatly in her notebook, improvising a cryptogram.

"A message from *Mr. Winters*," Cy announced, "means we're in a life-and-death emergency. Regular emergencies'll be Dr. Manchester. Be prepared. Get your visa today."

Even now the old man was so subtle. How could I get a visa if I didn't know where I would be going?

"And we'll need access to ready cash," he added casually. "You're a signatory on the important bank accounts. Charlée will call with wire instructions so you can transfer money on short notice." I nodded, fighting back shock and anger. How much more money did they plan to need?

In oppressive silence we barreled toward the airport. I wanted to dump them miles from the terminal, but drove on mechanically. I imagined myself watching from some high place: the van slowing, turning, rolling to a stop in front of the international departures area; me with the ski cap pulled over my eyebrows, piling the luggage on a sidewalk while Charlée went inside.

At the curb I reminded myself to breathe, and settled back into my body. I looked straight into one of several surveillance cameras and kept busy behind the van, re-taping a carton Cy had ripped open. Soon Charlée reappeared, leading a small army of redcaps. I hid my face by pretending to rummage in the empty van until she approached me. "Tell me where the hell you're going," I whispered.

She showed me her ticket, and I stared at it in confusion. "*San Jose?*"

She winked and kissed me on the cheek. "Costa Rica."

NO ONE AT BEDFORD DRIVE asked where I had been. I announced at breakfast that Cy and Charlée had decided on short notice to take a well-deserved vacation, and embarked on a cruise. Behind a tight smile, even Tobey concealed his knowledge that something monstrously heavy was happening.

Short of renting a post-office box and hiring the mob lawyer Felix Thornton, I covered the necessary bases. When I told Elsie she shouldn't expect to hear from Cy and Charlée for several weeks, she replied in a Theodora-like tone, "Whadja do with the bodies?" We both laughed. That afternoon I completed the past month's insurance billings but found myself desperately going through the motions as if there were a future to prepare for. I spent the weekend drafting proposals for the consultation projects with the L.A. Airport and Hilton Hotels, and tried not to think about Monday's staff meeting. Theodora or Ken would ask, *Where the hell are Cy and Charlée?* and I would elaborate on my last-minute-vacation story, which no one would swallow. I decided this was good practice for deceiving the police, but how could I live with Withholds between myself and the people I loved?

On Monday morning I sat at the head of the conference-room table, in Charlée's old seat. I took control of the meeting before anyone could launch into difficult questions. "Let's face it," I said, "Cy is out of commission. He went on vacation because he's exhausted and overwhelmed. After Charlée's process—"

Panic flashed in Willow's eyes. I detoured quickly, as unwilling as the others to discuss what we had done in the upstairs bedroom at Seabird. "Even if, you know, when they come back, Cy won't be able to handle everything. Without him to run the LAX and Hilton projects, all we've got is Ken doing Executive Trails. We can charge a lot for those, but he can only take so many people at a time."

Ken nodded and I went on excitedly, "But an article in Saturday's paper gave me an idea. Industrial psychologists say *substance abuse* is the number-one cause of lost profits in corporations today. They call it an 'epidemic.' We have the resources to evaluate thousands of employees for a company. We can refer those who need treatment somewhere else."

Elsie gave me a sharp look of understanding and finished my thought: "You mean without providing the treatment ourselves—just the evaluation and recommendations."

"Amen." I saw relief in the others' faces, and knew they all understood Cy wasn't coming back for a long time. "We can charge plenty for evaluations. Listen to this." I read segments of proposals I'd outlined over the weekend. Everyone added constructive suggestions. After the meeting adjourned I stayed at the office all night, polishing the results, and sent the completed packages to the clients in the morning.

I slept all afternoon and awoke with what felt like a revolutionary idea. Over dinner I declared, "We need to have some *fun!*" Soon twenty-two of us stashed bags of home-made popcorn and bottles of Joy Juice in our clothes and piled into the dump truck bound for Westwood. Tobey and I jostled among the others and cuddled in the balcony of the cavernous old Fox Theatre where we screamed through *The Exorcist*.

A MESSAGE FROM "DR. MANCHESTER"—Cy's code for a regular emergency—came at five-forty the next morning, and I suddenly realized how little I knew. Was "harboring fugitives" a bucket I either dunked my head in or didn't, a broad crime of which I was either guilty or innocent? Or did every phone call I made, every carton of typewriter ribbons I taped shut, every dollar I wired to a foreign bank, count as a distinct crime carrying its own penalty?

With no answers, I sucked on my last pilfered Valium and drove through Topanga Canyon looking for a pay phone. I found one outside a health-food store and called the international operator. Slowly and quietly I read her the number I'd decoded from "Dr. Manchester's" message, then began feeding quarters into the coin slot from a canvas tote bag.

Charlée answered briskly, "Bwayno?"

"It's me."

She sighed. "We're doing as well as can be expected." Immediately she went on about client contacts and business opportunities, including the airport consultation project. "Before we left I set up an appointment with LAX Personnel. I was taking Willow. You go with her instead."

I didn't have time to explain we had already taken those projects in our own direction. Cy came on, bellowing, "We're going to survive!" He had only one agenda item. "Write this down . . ." He dictated a letter instructing Tobey to call the next day.

My only protest was a tiny grunt of fear.

"Don't tell anybody," Cy added. "I don't want Willow raising hell. But Tobey is young and scared. He needs to hear from us."

"Okay," I promised, relieved and grateful. In the midst of Cy's panic he was treating Tobey's well-being as a priority.

"See Felix Thornton this week," Cy ordered. "And—oh! What's the new post-office box number? We've got the materials to send you for our photo album."

"I forgot to bring it," I lied, ashamed to admit I was dragging my feet on Cy's top-priority passports project. "I'll give it to you tomorrow when Tobey calls. I love you—guys."

"We're going to survive," Cy repeated.

Charlée came back on and said, "You're our lifeline. We're so grateful for all you're doing." Probably reading from a script, but at least she acknowledged me.

I hung up and counted my remaining quarters. The call had cost sixty-eight dollars, more than I had spent on a year of phone bills when I lived with Lydia.

I agonized over my next move. Dropping friends at the airport and returning phone calls were arguably innocent acts. But renting a post-office box under a phony name, for the purpose of receiving photographs needed to produce counterfeit passports . . . I may as well make a phony passport for myself, too, because I would need one before this was over.

I drove into town and cruised through quiet neighborhoods until a small, friendly-looking post office caught my eye, then decided I wanted more anonymity and headed for the federal building near UCLA. I made up a name—"Sam Kelly"—and paid cash for a one-year rental on the largest box available. The clerk didn't ask for identification or even look at me. I ached to be comforted, but was afraid to go to Bedford Drive. Once I saw Tobey I would want to tell him everything I'd done, but he had enough burdens already. Utterly exhausted, I drove to Seabird and called to tell him I had work to do there. Then I fell into the bed where Charlée's process had taken place, thinking I would enjoy watching the ocean until I fell asleep. Nylon straps still circled the legs of the bed. Memories of her writhing body and gagged mouth haunted me. Finally I moved downstairs to Tobey's little bed in the windowless servant's room off the kitchen.

I awoke trembling and drenched in sweat. Some wailing creature had chased me in my dream. Before leaving, Cy had overseen the flushing of every flake of marijuana down the master bathroom toilet, in case the police searched the house. With trembling fingers I rummaged in bathroom drawers, scrounged a loose Valium tablet, and nursed it. I tried to breathe deeply. After ten minutes I stopped shaking but nothing like serenity arrived.

An occasional tremor jolted me as I drove through the morning traffic to Beverly Hills. At the Bedford house I found Tobey cleaning the pool. "Let's go for a drive," I said, trying to sound casual. After we were in the car I explained, "Cy is real concerned about you." We drove to an abandoned-looking park in Mar Vista with a pay phone. Tobey looked more excited than afraid as we walked together through the playground.

Then I panicked—I had to give Cy my new alias and post-office box number, and didn't want Tobey to know. It was too late to explain. I dialed, and when Charlée answered I cheerily said, "Let me give you Sam Kelly's address," and recited the information. Then I handed the phone and my bag of quarters to Tobey, and forced myself to walk back to the car.

Ten minutes later he flopped onto the front seat and flung the money bag on the floor. "I'm going to help them move."

I gazed at him, too stunned to speak.

"They're in a villa and they need to go somewhere cheap. They've pre-paid my ticket out of San Francisco. Tomorrow."

"We have to stop pretending they're on vacation."

"You didn't think I believed that." he snorted. "They can't take care of themselves. I'm bringing the juicer. Can you see Cy juicing his own carrots every morning?" He made a noise that sounded like a giggle, but I saw tears in his eyes.

At the house Tobey loaded the Champion juicer, a quarter-horsepower machine that weighed more than an electric type-writer, into a bowling-ball bag. He then packed his own small suitcase, and insisted on saying goodbye to Theodora before we hopped into the little Mercedes.

I followed the same route I'd taken in the van a few days before, north on Interstate 5, and carefully observed the speed limit. We reached San Francisco in time for dinner. At an expensive Italian restaurant we held hands under the table and pretended we were on our first date. Later, in a plush little room at the Palace Hotel, we made love for the first time in months, and held each other all night.

In the morning, after Tobey dashed into the Flood Building for his visa, I circled the block and told myself it wasn't too late. I could get my own visa, use Tobey's plane ticket to join the fugitives, and send him back to Beverly Hills where he belonged.

But Tobey was flushed with excitement when he ran out to the car.

"You're braver than me," I said.

"This is my first vacation since the honeymoon cruise! I'm gonna make this fun."

In line at the airport I looked at his young face, so full of trust. The person I hoped to spend my life with was being yanked away by a rip-tide. The love I rarely expressed rose into my throat. "Are you sure about this?"

He nodded. We clung to each other and finally kissed quickly on the lips. "Once your mother said you idolized me," I whispered. "I was afraid to let her see how much that meant. You're the closest thing I have to a brother."

I knew the impish face so well. Tobey was holding back a smart remark about fraternal incest. We grazed cheeks, then he grabbed his carry-ons and bolted for the plane, lopsided, with the bowling bag weighing down one shoulder. *I should be going, not you*, I thought, but watched him disappear. I chewed on a clump of my hair until the jet eased away from the gate.

On the drive back to L.A. I had time to ponder the nature of betrayal and the myth of free will. *Tobey is thrilled to go*, I kept telling myself.

Yes, and Eric had submitted to Grand Silence. Elizabeth had been proud to give her virginity to Cy. Charlée had thanked a roomful of men for fucking her while she was tied and gagged.

I rehearsed a dozen ridiculous explanations for what had just happened. Unready to face the other Vistans and make up believable stories, I headed for Malibu.

When I approached Seabird I saw a taxi rumbling at the curb. I considered driving on, but Theodora stepped out and waved the driver away, then waited at the front door.

Once it slammed behind her she shouted, "I ain't as smart as you, but I ain't stupid." She pursued me as I backed toward the kitchen. "Where the hell is Tobey? He said goodbye yesterday like he was leavin' for Mars with a one-way ticket."

"How long were you waiting out there?"

"I know what's going on. You fuckers are afraid Cy's gonna get arrested for screwing Elizabeth, but they can't drag him back from Bolivia or Macedonia or some flea-bag country that doesn't have a U.S. extradition treaty."

"Don't tell me. You just got an 'A' in political science."

She kicked her sneakers across the floor and stalked out of the kitchen. I opened the refrigerator and began sniffing leftovers. "You know more than me," I called out. "Want some soup?"

I heard banging and grunting upstairs. A minute later she appeared, holding the nylon straps that had been tied to the bed. "Don't you think we should give these to Ken? I mean, in case some *Sunset Magazine* photographers drop by? Or the *cops?*"

"I won't try to hide anything from you again," I promised, meaning it.

MONEY HAD FLOWED THROUGH RANCHO VISTA like a mighty river. Without Cy generating insurance revenue, forty-eight thousand dollars of monthly income immediately dried up. Royalties from his book, *The Quest for Unconditional Love*, went into a special account only he had access to.

Elsie said she was "taking this situation in hand," and signed up for an advanced accounting class. She read the textbook in a weekend and consulted her professor to work out financial forecasts. At the next staff meeting she reported that the community could meet expenses, but only by living on a budget— something we had never done."

I announced that the Personnel Department for Hilton Hotels had accepted our substance abuse evaluation proposal, and the team went to work on making it happen. Willow helped me schedule meetings. Elsie arranged to submit monthly invoices for our work, but was already earmarking every dime.

We had either bought the mansions and luxury automobiles at foreclosure sales, or received them in payment from Cy's clients—but even these bargains had mortgages and balances due. The one potential source of ready cash was the Rolls, which was still in my name. It was paid for—a "liquid asset," Elsie called it—but Zoë still had it. The night Cy broke my ribs, he told her he would keep Wolfie as long as she kept the car.

I took the dog for a long walk on the beach, and said I was sorry I'd held onto him for so long. "You belong with Zoë," I said through tears, and knew I would return him to her even if she and her lawyers refused to release the car to me. The thought of losing him opened a well of pain. With Tobey gone, the wolf-dog was my only comfort. I often awoke in the morning with him standing over me. Not until my eyes fluttered open did he begin to lick my face.

Finally, after cuddling with him all night and putting a warmed-up slice of sausage pizza in his bowl, I called Zoë. "Etienne," she said, recognizing my voice immediately. "You are so loyal to Cy. He is lucky to have you." I offered to deliver Wolfie to her, and didn't mention the car. "I miss him," she said, and gave me her address in Sherman Oaks, then added, "Cy's car is in my garage. Please plan to take it with you." Theodora drove Wolfie and me to the modest suburban house, where we found an envelope containing keys to the garage and the car. "Forgive me," Zoë had written. "I cannot bear to see you kids." In the garage she had installed a dog door that opened to the fenced back yard—obviously hoping she would some day have Wolfie with her again. Beside the door were bowls of kibble and water. Wolfie went nuts, running around and sniffing everything, whimpering for the woman who had brought light into his life. And mine.

Later I dutifully checked my P.O. box in Westwood, and hesitated even to touch the padded package that I found there, a manila envelope sealed in about ten layers of strapping tape. Trying not to appear furtive, I strolled with it out to the parking lot, and waited until I reached Seabird to hack it open. The photographs that spilled out made me want to laugh—Tobey looked like a rock singer, with yellow-blond bangs hanging to his sable eyebrows. Charlée had dyed her hair Cleopatra-black and cut it in a pageboy. Cy's hair and eyebrows were a believable shade of russet, and he had a matching, close-cropped beard.

I stashed the pictures under my socks in Tobey's dresser and burned the envelope in the fireplace. Weeks had passed since Elizabeth joined her mother, and no indictments had come down. I would be insane to commit passport fraud in anticipation of some vague threat. Cy and Charlée could travel with Tobey for a while and then return home, rested and ready to move back to the Ranch.

In the morning I put the car on sale through a Beverly Hills consignor. "I'll have it sold within a week," the man said, and didn't blink when I told him I could accept no less than seventy thousand dollars. Four days later I deposited a check for seventy-six thousand in my personal account.

In the next phone call to Costa Rica I shared the news about the clinic's prospects. Though eager to talk to Tobey, I carefully answered all of Cy's questions. When I tried to reason with him about his choice of the Mafia lawyer Felix Thornton, he cut me off mid-sentence. Suddenly the call was over and neither of us had mentioned Tobey.

The Seabird doorbell rang at four-thirty the next morning. I bolted up in panic, threw on a bathrobe and ran to the door. Through the peep-hole I saw a pair of glittering handcuffs.

It was too late to pretend no one was home. I'd already turned on the porch light. When I opened the door, a man barked, "Dr. Cyrus Aaron?"

Two men glared at me, one in a cop's uniform, the other in a rumpled suit. "Are you Dr. Cyrus Aaron?" repeated the thuggish-looking officer.

"No. I'm house-sitting." I gave the men Vistan eye contact and invited them in.

The middle-aged plainclothesman introduced himself as a detective and explained, "Dr. Aaron has been indicted on several counts of statutory rape and infamous crimes against nature."

I replied as smoothly as I could, "Dr. Aaron and his wife are on their second honeymoon."

The two men exchanged a look. "Wife's been indicted too," the detective said.

The other asked, "They're out of the country, no doubt?"

"Well, yes," I said, trying to sound helpful. "But I don't know where."

The detective yawned. "If you hear from the honeymooners please have 'em call us." He handed me a business card that bore the logo of the Los Angeles County Sheriff's Office.

"Oh, of course," I replied, praying he and his partner would leave before I began sobbing. As they strode down the walk I knew they didn't believe anything I'd said.

Even at five a.m. there was a lot of traffic on Sunset. When I reached Bedford Drive the Vistans were gathered in the great hall, drinking warm milk with honey—Travis's prescription for nervous stomachs. The indictment story was on the wire services and the phone had been ringing—everyone from Theodora's Colorado probation officer to Wanda Richter had called.

Wishing I'd stolen more Valium from Charlée's purse, I phoned Cy's tax lawyer. When I tried to corner him for specifics—*What kind of trouble could someone get in for helping fugitives?*—the advice was sensible: "Just continue business as usual."

Finally I convened a meeting with the anxious Vistans. "This is scary," I said, hearing the raw edge of panic in my voice, "but it's not as bad as it sounds. Cy and Charlée are still on vacation. Tobey has joined them. When they find out about this, they'll come back and straighten everything out." Jesus, how I wished I could believe this.

I explained what I knew about the difference between an indictment, which involved prosecution and the threat of prison, and Vivian's civil lawsuit, whose worst result would be a judgment for money. "What we can do," I concluded, "is conduct business as usual, act like grownups. Make Cy proud of us. Then he and Charlée can come home to a fair trial."

Theodora asked, "Can you get in trouble for helping them leave the country?"

"I helped them go on vacation. We didn't know *this* would happen."

She nodded with a complicit smile that implied, *Oh, right, you've been talking to a lawyer.* "How about if someone wants to go and help them? Is that against the law?"

"We need another kind of lawyer to answer all our questions. A criminal lawyer."

Her face brightened. "Cy said one time if he was ever persecuted he wanted Felix Thornton to defend him. I'd hire the guy myself but I don't get my money 'til I'm twenty-one."

Despite her burst of enthusiasm, the air in the room reeked of dread. I hoped I could pull off one more pep-talk. My own fear was overwhelming, but I stood before the baronial fireplace and tried to draw courage from the trust in the others' faces. "The fair trial is everything. It's the chance for the community's rebirth from the ashes, with a greater future than ever. Some day we will again live in Paradise."

Theodora applauded, and everyone else joined in.

"BUSINESS AS USUAL" turned out to be a lot like "moving the body," Cy's prescription for difficult times. For Theodora, Elsie and the other students it meant getting straight A's. For Travis and the work crew it meant keeping the yards weed-free, the pool clean, and the Bedford house's six bathrooms functioning. Formerly the neighborhood eyesore, with broken windows and skeletal shrubbery, the mansion was now a showplace surrounded by lush gardens.

The staff went to the office every day, conducted Group several times a week, collected money, paid bills and promoted the programs and services of Rancho Vista Institute. We plodded ahead in the face of disaster, sitting together in meetings where I couldn't admit my role in the fugitives' flight although everyone knew. When Ken took a crowd of Hilton corporate leaders on Executive Trail, I stayed behind, pining for a breath of Colorado air. I quietly transferred hundreds of thousands of dollars into my own account, then wired most to Costa Rican banks and wondered where in hell all the money was going.

Despite everyone's dogged show of optimism, we were all suffering. One morning I found Willow's office door closed. I stood for a moment looking through the mail with Elsie, who seemed to have shrunk inside herself. She wore no makeup and her hair hung limp and dirty.

At the staff meeting Willow said, "He's abandoned us. He thinks he's running from the police, but he's run away from us."

I shrugged. "He's certainly left us with a lot of work to do. You ran a great Group on Thursday night." I pulled a letter from the stack of mail. "Gertrude Fitzimmons wrote the Board of Medical Examiners. She'll sponsor us under her license. Sixteen people have confirmed for this month's Marathon."

Elsie held up another envelope. "Good. 'Cause speaking of medical licenses, Cy's is suspended." She separated out another document. "And our liability insurance won't consider covering Vivian's lawsuit unless Cy appears for a deposition. If Rutherford College's insurance won't pay, he'll have to cough up a million bucks. If you don't show up for a lawsuit, you lose by default."

"Cy used to have sixty people at the Marathon," Willow said.

I smiled weakly, glad she'd brought up something that at least allowed us the illusion of control. I asked Elsie, "If we used the smallest meeting room at the hotel, how many Marathon participants would we need to cover expenses?"

She scribbled for a moment. "Fourteen."

"So the Marathon's in the black. Not by much, but we're holding our own."

Theodora burst into the conference room wearing a stylish dress and feminine, low-heeled shoes. Her soft brown hair was neatly pulled back and she had a small round Band-Aid under one eye. "I know you guys don't think of me as staff," she said, and sat beside me at the head of the table. "But Cy does, and in my book he still runs this joint."

"Are you okay?" I asked, and touched my cheek to mirror her Band-Aid.

"Oh, I got that dumb tattoo removed. And look, I got my chipped tooth fixed, too." She grinned, showing off her new smile. "Cy needs us to act like grownups. Elsie's our accountant now. I'm the new receptionist, except until ten on Tuesday and Thursday mornings. Anthropology class."

"Whatever you say," I murmured, feeling more supported than I had imagined possible.

THE MARATHON ATTRACTED FORTY-SIX PEOPLE, including some I hadn't seen since my first Beverly Hills Group. The gay couple, Gordon and Tim, reported some ups and downs but concluded, "We're happier than we've ever been." They and many others expressed shock at the charges against Cy and pledged to help in any way possible.

"Dr. Aaron saved my life," said a woman with an accent reminiscent of Zoë's. "In France where I grew up, the age of consent is twelve. Even if what she says is true, that girl should consider herself lucky to have had a man like Cyrus Aaron. My first was my uncle. He stank of cigars and passed out on top of me."

Those who spoke made clear that they didn't care whether Cy had done what he was accused of. When my turn came I said, "It's good to be reminded that we're all here because of a remarkable man who deserves a fair trial."

30

"TOBEY'S MOM ON LINE ONE," Theodora announced. "She wants him."

I closed my eyes. "God, what did you tell her?"

"I said, 'Please hold.' I do my job, handsome, you do yours."

I chewed a hangnail and watched a light cube flash on my phone. If I stared at it long enough it would stop. Alice Turner might be recording the call, or even phoning from the Sheriff's office. Desperately I wished for a Valium. I picked up the receiver, took a deep breath and punched the flashing cube. "Steve Susoyev."

"Tobey hasn't answered my letters." Alice sounded tired.

"I assume you've read the papers. He's out of the country with Cy and Charlée, on sabbatical. We'll forward his mail as soon—"

"Assume nothing," she said with an edge to her voice. "Where is my son?"

"Alice, I wish I *knew.*" I tried to sound spontaneous. "They were on vacation, a cruise, when we learned about this indictment thing."

"Leave it to the man who stole Josh Thurgood's wife to run like a coward."

I grasped the receiver in both hands. Jesus, she'd talked to Josh and Vivian. "When I find out where Tobey is I'll call you right away."

"You never were a good liar, but not for lack of practice."

I bit off my hangnail and sucked the oozing blood. Did she realize it was because of Cy that she'd grown bold enough to confront me? Finally she said, "I'm having Aaron prosecuted for kidnapping my boy." The line went dead.

Frantically I unlocked my briefcase and dug out the little manila envelope that contained my passport. I had never worried that Tobey would go to the police about our lovemaking a month before his "no more jailbait" birthday, but surely he had told Elizabeth. And his mother clearly *had* been talking to Vivian. Alice might already have reported Tobey as a victim of statutory rape, or something even more gruesome. Tobey was now twenty-two, but I had learned during anxious hours at the library that there was no statute of limitations on sex crimes: a person could be prosecuted twenty years after the fact.

I walked to the UCLA campus to find a pay phone I hadn't used before. From an old booth in the law school—with a fan that clicked on soothingly when I closed the door—I called the most notorious mob lawyer in the country.

I FILLED A CARTON WITH JOURNALS, staff-meeting minutes and photographs that included some of Cy's Polaroids. Then I dressed in a crisp shirt and fresh trousers and hauled the box downtown. In Felix Thornton's penthouse offices I stepped from a rosewood-paneled elevator onto a rug worthy of Ali Baba.

A receptionist sat at a horseshoe-shaped console that appeared to have been carved from a block of malachite. Rancho Vista would be paying for this opulence. Cy was going through money faster than anyone could keep track of. Charlée insisted no real estate be sold, placing the entire financial burden of the "sabbatical" on what the staff could earn.

I gave the receptionist my name, and sank into a buttery leather couch, with the box at my feet. Moments later Felix Thornton swept into the waiting area looking younger and more alert than in his newspaper photos. His hair was a contained, gentlemanly mane like Cy's, but a harder, silvery shade. When he smiled, his thin lips disappeared into a quizzical line. His shirt-sleeves were rolled up and his tie was loose, and he wore a tweed vest with no jacket.

I shot out of my chair and kicked over the file carton, dumping its contents onto the floor. Thornton leaned over the mess to offer his enormous hand, strong and firm, and gave me a frank, civil once-over, like a Great Dane sniffing a Chihuahua's ass. "Mr. Susoyev?" He established eye contact, scanning for clues, as direct as Cyrus Aaron at his best, and gave me another taut, lipless smile. "I'll call you when I've had a chance to study your materials. Do I have Dr. Aaron's telephone number?" He turned and left without waiting for an answer.

I reorganized the carton and gave Cy's number to the receptionist. I then drove straight to the Bedford house and holed up to write something for Cy's defense—a chronology of events as I wished they had occurred. Did criminals tell their lawyers the truth about their crimes, or concoct tales of innocence and stick to them against all logic? I crumpled page after page and burned the frustrating mess in the fireplace.

During dinner Theodora handed me a phone message: Felix Thornton had already called, and wanted me downtown at eight in the morning. While I fretted and picked at my food, Willow reported that the airport's Personnel Department had signed its contract with Rancho Vista Institute. "Every alcoholic, drug-abusing employee of LAX will be screened by us for referral."

Everyone cheered, but I wanted to cry. *She* had signed the LAX contract, and now enjoyed the privilege of announcing it. No one would applaud me if I stood to say, *Tomorrow I'll be hiring a Mafia lawyer, and right now I'm trying to figure out how to counterfeit some passports.*

I chewed on my lonely mission a while, then asked Willow and Ken to accompany me to Thornton's office in the morning. They readily agreed. "Hiring Cy's lawyer might be the most important thing you ever do," Ken said. "Don't go alone."

THORNTON ROSE BUT REMAINED BEHIND HIS DESK when the trio filed into his rosewood-and-glass corner office. He accepted Willow's hand first, and looked Ken up and down while shaking his. "Steve wore that shirt in here yesterday," he observed with a faint smile, then reached for my hand.

Abruptly he sat down and stopped smiling. We plopped into chairs facing him. "I'm willing to take this case," he said. "My retainer would be one hundred fifty thousand dollars."

I gulped and studied the infamous face. Surely the man had once, perhaps while still in law school, practiced saying such things in front of a mirror.

"If Dr. Aaron weren't a fugitive," Thornton continued, "he could retain me for twenty-five thousand. But I charge more to represent anyone who's pleaded guilty by skipping town."

The room seemed to be getting dark. "*If* we decide to go forward," I said, "I can write you a personal check. We'd rather it didn't go through the business." I eyed the beautifully-framed, oversized photographs that lined the walls—Thornton with distinguished-looking men, some popping champagne corks. Business and political leaders, I assumed, until I recognized one of Thornton's well-dressed companions as the chinless assassin, Ralph "the Roach" Ryan.

Thornton chuckled. "Let's cover some basics. Do you kids all keep that much loose change rattling around in your checking accounts?"

How could I explain? "Some clients pay their bills with things like cars, which we've sold. So we do have some cash on hand, for mobility." More softly I asked, "Can we *talk* about mobility?"

Thornton smiled as if the question entertained him. "As in preparing to become fugitives yourselves?" I stiffened. More gently he said, "We'll get to that. First let me ask another personal question. How old is each of you?"

Willow answered, "I'm twenty-six," and nodded to me.

"Twenty-six," I said.

Ken echoed, "Twenty-six. A month older than Steve."

"And how many years has each of you spent with Dr. Aaron?"

In the same order we answered, "Eight." "Little over seven." "Seven and a half."

"You're not the kids you were when you joined him."

We shook our heads.

"You're all shareholders in Rancho Vista Corporation?"

We nodded.

"Your accounting person—Elsie? From the sophisticated financial projections I've seen, she obviously knows what she's doing. Another basic question. Do you all simply grab money out of the same account, shirts out of the same closet?" We nodded again, and continued as he asked, "And Aaron trusts you to keep his money in your personal checking accounts in case you decide to become mobile and join him on his sabbatical?"

"We're preparing the way for Cy and Charlée to return to a fair trial," Willow recited. She shifted in her chair and looked at me. I was mentally tallying the money I had transferred to my own accounts and wired to Costa Rica. At a day in prison for each dollar, I would spend a thousand years behind bars.

"And we're earning money," she continued. "Doing very well, in fact. But Elsie has us on a budget and won't let us give Cy cash from under-the-table collections."

"Smart gal," Thornton said. "Al Capone lost his liberty for tax evasion, not murder." He made a little church and steeple with his meaty fingers. "Listen. I hate to discourage you kids, but there won't be any 'fair trial.'"

Willow gazed at him. Ken didn't move. Feeling as if I'd been slapped, I asked, "What do you mean?"

"You poor kids. This is the hardest part of my job. Here's a fifty-some-year-old Rolls Royce-driving psychiatrist accused of molesting a pubescent girl who's his patient. In this hypothetical trial of yours, he can expect to have trouble getting a jury enthusiastic about his side of the story."

Ken jumped in with an anxious glance at me. "Why 'hypo-thetical'?"

"No ethical lawyer would take Aaron to trial. People serve six months for stat rape. Many get probation. But Aaron is a psychiatrist, held to a higher standard. If he hadn't abused the public's trust—and run *away*, for God's sake—this case wouldn't be such a big deal. But he did, and it's an enormous deal."

"Cy will want to meet you," I said. "But if you find out where they are, will you have to turn them in?" I closed my eyes to hear the reply, recalling my enthusiastic words to the other Vistans, *The fair trial is everything.*

"I can't advise anyone to leave the country to avoid prosecution," Thornton answered dryly, "or to violate any law. But nor can I turn in someone who has retained me. Both are violations of the attorney's code of ethics." He watched the three of us a moment. "Your—whatever Cy Aaron is to you kids—he talks a lot about *reality*, 'The reality of the situation.' I had no idea what the hell he meant during most of our conversation. But I'll tell you the reality of *your* situation."

I rose from my chair. "You've talked to Cy?"

"After you left yesterday. I wouldn't have scheduled this meeting without a better idea than I got from your box of colorful material, and articles I've read over the years. I'm not entirely surprised Aaron needs somebody like me. To you kids, he's Ghandi. Florence Nightingale. To a jury, he's a man who abused his power over helpless children."

I sat down and opened my notebook and wrote, "Abused power" while Thornton warned that we should assume our phones were tapped. Police could record a conversation on a crowded street from a block away, and trace every call made from any telephone, even a pay phone, for the past year.

The lawyer paused while we absorbed this. Then, as clinically as a surgeon explaining the remedies for advanced gangrene, he summed up Cy and Charlée's situation. They were wanted in California for statutory rape and infamous crimes against nature. By fleeing the U.S., they had invited the federal authorities to become involved, and were now also wanted for unlawful flight to avoid prosecution, a charge that engaged the F.B.I. in tracking them down.

"They left before the indictments were issued," I protested.

"Dr. and Mrs. Aaron will have ample opportunity to explain

that." Thornton shook his head. "By the way, if they do anything crazy with passports, they'll really be in trouble. One count of passport fraud carries between ten and twenty years." I looked up from my notes. "What if the police ask us where Cy and Charlée are?"

"You and the rest of Aaron's inner circle are probably immune from questioning. The authorities won't waste their time interrogating somebody they assume will lie, but—"

"What kind of a crime is it to help fugitives?" Ken asked.

Thornton sighed at the interruption, looking more sad than annoyed. "You people go to the bathroom in committees. But my advice is to let Steve do his job. From what I've seen he's got the constitution for this international second-story work. The less anybody else knows, the easier it'll be for him and you."

We all wrote in our fat spiral notebooks. "One last thing," Thornton said. "The boy who answers Dr. Aaron's phone. He's the one whose father drove off the cliff?"

I nodded. This guy didn't miss much.

Willow and Ken sat looking straight ahead while I wrote out a check for one hundred fifty thousand dollars. Felix Thornton placed it under a malachite paperweight.

I TRIED TO PREPARE THE COMMUNITY in case the police did question us. Over meals and beside the pool I repeated the story of Cy and Charlée's long-planned vacation that had been underway at the time of the indictments. I told it so often and so well that I started to believe it, and to think everyone did—until Theodora whispered to me over breakfast, "Why not tape record that, and play it to us in our sleep?"

As Felix predicted, only people in the Vistan periphery underwent police interviews. The therapists Gertrude Fitzimmons and George Larkin, and the reporter Wanda Richter, called to say they'd been asked questions that implied Cy was suspected of operating a child-prostitution ring.

I felt I was waiting for something to happen, and wished to hell I knew what—for the Vistan First Couple to return? For Elizabeth to recant her Grand Jury testimony? For myself to find some courage and counterfeit the passports Cy wanted? Prompted by Elsie, who was doggedly completing her masters thesis for the Rutherford program, I submitted the final draft of my own thesis, "Sempre libera," on individual freedom—a ripoff of J.S.

Mill's slender volume, *On Liberty*, with a focus on life in an intentional community. The writing gave me comfort because it reminded me of what Rancho Vista had once been—and of what our life could again be, once this nightmare was over.

I skipped a few meals at the Bedford house, and no one seemed to notice. I missed staff meetings with the same result. The others apparently thought I was deeply engaged in fugitive-harboring, and left me alone. I began sleeping every night at Sea-bird, in Tobey's little windowless room. Each night I lay on my side and tried to figure out how to position my teeth. If I clenched them, my head began to throb. If I forced a yawn and tried to loosen my jaw, it felt about to unhinge. No position was right. On some nights this went on for hours and I wondered how anybody ever fell asleep.

I lived on macaroons and vodka, and went three days with no human contact. I woke up to "One Life to Live" and passed out after "Jeopardy." Once I'd wished for nothing more than to be like Cy. I was becoming like Cy, all right. A paranoid hermit.

A week after retaining Thornton, I went through my mail at the office and opened an envelope hand-addressed in my father's squarish script. Inside I found only a childhood photo of myself and my shirtless dad astride Sherry, my pet donkey. Six years old, I sat behind Alex in a striped tee-shirt, with my arms clasped around him. His long legs nearly reached the ground.

I had heard nothing from my parents since my mother's cryptic phone message the week of the Vistans' move to Beverly Hills. So much for direct communication, I thought, and dropped the photograph into a pocket of my briefcase.

Theodora stuck her head into my office and tossed an amber pill-bottle at me. I caught it and read the label—Valium. She'd gotten her own prescription. "Vitamin V for you, sweetie," she said. "You're pulling the heaviest load around here. This'll wrap you in a gauze of nonchalance." I jumped up to kiss her and she promised the bottle would never be empty.

At the staff meeting an hour later I had nothing to contribute, but Ken called enthusiastically from Keystone, having just finished the latest Executive Trail. Willow was excited about the new men's and women's groups. Elsie announced that the insurance company for Rutherford College had settled Vivian's lawsuit. Elizabeth would receive two hundred thousand dollars. The news gave me hope that she might drop the criminal charges.

I had to leave the meeting to answer a call from Felix, and

learned that the man known as "the Colonel," who had signed over the Rolls and the Seabird house, was under indictment for tax evasion. Cy had been subpoenaed as a witness. Failure to appear would put him in contempt of court, and open him to charges of conspiracy and fraud.

My panic screeched beyond the reach of Vitamin V. One more reason to stay away from here. My gaunt presence cast a shadow on the bright promise of new programs and financial independence.

31

I TRIED TO MUSTER A BRIGHT "HELLO!" AS IF
THE PHONE WEREN'T WAKING ME, though my forty
milligrams of bedtime Vitamin V still thickened my tongue.

"Who's this Dr. Manchester, anyway?" Theodora asked, in a
cheery tone that sounded as genuine as my own. "He left you a
message with the service at twelve-oh-five this morning. You got
some midnight disease?"

I had rehearsed for this eventuality, and sat up for my performance. A sliver of daylight from under the door of Tobey's
little room seared my eyes. "Manchester's an old patient of Cy's,"
I said. "I'll call him."

She read me the coded phone number. "Uh-*huh*. Sounds very
far away." She paused and I stayed silent, afraid to take any bait.
Finally she continued, "Then a Mr. Winters called at three a.m.,
and left the *same number* as Manchester. The plot thickens!"

In a conversation-ending tone I said, "Well, thanks." Poor Cy,
using the code name for a life-and-death emergency. The old guy
must be wild with anxiety.

"I'm not through with you. You've got a letter from Alex
Susoyev. Isn't that your dad?"

Bitterly I recalled my parents stomping out of the Marathon
and shouting that I could forget I'd ever had a family. Now they
were harassing me. "More donkey pictures."

"Coming into town any time this year?"

"Soon as, you know, I get some things done out here." In
response to her unconvinced grunt I said, "I better call those
guys," and hung up.

I dressed and gulped two one-ounce medicine cups of vodka.
Outside I groaned when I saw the little red Mercedes. I'd left it
out of the garage, and the windshield was caked with sea salt and
bird shit. I set out on foot to find a pay phone. A convertible full
of bronzed, nearly-naked teenagers flew past, hooting at the pallid
figure who shuffled like an old man along the side of the road.

I found a phone around the side of the wine shop a half mile
from Seabird. A true emergency could mean I was being followed, that the van parking across the road as I dialed the
fugitives' de-coded number was equipped with sensitive elec-

tronic ears. I took pleasure in the grotesque fantasy, the sweet prayer, that the stranger at the wheel of the van was tuning in. In Costa Rica, Cyrus and Charlée Aaron were exempt from extradition. But for Steve Susoyev, criminal accomplice, this could all be over very soon. In prison my anxiety would be predicable and manageable, unlike the chaotic terror that ruled my life when I performed even the most routine tasks.

Tobey answered softly, "Bueno?"

"Hi," I said, "it's me," and wrote the date on a scrap of paper. "Oh, hey! Happy birth—"

"There's a revolution going on down here!" Cy shouted into the phone. "They're confiscating Americans' property. You've got to help us. We need our passports. *Today.*"

The television had been my faithful companion, and I hadn't seen any news about a Costa Rican revolution. "I'm on top of it," I said in a rough whisper. "But do you know that every count of passport fraud carries a twenty-year prison sentence?"

Cy snorted. "We're in too deep to worry about that."

No, I wanted to explain, *I'm* the one who can get in trouble for this. But the stranger in the van across the street lit a cigarette, and his cold glance in my direction chilled me. After a silent moment I said, "Jesus, somebody's following me," and hung up.

I forced myself not to look over my shoulder at the van, and walked normally back to the house. Cy hadn't grasped that he was asking me to risk sixty years in prison. He understood only his own situation.

Near Seabird the van sailed past me. The driver had picked up a woman who looked about ninety—probably not an FBI agent. Inside the house I took enough Vitamin V to induce a nap, and surrendered gratefully to the cocoon of drugged sleep as it enveloped me. I woke up in time to watch Walter Cronkite at six. An earthquake in Ecuador, floods in Arkansas, nothing newsworthy in Costa Rica.

If only someone would tell me what to do! Felix was the only person who understood what was at stake, but he wouldn't recommend jaywalking, much less counterfeiting U.S. passports. "I'm a grownup now," I told the haggard face in the mirror.

I set up a TV in the bathroom and spent the evening in the tub, sipping vodka from the bottle. I ended the night with a rerun of "Dark Victory," and cried when the blind Bette Davis spurned the man who loved her because she mistook his love for pity.

For several days I managed to go without human contact. I

finished off the macaroons, but Charlée had left dozens of bags of pretzels in the pantry and there were still gallons of vodka. The phone rang one day at noon and woke me up. I let it ring ten times, trying to figure out what day it was, and finally answered.

"Gee," Theodora breezed at me, "I'm glad I caught you home. Out working in the garden?"

"Everything okay?"

"If you don't come to dinner tonight I'm sending a SWAT team after you." Her voice softened. "Travis is roasting turkeys, just like the old days. Want somebody to pick you up?"

I could have talked Willow or Ken into letting me rot in Malibu. Theodora might arrive to take me at gunpoint if I didn't promise to come, and so I agreed, but said I would drive.

"And you've been so busy," she went on, "you may have missed the story on page E-14 of today's *Times*. Something of interest to you there, I believe."

An icepick of fear stabbed my gut, but I carried in the newspapers from the driveway and found the most recent. I rolled off the rubber band, turned to the page and found the small headline: "Homosexuality Not Mental Illness, Psychiatric Association Declares." I sat on the kitchen floor. With the first true excitement I could remember, I read that the American Psychiatric Association had evaluated a "body of contemporary research" with the result that the upcoming edition of the *Diagnostic and Statistical Manual* would not catalogue homosexuality as a mental disorder. Only an individual's reaction to the condemnation of society would be treated as an illness.

The story was brief, and mentioned none of the heated debate of which I had seen a small part. Cy's name, and my own, were not among those mentioned in the story. Fugitives and those who harbor them are of interest only for their crimes, I realized, not their contributions. Still, we had made a difference. Kids who had grown up like Tobey and me might not have to feel like misfits.

I shaved, hosed off the car, and drove to the Bedford house. Theodora let out a whoop when I appeared. I ate the double portions Travis put in front of me, and talked with Ken about the chances that Gerald Ford would pardon Richard Nixon. Willow had a surprise: my masters degree diploma from Rutherford College had arrived, along with hers and Ken's. "Not much of a graduation," she said, but none of us felt like celebrating anyway.

Rainbow, Lucky and others gaped at me as if I were a stranger who had come to read the gas meter and been invited to stay for dinner. Puck sat beside me but had little to say. Theodora referred to Seabird as "the haunted house" and invited me to sleep "with a warm-blooded woman." Snuggling against her, I fell into a deep and dreamless sleep.

In the morning Willow convinced me to attend a staff meeting. *Let's pretend you're alive and well*, her concerned look said. Ken reported on his most recent Trail. "The Ranch is like a ghost town. Puck had to chop down an upstart cottonwood so we could drive in. The Hilton executives were real impressed."

Our home a ghost town. This seemed oddly appropriate because I felt like a wraith, coming and going unseen, bringing vague dread to the people I loved.

Ken mentioned, with a quick look my way, "There's a phantom gardener living up there. Guess he's had plenty of practice being comfortable in his own company. Mother nature is reclaiming the roads, but the small garden looks pretty good." My heart raced. Officially, Eric and I were still nonpersons to each other. But I was grateful to know he was thriving.

Finally, Ken passed around photos of Trail locations he'd scouted in Joshua Tree National Forest and Death Valley, locations that clients could reach in a few hours—places I would never see because I couldn't wander more than five feet from a telephone. Feeling completely unnecessary, I wandered into my office. Theodora had sorted my mail and removed the bills. I shuffled through psychological conference announcements and graphic arts catalogues, and opened a letter from my father. Alex's strong script had devolved into a scrawl I read with difficulty:

> *My dear and only son,*
> *The doctors tell me my days are numbered.*
> *My only real regret in life is that I didn't drag you out of that ballroom at the Beverly Hills Hotel.*
> *I'll leave it up to you if you want to say goodbye.*
> *I love you.*

The postmark was ten days old.

HOW COULD I WORRY ABOUT A MAN who was handicapping horses in his hospital bed? I stood in the doorway and watched him scribble notes in the margins of the *Daily Racing Form*. When he looked up I said, "Hi."

Alex lowered his reading glasses. "Praise God, if it isn't the prodigal son."

I perched on the edge of the bed. Close up, my father did look like someone to worry about. His skin was drawn tight like parchment over his sharp bones. He'd turned the color of putty in the years since I had seen him. His hair had grayed and thinned, and the unfamiliar bags under his bloodshot eyes were the color of raw liver. He'd always liked open windows, but the room was sealed up and about eighty degrees. He had on a heavy sweater.

"Afraid there's no fatted calf on the fire." He gestured toward an abandoned food tray. "Want my tapioca?"

"I'm sorry I didn't come earlier. I didn't know—"

"Your mother finally convinced me that if I wanted to see you I'd better let you know what the hell was going on."

"Daddy, I—"

His smile, and the tears at the corners of his eyes, stopped me. I had begun calling him and my mother by their first names when I was six. He reached for my hand and gazed out the window with a daydreamy expression. I followed his gaze, and saw nothing but the lentil-colored sky.

"I worried about you when Dr. Aaron was the darling of the society pages," he said. "I'm seriously concerned now that he's moved to the True Crime section. Wish I'd given him my father's advice: the two most overrated things in the world are home cooking and teenage pussy."

I laughed too hard at the feeble joke, and he nailed me with eye contact worthy of a Vistan. "While you're in this contrite state I want you to promise me you'll take care of your mother."

"Of course," I agreed, though I had no idea what "taking care" of Susi meant. Buying her good liquor? An AA book?

"And I don't mean by putting her away! I'll come back and haunt you if you even think of having her committed."

I nodded.

"You never had diaper rash when you were a child. Never. Because she took such good care of you." He removed his glasses. "I told her you probably wouldn't come."

I fell into my father's arms and wept.

He stroked my hair. With my head on his chest, I could hear the effort of every word as he asked me, "Can you stay 'til this is over? I won't take long. You haven't been much of a son to Susi, but she needs you at least as much as Dr. Aaron does."

Stung by the truth of this, I sat up and looked into his tired face. He hadn't told me what was killing him, but I asked now.

He tapped his chest. "Got too excited at the races, I guess. Heart's on the fritz."

"Isn't there something they can do—"

"To torture me before I die? Oh yes, they have methods." He squeezed my hand. "Sometimes we just have to accept what life gives us."

An idea was hatching in my mind. "Is your passport current?"

"What—you want me to go on the lam with you?"

I watched him drift into sleep, then found a pay phone near the elevators. I phoned the answering service and learned that "Dr. Manchester" had called to demand I appear "at the southern office" for an emergency meeting. I asked the service operator to let Dr. Manchester know, if he called again, that I was involved in an emergency of my own, with my dying father.

I stood paralyzed after hanging up. Cy needed me and was counting on me to show up at a designated time and place. A gentle voice spoke inside my head, telling me this was my only chance to show my father I cared about him.

Can I say I "decided" anything at that moment? I reached for the phone, knowing, not deciding, that I would take Alex to the horse races, somewhere warm where we could be alone for a few days. I called information and tracked down his friend Larry, who owned a bar and happened to be a bookie. He liked my plan. He said the season had recently opened at El Comandante, in Puerto Rico. I stayed on the pay phone for an hour, making plane and hotel reservations. I wasn't too late to show my father I cared.

I was napping in the waiting area when a nurse found me. "We think your father was just waiting for you," she said, and her tight smile told me there would be no trip to Puerto Rico, or anywhere else.

WILLOW AND KEN CAME TO THE FUNERAL, and kept Susi occupied on the day after the service so I could get some time alone. I walked to the world's largest shopping mall, in roughly the area where we had kept donkeys in the late fifties. I walked the perimeter of the parking lot until I found a sewer grate and heard rushing water. The creek I'd swum in as a boy still flowed, now under the asphalt. One eucalyptus grove remained on an adjacent homestead the developers hadn't ravaged, and I used it to orient myself. The dirt lane had run *here*, parallel to the creek. Along the lane Alex had trotted beside me while I learned to pedal my bicycle. The donkeys had grazed *there*.

I'd been so proud to introduce Alex to Lydia. She'd been charmed by him, and moved by his political commitment— spending his free time registering migrant farm workers to vote. She called him a fox.

A security guard was studying me. I took a final look around, said, "Goodbye, Daddy," and walked away.

I set myself up in the room of my boyhood, which my mother had turned into a library. Her grief was translating itself into rage. "You showed up with too little, too late," she said again and again, while I repeated to myself Alex's favorite line from my childhood: "'That's not your mother talking, it's the gin."

More rage came at me by way of the answering service. Dr. Manchester was "profoundly concerned" that I hadn't shown up for his emergency meeting. Theodora had packed me off for my father's funeral with a double-prescription of Valium, but I found myself unwilling to become numb.

One night I suggested to Susi that we go out to dinner, to a place my father had liked. I made a fuss over her pretty dress, and drove her in the little red Mercedes. At the restaurant, when the waiter first appeared, she ordered two double martinis—a practice I recalled from my childhood, which she always explained was meant to save the waiter from making extra trips back and forth. But by the time her lobster tail arrived, the martinis were gone, and soon she slid under the table.

My father was six-feet-three. In my memory, he scooped her up whenever this happened, like the groom carrying his bride over the threshold. I am five-six, no match for my father—and when I confronted the spectacle of my mother sprawled on the floor under our horseshoe-shaped booth, I realized what Alex's final admonition had meant: "Take care of your mother" translated into "Carry her out of the restaurant when she passes out." I managed to do this with the help of two waiters and a busboy, tipped them each five dollars, and swore never to enter a restaurant with her again.

Within a few more days she was sick of me, and truly didn't need me—her sister Jane arrived for an extended stay, and my mother's friends stepped up their bridge schedule to four games a week, as was their routine when a husband died. Friendly Spirits

Liquors carried milk, eggs and bread, and delivered.

"Too little, too late," my mother repeated when I hugged her goodbye, then she added a twist: "Don't you understand anything? He died of a broken heart. God damn your soul to hell."

I listened for my father's assurance, *That's the gin talking*, but heard only the thumping of my own heart. Had I been too stubborn or too selfish to see that my father truly loved me? Could Cy have prevented this and saved our relationship?

BACK AT SEABIRD I DUG THROUGH MY BRIEF- CASE. In the pocket where I kept my passport I found the picture of myself and my father on the donkey, Sherry. I propped it on Tobey's little dresser and made a sort of shrine from a Rancho Vista bristlecone, an eagle's feather and a snapshot of me and Tobey with Wolfie, taken at the last Colorado Christmas. In the background of the photo, Cy beamed at us.

That night I dreamed of being back in Orange County with Lydia, sheltering Chilean refugees. In my hands I held a passport that bore my own photograph below a stranger's name. I awoke recalling a phrase, *to make bomb with household cleaning products*.

I'm harboring fugitives in my sleep, I thought. But I wasn't trembling as I did most mornings, and knew what to do. The man who married Lydia to get himself a green card had once explained the process over a pan of her enchiladas. I had severely disappointed one father, barely showing up in time to hold his hand before he died. I would not let Cy down.

I dressed in my most boring tan trousers and a gray knit shirt. In the car, I obeyed every traffic sign like a man on parole. I would do nothing to draw attention to myself.

My first stop was the office of the Santa Monica *Evening Out- look*, where I hunted through microfilm of fifty-year-old newspapers for children's obituaries. These were more plentiful than I expected, and easy to spot, invariably framed with engravings of lambs or angels. In the summer of 1922 several young boys had died. I paid a nickel each to photocopy two obituaries. Cy could be reborn as Harold Novotnik or Addison Sommerfield.

I moved on to papers from the mid-forties and late fifties, approximating Charlée's and Tobey's birth years, and fed more nickels into the microfilm copier. Finally, as I'd known I would do eventually, I looked for obituaries of boys who would be my age if they had lived.

Gerald Ezekiel Sawyer's family had called him "Zeke." I was enchanted with the boy's earnest face, encircled by angels in a 1958 edition of the *Outlook*. Something utterly trusting in his smile reminded me of childhood pictures of myself. Zeke had "joined his Heavenly Father at age six to receive an early reward." The cause of death wasn't named. I slipped another nickel into the copier.

I spent the afternoon in downtown L.A., at the office of the county clerk—again reading microfilm, but now I studied death certificates. I deleted from my list of available identities any child whose death had been officially recorded. Few had been. After re-reading the cherub-adorned obituaries, I decided parents simply couldn't bear to officialize their toddlers' deaths. And that worked in my favor.

How would my parents have grieved for their only child if I'd pursued my suicide mission before Cy had the chance to rescue me? Would burying his only son have been worse for Alex than dying with the belief that I didn't give a shit? Had my last-minute appearance made any difference to him?

I shook off these thoughts and made my choices: Cy would be reincarnated as Addison Sommerfield, born in 1922 and dead at three months from unspecified causes. For Charlée's alter ego I chose Linda Ruckster, born in 1946, dead from diphtheria in 1950. Tobey would become Derek Hamilton, killed in a car crash in 1960 at age two. And Steve Susoyev would assume the identity of Zeke Sawyer.

I slept well that night, awoke early and drove to distant areas of greater Los Angeles to rent four post-office boxes, one in the name of each dead child. At an obscure bank I purchased a cashiers check payable to the county clerk. In the space for "Purchaser" I wrote, "Addison Sommerfield." At my office I typed a letter from Mr. Sommerfield, requesting a duplicate birth certificate, and gave it a business-like signature. Once that was in the mail I used different typewriters to prepare the other requests. I would send them in different types of envelopes with different kinds of stamps, enclosing money orders bought from separate vendors on various dates. I would not allow carelessness or haste to arouse suspicion among the county's petty bureaucrats.

At Seabird I watched the sun set over the Pacific and dialed my mother's number. My Aunt Jane answered. "Isabel showed me newspaper stories about what you're involved in," she said coolly. "When I saw you last week I didn't understand." The line went dead.

Some day, I wanted to believe, my mother *would* understand, and forgive me. In the meantime she had her sister for comfort, and I had work to do. I wrote her a card with the Seabird phone number, relying on Relationship Workbook language to guide me: ". . . Daddy may have felt hopeless and abandoned . . ."

Weeks of waiting for something without knowing what it was had plunged me into a grinding terror that felt endless. But now I rose each day with purpose and direction, and left early to check my post-office boxes for the birth certificates of four long-dead children. I lost interest in alcohol, and used Vitamin V only to sleep. I still avoided the office and the Bedford house, feeling more than ever like a threat to the other Vistans' mental stability.

EVENTUALLY MY TERRIFYING SUCCESS AT FRAUD drove me to the office of my confessor. "Waiting for the Social Security cards was scary," I told Felix Thornton one icy-clear morning. I could see snow on the San Gabriels through his window. "The last one took six weeks, and every morning I shook in bed."

How ironic that this walking shark was the only person I could talk to. Unlike the Vistans, Felix seemed to have nothing to compromise. Unlike Cy, he could listen attentively.

"The passports were tricky, but I was able to use real photographs of everyone." I heard the giddy rush in my voice. Tricky, indeed. One of Lydia's old contacts in Orange County had charged me fifteen thousand dollars for realistically back-dated passports, complete with Costa Rican visa and entry stamps. "The fingerprints could be a problem," I admitted.

Felix closed his eyes as if in prayer. "You're not my client, and so I'll only comment on my concern for Dr. Aaron. If you give him those passports it will be like handing a loaded gun to a man who's threatening suicide. Your mentor thrives on fame and exposure. He's known everywhere. I don't care what color he's dyed his hair. If he moves that little fugitive operation into the U.S., how long do you think it'll take him to attract the attention of the authorities?"

"But you've always said the best thing is for him to come back and face the charges."

"Significant difference between turning himself in and getting

sniffed out." Felix shook his head. "Got a passport for yourself?"
I shrugged. No point in lying to this man.

"You may need it." He opened his big hands in a protective
gesture. "You're risking an eighty-year prison sentence."

"I love Cy that much," I said. But what did "love" mean to an
attorney whose best-known client was currently under indictment
for murdering four people, including a fourteen-year-old girl?

Felix nodded seriously. "I don't see this kind of loyalty, even
in the strongest families."

"Crime families, you mean."

"What you've done is like a blood oath." He shook his head
again, very slowly. "What's your new name?"

"Zeke. Gerald Ezekiel Sawyer." I sighed, looking into those
cold eyes, regarding that sharp smile—the notorious features of
the one person who understood what I was going through. "I've
got to join them. Tobey must be exhausted. I'm the only one who
can take over for him."

"Nonsense. Your work is here where you have mobility.
When that kid's my age he'll look back on this as the most
exciting time of his life."

He stood, dismissing me. The most hated lawyer in the country had reassured me it was wise and proper to let Tobey rot in
exile. Sympathy from the devil felt like icy comfort.

WITH EACH NEW FELONY I compounded my withholds
on my friends. I drifted toward Felix for comfort and distanced
myself further from Ken and Willow and Theodora, whose
spiritual and psychic sustenance I craved, but with whom I rarely
shared meals or even conversation. Concern shone through their
tight smiles at increasingly alien staff meetings where I contributed nothing and daydreamed about prison.

I trimmed Zeke's newspaper photo, sealed it in tape and set it
among the snapshots and feathers at my little shrine. Each
evening, by flickering votive-light, the dead boy's face shone into
the yawning pit of my loneliness. I re-read *The Spy Who Came in
From the Cold* as if it were a training manual, and understood for
the first time the passages concerning the importance of living
one's role. Like a double agent, I had to protect myself not only
from external threats but from my most natural impulses, particularly by avoiding the people I loved. I lived my role even in my
sleep. During my early months as a growth case, I had given up

my identity to become Sneevie, to become Gollum. For the sake of an even greater cause I now was becoming Zeke Sawyer, and imagined forgetting my birth name.

During the next phone call Cy insisted I deliver the passports in person. "Tobey's dying to see you," he said. I recognized the manipulation but watched myself succumb. I was dying too.

Elsie had recently written a memo cataloguing the staff's chief concerns. Control of the fugitives' spending topped the list. Over four hundred thousand dollars had disappeared from Rancho Vista's investment accounts, drained away by me for wire transfers to a Costa Rican bank. I felt encouraged when the fugitives told me they had moved to a yoga retreat on a remote peninsula, which I imagined had to be much cheaper than the villa they had first occupied.

The woman at the Costa Rican consulate, who stamped a visa into my Gerald Sawyer passport, never looked up. How disappointing! *That is my picture and those are my fingerprints*, I wanted to brag, and I walked out wondering why more people didn't adopt second identities.

Because, I reminded myself when the Vitamin V wore off, one identity is all most people ever need. For the next twenty-two hours everything happened in a dull haze. Bank, ticket office, packing a bag and briefcase, taxi to the airport, sitting on the plane among excited tourists and bored businessmen—and, perhaps, a few like me who were traveling to Costa Rica because it was the nearest country that refused to allow the extradition of fugitives from U.S. justice.

The trio met me wearing tennis whites that glowed against their deeply-tanned skin. They could have been a visitors bureau commercial, laughing and waving as I descended the steps of the prop-jet into the swelter of the Nicoya Peninsula. I embraced Tobey first and kissed him on the forehead, then quickly hugged Charlée and Cy.

On the bus to the yoga retreat we chatted like tourists. Charlée wore clunky native jewelry and a big sun hat over her raven-black hair. Cy wore simple sandals. He'd kept his full beard dyed rusty-brown like his hair and eyebrows. Tobey had grown a downy-soft moustache as dark as his eyes, in sharp contrast to his bleached-yellow hair. His face was drawn and marked by crow's feet. He laughed too hard at stories about Theodora and other news from Beverly Hills. When I tried to look into his eyes, I noticed that the right side of his face was twitching.

As soon as we reached the yoga cabin, Cy sent Tobey out to shop. I had no choice except to sit down with him and Charlée in their modest room, but was determined to get some time alone with Tobey.

"Item one on the agenda," Cy said.

I handed him three crisp manila envelopes. Each contained a passport with matching birth certificate and Social Security card. Against all logic I felt a glow of pride in my work, and recalled the Open House invitation of a lifetime ago, and my excitement when Cy had smiled and said, "You're an artist, my son."

Cy opened the Addison Sommerfield passport first, and held it like a sacred object. In a hushed tone he said, "We can go anywhere in the world. We can stop living like hunted animals."

Charlée was equally thrilled. I received kisses and hugs like a man delivering Christmas toys to orphans. My main goal was accomplished, but I had my own agenda, stated in harsh terms in Elsie's memo, which I would have to translate into a softer approach. But if I didn't confront them with the memo, which felt like suicide, was there a "softer" way to address money or the fugitives' eventual surrender?

Charlée poured three glasses of wine and became chatty. "We've started a couples' group with some of the yoga teachers here. You might like to meet them."

I marveled, "Do you do therapy on everybody who walks by?"

Her eyes went cold. "We will not be defied like this! You know nothing of our life here. These young people love us. Don't tell me you're *jealous!*"

Her naïveté stunned me. "Do they know you're fugitives?"

"You *are* jealous," Cy snarled. "We go into exile, and in spite of our situation we attract growth cases. Meanwhile you squat on our property in L.A., inventing reasons why we should submit to the dungeon and the iron maiden."

I sucked at a tuft of my hair and wished I'd kept my mouth shut. Cy raved on until Charlée said something that enraged him. They got into their own argument and I found myself off the hotseat, wondering how Tobey could stand living with no privacy, always at their mercy.

Eventually he returned with a basket of fruit and hot *pan de queso*, rolls made with pungent cheese melted into the dough. Cy and Charlée argued while we ate. At about nine o'clock Cy suddenly said, "You boys should go to the village. There's a big celebration, festival of the local Coconut God." His tone and expression were those of a gracious host.

"Yes," Charlée said with equal courtesy, "go on over. It'll be fun for you two."

Tobey led me out to the beach, where we watched the dancing lights across the channel. "At home they're worried about money," I told him. "I'm relieved you're staying here."

He nodded and kicked sand.

"Don't tell me. That little cabin is a front for my benefit. You're really living at the Sheraton in town."

"Where do you suppose we've got all the shit you packed the day they left the U.S.?"

"And is Cy stashing money in Swiss bank accounts?"

"You know him better than he thinks you do."

"How is it, being with them?"

"They're constantly at each other's throats." The tic on the right side of his face was now out of control. He held his shapely lips tight, like a shy kid trying to hide braces.

I stroked his face. "And you have to listen to it."

"Usually I sit in the same room and read. I jump in if it looks like they're gonna hurt each other, and say as little as possible if he makes me give her feedback."

I dreaded the answer to my next question. "How long can you stand this?"

"I don't know. It's uglier than you can imagine."

"Use my ticket and go home. I'll stay here."

"Cy warned me you'd say that. Felix Thornton told him you felt guilty and wanted to trade places with me. I can't leave. You need to be back there, handling the stuff you're good at. And I need to be here to—you know." His sad eyes explained he was still servicing Charlée.

"If I ever become a fugitive," I whispered, "I hope there's some money left."

"This fugitive shit is nothing to joke about."

"That wasn't a joke. Getting those passports, I've committed more crimes than they have. Not to mention the *same* crimes."

Tobey stiffened and pulled away. "You mean with me."

"Well, yeah."

"And you think—"

"I'm not sure of anything any more." I pictured Elizabeth, revealing all she knew about us to a spellbound detective.

"Jesus," he wailed, "you don't know me at all!" He started down the beach. I ran after him, and he swung around. "You

don't love me, you've just been nice to me because you're afraid
I'll hand you over to the cops. You sent me into this nightmare
so I'd be out of the way. I can imagine what you thought the day
you dropped me at the airport—'Thank God that brat's gone.'"

I touched his arm and he wrenched free, yelling, "Get the fuck
away from me!" He ran inland and disappeared into the trees.

I lunged after him, fell in the sand, got up, stumbled a few feet
and fell again. The pale moonlight didn't penetrate the overhanging trees. Farther on I tripped through a jumble of waist-
high vines and shouted, but heard only the roaring surf and the
popping fireworks from across the channel.

I trudged through the palms and finally found the path back
to the cabin. The door stood open, and Cy and Charlée's muted
voices drifted out. Before I was fully inside I knew I was in
trouble: my briefcase lay open on the floor, its brass latches
smashed, the balance of power reëstablished. The Vistan First
Couple glared at me. They had crumpled Elsie's memo, then
smoothed it on a low table. Cy picked it up and read in an oily
voice, "*Item four. Control of money and spending.* Honey, the people
we're depending on for our survival have written that they must
'*plug up all the rat holes.*'" He grasped Charlée's hand. "That's an
important issue for our conference with Steve, don't you agree?"

"Vitally important."

"We may have to travel north. Certain parties have forgotten
who *earned* the money that requires such careful control."

I knew better than to argue. While they ranted, I lay a pad on
the floor and tried to sleep. Even after they fell silent and turned
off the lights, I clutched my pillow, trembling.

Tobey padded into the cabin at sunrise looking as if he had
cried all night. Cy and Charlée didn't question his dark attitude
toward me, so similar to their own.

"By the way," Cy asked me, after a silent breakfast of fruit and
juice, "is that father of yours dead yet?"

I shook my head. Soon they put me on the jitney for the airport. Tobey gave me a perfunctory hug, but refused to look me in
the face. I stepped onto the plane feeling as battered as my
briefcase, which I had tied shut with twine. My morning tremors
overtook me, and my hands shook so badly I had to go into the
restroom and gnaw the lid off my Vitamin V bottle.

32

THE NEWS FROM THE "REAL WORLD" WAS EVEN MORE DISTURBING THAN USUAL. "Hundreds died last night in an apparent mass suicide," Cronkite reported. The television displayed heaped corpses, including those of many children—members of a religious group who had lined up to drink sweetened cyanide. I watched the footage with grim fascination while Cronkite updated the body count: six hundred and rising.

The phone rang for the first time in weeks. I stared at it. Even Theodora rarely reached out to me. Finally I answered and heard my mother's voice. "That could be you and your friends on the front page," she said, "when you're all found dead in your tents."

Never before had I welcomed alcohol's effect on her. Without it she wouldn't have called. "Actually," I said, trying to sound upbeat, "they weren't *tents* and we don't live in them any more. I'm staying at a beach house in Malibu. Would you like to come up and—"

The line went dead. I began to cry. Reconciliation would take time. But she had saved my phone number, and that meant she cared whether I lived or died.

Each morning I called the message service but there had been nothing from down south for over a month. I began to think I might never hear from the fugitives again, but today "Mr. Winters" wanted me to call. I had gotten dulled to the possibility of a life-and-death emergency, but drove to the village and found a pay phone I'd never used, in back of the only bar in town. I barely had a chance to say "Hi" to Tobey before Cy asked in a gravelly voice, "Where are you?"

"What's the emergency?"

"We will not tolerate this! Where the hell are you?"

"California."

On an extension Charlée said with strained mellowness, "Steve, you do sound evasive."

Cy barked, "I can tell him how he sounds." He made an exasperated noise with his sinuses and admonished Tobey not to chop the celery into such tiny pieces. There was a tinkle of ice, the fizz of soda and the glugging, splashing sound of a bottle being emptied into a glass.

"Okay, fellahs," Charlée said, "we've got a lot to cover. Steve, you've seen the news about that religious sect?"

So this was the life-and-death emergency. "Those people who made friends with Kool-Aid?"

"Goddammit," Cy roared, "this is very fucking serious."

I replied in my most mollifying tone, "The news proves that everything you've taught us about preachers is true."

"Listen to me. This incident fans the flames at the office of the Inquisition. Our enemies will take advantage of our situation and compare us to that cult. If I could, I'd hold a press conference tomorrow in Beverly Hills. But you've got to do it for me."

I had never realized so clearly that making Cy angry could speed things along, because it got him to organize his thoughts. "Okay," I said, ready to promise anything if it would end this conversation. "A press conference."

Charlée faked a breezy laugh. "Cy's exaggerating. But talk to the *community*. The Vistans, the people who come to the Marathons, whatever else you guys have going on up there, all that good P.R. work you're doing so Cy and I can get a fair trial when we come back."

It's not just P.R., I wanted to say. And nobody but me is doing it for you two anymore. We all know you're never coming back.

Cy mumbled away from the phone, then said clearly, "Jesus. Tobey's watching a news bulletin. They've counted over nine hundred bodies. Some have gunshot wounds." He slurped at his drink. "Okay. Charlée's will read some notes we've made. Take this to the Vistans *tonight*. Tell them you saw the news and came up with this analysis." He explained the subtle connections between his political persecution and the mass suicide in South America. "I can just hear that twat telling the papers her daughter was in a *sex cult*."

"First," Charlée said, "remind people that Vista was *never* a religion. Nothing like this Jonestown outfit. Cy is a highly-respected psychiatrist."

"That's right," I said, trying to sound enthusiastic. "Those people were like slaves. We're your *students*."

"Exactly!" Cy cried. "My God, I've cured schizophrenics." He allowed Charlée to list several particulars regarding the Ranch's legitimacy, then interrupted, "Steve. Listen carefully. If we go to prison, I must know one thing will be taken care of. Steve? Are you with me?"

"Sure. What do you want me to do?"

"There's a certain pretty *jeune fille* whose lying little face has a date with hydrochloric destiny."

"What?" Jesus, what was he asking me to do?

"And that girl's mother needs to be put out of her misery, and everybody else's."

I swallowed my horror and tried to stay calm. "When shall I call you next?"

"Tomorrow. Let us know if everyone understands about Jonestown and Vista."

The thought popped into my mind that the person who understood best was my mother. I hung up knowing I wouldn't talk to the Vistans or the press or anyone else about the purported differences between Rancho Vista and the Jonestown cult. And as much as I wanted to forget them, the words "hydrochloric destiny" kept swimming through my head.

The next night I tried the fugitives' number and got a Spanish version of "The number you have dialed is not . . ."

THE TELEPHONE HAD LONG BEEN MY ENEMY, but when I was alone at Seabird I answered reflexively in case Felix or my mother called. On the rare occasions it did ring, Theodora was checking on whether I'd remembered to eat breakfast. Weeks passed with no word from Felix or any of Cy's cast of alter egos. I still held out hope for a miracle—though even in my wildest fantasies I couldn't imagine what would bring back all that had been lost.

During the evening news on a foggy Monday, the phone jangled and I grabbed it.

"Don't hang up," Charlée said. "I'm in jail."

I asked, "Where's Tobey?" without thinking, then added, "What happened?"

"We had to cut the Gordian knot." She spoke as if reciting a memorized speech, and explained that Tobey had called Elizabeth and found her friendly. "So I got on the phone and told her we wanted to send her to art school in London or wherever she decided to study. She said she was sorry we were suffering, and agreed to have lunch with me today."

"What? Wait, where the fuck did this happen? You're all back in the country?"

"Yes," she said matter-of-factly. I punched the wall and she went on, "I met Elizabeth in Laguna. We had a lovely lunch and talked about her education. She agreed not to testify against Cy and me, and I handed her a package containing fifty thousand dollars. Then two men in suits walked over to our table and arrested me." In a guttural tone she added, "She was wearing a *microphone*. I'm in Orange County Jail."

"Does Cy know?"

"It's like the movies. You're my one phone call."

Me? *Why me?* Well, I was still their caretaker. "I'll come and bail you out. Will they give you back the money?"

"They confiscated it. And thanks, but they're holding me without bail until Cy turns himself in." In a child's voice she added, "But I *can* have visitors."

"You must be scared, but this is a wonderful development. Cy'll plead guilty or whatever, and you'll both get probation. The nightmare is over." My heart thudded. I was already planning my call to Felix. *It's over* was going to feel so good to say.

"IT'S JUST BEGINNING," FELIX BARKED OVER THE PHONE. By the time I reached him, the DA's office had already alerted him to Charlée's arrest. "Cy and Tobey used those magic-carpet passports to make themselves scarce."

"Oh," I murmured, then thanked him and hung up. Now I understood why Charlée had used her one phone call to reach me instead of Cy: she'd *known* Cy would run if her bribery attempt backfired. The old fuck had abandoned her, and she'd known he would.

Felix disposed of her no-bail order before noon the next day, and she clung to me outside the jail. I let her cry in my arms, then drove her to Malibu. Travis organized a shuttle from Beverly Hills so a few Vistans at a time could visit to welcome her home. I moved back to Bedford Drive and looked forward to sharing meals with a houseful of people.

In the morning Felix called and announced, "Your Mr. Wanderer is overseas. Skipping the country to avoid prosecution was bad enough. Leaving his wife to stand trial on her own makes him look like a selfish bastard."

I didn't bother trying to argue with this evaluation.

"Every minute he stays away," Felix went on, "the worse it'll be when he's finally sentenced."

"You've told him that?"

"Ever tried telling that man anything he didn't want to hear?"

I groaned.

"One more thing," said Felix. "Your extraordinary loyalty. Your blood oath. Charlée's in even deeper than you. The head of a crime family never hangs his faithful assistants out to dry like this. He may kill them for betrayal, but he never betrays *them*. Aaron doesn't deserve you kids. I'm not the psychiatrist here, but that man needs therapy."

I decided to close Seabird immediately and put it on the market before the next mortgage payment was due. Charlée readily agreed the place should be sold. She asked to help, with an attitude that struck me as humble and shy. I understood that her life would be over if she went to prison. Whatever charges I faced, I was at worst an accessory after-the-fact and would get off with a lesser sentence. She had no such hope. For the first time I looked forward to being with her.

"It meant a lot," she told me, while we shopped for cleaning supplies, "when you offered to come right down and bail me out of jail."

I took my time and looked her full in the face. "I've done a lot of thinking since you guys went on sabbatical. You're sort of like a battered wife."

She stiffened. "What's that supposed to mean?" Then her voice softened. "Cy's not an ordinary man. I always knew there'd be a cost to marrying him. I guess part of the cost is being misunderstood by the people I have to depend on."

We spent a week cleaning, packing, and talking as never before. She scrubbed toilets and scoured the oven—determined to get top dollar for the house. I climbed a ladder to wash the twelve-foot living room windows, and she stood below, rinsing the sponges. "I've taken you for granted," she confessed. "This place is a palace. I feel like I'm coming out of a dream."

Her unprecedented apologies amazed me. After I finished the windows I climbed down and embraced her. I admitted I'd been jealous when she came to the Ranch, that I'd enjoyed her vulnerability during her months of degradation. "It's like we gang-raped you."

She pulled away. "It was my *process*. No need for melodrama."

THE FIRST CALL I RECEIVED back at the office was from Puck's mother. From a family marathon I remembered her as a tense little woman.

"Dr. Aaron just phoned me," she said in an unsteady voice. "He asked for money and told me, 'I saved your son's life.' I said I appreciate everything he's done, but I'm a widow on a fixed income."

"Of course," I replied politely.

"The bastard! He said, 'Now I understand why your son slashed his wrists when he was living with you.'"

While she cried I repeatedly apologized. *Cy out of control*, I scribbled on my pad. She threatened to report Cy's call to the police, and I didn't try to dissuade her. Once Charlée was settled, I would be able to refer calls like this to her.

The next day Wanda Richter phoned, even more upset than Puck's mother. She'd published nothing about the Vistans since the indictments. "I would do anything for Cy," she said, "but he's gone too far. He and Tobey stayed with my father in Tel Aviv. I set it up to be helpful, when Cy called me after Charlée's arrest. My father didn't know they were wanted by the police." Her voice shot up. "Cy left Papa with a three-thousand-dollar phone bill! If you don't pay your phone bill in Israel you go to *jail*."

I assured her I would send a money order, and scrawled *Old man dangerous*. "Did Cy mention where he was going next?"

"If I knew, I'd be talking to the F.B.I. right now, not to you. Papa said he asked a lot of questions about Egypt, but that might have been a ruse."

Egypt, I wrote. *Anywhere*.

That evening Charlée and I sipped white wine beside the Bedford house pool. Trying to sound casual, I asked, "When do you think you'll talk to Cy again?" She was the second-sharpest person I knew, and I didn't want her to guess what I was up to. "I have some money freed up I'd like to send him."

"Felix thinks he can get my charges dropped. Because I was *brain*washed. But for that to happen, I would have to agree to testify against Cy. Clever system we've got, huh?"

"So you don't know where he is?"

Her face was drawn, without makeup, and her mousy roots were growing out, yet she looked younger and prettier to me than the day I'd met her. She studied me from behind her sunglasses. "I've had several sessions with a court-appointed counselor. It's required because I'm considered a sex offender."

I placed a hand on her shoulder.

"The counseling's helped me understand I *was* a battered wife, like you said. Physically, emotionally. Sexually. If I let Cy use me like he's used you, to run money and information, I would continue the abuse and open myself to more legal charges. And I will agree to testify against him, because I know I won't have to do it. He'll never surrender."

She pulled off her dark glasses and looked into my eyes. "Okay. He called two nights ago from his suite at the Royal Mansour Hotel in Casablanca, begging for money. I pretended I couldn't hear him. Then I unplugged the phone."

"Well, I should get this cash to him."

"Do. Please." She put her sunglasses back on and squeezed my hand so hard it hurt. I saw tears leaking out from behind the dark lenses.

WHEN I PHONED FELIX'S OFFICE in the morning, the secretary said he wouldn't return my call for at least three days. I persisted and she told me to look at the morning paper.

I retrieved it from the driveway. The *Times'* front page proclaimed, GRISLY MOB MURDER. An Indiana farmer's dog had unearthed a human head from a soybean field. Forensic tests confirmed it was the head of Ralph "the Roach" Ryan, Felix's client.

A warm calm descended over me. I knew what to do even without Felix's guidance. Cy had been taken over by a dangerous creature—the creature that had used my resentment against Charlée, and my fear of Gollum, to corral me into unspeakable crimes against others. But inside Cy a compassionate man was hidden. He was in my life because, when I met him, his kindness overwhelmed me. I had to find that man.

I called the American Embassy in Casablanca and asked where a U.S. fugitive should go to surrender. An official explained that the local police were "very coöperative." Then I phoned the Royal Mansour hotel and learned that Addison Sommerfield was still registered. After that I spent several intense hours making arrangements. I flew to Paris under my own name, taking return tickets for Cy and Tobey, in their real names. During the flight I slept little and quietly rehearsed what I must tell Cy. *We've gone too far,* I kept repeating under my breath. *We're hurting people.*

On the short flight to Casablanca, the path before me was clear for the first time since I'd hitchhiked into the wilderness through a blizzard. Cy and I had made choices that carried fearsome consequences. Running away created soul-crushing anxiety far worse than the consequences we had avoided. I would take Cy back to L.A. and we would turn ourselves in. No felony would go unconfessed. We might serve some prison time, but more likely the judge would recognize Cy's contribution to society, and my desire to serve my mentor, and we would be released—finally free to return to Rancho Vista and the life we were meant to live.

I took a taxi to the hotel, which stood back from the street like a grand mosque. The desk clerk called the Sommerfield suite and was told to send up the American visitor.

"Well," said Cy when he opened the door. "It's the reprobate remainder, come to buy back his place in heaven." He walked across the room, sank into the cushions of a divan and sipped a cold drink.

I stepped inside. The place was a mess—not his usual creative mess of papers and books, but a chaos of dirty clothes and newspapers. I shut the door and put down my small suitcase. My hands curled into fists but I leaned over the old man and kissed him on the cheek. "Where's Tobey?"

"Don't insult me by playing dumb. I know you engineered his desertion."

"His *what?*"

Cy had had gained weight and his skin was sallow, but the cobalt eyes bored into me as they always had. "Either you've become a better liar or you really don't know. Your little catamite has flown the coop. If you didn't do it, his sainted mother must have sent him money."

Why had I been foolish enough to think I could determine the agenda for a meeting with Cy? I felt dizzy and forced myself to sit beside him. "When did he leave?"

"Ask him on *your* time. Did you bring any of the money you've embezzled from me?"

The question roused me like a kick in the head. "It's over," I said. "We're going back to L.A."

"I thought as much," he said smoothly, but his eyes betrayed a flash of panic. He held up his hands in surrender. "It's been a grand adventure. But I'm tired. You can't possibly understand what tired really means. You're too damn young and selfish."

"We've hurt too many people, Cy."

"Speak for yourself. I saved your life, in case you've forgotten. Charlée hurt people. I let the cunt hurt you, and I regret that. But if you understood me you could not judge me."

"We *tortured* her! You've said yourself that power corrupts—"

"And a twenty-year-old faggot corrupts a sixteen-year-old child. Are you ready to face Tobey's mother on the witness stand after I face Elizabeth's?"

I flushed, but refused to take the bait. I had never won an argument with Cy. "It's time," I insisted.

"Time for you to get out of my life, you little psychopath." He adjusted his cushions.

I heard the pistol click before the silver zero of its barrel flashed.

I locked eyes with Cy, stood, and moved toward the phone.

I picked up the receiver and a woman said, "*Bonjour.*"

Across the room Cy held the pistol firmly. With one eye closed, he had the gun trained on the spot between my eyes.

Sweat trickled down my back, but I felt strangely calm. I'd never imagined it would end like this, my head blown apart by the man who had saved me. "Please send the police to Dr. Sommerfield's room," I said to the operator. "*Les gendarmes immédiatement, s'il vous plaît.*"

Cy slowly swung the gun around to his temple and pulled the trigger. It clicked smoothly. "You little prick," he said. "Do you think I'd point a loaded gun at you?"

33

THE PRISONER HUNCHED over the defense table in a rumpled suit. I spotted him from the rear wall of the packed courtroom and wondered why someone in Felix's office hadn't gotten the jacket pressed. At one time that would have been my job. I would have done it gladly, and given the old man's hair a trim. I ached to call out, Please, Cy, sit up straight. Turn around and see who's come. It's not too late to show you can face your mistakes.

But the miracle worker, the healer, was humbled beyond recognition. I wished the judge and this crowd could experience the magnificence I had witnessed the day Cy strode before the mourners at a young suicide's funeral, condemning the psychiatric establishment and showing that the fallen youth was a victim of society's fetish with conformity. If these people could see the courage of the man who had summoned Gollum and other demons to the surface—not to cast them out, but to welcome them into the human family!

The courtroom hummed with the murmurs of the curious, the concerned, the angry and the vindicated. Charlée and Zoë whispered head-to-head like lifelong girlfriends. Elizabeth, her flaming hair in tight pigtails, sat between her mother and a man who looked like a less expensive lawyer than Felix. Wanda Richter spoke into a tiny tape recorder. Beside her, the gay psychiatrist Nelson Christopher sat with arms folded.

Travis wore a defiantly flowered shirt and stood near a side wall, as if ready to denounce the proceedings—supportive to the end of the man who had believed in him. Theodora sat near him in a dark suit whose skirt reached past her knees, with stockings and a stylish hat. Her posture and outfit proclaimed, *Cyrus Aaron rescued me from a life of crime!*

She and Travis acknowledged me only by lowering their eyes. To them and many others I imagined I was Judas, a beloved disciple turned traitor. Vivian and Elizabeth gazed past me as if I were a stranger. I imagined they felt I'd done the right thing, but far too late and probably for the wrong reasons. Josh, stiff in a polyester suit, did nod to me. But I didn't see Ken or Willow or Elsie, who might understand why I had made this happen. The one person I really wanted to see, Tobey, was probably in the care of a cult deprogrammer.

Under headlines that varied little from a single theme—*SEX CULT LEADER SURRENDERS!*—all the focus was on punishing Cy. His followers were considered pathetic dupes. My attempt to surrender for passport fraud amounted only to a colorful footnote to the story of Cy's arrest. "Go and sin no more, kid," an assistant federal prosecutor had told me.

On the bench the judge turned the pages of a document, and I thought even he must be nervous. If Cy received probation, the press would crowd around Vivian on the courthouse steps. She would brand the judge an accomplice in the crimes of a pervert who had preyed on a young girl in her family's darkest days. If Cy got anything near the maximum sentence, Felix Thornton would protest that the court had dispatched a penitent man to certain death among killers whose sole claim to humanity was that they exterminated child molesters.

Who would declare for the court record that something wonderful had happened at Rancho Vista? And that Cyrus Aaron was responsible? Yes, he was a damaged human being who had allowed power to corrupt him—but it was power we Vistans had gladly given him. I imagined writing on an index card and passing it to the judge: *Why don't we just tie Cy up and throw a few tons of horseshit at him?*

The bailiff announced the case number and intoned, "The People versus Cyrus Aaron." The judge removed his glasses and looked straight at Cy, as if he'd read about the importance of eye contact to the Vistan leader. The crowd silenced itself.

"Doctor Aaron, you have submitted to this court's jurisdiction by pleading guilty to several charges against you, including statutory rape, infamous crimes against nature and kidnapping. Your case is one of the most difficult of my career. That is saying a great deal."

Felix extended an arm around the back of Cy's chair in a protective gesture. Cy's shoulders remained hunched but he tipped his head up toward the bench.

"As a psychotherapist you have violated your professional trust in the utmost manner." The judge consulted his papers, then added, sounding puzzled, "You have written me a thirty-four-page letter." Felix slowly shook his head while the reprimand went on. "In carefully-chosen language you say, 'There's no denying I did a wrong thing' and you ask me for mercy. You

admit your actions 'constituted a departure from society's trust.' "
The judge again zeroed in on Cy's face. "A 'departure'? You
violated troubled people who trusted you with their lives, their
children, their souls." His passionate tone shocked me, yet the
lecture seemed to suggest tolerance. He could have banged his
gavel and said, *Forty years in the big house! Next case.* Instead he was
taking time to scold Cy, then could give him a suspended
sentence without appearing soft on crime.

For years my only goal had been to keep Cy out of prison.
Now I dreaded the fruit of that labor. On probation and stripped
of his career, Cy would demand more than ever, if he spoke to
me. Which would hurt more: to continue as the center of his
support system or be flung into outer darkness?

"I am impressed by your accomplishments," the judge went
on, "and the twenty letters submitted by respected professionals
in the legal and medical fields, and even the clergy, who have
implored me not to send you to prison." He shuffled through
more papers. "I have sentenced hundreds of child molesters. But
for the first time I've received clemency recommendations from
juvenile court officers, college deans, a Nobel Laureate and a
Jesuit professor."

He surveyed the room over his reading glasses, probably wondering how many of the luminaries who had written to him were
present today. "These letters have forced me to wrestle with my
decision. But I am more interested in *your* letter, Dr. Aaron. You
cite your childhood problems as if they caused your aberrant and
destructive behavior as a psychotherapist. You write, '*My mother
was killed when I was five years old. I have sought women's love in inappro-
priate ways ever since.*' You have entered a guilty plea, no doubt on
the advice of your attorney, but nowhere in your thirty-four page
statement do I see any understanding that what you did was truly
wrong. You harmed a young girl and her family. Your violations
of trust cannot be explained away in psychological terms."

The truth of the words burned into me. I wanted to shout, *Cy,
are you listening?* A loyal friend would have said these things long
ago. A friend who wasn't complicit in the violations of innocent
people's trust.

Vivian stroked her daughter's hair, adjusting the barrettes just
as she had the morning I first saw her—when she came to
believe, at her son's funeral, that her wounded family might be
healed at Rancho Vista.

The courtroom rustled with whispers while the judge consulted more documents. He silenced everyone with a quick rap of the gavel and announced, "I find that a prison sentence is necessary to instruct you that you cannot take advantage of your professional position to exploit children for your own pleasure."

Cy's head fell into his hands. The air was filled with cries of outrage and vindication, of pity and wrath, and the crowd ignored the banging gavel. Travis, his hair flying behind him, charged forward, but a guard quickly wrestled him outside. The crowd silenced itself as the judge dryly detailed the charges and corresponding sentences. "For count one of statutory rape, six years; for count two, four years . . . ." On and on, a jumble of concurrents and consecutives I couldn't follow, enough to keep Cy behind bars until he was a very old man, with obscure possibilities for reductions and clemency. The numbers swam in my mind as the bailiff announced the next case.

Cy's head sank to the defense table and he looked as if he would need to be carried out. The courtroom doors clacked open. Briefly I caught sight of the few people who might be willing to talk to me—Charlée and Zoë, Wanda Richter, Nelson Christopher—but I ran for the hallway and slid along a side corridor, in terror of getting caught in an elevator with anyone who had shared my world. I couldn't stand the thought of being interviewed, or comforted, or scolded. I wanted to run where no one had ever heard of Cyrus Aaron, if such a place existed.

Finally I found a narrow stairway down to an exit. At the bottom I nodded to a guard, followed a corridor away from the grand entrance of the courthouse and slipped out through a janitor's door. A morning fog had burned away, and I squinted into the sun. At my side the traffic noise pummeled me. I walked furiously for a few blocks, then slumped against a mailbox feeling I might pass out. Slowly my mind clunked through the numbers: with all the consecutive sentences, Cy was going to spend at least three years in prison—could he use that time to meditate on what the judge had said, or would the experience harden him even further?

My beloved community had crumbled, but my relief intoxicated me. I had nothing in particular to live for, beyond the overwhelming prospect of trying to make peace with people I had hurt. But I had no compelling desire to die. Certainly I must thank Cy for that.

I had worked for so long to protect him from prison, but then forced him to surrender because living like a hunted animal had made the old man dangerous. But wasn't the point of the judge's lecture that Cy had already been dangerous? Hadn't people I should have trusted sensed something wrong and tried to warn me—Lydia and my parents, even Eric, Josh and Vivian, by leaving? Suddenly I ached to see Eric, who, I imagined, was still planting pumpkins in the gardens of Rancho Vista. And Lydia! I even had the time to find her in Chile or wherever she might be.

From somewhere behind me I heard a shout. I froze at the sound of my name, then sprang through an oleander thicket and into a parking lot. Someone was running up behind me, crashing through the shrubbery, yelling, "It's over!"

Tobey threw himself on me and sobbed. Our arms tangled in wild, wrestling recognition, and we fell together against a parked car.

I straightened up and cradled his head against my chest. "Were you there?"

Gradually his sobs subsided into long, low gasps. "I was waiting outside. For you."

Both of us panted, catching our breath, still stumbling a little. I couldn't speak. Tobey had not given up on me. "I've waited my whole life for someone who would wait for me," I finally whispered.

He seemed to melt against me. "I'm scared."

"Me too." I gripped his hands, muscular and warm, and raised them to my lips to kiss each finger. The power of my love for this young man made me light-headed, and I believed suddenly that anything was possible. I recalled a magazine photo—a white tipi against a violet sky, the vision of a beginning. "I heard about an enchanting resort in the Colorado mountains. I think this is the off-season."

"Two weeks, max," he said. "I'm going back to school this fall. UCLA. How about you?"

"You mean we can't disappear into the wilderness?" I kissed him again. "Oh, hell. I *was* thinking about law school or something. After I see my mother and track down an old friend in South America."

THE FINAL SESSION

The Cult of the Victim-Perpetrators

It should be very obvious that someone who was
allowed to feel free and strong from childhood
does not have the need to humiliate another person.

Alice Miller
Thou Shalt Not Be Aware

WE ARE ALL FAMILIAR WITH THAT SPECIES OF ABUSE whose participants can be identified readily either as perpetrators or as victims. This story is full of appalling examples—Charlée's gang rape, the alienation of Elizabeth from her mother for pederastic purposes, Eric's shunning, and old-fashioned wife-beating and child-endangerment, all camouflaged as psychotherapy.

I cannot claim to have suffered much of this readily-recognized nature of mistreatment, despite the episode recounted in Chapter 23, when Cy broke my ribs. But far beyond that dark night, I consider myself a victim, and cry out for understanding, because throughout this time I was an apprentice perpetrator—ready to rape and alienate, to shun and endanger, at the request of the man whom I had adopted as my father, mentor and savior. And I choose the word "request" here consciously: by now the reader knows that Cy didn't have to command me to do anything, so eager was I to please and support him.

Stanley Milgram's notorious 1962 obedience study at Yale, timed to coincide with the trial of Adolph "only following orders" Eichmann, involved subjects called teachers who believed they were administering electric shocks of up to 450 volts to slow learners in a memory experiment. The study shocked the world—*How horrible human beings can be!* Milgram "debriefed" his subjects with assurances that no one had really been injured, that the screaming learners had been acting, and he sent the subjects on their way with four dollars and fifty cents for each hour of their participation. In Milgram's authoritatively titled book on the study, *Obedience to Authority*, little can be found concerning the effect of the experience on the "teachers" who discovered this capacity for evil residing within them.

Milgram silenced his own conscience by administering to the "teachers" a questionnaire whose results showed that most did not regret having participated. What he failed to understand was that they were *still* obeying authority while they filled out the questionnaire! I can only guess that some of them continue to have nightmares about their participation.

When I am offered positions of authority, I think, *Please, don't trust me. Given the chance, I will rape, alienate and injure* . . . Like the Milgram subjects, like soldiers who commit atrocities for their fatherland or to avoid court-martial, I occupy a terrain where victim-perpetrators are known only for their monstrous deeds, not for their own suffering, where they live silently with a knowledge that finds few advocates. Whatever I do, some people who knew me when I was nineteen years old will distrust me until the day I die. Those people particularly fear what I write here, because even my act of contrition threatens their privacy.

TO THOSE WHO LIVED at the place I'm calling "Rancho Vista" and dispute the veracity of anything they find in these pages, I say Okay, it's true, Puck and I did jack off into the cake batter that night. I did a lot of demented things that I can't blame directly on the old man and that didn't make it into my memoir. Also, you won't find Hermione Pitt in an Internet search, because the woman she is based on has living children whom I don't want to hurt with further publicity.

"Vistans" who have read pieces of the manuscript have already protested, "But it didn't happen like that!" and here's the irony: In spite of my bluster about protecting myself, I've tried like hell to protect the privacy of others—married men who would prefer I didn't advertise their youthful prowess at fellatio, women who insist their childhood incest stories belong to them, not to me . . . and people who, like me, committed countless felonies in service of a cause that we believed was far more important than our own liberty, safety and sanity. Even the man I call Felix Thornton, a Mafia lawyer who counts convicted murderers among his close friends, would prefer anonymity in the case of our wilderness sex commune. Such notoriety might taint his burgeoning political career.

And I've left out a lot of things I just couldn't figure out how to write about. Cy did conduct LSD therapy at the Ranch, at least once—Willow was the guest of honor, and I saw her swallow ten pink Sandoz capsules. Someday she might decide to write about the experience. I wouldn't know where to begin. And I've chosen not to include "Harem Night," an event I didn't attend because it was a women's thing—the most beautiful and trustworthy of the Rancho Vista women provided a night of sensual fantasy-fulfillment for a visiting businessman, who paid about ten thousand dollars for the privilege—an amazing sum considering (at least according to the whispers I overheard later) that he never had an orgasm.

In spite of our diligent journal-keeping, I've had to rely on memory. When I found myself ready to start telling the story of my life at Rancho Vista, my writings were unavailable. Cy and Charlée burned them in the fireplace at Seabird. They burned thousands of journals and letters, belonging to eighty-some people. I was present to help determine what to burn and what to keep. Cy saved materials that could incriminate people who, he feared, might turn against him some day. How honored I felt, because he trusted me enough to burn everything I had written!

HAVE I REACHED YOU, "DR. AARON," OR MERELY EXACTED REVENGE? About a hundred and fifty thousand words ago, I said I wanted to thank the man who had saved my life. Thank you, Cy. And I want to acknowledge how much I sometimes miss you. After living for ten years with a man who could make a vibrant anthropology seminar out of a commercial for toilet-bowl cleaner, I admit my daily life can be a bit colorless.

Are you truly a psychopath, beyond humanity's reach? Prison certainly didn't reach you—you came out of there bitterly blaming Charlée, Vivian, me, Tobey, even Felix. But in a deep part of my soul, I want to believe it is possible for the hand of God to stroke your now-eighty-year-old head and for you to say, *I hurt people and I want to make things right before it's too late.* If that can happen, I'll be glad, but you trained me well in the meaning of Greek legend, so I recognize the hubris in this. If God has a plan for you, who am I to appoint myself the executor of that plan?

I have told what I know, but I cannot curse your name or your legacy. In spite of your rapacious self-indulgence, you rescued me from my pathetic suicide fantasy and managed to generate hope in many young hearts, including mine. You taught me far more about humankind than I wanted to know, and I am sad to report that nothing you taught me was untrue. But I also learned that human beings have the capacity to become better than they are, sometimes in response to inhuman challenges. A few of your followers have killed themselves or otherwise failed to thrive, but most of us have stayed close to at least a few members of our tribe, and developed rewarding lives. Considering where we were when you found us, how could we deny your part in this miracle?

My passion for telling this story has given my life meaning and shape for over twenty years. Now I must release myself, and you. May God be with us both.

THE END

EPILOGUE

THIS BOOK BEGAN TO POUR OUT OF ME IN 1987 as the gruesomely **TRUE STORY**. Five years later, a therapist pronounced me free of trauma, and I pronounced my manuscript complete. I expected everyone who had lived at the Ranch to be thrilled that our story was finally being told. I thought it was an important story, and I intended it to be helpful to others. Here are excerpts from some of the responses I received to my request for people's blessing:

> *What you have written imperils everything important to me. How could you possibly expect my "blessing"?*

and:

> *Think what this book will do to other people who lived at the Ranch. If you follow through with this thing it will probably be a best-seller. I can picture you on daytime talk shows, revealing intimate details of other people's lives and claiming you have our blessing to do so.*

A Vistan with a political career appealed to me to protect her livelihood:

> *My job requires a security clearance. The Senator's office knows I worked at a therapy ranch in Colorado. Before my last promotion, FBI agents went to Keystone and interviewed some locals . . . In this environment, but how could I possibly explain what went on at the Ranch?*

Here's the closest anyone came to threatening a lawsuit:

> *Since we were all patients, anything you reveal is protected as confidential therapeutic communication. Even if you write the truth, which is difficult to imagine, you can be sued by every one of us if you reveal anything of an even remotely personal nature.*

I had asked for the blessing of so many people! I received lots of other letters, and some phone calls, and for a while I feared that someone might even be causing me to have bad dreams.

I dumped my important and helpful book into the bottom drawer of my filing cabinet and went off in search of a hobby. One night, a year later, the filing cabinet started to glow with a rich, pulsing light. I excavated the single letter that all along had prevented me from throwing the whole nine-hundred page mess into the fireplace:

September 21, 1992

Dearest Steve,

The book you are writing will open old wounds, for me and anyone who lived at the Ranch. But doesn't someone need to tell this story and make it a part of history? Doesn't the world need to understand how easily normal people can be drawn into something dreadfully abnormal and destructive?

Honey, I always knew you were a victim too. If your healing requires you to write about what happened to you, who am I to stand in your way? I pray that what you write will help others to heal as well. You don't need my blessing to do anything, but since you asked, it's yours.

With my love always,
Vivian

Thank you, Vivian. I changed your name and a few other identifying details, but like most people who appear in disguise here, you'll know who you are.

FINALLY, I RECEIVED an offer of collaboration:

Transcription of Answering Machine Message
from Cyrus Aaron
October 23, 1992

Steve, is that really you? Willow just told me you're writing a book about our noble experiment. You're absolutely the right person for this project, the one I could always count on to get things organized and finished. Remember when I appointed you our community's official scribe?

Since I got out of the big house I've been overwhelmed with the fucking work of putting my life back together. I'm dying to write our story but where do I start? Listen, you're a rich lawyer now and you can afford a long-distance call a lot better than I can. My son, call your old man and let's talk about how to go about this. Leticia and I have just moved. Our new number is [_____] *(Believe me, dear reader, I was tempted, but the lawyer in me counseled against printing his phone number.)*

THAT WAS TEN YEARS AGO. Since then I fictionalized the story, unfictionalized it, workshopped it, gave up on it, and, finally, published it. Now what?

CONCERNING THERAPY CULTS

Perhaps no one in contemporary society is confronted by greater temptation to abuse power than the psychotherapist. We reveal to therapists personal information we do not share with our families or trusted friends. We rely on them for guidance when in turmoil. Most therapists avoid the temptation to abuse the power they are given over clients' hearts, minds and souls.

But some therapists, less rigorous about ethics or less conscious of their own need for personal validation, fall into the power trap and take advantage of needy or frightened clients. In a group setting, the temptation is magnified—a charismatic group therapist may become intoxicated with power when several clients willingly relinquish control over their lives.

And when a client, particularly a young person or anyone whose life is in serious transition, observes a group of intelligent people relying on a charismatic, bigger-than-life being, the temptation to join up can be as seductive as the therapist's temptation to play God.

When the therapist and the clients succumb to their respective temptations, a cult is born.

At **peoplefarm.com**, the reader will find links to a variety of online resources concerning therapy cults.
Offline, the author highly recommends these books:

Appel, Willa. *Cults in America: Programmed for Paradise.* New York: Holt, Rinehart & Winston, 1983.

Sargant, William. *Battle for the Mind: A Physiology of Conversion and Brainwashing.* Cambridge, MA: Malor Books, 1997.

Singer, Margaret Thaler with Lalich, Janja. *Cults in Our Midst: The Hidden Menace in Our Everyday Lives.* San Francisco: Jossey-Bass, 1995.

Singer, Margaret Thaler with Lalich, Janja. *"Crazy"Therapies. What are They? Do They Work?* San Francisco: Jossey-Bass, 1996.

THANK YOU . . .

To **Waimea Williams**, *People Farm's* editor, who read the 1996 draft of Chapter 1 and wrote, *"I've identified 17 subplots and can't figure out who your main character is. These are serious problems . . ."* Since then, Waimea, I've trusted your praise as well as your criticism. Thank you for taking a chance on me, and for teaching me so much along the way.

To **Judy Betts**, who has treated every draft of every chapter as a gift. The gift, Judy, has been your enthusiasm.

To **Jane Staw**, who never stopped trying to persuade me to write *People Farm* as the true story.

To my mentor **Sands Hall** of Squaw Valley, who reminds me often that writing this book can, and should, serve a higher purpose than getting even.

To **Moira Johnston** of the Squaw Valley nonfiction program, who has elevated investigative journalism to a form of high art, and inspired me to stick to what I know is true.

To **George Birimisa**, who, at 78, has taught me that writing is the cheapest way to stay young.

To **Traci** and **Walter Hjelt-Sullivan**, the gentle hosts of the **Quaker Center** in Ben Lomond, California, in whose Sojourner Cottage *People Farm* completed itself.

To **Susi**, my mother, who gave me a grownup typewriter when I was six so I could produce my fledgling literary magazine, and wept in disappointment when I was accepted into law school because she didn't believe God meant me to be a lawyer. Susi, I miss you. I still have the typewriter.

To professors **Margaret Thaler Singer** and **Willa Appel**, whose courageous research concerning therapy cults helped me to understand what the other "Vistans" and I had experienced.

To **Muni**—The San Francisco Municipal Railway—at whose bus stops, and on whose conveyances, much of this book was drafted while I commuted to my day job. If the politicians had kept their promises and made you run on time, I might never have finished this book!

and

To the **"Vistans."** Your collective ascent from the ashes of our wilderness home is the greatest triumph of the human spirit I have ever been privileged to witness.

BIBLIOGRAPHY

Cavafy, Constantine. *Collected Poems*. E. Keeley & P. Sherrard, trans. G. Savidis, ed. Princeton: Princeton U. Press, 1975.

"Cripple Creek," American folk song. Lyrics as recorded by Buffy Sainte-Marie on the LP *It's My Way!* Vanguard Records, 1964.

Fogerty, John C. "Proud Mary." Lyrics as recorded on the LP *Bayou Country*. Fantasy Records, 1969.

Freud, Sigmund. *Complete Psychological Works*, Vol. 2. London: Hogarth Press, 1895. (For the curious or incredulous, the "change your hysterical misery into common unhappiness" letter appears on page 305).

Hendrix, Jimi. "Red House." Lyrics in *Jimi Hendrix: A Musician's Collection*. Milwaukee, WI: Hal Leonard Pub. Corp., 2001.

Hesse, Hermann. *Beneath the Wheel*. Translated by Michael Roloff. New York: Farrar, Straus & Giroux, 1968.

Johnson, J.R. and J.W. "Motherless Child." Lyrics in *American Negro Spirituals*. New York: Viking, 1925.

Jung, Carl Gustav. *Memories, Dreams, Reflections*. New York: Random House, 1965.

Kyayyám, Omar. *The Rubáiyát*. E. Fitzgerald, trans. Garden City, NY: Garden City Books, 1952.

"Lie Low Little Doggies," American folk song. Lyrics as recorded by The Sons of the Pioneers on LP *Cowboy Country*. RCA, 1947.

McCartney, Paul. "In My Life." Lyrics as recorded by the Beatles on the LP *Rubber Soul*. EMI, 1965.

Milgram, Stanley. *Obedience to Authority: An Experimental View*. New York: Harper & Row, 1974.

Miller, Alice. *Thou Shalt Not Be Aware*. New York: Farrar, Strauss and Giroux, 1984.

Perls, Frederick S. *Gestalt Therapy Verbatim*. Lafayette, CA: Real People Press, 1969.

Rogers, Carl R. *On Becoming a Person: a Therapist's View of Psychotherapy*. Boston: Houghton Mifflin, 1961.

Standal, Stanley. "The Need for Positive Regard: A Contribution to Client-Centered Therapy." Unpub. Ph.D. dissert., U. of Chicago, 1954.

Tolkien, J.R.R. *The Hobbit, or, There and Back Again*. Boston: Houghton Mifflin, 1938.

SNOWBOUND RANCHO VISTA TIPIS, 1971

THE AUTHOR TODAY
(photo by the little guy's papa,
a pseudonymous former Vistan)